American Studies, Ecocriticism, and Citizenship

This collection reclaims public intellectuals and scholars important to the foundational work in American Studies that contributed to emerging conceptions of an "ecological citizenship" advocating something other than nationalism or an "exclusionary ethics of place." Co-editors Adamson and Ruffin recover underrecognized field genealogies in American Studies (i.e., the work of early scholars whose scope was transnational and whose activism focused on race, class, and gender) and ecocriticism (i.e., the work of movement leaders, activists, and scholars concerned with environmental justice whose work predates the 1990s advent of the field). They stress the necessity of a confluence of intellectual traditions, or "interdisciplinarities," in meeting the challenges presented by the "anthropocene," a new era in which human beings have the power to radically endanger the planet or support new approaches to transnational, national, and ecological citizenship. Contributors to the collection examine literary, historical, and cultural examples from the nineteenth century to the twenty-first. They explore notions of the common—namely, common humanity, common wealth, and common ground—and the relation of these notions to often conflicting definitions of who (or what) can have access to "citizenship" and "rights." The book engages in scholarly ecological analysis via the lens of various human groups—ethnic, racial, gendered, coalitional—that are shaping twenty-first century environmental experience and vision. Read together, the essays included in American Studies, Ecocriticism, and Citizenship create a "methodological commons" where environmental justice case studies and interviews with activists and artists living in places as diverse as the U.S., Canada, Haiti, Puerto Rico, Taiwan, and the Navajo Nation can be considered alongside literary and social science analysis that contributes significantly to current debates catalyzed by nuclear meltdowns, oil spills, hurricanes, and climate change, but also by hopes for a common future that will ensure the rights of all beings—human and nonhuman—to exist, maintain, and regenerate life cycles and evolutionary processes.

Joni Adamson is Associate Professor of English and Environmental Humanities at Arizona State University, U.S.

Kimberly N. Ruffin is Associate Professor in the Department of Literature and Languages at Roosevelt University, U.S.

Routledge Interdisciplinary Perspectives on Literature

1 **Environmental Criticism for the Twenty-First Century**
Edited by Stephanie LeMenager, Teresa Shewry, and Ken Hiltner

2 **Theoretical Perspectives on Human Rights and Literature**
Elizabeth Swanson Goldberg and Alexandra Schultheis Moore

3 **Resistance to Science in Contemporary American Poetry**
Bryan Walpert

4 **Magic, Science, and Empire in Postcolonial Literature**
The Alchemical Literary Imagination
Kathleen J. Renk

5 **The Black Female Body in American Literature and Art**
Performing Identity
Caroline A. Brown

6 **Narratives of Migration and Displacement in Dominican Literature**
Danny Méndez

7 **The Cinema and the Origins of Literary Modernism**
Andrew Shail

8 **The Gothic in Contemporary Literature and Popular Culture**
Pop Goth
Edited by Justin D. Edwards and Agnieszka Soltysik Monnet

9 **Wallace Stevens and Pre-Socratic Philosophy**
Metaphysics and the Play of Violence
Daniel Tompsett

10 **Modern Orthodoxies**
Judaic Imaginative Journeys of the Twentieth Century
Lisa Mulman

11 **Eugenics, Literature, and Culture in Post-war Britain**
Clare Hanson

12 **Postcolonial Readings of Music in World Literature**
Turning Empire on Its Ear
Cameron Fae Bushnell

13 **Stanley Cavell, Literature, and Film**
The Idea of America
Edited by Andrew Taylor and Áine Kelly

14 **William Blake and the Digital Humanities**
Collaboration, Participation, and Social Media
Roger Whitson and Jason Whittaker

15 **American Studies, Ecocriticism, and Citizenship**
Thinking and Acting in the Local and Global Commons
Edited by Joni Adamson and Kimberly N. Ruffin

American Studies, Ecocriticism, and Citizenship

Thinking and Acting in the Local and Global Commons

Edited by Joni Adamson and Kimberly N. Ruffin

With a Foreword by Philip J. Deloria

LONDON AND NEW YORK

First published 2013
by Routledge

Published 2016 by Routledge

711 Third Avenue, New York, NY 10017

Simultaneously published in the UK
by Routledge
2 Park Square, Milton Park, Abingdon, Oxon OX14 4RN

Routledge is an imprint of the Taylor & Francis Group, an informa business

First issued in paperback 2015

Library of Congress Cataloging-in-Publication Data

American studies, ecocriticism, and citizenship : thinking and acting in the local and global commons / edited by Joni Adamson and Kimberly N. Ruffin.

p. cm. — (Routledge interdisciplinary perspectives on literature ; 15)

Includes bibliographical references and index.

1. Ecocriticism. 2. Citizenship—History. 3. Ecology in literature. I. Adamson, Joni, 1958– II. Ruffin, Kimberly N., 1969–

PN98.E36A44 2012

809'.93355—dc23

2012032780

ISBN13: 978-0-415-62823-5 (hbk)
ISBN13: 978-1-138-64556-1 (pbk)

Typeset in Sabon
by IBT Global

This book is dedicated to the activists, academics, public intellectuals, and artists around the world who are shaping the terms of diverse forms of ecological citizenship.

Contents

Figures

Foreword

"It is interesting to contemplate a tangled bank," Charles Darwin famously observed, "clothed with many plants of many kinds, with birds singing on the bushes, with various insects flitting about, and with worms crawling through the damp earth, and to reflect that these elaborately constructed forms, so different from each other, and dependent on each other in so complex a manner, have all been produced by laws acting around us" (Darwin 440).

The passage is often quoted, and with good reason. It captures in concrete terms both the essence of evolution theory and the complex interdependence underpinning ecology. Two tenets of modern biological science come together in the passage, and they do so with a flash of bewitching coherence—something like Einstein realizing the theory of relativity while looking at a clock as he rode in the Bern trolley. In the figure of the "tangled bank," Darwin offers not only a rich observation, but also a compelling metaphor for complexity and change, for thinking in terms of both structure and development over time (Hagen). One might easily apply the metaphor to this collection as well. Imagine this book as a sort of tangled bank of its own, rich with disciplinary structures and field genealogies. Ecocriticism sings like a bird on a bush, and environmental history flits about, while American studies (AS) plays in the shadow of the global and local, the cosmopolitan, the political and the planetary, the transnational. So different from one another. Usefully and interestingly interdependent. Complex in their interactions. If we follow this mapping of interdisciplinary imaginaries onto Darwin's words to the last extreme, we are left only to articulate the question that drove his own inquiry: what are the laws and the rules that might make sense of this tangle of intellectual complexity?

Scholarship is not exactly governed by natural selection, but the parallels are close enough that we can fairly say that we too are looking at evolution and development over time. Like new species, emergent interdisciplinary fields evolve from what *was* into what *is* and what might be. At the same time that we consider development, though, it's as important to consider structure—the relationships *within* the tangled bank that might knit together interlocked fields of study, keywords and concepts, and questions that carry bite and heft. What evolves, in this case, are individual fields such as AS, ecocriticism, environmental history, and global studies—but also the very nature of their interrelationships.

It is not easy to think reflectively about intellectual practice within the current environmental moment. A series of unrelenting crises—oils spills, reactor meltdowns, pipelines, frackings—seem to require our immediate attention, which is constantly drawn from one site to the next. Then layer on top of these issues long-scale problems—climate change, energy geopolitics, environmental social inequality. Factor in what seem to be pressing debates in different fields of intellectual inquiry, and one can see just how difficult it is to find the time, space, and energy to pause and think systematically about the ways fields themselves cohere, pull apart, and collide. In *American Studies, Ecocriticism, and Citizenship: Thinking and Acting in the Global Commons*, Joni Adamson and Kimberly Ruffin have brought together recent work that prods us to reflect on exactly these issues of intellectual practice. They ask us to consider the ground rules that might make sense of new forms of community-centered scholarly work, designed for and addressed to the global commons and contemporary environmental crises.

To clear the ground, Adamson and Ruffin ask us to quickly revisit familiar genealogical narratives of field formation. AS, they argue, has a powerful tradition of environmental and ecological thought, implicit in nineteenth century foundational writers. For instance, buried beneath the celebratory nationalism of Frederick Jackson Turner's frontier thesis was an analytical power stemming from the material and cultural dialogue that unfolds between human beings and the places they occupy (Cronon, "Revisiting"). AS scholars such as Henry Nash Smith, Leo Marx, Roderick Nash, and Annette Kolodny would elaborate on this insight, creating a strand of AS work that elaborated on this human-nature dialogue, especially to the cultural questions of human meaning and its creation, communication, reception, and transformation over time. Yet this strand was easily submerged by larger currents of the field.

Over time, scholars recounting AS field imaginaries came to look askance at some of these earlier roots, seeing in them Cold War nationalisms, white heteropatriarchy, and the drive to constitute institutional academic authority and power. Markers of the "state of the field" came to note instead the sustained growth in excellent scholarship interested in literary theory, gender studies, ethnic studies, transnational and then global studies, and a range of smaller field interests, all on display at an annual meeting that was more diverse and varied than perhaps any other (Davis; Deloria "Broadway"; Fishkin; Washington "Disturbing"; Wise). The result, Adamson and Ruffin suggest, was a field well positioned to advance environmental thinking in sophisticated but particular ways, configured in terms of ethnic studies, citizenship, transnationalism, and the global world. Ironically, however, over the last decades AS has not often been attuned to environmental issues, as the early possibilities for environmental cultural critique were overwritten and subsumed. And then came the Hurricane Katrina disaster—a social catastrophe that cried out for AS analysis—that was at the same time an undeniably environmental and ecological catastrophe, and that pushed more AS scholars to turn the interdisciplinary tools of their craft back toward matters ecological. This volume joins together work that has sought to do exactly that.

While AS was deemphasizing environmental possibilities, literary scholars were feeling their way toward the congealing of a field called "ecocriticism." Beginning with a disconnected series of individual forays in the 1970s, a reclamation of "nature writing" and the American West in the 1980s, the 1992 founding of the Association for the Study of Literature and the Environment, and a set of field-foundational writings in the 1990s, ecocriticism looked to bring interpretive weight to the relationship between literary expression and environmental and ecological subject matter and consequences (Buell "Environmental Imagination"; Glotfelty and Fromm; Kroeber). Strongly rooted in both nature writing and the critique of "nature" as a reified object, ecocriticism has sometimes wavered uncertainly between the celebration and the deconstruction of nature—which has, in the end, turned out to be a challenging analytical position that has posed problems for the coherence of the field. For those concerned with the link between environmental politics and the experience of nature and place, the move to critical, theoretical, and deconstructive scholarship might look downright destructive and politically naïve, while for those in the critical camp, the (less-than-critical) celebration of "nature" might seem intellectually naïve and willfully shallow (Buell *Future*; Garrard; Phillips *The Truth*). Engagement with the angular fields of environmental justice scholarship and environmental history helped transform these debates, bringing ecocriticism into a broader realm of materialist critique.

And here we can push "reset": The result of this genealogy, Adamson and Ruffin suggest, was a field that was well positioned to advance environmental thinking in terms of the meanings and experiences of nature—that area that had been somewhat fallow in AS—while only beginning to think about the material social relations and histories embedded in ethnic studies (and, thus, in environmental justice) and perhaps less well equipped to problematize a notion of "the global" in relation to national and transnational studies (Heise). At this particular point of intersection, then, AS and ecocriticism present themselves as tangled genealogies likely to tangle further in new inter- and cross-disciplinary formations. What, we might ask, can a new AS environmentalism look like? And what might a new ecocriticism look like as well? And is this particular intersection perhaps the best candidate for the creation of new forms of politically and intellectually productive discourse well suited to the crises at hand?

Adamson, Ruffin, and the contributors to this volume ask us to step through the nature of the tangle: not simply the rules of tangling (if such can be named) but the particular kinds of tangles that will prove most useful and evocative to the discussion. And they give us hints and roadmaps in the words they use: commons, global, transnational, citizenship, planetary, community, cosmopolitan, cosmopolitics, place, among others.

This idea of the commons, for example, comes to us in distinct, overlapping, and evocative guises. Consider, for example, the commons of E. P. Thompson and Garrett Hardin; both shared spaces in which local social and political understandings govern the tension between collective management and individual opportunism (Thompson *The Making of the English Working Class, Whigs and Hunters: The Origin of the Black Act*; Hardin "The Tragedy"). Hardinesque humans create rules on the commons, and they submit to them or they destroy the resource. For Thompsonians, the metaphor evokes not the challenges of the shared management of common space but the sheer exercise of power and domination that comes with the *enclosure* of the commons—the rejection of communal and shared space in favor of privatization, profit, and human dispossession ("Introduction to the New Enclosures" 1–9). One might wonder how we begin to scale "the commons" across a range that extends from pastureland to the planet.

Hardin framed the commons as a pasture, the site for a thought experiment focused in precise terms around the marginal return to individuals and the costs to groups when everyone quietly overloaded shared grazing land. One of his conclusions—"mutual coercion, mutually agreed upon"—points to the larger structures of common property resource management, which might be said to scale up quickly from the local to the global. Imagine, first, a shift from local *tradition* to local *law*, which suggests a new category of person: the citizen. Using the concept of the citizen—who participates in the creation of non-local rules and structures of coercion and who consents to be governed by them—it is not difficult to move up the chain. "National citizen" comes somewhat easily (as it remains contested), and the possibility of a "global" or "planetary" citizen comes into soft focus, a category created explicitly to address problems that exist at earth level.

If only it were so easy. How, one might ask, does one build a planetary imaginary when it is almost impossible to build a shared identity on a concept like the nation? The contributors to this book understand that the nation is at once an unavoidable obstacle and an object to skirt—at least for the time being. More pressing and perhaps more productive are concepts that stand in critical relation to "the global": the transnational and the local. The first of these puts a paradoxical spin on the globe, leading us to consider both the concrete materiality of existence between nations *and* the immaterial placelessness of such in-betweens. Migrants move from place to place to place, and what comes to matter most is their "transient" being—the motion between localities that locates them someplace outside the context of "the nation." Corporations think globally with little concern for such things as nations. Money and goods become electronic, and they exist placelessly in digital strings floating outside nations.

At the same time, people—maybe even global citizens—realize that the experience of the global is inevitably played out in specific localities. No matter the extent to which a problem or an opportunity is conceived on global scales, its human experience will exist in "the local," a particular place with particular people and particular histories and structures. Environmental action and thought has been most effectively practiced on the local scale of the community. And so this book directs our attention to a complex question: Can one truly act as a planetary citizen in the context of local knowledge and local politics that are structured by transnational flows of capital, goods, and people—even while the power of the nation-state exerts itself on local (and thus global) life? What would such acts look like? How would one recognize and understand the various scales of citizenship at play? What would be the tools and strategies to enjoin a conversation?

Such a conversation faces multiple challenges. Our categories always threaten to reduce themselves to dualisms: global-local, city-country, nature-pavement, citizen-government, public-private, and so on. The scales are so huge it becomes almost impossible to move a concept across the full range, and so ideas like "planetary citizen" or "ecological citizen" threaten instantly to become metaphoric rather than possible. Cases, defined by specificity, seem to defy generalization. And looming always overhead are the challenges, which call for speed, certainty, and action rather than just more talk.

Acting, however, is best preceded by thinking, and the role of scholars is to do that work—always with an eye cocked for the action. Joni Adamson, Kimberly Ruffin, and the contributors to this volume have been hard at work on both fronts. In the end, the thinking that takes place between these covers does not boil down to individual writings, but rather comes out of their placement together, as a constellation of thought and possibility, engaged with similar questions and situated at the intersection of AS and ecocriticism.

That location is rich with possibility. But it need not be defined only through these two fields. Laced just as tightly into this tangled bank are other possibilities not to be ignored. Whenever ecology is on the table, for instance, economics (joined through their common root word) can and should never be far behind. And while both AS and ecocriticism have engaged environmental history, such engagements have taken place primarily around the cultural studies wing of that field. From its earliest beginnings, environmental history has taken seriously the integration of scientific knowledge into its explanatory frameworks. When William Cronon—a longstanding key environmental writer—left Yale University for the Frederick Jackson Turner Chair at the University of Wisconsin in 1991, he noted with some small regret not simply his departure from an excellent History Department, but also the fertile presence of the United States' foundational School of Forestry and, just down the hall, one of the best AS programs in the world. It was the longstanding interdisciplinary practice of that AS program that helped many scholars align other departments with the expansive study of literature, history, art and material culture, politics, and society.

So too with both AS and ecocriticism. Both fields have been structured by certain kinds of interdisciplinary conversations and not others. That means certain kinds of critical insights and not others. And that, in turn, means opportunity. The new emergent interdisciplinary constellations found in *American Studies, Ecocriticism, and Citizenship: Thinking and Acting in the Global Commons* offer a tangled bank for our contemplation, something akin to the hillock in Kent where Darwin gained inspiration, a metaphor, and a striking picture to illustrate the theory of evolution. Read here and see histories of change, moments of possibility, and structures and frames for further thought—and, in thought, the opportunity for action.

—Philip J. Deloria

Acknowledgments

This collection is the tangible outcome of more than a decade of organizing and research by members of the American Studies Association's Environment and Culture Caucus (ASA-ECC), which was organized by Joni Adamson to call attention to long-existing and emerging synergies among the fields of AS, ecocriticism, ethnic studies, and environmental studies. We thank the founding members of the ASA-ECC, Lawrence Buell, Giovanna Di Chiro, William Gleason, Jurretta Heckscher, Annette Kolodny, Charles Mitchell, Mary Kate Nelson, T. V. Reed, Amanda Rees, Noël Sturgeon, and Adam Sweeting. We also thank the entire membership of the ASA-ECC for their research and organizational work, which has inspired us and strengthened this collection. Most chapters in this collection were first presented at linked 2008 and 2009 ASA conferences sessions which were clustered thematically around the keywords "environment," "citizenship," and "belonging." We would like to thank Dennis Moore and Karen Salt of the ASA's Early American Matters Caucus for helping us expand the scope of these presentations across broader histories and scales of time and, ultimately, strengthen the book.

We thank our contributors for their writing, for their professionalism in responding to our feedback, and for offering collaborative responses to each other's work. Stephanie LeMenager, Claudia Sadowski-Smith, and Sarah Wald not only read and commented on the introduction but offered especially insightful comments on the confluences among AS, ecocriticism, and citizenship. Rob Nixon's notion of "slow violence" was important to our thinking, and he generously offered us comments on the introduction that helped us rethink and strengthen key claims. Philip Deloria, Shelley Fisher Fishkin, and Priscilla Wald not only led the ASA in ways that encouraged transnational "interdisciplinarities," they were each willing to engage in discussions that helped us shape the project in ways that we did not anticipate. Frederick Corey, Dean of the School of Letters and Sciences, and Ian Moulton, Head of Interdisciplinary Humanities and Communication at Arizona State University, funded the work of our Arizona State graduate assistants, Sarah Grieve and Kyndra Turner, who worked professionally and effectively with contributors to copy-edit each chapter and ensure accurate citations. We also thank Blaine Washington of Roosevelt University for compiling our references and Kydra Turner for creating the index.

We wish to thank the Association for the Study of Literature and Environment (ASLE), which has offered us a vibrant scholarly home in which to test our ideas and receive constructive feedback. Finally, we thank Deryl Smith and Kenneth Pozehl for surrounding us with the love, support, time, and space that make completion of rewarding projects like this one possible.

Introduction

Joni Adamson and Kimberly N. Ruffin

In the summer of 2010, the Deepwater Horizon oil rig in the Gulf of Mexico exploded and set off the largest accidental release in history of oil into marine water. For over three months, U.S. federal scientific teams estimate, about 4.9 million barrels—or 205.8 million gallons—of thick crude spewed from a ruptured pipe into the ocean.[1] Other large-scale disasters such as Hurricane Katrina, which hit New Orleans in 2005, the earthquake that decimated Haiti in 2010, and the 2011 tsunami, earthquake, and nuclear disaster in Japan, have also drawn the world's attention to questions of ecological ethics and vulnerability that are placing both rich and poor nations and their citizens at risk. Whether the primary culprit is corporate malfeasance, government neglect, or climactic or geologic change, it is becoming increasingly clear that while disasters such as earthquakes are acts of nature, extreme vulnerability to these disasters is human-caused.

As Priscilla Wald observes in her 2011 Presidential Address to the American Studies Association, our understandings of "natural disaster" are challenged as we learn more about structural violence and institutional racism that often take shape in the disproportionate effects of "hurricanes or pandemics on different populations—by income level, race, gender, sex, or another marker" (191). Wald grounds her contention that "disasters" may not always be completely "natural" in a history of criticism stretching from Hannah Arendt's and Frantz Fanon's critiques of structural violence that deprives humans of their status as "humans," to Stokely Carmichael and Angela Davis's work on institutionalized forms of racism that "structured the relationships, interactions, and institutions of social, political, and economic life in the United States" (Wald 190).

Many of the contributors to *American Studies, Ecocriticism, and Citizenship* explore how human activities around the world are increasing the vulnerability not only of humans to environmental disaster and risk, but of all life on the planet. Atmospheric chemist Paul Crutzen and biologist Eugene Stoermer have coined the term "anthropocene" to describe this new epoch in earth's history. They argue that a key transformation in the planet's life began some two hundred years ago, or about the time the steam engine was invented. Since then, human activity has grown into a "significant and morphological force" (17). Wald argues that American Studies (AS) "is and ought to be a meeting ground in which a range of overlapping and sometimes contradictory theories come together to sharpen our insights" into these risks and to offer us opportunities to discuss "the politics of life" (192). Wald's use of this phrase invokes theorists who have engaged with "biopolitics" and "biopower," terms Michel Foucault coined to "name the exercise of state power through the administration of bodies and the calculated management of life" (Wald 189).

Wald's address is noteworthy for signaling something like an "official," or presidential-level, return of debates surrounding the politics of "nature" to the AS annual conference program after an absence of nearly a decade. This is not to say that individual scholars were not researching and presenting on environmental topics, but rather to observe that, in 1992, at the same moment when scholars with an interest in literary ecology were gearing up to form the Association for the Study of Literature and Environment and argue for the relevance of environmental approaches to cultural production, it was becoming apparent that, within the American Studies Association (ASA), projects taking environmental approaches to history, literature, ethnic studies, cultural geography, and anthropology were increasingly hard to get placed on the annual program.[2]

The chapters in *American Studies, Ecocriticism, and Citizenship* illustrate that even in a seeming absence, AS has provided an important "meeting ground" for scholars to come together to address the "politics of life," "nature," "environment," "justice, "citizenship," and "belonging."[3] Questions of citizenship have long been at the heart of the AS field imaginary and central to debates about the interrelations of cosmopolitanism, nationalism, localism, and environmentalism. In a special issue of the *Journal of Transnational American Studies*, Günter Lenz surveys key texts and scholars that have centered on the meaning and promise of definitions of cosmopolitanism.[4] He observes that this work is energizing the potential for "newly defined conceptions and practices of governance, justice, [and] citizenship . . . in a multi-polar world of unequal distribution of power and resources" (9). In the same issue, Alfred Hornung notes that new interpretations of cosmopolitanism are leading to recognition of multiple new dimensions of "cultural citizenship, minority rights, [and] the right of ecological citizenship" (6). William Boelhower, another contributor to the issue, concludes that we have reached a historical moment in which humans are "possessed of an agency scaled up to embrace and endanger a planet," and for this reason, recent notions of "common humanity, common wealth, and common ground" hinge on a highly appealing and irrepressible planetary point of view, often expressed through the new conceptual figure of a planetary *commons* dependent on the health of non-human nature as well as on human recognition of belonging to local, national, global, and ecological communities (47).[5]

While many AS scholars are exploring planetary approaches, scholars taking transnational ethnic studies approaches have been particularly insistent about the importance of interrogating how definitions of legal citizenship, within a region or nation, can be wielded in exclusionary regimes to bar whole groups of people from access to the rights and privileges of "citizens." As Lauren Berlant points out in a concise definition and history of citizenship, in many places, including the U.S., the "historical conditions of legal and social belonging have been manipulated to serve the economic, racial and sexual power in the society's ruling blocs" (37–38). This history complicates notions of a "global cosmopolitanism" and raises questions about who has access to "the commons."[6] Once understood as a centrally located tract of land or resource used by a community as a whole, the word "commons" has, since 1968, become associated with a metaphor devised by American ecologist Garrett Hardin in a much-cited paper, "The Tragedy of the Commons." Warning of the ecological dangers of human overpopulation, Hardin describes the future metaphorically as an "over-grazed pasture" and calls attention to the damage that innocent actions by individuals, in increasing numbers, can inflict on the environment. In a subsequent paper subtitled, "The Case Against Helping the Poor," Hardin went on to popularize the notion of an environmental "lifeboat ethics" which held that sharing resources with the world's poor would capsize any effort to develop the nation sustainably. In 1979, Hardin helped found the Federation for American Immigration Reform (FAIR), one of the best-established anti-immigration groups in the U.S.[7] These events are significant for anyone interested in the issues surrounding "citizenship" and "environment" or competing notions of "ecological citizenship" wielded by groups interested in either building protectionist walls around "natural resources" for exclusive communities or providing broader "rights" or access to resources for "communities" recognized as including both human and non-human beings. As Andrew Ross explains, in the U.S., FAIR and other international groups like it are finding new acolytes by contributing "warmed over" versions of Hardin's ideas to fractious debates about climate change that are fueling a blacklash against the notion that rich nations owe "a humanitarian lifeline to swimmers trying to catch up" (242).

Ross notes the irony of Arizona Governor Jan Brewer signing Senate Bill 1070, one of the strictest anti-immigration laws in the U.S.,[8] on the same (Earth Day) week that Bolivian President Evo Morales convened the World People's Conference on the Rights of Mother Earth and Climate Change in Cochabamba, site of a famous popular movement in 2000 to resist privatization of the city's water supply. In a Universal Declaration on the Rights of Mother Earth (UDRME) that emerged from the conference, delegates not only claimed civil and human rights for all people, they advocated for the rights of "ecosystems, natural communities, species and all other natural entities" to "continue and maintain their existence" (UDRME, Art. 4.1

n.p.). This 2010 meeting could be associated with the earlier 2008 revision of Ecuador's constitution, which granted "Pachamama" or "Mother Earth" the right to maintain and regenerate its "life cycles, structures, functions, and evolutionary processes."[9] The Conference also energized the passage in 2011 of Bolivia's Law of Mother Earth which establishes a ministry to provide water, air, and all living organisms with an ombudsman to advocate for their rights to maintain vital life cycles (Vidal n.p.). These global conferences and legislative innovations offer high-profile evidence that notions of "an environmental commons" and "environmentalism" are decisively "outgrowing their reputation as either a feel-good cause for the affluent, or a battle cry for exclusionary states and nations" (Ross 204). As Daniel Fischlin and Martha Nandorfy emphasize in *The Concise Guide to Global Human Rights* and in *The Community of Rights: The Rights of Community*, in a globalizing and corporatizing world, the notions of "rights," "citizenship," and "community" are being pushed beyond the confines of legalistic and political structures, since these terms often problematically promote notions of identification, symmetry, totality, and unity employed to justify hegemonic and totalitarian actions, by both state and corporations, in the name of community. In their work, Fischlin and Nandorfy seek to understand how "community" might suggest a complex allegory for relational identities that unravel generally accepted notions of "human rights" that pay scant attention to the environmental conditions that make "humanity" possible.

In "*¡Todos Somos Indios!*," Joni Adamson explores the significance of social justice and environmental activism emerging in Latin and South America that is undergirding calls for new understandings of citizenship, community, and rights in AS, ethnic studies, and ecocriticism.[10] From the 1960s to the 1990s, a number of important indigenous-led meetings represented several decades of struggle for self-determination, self-representation, and capacity-building. The declarations and manifestos written at these events drew global media attention to the deleterious social and environmental effects of unregulated multinational corporate power, expanding international trade agreements, and deregulated financial markets. These meetings illustrated that discourses on environmentalism do not all derive from 1960s–1970s Euro-American or Global North forms of environmentalism. They also illustrated that transnational indigenous groups in the Americas have long been working with diverse minority ethnic groups from around the world that self-identify as indigenous even though they may not be formally recognized by a nation-state, and their allies, non-native and civil society groups with overlapping interests in social justice and environmental protection.

Diverse forms of global environmentalism have important implications for the ways in which we understand the relationships among AS, ethnic studies, and ecocriticism and for the ways in which we understand what shared management of local and global "commons" and "ecological citizenship and belonging" might mean for both human and non-human species. In *Postcolonial Ecologies*, Elizabeth DeLoughrey and George Handley rightly point out that most descriptions of what Lawrence Buell has described as the "environmental imagination" have, for the most part, been produced in the northern hemisphere and focused on Anglo-American writing (8). Buell's seminal study, *The Environmental Imagination*, for example, makes the work of Henry David Thoreau a touchstone, as it provides a far-reaching account of environmental perception and the place of nature in Western thought. Ten years later, in perhaps the most cited and influential of ecocriticism's field genealogies, *The Future of Ecological Criticism*, Buell notes that the field is fast moving beyond its "first wave," which focused on Anglo-European environmental writings and genres into a "second wave" focusing on ecofeminism, environmental justice, and postcolonial studies.[11]

DeLoughrey and Handley note that most intellectual histories of ecocriticism have accepted the "wave" rubric. Whether they are written along the lines of thematics, chronologies, epistemologies, or pedagogies, their predominant focus on American or British literatures has tended to elevate forms of criticism that question the normative ecological subject (the white man or "discoverer" in wilderness) and the human's "relation to place (including nation)," while suggesting ecofeminism, postcolonial ecologies, queer ecologies, and environmental justice revisionism are secondary developments (DeLoughrey and Handley 11). Deloughrey and Handley question this genealogy, noting that many of the books and articles written by ecofeminists and environmental justice critics predate the work of some of the most important critics assigned to the "first wave" of ecocriticism (DeLoughrey and Handley 14).[12]

In *Slow Violence and the Environmentalism of the Poor*, Rob Nixon explains the "belatedness" of early ecocriticism to environmental justice organizing forms emerging in the Global South decades before ecocriticism appeared on the scene. Ramachandra Guha's influential essay, "Radical American Environmentalism and Wilderness Preservation: A Third World Critique," published in 1989, had already been widely disseminated through the social sciences and philosophy studies before ecocriticism got its start in the early 1990s (Nixon 253–255). For this reason, Guha's article was largely missed by some of the earliest practitioners of ecocriticism. Guha, along with Joan Martinez-Alier, went on to write *Varieties of Environmentalism* and develop the concept "environmentalisms of the poor" to describe movements that had been emerging in the Global South, many of which predated the mainstream conservation movement in the U.S. Also calling attention to this belatedness, Deloughrey and Handley urge ecocritics to reconfigure the intellectual histories of their field "in broader, more rhizomatic terms" that can account for forms of environmentalism that have developed in the Carribbean, India, or Africa and that will draw inspiration from ancient thinkers, indigenous and non-Western traditions (15).[13]

We agree that broader, more "rhizomatic" accounts of environmentalism(s) are needed in ecocriticism. However, on one small but important point, we would disagree with DeLoughrey and Handley. They describe a "communication barrier" between groups of ecocritics focusing on AS concepts of pastoral, wilderness, and frontier and those studying postcolonial, ecofeminist, and environmental justice approaches. They attribute this barrier "to the predominantly national framework for literary studies in general" and the "persistence of a lingering insular and/or exceptional vision of American Studies" (20). While it is true, as Rob Nixon puts it, that ecocriticism developed "de facto as an offshoot of American Studies" (235), it is not accurate to ascribe to all AS work, or even to all its early work, or all work focused on American subjects and authors, a narrow nationalism or exceptionalism. As Joni Adamson observes in a study of the environmental justice movement's influence on American literary studies and ecocriticism, to do so may be to miss some of the important legacies in AS that we may want to reclaim.[14] Adamson maps the blind spots in AS work with an environmental focus that clearly *does* focus on nationalist objectives and questionable assumptions about European and American "discoverers" or immigrants becoming "American" as they moved from cities or urban areas to the unsettled "wilderness." However, a narrow attention to these trends alone obscures the social justice and environmental activism of founding AS scholars, including F. O. Matthiessen who wrote *American Renaissance*, Henry Nash Smith who wrote *Virgin Land*, and Leo Marx who wrote *The Machine in the Garden*. As a literary critic, public intellectual, and teacher who worked to situate his own practice in ways that might be seen today within the frame of "environmental justice," for example, Matthiessen wrote about early American notions of the pastoral, but he was also working as an activist from the 1920s through the 1950s in support of teachers' unions, New Mexican miners, and longshoremen. He worked to bring, Paul Lauter argues, self-serving AS "ideologies under scrutiny and illuminated alternatives" (50). Mattheissen is currently being reclaimed not only for his distinguished scholarship and committed activism, but because he was an unusual example of a gay man who lived with his sexuality as an "open secret." He and his partner, artist Russell Cheney, lived together for 23 years until Cheney's death. Because of this legacy, Harvard is currently raising funds to endow a Distinguished Visiting Professorship in Gender and Sexuality named in his honor.[15]

Adamson notes that Annette Kolodny's *The Lay of the Land*, Patricia Limerick's *The Legacy of Conquest*, and Gloria Anzaldúa's *Borderlands/La Frontera* followed in the tradition of social and environmentally committed AS scholars who consider(ed) themselves not only academics but public intellectuals who take activist stances in their teaching, public speaking, and scholarship as they work to bridge multiple publics. Each brings/brought gender into their intersectional analysis of race, class, and environment to show that conceptions of the environment held by many

European Americans were not gender-neutral and were far older and more diverse than most mainstream conservationists (who dated the beginnings of the environmental movement to John Muir's fight to establish Yosemite National Park) had acknowledged (Adamson, "Literature" 598).

Despite these powerful examples of research and activism by founding AS scholars, by the late 1990s, overly simplified connections between environmental or ecological research and nationalism—inside and outside of AS—were leading to a disappearance of these subjects from the ASA's programmatic emphases in the first decade of the twenty-first century. In his 2007 presidential address, Philip Deloria refers to easy assumptions about the field's "creation story," which narrowly focus on U.S. white people and confine themselves within an intellectual project that accompanies "cold war containment culture" (10–11). The field bears unmistakable traces of this history, Deloria agrees, but if we take a second look, we might see the AS past as more variegated (11). As he asks in the "Foreword" to this volume, "How do we begin re-mapping these interdisciplinary imaginaries?" "How do we make sense of this 'tangle of intellectual complexity'?"

The usual place to start making sense of an intellectual tangle is to rewrite field genealogies and list ground-shifting texts and scholars. Both Wald's and Deloria's presidential addresses do this work for AS so concisely that we will not replicate their work here.[16] Instead, our purpose is to reclaim the rich ground in which environmentally-focused AS began growing, rhizomatically, in the 1930s, then more broadly and deeply in the 1970s and 1980s, until it became unmistakably visible in the first decade of the twenty-first century. Deloria's presidential address helps to explain how a "tangled bank" of new or re-emerging branches of study in AS were taking hold, receding, and/or reappearing. As a field, AS has offered a capaciousness in which to rethink categories of the "human," often discussed as "race," "class," "gender," "sexuality," and "ethnicity," and to rethink the relationship between people and place both locally and globally. Research of these categories has required the field to structure itself as interdisciplinary since one cannot talk about the construction of race and place without engaging with political structures, legal mechanisms, economic situations, social relations, and cultural systems that codify, manage, interpret, create, and convey the "meanings about race that will become common sense" and even the "environments and landscapes" that will be racialized by these "common" political structures and identity categories (Deloria, "Presidential" 7). An *analytic* imaginary connected to communities—racial, ethnic, or gendered—immediately invites a theory of intersectionality that puts these categories in relation to one another, either as a "*problem*-based multidisciplinarity or a *discipline*-based interdisciplinarity" (Deloria, "Presidential" 7). In Native American and indigenous studies, for example, the central problem for the field has been "how to help Indian communities" (Deloria, "Presidential" 9). Meeting this objective has required academics and activists to pull together "social science, literature, and folklore" and bridge "anthropology, history, and law and policy" while linking their research to other ethnic studies in African and African American and Asian and Pacific Islander studies which are often linked to "distinctive histories of Chicano, Mexican, Hispano, and Latino studies that sometimes do (or do not) congeal into that 'field'" (Deloria, "Presidential" 8).

In her presidential address, Priscilla Wald concisely describes and links the growth of ethnic studies in AS to an emerging post-1960s consciousness of the ways in which institutional racism and structural violence would need to be critiqued. Nourished by the writings of Franz Fanon, Aimé Césaire, Eldridge Cleaver, and Angela Davis, this emerging consciousness fueled the earliest calls for "ethnic studies that challenged the disciplinary canons and paved the way for new methods and approaches to the study of the relationship of cultural expression to social hierarchies and political structures—to the material impact of how as well as what we study" (Wald 194). Deloria adds that we might think of ethnic studies as "emergent interdisciplinarities" in AS or interlinked fields that might be described as "institutional, intellectual, and political" methodologies, or sites for the production of knowledge developed from activist conceptions of intellectual and theoretical work as political practice (Deloria 2009: 11). As Nikhil Singh observes in his response to Deloria's address, thinking of AS as a methodology also does away with the requirement of an ethic of consensus "based in accounts of a shared [national] past" (Singh 31).

Conceiving of AS as an intellectual and "methodological commons" has facilitated the recuperation of AS legacies of public intellectualism, scholarship, and activism that have focused on local and global ethnic communities and/or environmentalism (s) and resulted in the appearance of what David Pellow and Robert Brulle have named "critical environmental justice studies."[17] For example, Rob Nixon's *Slow Violence and the Environmentalism of the Poor* goes well beyond the "American Studies creation story" to reclaim important public intellectuals and scholars who were conceiving of an "ecological citizenship" that advocated something other than an "exclusionary ethics of place" (Nixon 239). Nixon examines how the publication of Aldo Leopold's *A Sand County Almanac* inspired the creation of the American Wilderness Society, which put into place a Committee on Foreign Relations, chaired by Leopold. The committee charged Leopold with overseeing the creation of a plan for world peace that recognized the slow violence and attritional lethality of nuclear weapons and other weapons of war (251). Leopold, whose work will be considered in this volume by Susan Scott Parrish, was working very much in an AS tradition that reflected the public intellectual energies of a figure like Matthiessen while also foreshadowing the work of the contributors to this collection. Leopold was clearly aware of the transnational, which is exactly the direction in which AS has more recently taken a "turn," as Shelley Fisher Fishkin terms it in her 2004 presidential address. Today, AS scholars are routinely focusing on networks or webs of contact that have "increasingly superseded 'the nation' as 'the basic unit of, and frame for, analysis'" (Fishkin 21).

Many of the contributors to this volume have been leaders in the production of scholarly work with a strong, critical interest in the significance, for academic study and activism, of emerging forms of environmental justice, citizenship, and coalitional politics both inside and outside the U.S. Since the early 1990s, Giovanna Di Chiro has been active in both the AS and ecocritical communities. She has produced a large body of work analyzing grassroots activism from the perspective of intersectional gender, race, and class analysis that theorizes why women are drawn to environmental causes in numbers that, in some cases, make up 90 percent of an organization's membership (Di Chiro 109). David Naguib Pellow and Robert Brulle, writing in the introduction to *Power, Justice and the Environment*, have also analyzed extensive social science-oriented literature proving that environmental risks have been inequitably distributed, with poor people, people of color, and people of the Global South bearing a greater share of the burden than richer people and people of the Global North. They describe how the growing pressures of global capital encourage grassroots ethnic minority and indigenous groups to forge transnational links with one another.

Another collection, *The Environmental Justice Reader*, edited by Joni Adamson, Mei Mei Evans, and Rachel Stein, brings ecocritics, activists, and artists together to explore possibilities for bridging academia and the multiple publics interested in linking social justice and environmental concerns. What sets this book apart from other early ecocritical field genealogies and collections, and lays the foundation for *American Studies, Ecocriticism, and Citizenship*, is the collection's interdisciplinary juxtaposition of literary analysis with critical environmental justice studies and the acknowledgment that *theory* can be produced outside the academy in communities and activists contexts. In a chapter published in *The Environmental Justice Reader*, Julie Sze, one of the contributors to this volume, argues that literature sets the issues at stake within more flexible, local, and global contexts while illuminating connections to history and, often, to imagined futures. It allows environmental justice to be seen not only as a political movement concerned with public policy but also as a cultural movement interested in issues of ideology and representation (Sze 163). Other contributors to *The Environmental Justice Reader* question the convention of arguing only within the frameworks of science, technology, ethics, policy, and law as they reclaim environmental traditions and histories from Nigeria, the Pacific Islands, Mexico, and the U.S. that predate 1960s U.S. environmental conservationism and show academics and activists thinking and acting in the local and global commons.

Our own individual monographs, *American Indian Literature, Environmental Justice, and Ecocriticism: The Middle Place* (Adamson 2001) and *Black on Earth: African American Ecoliterary Traditions* (Ruffin 2010), offer, respectively, one of the first and most recent book-length examples of the fusion of AS, ethnic studies, and ecocritical methodologies that set the tone for the chapters in this volume. Each of these books illustrates how scholars working across disciplines are contesting globalizing or universalizing meanings of a "common good" that excludes long-held local and indigenous knowledges about human relations to the more than human world. In *American Indian Literature, Environmental Justice, and Ecocriticism*, Adamson examines the environmental justice movement from a transnational perspective, moving from poems by Joy Harjo (Creek) addressing the violence and socioenvironmental degradation authorized by the Reagan administration in Nicaragua in the 1980s to a novel by Leslie Marmon Silko (Laguna Pueblo/Mexican/Anglo) linking the Zapatistas of Chiapas, Mexico (a mostly Mayan group of farmers who mounted a resistance movement to the North American Free Trade Agreement) in the early 1990s. She argues that Silko's *Almanac of the Dead* and movements such as the Zapatista rebellion push the advent of "environmentalism" back (at least) to the Pueblo Revolt of 1680 in the Southwest region of North America and to every slave revolt in the Americas. Exploring why varieties of American environmentalism based on U.S. deep-ecology models of conservation-oriented activism were being dismissed by indigenous groups like the Zapatistas, Adamson argues that, after the 1980s, indigenous, ethnic minority, and economically disadvantaged groups throughout the Americas were consistently rejecting clichéd stereotypes of "ethnic purity" or "Indian authenticity" as they organized to oppose economic development models that were causing environmental degradation and displacement in their communities (31–50, 128–179). Anticipating Deloria's and Wald's notions of AS as a "methodological commons" or "meeting place," Adamson calls on AS scholars and ecocritics to recognize that addressing our most challenging social and environmental problems will take more than savvy literary analysis; it will take coming into a "middle place" where political consensus, however contingent and subject to change, will allow intercultural, interdisciplinary and international groups to find common ground in their advocacy for new definitions of an ecological "community of rights".[18]

In *Black on Earth*, Ruffin brings ecocriticism and ethnic studies together to forge a "human groups approach"[19] to literature and activism which acknowledges that human beings are animals who form groups that influence and sometimes delimit ecological opportunity. Human group identification grows out of experiences such as genealogy, geography, affinity, oppression, and/or social construction. Groups can be imposed, voluntary, local, national, and/or transnational, and they have the power to shape interactions among humans and with non-human nature. This approach does *not* rest on assumptions about the natural constructedness of any group but rather allows all groups a "point of entry into ecological discussion that includes but is not limited to domination" (Ruffin 16). Acknowledging the variety in human experiences not only yields a better understanding of the ecological implications of marginalization but also illuminates the multiple and changing conceptual legacies within the human family. For instance, the primary human group of her study, African Americans, provides evidence that pervasive negative grouping as racial "others" yields limited access to environmental privileges that other groups enjoy. However, *Black on Earth* also demonstrates that imposed racialization and marginalization did not prevent African-American authors from formulating their own ideas about their heritage, nature, and built environments. Taken together, both the negative and positive consequences of imposed and voluntary human group identification form an "ecological burden-and-beauty paradox" resulting in a complex perspective that records both social and environmental burdens along with environmental desires and joy. African Americans' artistic record shows how this group has moved beyond the limitations of injustice to reflect on the advantages of long-held and emerging ecological traditions and knowledge. When the realities and diversity of human group experiences are ignored, scholars fail to illuminate the ways in which subcategories of "the human" driven by race/ethnicity, region, class, gender, and sexuality can be used to grant or restrict environmental access, perspective, and experience. Thus, *Black on Earth* records the merit of combining AS and ecocritical methodologies in aesthetic and social analysis.

The chapters included in *American Studies, Ecocriticism, and Citizenship* create a "methodological commons" where environmental justice case studies and analysis, together with interviews with activists and artists living in places as diverse as Washington, DC, Kentucky, and Taiwan, can be considered alongside literary and social science analysis that contributes significantly to current debates about the future of places as different as the Navajo Nation, New York City, and Haiti. While the majority of contributors to the volume are environmental literary critics, the volume is necessarily multidisciplinary because interlinked social justice and environmental issues cannot be described from the perspective of the humanities or cultural studies alone or the social sciences or sciences alone. Contributors take a "human groups approach" rather than a necessarily racialized approach, which emphasizes that each of us, as individuals and as groups, is a crossing point for a variety of political orders, from the local, state, and regional to the hemispheric and the global and that each of us has a stake in imagining our common local and global futures. They show how human groups are mobilizing around new concepts of ecological citizenship and belonging catalyzed by nuclear meltdowns, oil spills, hurricanes, climate change, and histories of privilege or social and environmental injustice.

Contributors engage in scholarly ecological analysis via the lens of various human groups—ethnic, racial, gendered, activist—that are shaping twenty-first-century environmental experience and vision and contributing to new concepts of citizenship. Together, these 15 chapters (1) illuminate the ecological impact of how humans organize themselves; (2) clarify the impact on both human groups and non-human nature; (3) locate patterns and changes in human group affiliation; (4) acknowledge areas of conflict and exclusion within the human species; (5) illustrate the role of diverse human groups in building coalition politics; (6) bring more nuance to discussions of human ecological impacts; and (7) offer new understandings of both ancient and new trans-species understandings of who and *what* can be granted the right to exist, maintain, and regenerate life cycles and evolutionary processes.

PART I: INTERDISCIPLINARY PERSPECTIVES ON CITIZENSHIP AND BELONGING

The chapters in Part I of *American Studies, Ecocriticism, and Citizenship* illustrate how greater sophistication about human group dynamics may catalyze deeper understandings and inquiry about relations between humans and non-human nature, which in turn may illuminate why questions of belonging have long been central to the interdisciplinarities among AS, ethnic studies, and ecocriticism. They also demonstrate how fictional narratives negotiate the complicated terrain of the Americas and the Caribbean, exposing the collisions of race, ethnicity, gender, place, and national or global affiliations that have defined and redefined people and places, together with the multiple nonhuman species with which they interact.

The first two chapters illustrate, as Elizabeth DeLoughrey and George Handley have argued in *Postcolonial Ecologies*, that landscapes (and seascapes) can participate in historical processes and are not simply "bystanders" to human experience. In "Zora Neale Hurston and the Environmental Ethic of Risk," Susan Scott Parrish (Chapter 1) examines people of African descent in the (U.S.) rural south and the Caribbean. As mediated in Hurston's oeuvre, she argues, these people rarely espoused a worldview based on steady-state equilibrium; rather, they demonstrated an environmental ethic based on risk. They thus offer a significant reservoir of nature-experience and nature-conceptualization, produced in a region of intense disturbance regimes, which, in our latter-day moment of ecological modeling, appears to have been remarkably insightful. In her analysis of nineteenth-century concepts of "racialized citizenship," "Haitian Soil for the Citizen's Soul," Karen Salt (Chapter 2) contends that in response to France's edict requiring post-revolution Haiti to pay for their freedom, Jean-Pierre Boyer—the president of Haiti from 1818 to 1843—set about revitalizing Haiti's economy by first marshaling its image within the Atlantic World as a bountiful, rich black nation and then marketing its supposed ecological and political abundance to people of African descent within America. She shows how Boyer's citizenship scheme, which could be described as an eighteenth-century form of what we today call "place-branding," is a rationale that continues to be marshaled today.

Working at the "emergent interdisciplinary" intersections of ethnic studies and environmental studies, Traci Brynne Voyles's "Intimate Cartographies: Soil Conservation, Livestock Reduction, and Navajo Ecological Citizenship" (Chapter 3) explores federal conservationists' work to transform Navajo sheepherding, land use, and family life through soil erosion control in the 1930s and 1940s. Voyles explores how the aftereffects of this conservationist program have shaped the course of Navajo environmental self-determination today. In "Getting Back to an Imagined Nature: The Mannahatta Project and Environmental Justice," Jeffrey Myers (Chapter 4) analyzes *Mannahatta: A Natural History of New York City*, an interactive website that reconstructs the "original" ecology of early seventeenth-century New York Harbor. Myers examines why it is problematic for those seeking to solve twenty-first-century environmental challenges to take an "anti-urban" stance toward the "concrete jungle."

"The Oil Desert" by Michael Ziser (Chapter 5) moves readers of the collection to immediately recognizable desert locales—distinguished by their relative aridity, lack of vegetation, and overall horizontality—that have come to be associated with the modern "petroscape." Ziser argues that oil discourse is the result of a millennia of cultural depositions, accumulations, compressions, and conversions. He asks whether naturalized petro-histories can be combusted in the engines of a new paradigm, one that can see the desert as more than a dumping ground for the consequences of present wealth. The final chapter in Part I, "Japanese Roots in American Soil: National Belonging in David Mas Masumoto's *Harvest Son* and Jeanne Wakatsuki Houston's *The Legend of Fire Horse Woman*," by Sarah D. Wald (Chapter 6), focuses on David Mas Masumoto's non-fiction essay collection *Harvest Son: Planting Roots in American Soil* (1999) and Jeanne Wakatsuki Houston's novel *The Legend of Fire Horse Woman* (2004), two contemporary narratives about Japanese American internment. Wald examines Masumoto's use of agrarianism and Houston's claims to indigeniety as the basis of alternative forms of ecological citizenship defined outside of the racial logic of U.S. legal citizenship. Exploring Japanese American interactions with nature, these texts contest the racialized nationalism manifest in many representations of Western U.S. landscapes.

PART II: BORDER ECOLOGIES

Part II takes its subtitle from inter-AS scholar Claudia Sadowski-Smith's discussion of "border ecologies" in her 2008 monograph *Border Fictions*. Chapters in this section assert that it is important for human beings to recognize their embeddedness in cultural and racial systems and hierarchies as well as their embeddedness in ecosystems that transcend national boundaries. In "Our Nations and All Our Relations: Ecological Community in

William S. Yellow Robe, Jr.'s *The Council*," John Gamber (Chapter 7) examines Assiniboine (or Stone Sioux) dramatist, director, actor, and poet William S. Yellow Robe, Jr.'s play *The Council* in terms of its environmental ethics and in the context of transnational, transcontinental, and transcultural indigenous organizing that is mobilizing around the world, working within and without the framing conceptions of the "nation." In the play, citizenship is a critical trope, with Eagle representing North America and Condor representing Central and South America. Gamber examines how Eagle and Condor come together to eschew dichotomous relationships between Native Americans and Europeans within a tribal "nation" of international, interspecies, and thoroughly global life.

The next three chapters explore U.S. borders, both north and south. In "Preserving the Great White North: Migratory Birds, Italian Immigrants, and the Making of Ecological Citizenship across the U.S.–Canada Border, 1900–1924," Ivan Grabovac (Chapter 8) examines concepts of "racial nativism," arguing that the Migratory Bird Acts of 1913 and 1916 and the U.S. Immigration Restriction Act of 1924 passed in the U.S. helped to construct an ecological conception of American citizenship that targeted supposed "aliens," especially Italian immigrants in the Northeast as threats to the national environment. In "Boundaries of Violence: Water, Gender, and Development in Context," Julie Sze (Chapter 9) focuses on novels by Kem Nunn and Linda Hogan that examine how conflicts over water and pollution are gendered in the context of globalization and how this is particularly clear at the borders the U.S. shares with both Mexico and Canada. Sze argues that water symbolizes the contested politics and the geographic and cultural spaces between nations and communities that hold unequal power as a result of large-scale economic development and the cultural changes and gendered effects this development provokes.

Claudia Sadowski-Smith's "U.S. Border Ecologies, Environmental Criticism, and Transnational American Studies" (Chapter 10) explores why debates about U.S. land borders that have centered on migration, terrorism, and smuggling have recently also turned to examine ecological degradation at the Mexico–U.S. border. Focusing on Jim Lynch's novel *Border Songs*—with its comparative perspective on the Canada–U.S. border, Sadowski-Smith posits that while AS scholars are becoming increasingly involved in social movements, environmental activists have also become strong voices in the struggle against border militarization and immigration restrictions that combine concerns about environmental preservation with human health. The final chapter of Part II, "Climate Justice and Trans-Pacific Indigenous Feminisms," by Hsinya Huang (Chapter 11), examines indigenous women's literary works in the context of environmental and trans-Pacific histories. It centralizes the role of gender, drawing on indigenous authors with links across the Pacific, from Mexico to Taiwan. The chapter goes beyond the U.S. and its readily identifiable, cultural anxiety about the geopolitical rise of China, as Huang analyzes trans-Pacific indigenous women's narratives, providing literary and activist examples of how environmental damage is mobilizing tribal groups who are seeking redress and reform.

PART III: ECOLOGICAL CITIZENSHIP IN ACTION

The chapters in Part III are important for revealing how societal marginalization often informs ecological vulnerabilities. In "Roots of Nativist Environmentalism in America's Eden," Lisa Sun-Hee Park and David Naguib Pellow (Chapter 12) focus on Aspen, Colorado, as they consider the flipside of crimes associated with environmental inequality and environmental racism: *environmental privilege*. Their research highlights the nativist (anti-immigrant) logic that runs through environmentalist arguments against low-wage immigrant Latina/o workers. "Wielding Common Wealth in Washington, DC, and Eastern Kentucky: Creative Social Practice in Two Marginalized Communities" by Kirsten Crase (Chapter 13) draws from interviews with residents of two historically marginalized communities. Crase explores how concepts of place, home, and environment are marshalled as tools by community members who actively ground themselves in their own "common wealth" as they address a variety of challenges that threaten their community's social and ecological integrity.

The next two chapters are particularly rich for exploring creative social and ecological practices. In "Climate Justice Now! Imagining Grassroots Eco-Cosmopolitanism," Giovanna Di Chiro (Chapter 14) examines environmental activism focused on community-based solutions to global problems. She explores why activists from around the world who are calling for "climate justice" are arguing that dominant cosmopolitan approaches to climate policy (e.g., UN's Clean Development Mechanism) disregard locally grown innovations supporting sustainable development produced by small farmers, indigenous communities, and grassroots environmental justice organizations. Di Chiro provides examples of how climate justice activists are building a *grassroots* version of cosmopolitanism in diverse efforts to create healthy and sustainable communities. Stephanie LeMenager, in the final chapter of the collection, offers a conversation across the cultures of academia and public art as a means of promoting AS as a mode of environmental action. In "The Los Angeles Urban Rangers, Trailblazing the Commons" (Chapter 15), she focuses on how an art collective, the Los Angeles Urban Rangers, can be understood within the traditions of community arts practice, temporary public art, and relational aesthetics. Their performance of environmentalism as a commitment to "common" places makes for a generous conclusion to this volume.

As a whole, *American Studies, Ecocriticism, and Citizenship: Thinking and Acting in the Local and Global Commons* helps clarify why both AS and ecocriticsm have taken on the subjects of race, class, and gender during the past twenty years (in transnational or globalizing contexts) and why this work often remains strongly regional and community-oriented, and often continues to prioritize local place allegiance and ecological distinctiveness. The volume speaks to the urgency of coming into a "middle place" or creating a "methodological commons" where academic and public discourse about citizenship and belonging in both local and global contexts might become more accessible and clear, and thus, more transformative. The book illustrates how we can fight for ecological justice both inside and outside national borders, how we can insist that nations contribute to dialogue and action that expands notions of what constitutes "the community of rights" and the "rights of community" and how we might better support individuals and groups who are part of nations *and* planetary citizens in creating and enacting policies, laws, and community practices that will have positive ecological consequences around the globe.

NOTES

1. See CNN Wire Staff, "Gulf Oil Spill Is Worst Accidental Spill Ever," n.p.
2. To address this challenge, in 1999, a small group of scholars from the Association for the Study of Literature and Environment (ASLE) came together with environmental studies scholars at the ASA to form the Environment and Culture Caucus of the American Studies Association (ASA-ECC) and to work for increased placement of sessions on the program.
3. Many of the chapters in this volume were first presented at the 2008 and 2009 ASA meetings which focused on these keywords.
4. For a history and definition of "cosmopolitanism," see Günter H. Lenz, "Redefinitions of Citizenship and Revisions of Cosmopolitanism—Challenges of Transnational Perspectives." See especially, page 5, n. 5.
5. Wai Chee Dimock and Lawrence Buell's edited collection, *Shades of the Planet*, for example, provocatively suggests how American literature might be studied from "planetary" perspectives that do not "begin with the United States as center, but with the world as circumference" (back cover description).
6. For more on how ethnic minority groups, and specifically ethnic climate justice activists, build a *grassroots* version of cosmopolitanism, see Giovanna Di Chiro, Chapter 14, this volume.
7. FAIR is discussed at greater length by Claudia Sadowski-Smith, Chapter 10, this volume.
8. The 2011 passage of an anti-immigration law in Alabama, which was upheld by a federal judge, while Arizona's law is being considered before the U.S. Supreme Court, makes Alabama's law the strictest.
9. See Constitution of Ecuador, *Asamblea Nacional Constituyente*, Chapter 7, n.p.
10. For a genealogy of this organizational work, much of which predates 1960s U.S. articulations of "environmentalism," and leading up to the World People's Conference the Rights of Mother Earth and Climate Change, also see, Marc Becker, "Third Continental Summit of Indigenous Peoples and Nationalities of Abya Yala: From Resistance to Power," page 85. For a broader discussion of indigenous and ethnic minority environmental movements in global contexts, see Fischlin and Nandorfy, *The Community of Rights* and *The Concise Guide to Human Rights*.

11. For other important field genealogies, see Cheryll Glotfelty and Harold Fromm, eds., *The Ecocriticism Reader*, and Greg Garrard, *Ecocriticism.*
12. As examples of important work that predates the "first wave," DeLoughrey and Handley cite critics important to both AS and ecocriticism who have also been strong influences in the activities of the ASA's Environment and Culture Caucus (ECC), Annette Kolodny (*The Lay of the Land* and *The Land Before Her*) and Noël Sturgeon (*Ecofeminist Natures*). We would add Louise H. Westling (*The Green Breast of the New World*) to this list and other scholars whose early work and presentations on ASA-ECC panels has been important to the work of the Caucus and to ecofeminists and environmental justice critics in general: Rachel Stein (*Shifting the Ground*), Catriona Sandlilands (*The Good Natured Feminist*), and Stacy Alaimo (*Undomesticated Ground*).
13. DeLoughrey and Handley refer to the metaphor of the "rhizome" that Gilles Delueze and Felix Guattari develop in *A Thousand Plateaus: Capitalism and Schizophrenia.*
14. See Adamson, "Literature-and-Environment Studies and the Influence of the Environmental Justice Movement."
15. See "F. O. Mattheissen Distinguished Visiting Professorship of Gender and Sexuality Fact Sheet."
16. For a concise field genealogy of AS, see especially Deloria's "Presidential Address," notes 6 and 9.
17. This term is coined by Pellow and Brulle in *Power, Justice and the Environment.*
18. The term "middle place" is taken from anthropologist Dennis Tedlock's translation of the Zuni concept of "home" as a "middle place," (See Adamson, *American Indian*, 46–48, 156–59; 190, n. 13; also see "The Beginning," *Finding the Center*, Dennis Tedlock, Trans., (275–98).
19. This phrase was coined by Kimberly Ruffin and used for a 2011 Association for the Study of Literature and Environment (ASLE) Preconference Seminar she led in Bloomington, Indiana.

Part I

Interdisciplinary Perspectives on Citizenship and Belonging

1 Zora Neale Hurston and the Environmental Ethic of Risk

Susan Scott Parrish

The verb "to belong" became a key term in environmentalist thought when, in his 1948 introduction to *A Sand County Almanac*, Aldo Leopold wrote,

> Conservation is getting nowhere because it is incompatible with our Abrahamic concept of land. We abuse land because we view it as a commodity belonging to us. When we see land as a community to which we belong, we may begin to use it with love and respect. There is no other way for land to survive the impact of mechanized man. (viii)

Land could no longer be construed as alienated chattel, Leopold urged, but instead had to be understood as a "biotic community" to which we humans belong, as "members" (210), with an "ecological conscience" (221). Others would fill in this genealogy of error, between the biblical, pastoral Abraham and Leopold's "mechanized" "modern" (223), by pointing to the Enlightenment and its disenchantments of nature, and especially to Descartes's detached human *cogito* or Locke's linkage of political subjectivity with property ownership.[1]

The way forward, for Leopold, was not to see land as "the slave and servant," but rather as "the collective organism" (223). Though this organism may appear to be a "disorderly tangle" (215), Leopold asserted that, in fact, "the stability of the system proves it to be a highly organized structure" (215), able to "adjust" (216) to "slow and local" (217) evolutionary changes. Modern "man-made changes are of a different order" (218), threatening "wastage" (219) on a global scale, he averred. Active belonging requires that humans no longer introduce disorder to this system but instead find their natural function in such a stable organism.

The history and cosmology of early twentieth-century, rural, southern, African-American men and women, as mediated by Zora Neale Hurston, offer a telling alternative to the human and natural history contained in Leopold's land ethic. These "folk" labored in agrarian monocultures and a variety of extractive industries, including phosphate mining and, most prominently, logging. They saw nature as neither a disenchanted belonging nor as a stable, slowly changing system to which they belonged. Rather, nature was shot through with chance and risk, acted on by an ever-involved and potent God and only sometimes respondent to human propitiation. One did not so much "belong" to such a volatile matrix as one developed and hazarded one's skills within its flux. Though Leopold's sense of belonging and citizenship continues to offer vital working concepts today, the black rural "folk" experience that Hurston explores offers a cosmology that is closer to much contemporary ecology in its emphasis on instability and chance. This "folk" cosmology is traceable, loosely and in part, to African retentions and, more certainly, to the experiences of diasporic Africans in the Atlantic world over the *longue durée*; it also stems from the involvement of African-American laborers in dramatic anthropogenic disturbances to the southern landscape in the post-bellum period, disturbances they both enacted as laborers but also disproportionately suffered from when these disturbances turned catastrophic. Moreover, in as much as Hurston not only isolates but also critiques her subjects' ethics within such a world, her work opens up important questions for our current moment.

Hurston's mediation of black southern folk culture was fraught with complexity. She understood that "the folk" was a potent, ideologically infused category used to naturalize movements as diverse and opposed as fascist nationalism in Europe, white Southern Agrarianism in the U.S., and even Booker T. Washington's program of racial uplift.[2] Hurston demurred from the cultural geography implicit in these usages of "the folk." For her, the rural was not a static "solid" starting point that a culture could cling to for authentication or return to for re-beginning, nor was the northern city the only locale that could enable cultural motion. Rather, she understood folk culture to be both migratory and constantly evolving. For Hurston, the concept of folk dynamism came in part from her own, constant and precarious, mobility, but also from her conception of America as a rough jumble of voluntary migrations and involuntary diasporas, "blending and contending" (*Go Gator* 66–67).[3]

It was not only rural folk culture that Hurston saw as subject to change. While studying at Barnard, off and on from 1925 to 1934, Hurston encountered an intellectual milieu in which concepts of flux and contingency, both cultural and ontological, were espoused by the likes of Franz Boas and John Dewey. Boas theorized in 1920 that, rather than driving toward a civilizational telos, "all cultural forms . . . appear in a constant state of flux and [are] subject to fundamental modifications" (284). Dewey's philosophy—thus far not associated with Hurston by scholars—involved a refutation of the concept, which he found both in classical Greece and in Descartes, that the human *cogito* existed as the end product of a servile nature. In *Experience and Nature*, Dewey sought to redefine this apparently superior "end" (369) term, as instead a "consequence" (370), an outflow, in which the human or natural "means" (369) continues to be active. It is only this way, by acknowledging "means-consequence" (370), that humans can recognize and further develop an "operative technique" (133) for behavior and for science. Moreover, rather than denying the "contingency" (46) fundamental to the universe—and hence the "risk" and "gamble" (41) inherent in human life—with philosophies of end-fixity, an operative, artisanal, and experimental epistemology, Dewey argued, makes the most sense in our "aleatory world" (41).[4] Both Dewey and Boas, as well as the larger group of Pragmatic philosophers and social scientists to which they respectively belonged, were deeply indebted to Darwinian theories of evolution, theories that postulated open-ended biological change. What Dewey, Boas, and others took from Darwin was a conviction that contingency, accident, and dynamic flux were natural and inherent.

The equally—if not more—important early twentieth-century source for Hurston's fluxional view of nature and culture came from the spectrum of vernacular southern African-American and Afro-Caribbean plantation and post-plantation experiences and modes of thinking she studied. That findings from these vernacular sources dovetail with academic theorists is less surprising than one might think given that Boas derived his theories from his own anthropological fieldwork and given that Dewey sought to bring "operative"—basically, tool working—agents into consequence and saw those agents as working things out in an aleatory world. Hurston, Dewey, Boas, and Leopold were all, in their own ways, trying to un-think the conservative strains of Enlightenment thought and the various modern cleavages—man-land, European-non-European, free-slave, subject-object—it wrought or codified as science. (Leopold diverged from the rest, though, in espousing a vision of a stable biotic system as providing a reformative model for humans.) In addressing African-American rural vernacular culture, Hurston spent time with men and women who had always been found to be on the wrong side of such cleavages. Because modernity had grown out of the very Atlantic experience that had spelled their subjugation, modern thought, as such, was something with which these men and women had a skeptical, ironic, and often subversive relationship. As such, these subjects offered Hurston the means for analyzing modernity's cleavages.

A friend and colleague of Hurston's at both the Federal Writers' Project and the Library of Congress, and a fellow Columbia-trained ethnographer, Benjamin Botkin explored, in his *Lay My Burden Down: A Folk History of Slavery*, the way that experiences of slavery conditioned a risk-centered epistemology. In his introduction to the section on "Mother Wit," Botkin explains that in "slavery's 'state of perpetual war' . . . [t]hrough the whole code of luck signs, of omens, charms, and taboos . . . , the master kept a fearful and restless people in hand." "At the same time," Botkin continues, "the slave used the power of luck for his own protection, as in conjuring the hounds or carrying a rabbit's foot in his pocket to keep from getting whipped" (2). The profound uncertainty built into all agriculture-based enterprises—and particularly those dedicated to monocultures like cotton, sugar, and tobacco—exacerbated ten-fold by the "perpetual war" of the antebellum plantation, combined to make all parties aware of risk at every turn and of operating in such a way as to play within such risk to one's best advantage. One way this situation was expressed theologically by African Americans was to see divine influences as always at play. As Orleans Finger, a Mississippi-born informant of Botkin's collection, put it when describing being physically healed through prayer: "God is a momentary God" (34). He does not mean that God's influence is only temporary, but rather that one can appeal to God in the moment; God works *in* time and *in* biology, not merely before an automated time/nature commenced (as per Enlightenment mechanical philosophy).

What agricultural labor also entailed for its laborers was a diurnal and accumulative empiricism about biotic change. Another informant, Texan John Love, observed:

> I knows why that boll weevil done come. They say he come from Mexico, but I think he always been here. Away back yonder a spider live in the country, 'specially in the bottoms. He live on the cotton leaves and stalks, but he don't hurt it. These spiders kept the insects eat up. They don't plow deep then, and plants cotton in February, so it made 'fore the insects git bad.
>
> Then they gets to plowing deep, and it am colder 'cause the trees all cut, and they plows up all the spiders and the cold kill them. They plants later, and there ain'tno spiders left to eat up the boll weevil. (13)

What this conjecture about the etiology of insect infestation shows is Love's long temporal and varied topographical awareness of multiple, mutually impacting factors: deforestation, microclimate change, vulnerable plant-insect symbiosis, and technological practice. Moreover, multiple actors influence these events: spiders, boll weevils, cotton plants, plows, humans, weather. Love thinks in terms of a complex network of human and non-human agents. Balance is temporary and fragile, and it does not reestablish itself. Though Love is remarkably observant about this fragile network, one suspects that, without economic power, he had to be knowing one thing with his mind and doing a different thing with his body. He thinks like a member of a biotic (and abiotic) community but must abet, in Leopold's terms, "the conqueror."

Hurston's decades of folk-gathering strongly verified what John Love here attests—namely, that "the field," both anthropological and environmental, was profoundly characterized by a pattern of disturbance. That is to say, the southern and Caribbean environments in which she gathered material were marked by physical, biogenic, and anthropogenic disturbance.

Moreover, her human subjects were, to use Dewey's phrase, the "means" whose labor was undertaken within these disturbance patterns and whose labor eventuated in further disturbances.[5]

Hurston did her anthropological work in the Gulf States and Caribbean, where hurricanes and flooding are signature physical disturbances. As John Love explained, the lower South was likewise the terrain of the biogenic and anthropogenic disturbance of the boll weevil. Moreover, Hurston witnessed the particular anthropogenic disturbances occurring in this region in the form of logging, turpentining, phosphate mining, wetlands drainage, and monoculture farming. The work and culture of black forestry laborers in particular is recorded in her short story "Spunk" (1925), her anthropological collection *Mules and Men* (1935), her documentary film work (ca. 1940), her autobiography *Dust Tracks on a Road* (1941), her unpublished play (written with Dorothy Waring) *Polk County: A Comedy of Negro Life on a Sawmill Camp* (1944), and the posthumously published *Every Tongue Got to Confess: Negro Folk-tales from the Gulf States* (2001).

Though forest modifications had been occurring in the south for millennia, it was not until the 1880s that, as historical geographer Michael Williams has put it, "the acceleration in commercial lumbering came with the sudden and massive transfer of capital, technology, and know-how from the North," especially from lumber barons in the Great Lakes states who were gradually exhausting their own once-extensive forests (238). Southern governments failed to check absentee extraction and exportation of their major resources, allowing a situation to develop of "semi-colonial dependency" (Williams 243). Highly efficient machines, like the steam skidder, could pull six hundred trees out of the forest in eight hours (see Figure 1.1).

This machine worked, as one observer noted in the early 1920s, like "an octopus of steel with several grappling arms running out 300 or more feet. These grapple a tree of any size that has been felled, and drag it through the wood to the tram road. These [felled trees] become enormous battering rams and lay low everything in their way. Standing trees that are not pulled down are skinned so badly as to be worthless. The remains of the forest [are] like the shell torn area of France" (qtd. in Williams 252). By 1930, the old growth forest was almost depleted.

In *Mules and Men* and *Polk County*, Hurston studied the mind consequences and the hand and tongue skills that developed while loggers enacted the anthropogenic disturbance of deforestation. Hurston lived at a boarding house at the Everglades Cypress Lumber Company in Loughman, Florida (west of Kissimmee), in 1928. The mill at the center of "the job" announced itself by "a huge smoke-stack blowing smut against the sky" (*Mules* 59). And all around it were the woods. One night a "grim-faced" traveling preacher, or '"stump-knocker,"' sermonizes to the camp from Genesis 2:21 (*Mules* 139). Though the preacher brings a sepulchral

Figure 1.1 "Brooks-Scanlon Corporation logging." Reproduced courtesy of State Archives of Florida; Image #RC04286.

aura along with him, he, like the loggers, speaks about a God for whom the world is something always in the making. The preacher intones:

> Wid de eye of Faith
> I can see him

Standing out on de eaves of ether
Breathing clouds from out his nostrils,
Blowing storms from 'tween his lips
I can see!
Him seize de mighty axe of his proving power
And smite the stubborn-standing space,
And laid it wide open in a mighty gash—
Making a place to hold de world
I can see him—(*Mules* 139–141)

Here is a God of generative violence who "makes" with a "mighty gash." This God creates through the physical disturbances of "storms" and geological fissures. It seems no coincidence that on a Florida logging camp (near massive drainage canals) that the power of the Almighty is described in terms of storms and land gashes, nor that the instruments of creation are cutting blades. Hurston's description of the loggers' arm-work makes the connection apparent: "Not only do they chop rhythmically," she wrote, "but they do a beautiful double twirl above their heads with the ascending axe before it begins that accurate and bird-like descent. They can hurl their axes great distances and behead moccasins or sink the blade into an alligator's skull. In fact, they seem to be able to do everything with their instrument that a blade can do" (*Mules* 66).

In the sermon, the power of God is imagined in terms of both physical (storms) and anthropogenic (earth and tree cutting) disturbances. Hurston sustains this confusion as she compares human axe work to bird flight. Given these instances in which anthropogenic disturbances are not distinguished from natural behavior or natural disturbances, it would seem that neither Hurston nor her subjects see southern forestry labor of this period as running contrary to nature. Because divine power itself (even in its creative acts) is seen as so thoroughly violent, human violence within and against the natural world is not singled out as introducing a new and catastrophic order of destruction. Hurston produces a cosmology in which divine creation and destruction go on without end, and the loggers—in other words, the axe and language handlers—participate in (and come to see as natural) this work of making and unmaking. What God does on a grand scale with the elements, the loggers do with saws, stories, and, in the juke at night, with music and games of chance. Living in a natural world so conceived is such a gamble that these subjects' creative forms are surged through with risk and violence. Hurston shows how her subjects internalize the anthropogenic disturbance (of which they are instruments) into a cosmology and a culture of creative violence.

She further explores this cosmology of "the job" in the play she co-wrote with Dorothy Waring in 1944: *Polk County: A Comedy of Negro Life on a Sawmill Camp* set at the Lofton Lumber Company. When the female hero of the story, "Big Sweet," a figure who first appeared in *Mules and Men*, is told she has to get off the job, she speaks a doleful soliloquy: "I aint nothing," she laments. "None of us aint nothing but dust. Saw dust. Piled up round the mill. What is left over from standing trees. Sometimes . . . the sawdust shines like diamonds, and glints like gold. Then the light goes out and we are dust again. Dust from God's Big Saw" (*Polk County* 125). At this, the nadir of the play, the hero imagines the black community to be surrounded by a hostile mechanized environment, to be a mere waste product of the mill and, in larger terms, of God's own destructive engines.[6]

Another way to put it is that Hurston imagines that her characters come to perceive the existence of physical disturbance (which they imagine to be authored by God) through the metonym of the lumber industry's instrument of anthropogenic disturbance. The "Big Saw" of "the job" becomes, for the characters who know their world through the logging work they perform, "God's Big Saw." The ecological structure of the universe is that of "the job" amplified. Hurston implies here and in *Mules and Men* that because the laborers extrapolate from the logging industry's operations in order to conceptualize divine and natural operations, the loggers do not perceive that they are the instruments of a different order of destruction and hence do not see their work as *un*natural. In Dewey's terms, they do not understand their own particular instrumentality or "means-consequence" because they see the world (nature, God, earthly power) as inherently cataclysmic.

The phosphate mining area of Central Florida was another site of anthropogenic disturbance at which Hurston observed African-American

Figure 1.2 Stripping overburden from soft phosphate, Phoslime Company, Phoslime, near Ocala, Florida. March 4, 1919. Reproduced courtesy of U.S. Geological Survey; ID. Stone, R.W. 859 srw00859.

"means" culture. Beginning in the 1920s and 1930s, workers operated large draglines, or earth-lifting cranes, to remove the top-most layers of earth (or "overburden") in order to get down to the phosphate matrix lying some fifteen to fifty feet below the surface (see Figure 1.2).

This matrix was a combination of phosphate rock, sand, and clay that was then processed to isolate the rock, which was, in turn, chemically treated to produce phosphorous, a fertilizer used in agriculture to restore soil productivity (Zhang). The Florida mines, in particular, housed the skeletal remains of ancient life. In her autobiography, Hurston describes the laborers' process of mining as an archaeological encounter with violent evolutionary "chance and change":

> Polk County. Black men laughing and singing. They go down into the phosphate mines and bring up the wet dust of the bones of pre-historic monsters to make rich land in far places. . . . But, all of it is not dust. Huge ribs, twenty feet from belly to back bone. Some old-time sea monster caught in the shallows in that morning when God said, "Let's make some more dry land. Stay there, great Leviathan! Stay there as a memory and a monument to Time." . . . Gazing on these relics, forty thousand years old and more, one visualizes the great surrender to chance and change when these creatures were rocked to sleep and slumber by the birth of land. (*Dust Tracks* 147)

New "birth" (punningly) rocks old forms "to sleep" in death. As Orleans Finger put it, "God is a momentary God" (34). Hurston also suggests here that God is an aleatory God, operating through "chance." God keeps making and destroying the world every day without a game plan.

During this same time period, massive drainage projects focusing on Lake Okeechobee radically transformed nature in South Florida. Lake Okeechobee covers over seven hundred and twenty square miles, making it the third largest freshwater lake within U.S. borders. Okeechobee draws its waters from the floodplain of the Kissimmee River and used to release its waters southward in a slow cascade through saw-grass prairies stretching all the way down the Everglades to the Bay of Florida. Beginning in the 1880s, entrepreneurs not only redirected the flow of the Kissimmee River but dug massive canals west, east, and south of the Lake to drain off the vast and arable acreage to the south. What was laid bare south of the Lake was nine-foot-deep fertile earth—"the muck"—which in turn yielded large crops of beans, citrus trees, tomatoes, and, most of all, sugar cane. Aware, though, of the risk of flooding, the state built, between 1923 and 1925, a five-foot-high dike along forty-seven miles of the Lake's southern border. Again, it was largely Northern and British concerns that had purchased massive tracts of initially "worthless" marshland to see its value increase dramatically after completion of the drainage projects. Promotion to northern (and British) investors clearly played on a history of British imperial venturing in the

Figure 1.3 Pamphlet and photographs relating to the sugar industry, 1921. Reproduced courtesy of HistoryMiami; Accession #RTjj00080011a.

tropical East; the goal was to create an internal plantation colony that could rival the other sugar-producing locales of the world (see Figure 1.3).

In 1880, here was a still changing wetlands landscape of perpetual flooding situated in the realm of the hurricane. White developers engineered the redirection of the natural water flow, creating an agricultural region of monocultures, and sited housing for migrant agricultural laborers right up against the presumably contained lake (Kleinberg 8–15; Douglas 312–328). White developers bet that the gains from crop sales would outweigh the risks resulting from both the physical and their own anthropogenic disturbances. Black harvesters also gambled that their wage earnings as day laborers would exceed these risks.

On September 12, 1928, the *Palm Beach Post* ran a report in its weather column, announcing that, through the Caribbean Antilles, a "tropical disturbance of considerable intensity . . . [was] moving west or west-northwestward" (qtd. in Mykle 115). The hurricane touched land on the eastern coast of Florida at Lake Worth with 130 mph winds on the 16th. With an eye 25 to 30 miles across, the winds pummeled Palm Beach around 6:45pm and then, moving as a counter-clockwise spiral in the darkness, came at Lake Okeechobee from the northwest corner, sloshing a 10-foot wall of water over its bottom rim and breaking down the paltry dike across a 21-mile expanse. As Marjorie Stoneman Douglas put it, "The lake with a long howling swept over everything. . . . When the light came back . . . there was one wilderness of water everywhere, in which the dead lay like logs" (345–346). Between 2,500 and 3,000 people died that night, almost half of the local population. More than three-quarters of the dead were African American and Afro-Caribbean. Six hundred and seventy-four black bodies were placed in a mass grave in West Palm Beach; another sixteen hundred were interred in Port Mayaca on high ground to the east of Okeechobee; scores of corpses were lost in the Everglades, and scores more were burned in funeral pyres. As one survivor noted, "After the first few days colored and white were indistinguishable. All had lost their skin" (qtd. in Mykle 199). White bodies turned black through lack of oxygen, and these racially indistinct bodies had, in turn, been covered by whitening dowses of lime (Mykle 189, 211–213; Kleinberg 19–21, 77, 82, 99).

News of the flood's devastation south of Okeechobee traveled slowly. Relief was therefore slow to come and distributed in a controversial manner when it arrived. A New York-based group, the Negro Workers Relief Committee, released reports that were picked up by Black newspapers across the country, about Jim Crow discrimination by the National Guard and the Red Cross. Mary McLeod Bethune, W. E. B. Du Bois, as well as the Associated Negro Press all ultimately exonerated the Red Cross of wrong doing in this instance, though Du Bois faulted the Red Cross's Negro Advisory Committee with being too conservative. Even if quantities of relief goods and monies were equal, the vile and grueling work of clean-up was, by all accounts, unfairly placed in the hands of black men and often through violent coercion. A National Guardsman, Knolton Crosby, shot and killed an African-American man, Coot Simpson, for apparently resisting conscription into a work gang. The jury found that Crosby had been lawfully discharging his duty, and the state later gave him the customary medal for service rendered after a natural disaster. One 14-year-old white witness wrote to his aunt on October 3: "Negroes ordered to load bodies at Pahokee and other Everglade towns were forced to do so at the point of a gun. . . . One negro in town was shot for disobeying. They were better then" (qtd. in Kleinberg 187). Not only do this adolescent's remarks speak to a white consensus about the cause of the shooting—black disobedience rather than white illegitimate violence—but they reflect a tacit approval of the action based on its disciplinary effect.

Zora Neale Hurston was not in harm's way during the September 16th hurricane and flood, but she heard oral accounts when in Florida the following spring. In 1935, she then spent time in Belle Glade, when she was gathering music for the Library of Congress, where she surely gathered more oral testimony of the flood and its aftermath (*Dust Tracks* 159). It was precisely the intense risk regime that characterized the drained Everglades region that Hurston described when she wrote a correspondent in 1936 that the novel she was then designing in her mind entailed the story of a woman who finally "got her chance at mud," down in "the Everglades where people worked and sweated and loved and died violently" (*A Life in Letters* 366–367). That novel was *Their Eyes Were Watching God*, which she wrote in Haiti in the last weeks of 1936. This particular "mud" was full of "chance," not only because of the violent culture of gambling, alcohol, and knives in the jukes, but because it was a drained wetland located next to a massive body of water.

In one of the earlier scenes of the novel, characters are debating the possible existence of a "great big ole scoundrel beast" who, as one speaker claims, "eats up all de folks outa de house and den eat de house." His interlocutor is skeptical: "'taint no sich a varmint nowhere dat kin eat no house!" He sure does exist, the first man, Sam Watson, claims: "Dey caught him over dere in Egypt. Seem lak he used tuh hang around dere and eat up dem Pharaohs' tombstones." Sam, who has been arguing for the overarching power of nature throughout the debate, concludes by saying, "Nature is high in uh varmint lak dat" (Hurston, *Their Eyes* 66). What Sam is describing here is the power of water operating in a floodplain. He points to the Nile's cyclical inundation of its banks and, without knowing it, presages Lake Okeechobee's own flooding. The narrator will take up this figure again to describe the power of the water in the lake to exceed humanly engineered constraints: the storm "woke up old Okechobee and the monster began to roll in his bed" (158). The danger, south of Okeechobee, results not directly from the physical disturbance (the hurricane) but from a grossly miscalculated anthropogenic disturbance (drainage, dikeage, large-scale monoculture planting involving a high-density human population). Before the dike breaks, the white "people felt uncomfortable but safe because there were the seawalls to chain the senseless monster in his bed. The folks let the people do the thinking. If the castles thought themselves secure, the cabins needn't worry. . . . The bossman might have the thing stopped before morning anyway" (158). Hurston is using free indirect discourse here to articulate—and simultaneously critique—black abdication of a skeptical risk epistemology. The black "folks," because of their greater experience at the flashpoints of a disturbed nature, should know that they are *not* secure; they should remember that the "bossman" does not live to protect them; they should remember that even when white "people" are safe in well-built physical structures on higher ground, that is no guarantee for black "folks" in shoddily built, low-lying "cabins."

The protagonist Janie, who had wanted her "chance at mud," had stayed at the lake's edge with her husband Tea Cake and their friend Motor Boat. Up until this scene in the novel, Tea Cake had shown himself to be, in a sense, *made for* Janie because they both possess an aptitude for listening to and knowing nature. Janie, who was conceived in the woods to a mother named Leafy, took her love lessons from the "alto chant" (11) of pollinating bees, "often spoke to falling seeds" (25) because she understood their language, "saw her life like a great tree in leaf" (8), and ceased to love the husband she had before Tea Cake because, as she said, "we ain't natural wid one 'nother" (46). Unlike that husband, who is associated with logging, drainage projects, and transforming nature into commodities, Tea Cake, alias Vergible Woods, is bio-sentient like Janie. He "know where de bream is beddin'" (102) and where wild strawberries are growing; he was "a bee to [her] blossom" (106), and their talk together runs "from grass roots tuh pine trees" (106). They don't merely know nature in its sweet equilibrium, though; both are drawn to its risk regimes as well and are pulled toward the muck for this reason.[7]

When the hurricane is blowing, Tea Cake and Motor Boat gamble in front of an audience, playing "Florida flip," and rolling dice (157). Tea Cake believes he lives in an aleatory world. Tea Cake's "art" of living in that world, up until this point, has involved a cosmically knowing kind of play (158). What is striking about this scene, however, is that Tea Cake's "art" of gambling has lost its grounding; he has allowed his bio-sentience to be smothered, putatively in deference to the white "bossman" (156). He has abjured his risk-trained epistemology. So that as Tea Cake rolls the dice, God will outdo him when he "roll[s] the dikes" (162); as Tea Cake plays "Florida flip," God will outdo him by flipping the Florida landscape rightside out again (returning earth to its wet state). Tea Cake and Motor finally stop gambling because, as Janie says, "Ole Massa is doin' *His* work now" (159). Tea Cake only regains his knowledge of disturbance regimes when he forgets about the "white folks['s]" (159) version of events and begins anew "watching God" (160) at work in nature. In this scene, Hurston is trying to distinguish between the illegitimately enshrined authority of the bossman and the ultimate, real, and dynamic power of a cosmic Ole Massa, a "high" "Nature":

> When finally evacuating, Janie and Tea Cake look back at the lake and see that a huge barrier of the makings of the dike to which the cabins had been added was rolling and tumbling forward. Ten feet higher and as far as they could see the muttering wall advanced before the braced-up waters like a road crusher on a cosmic scale. The monstropolous beast had left his bed. . . . He seized hold of his dikes and ran forward until he met the quarters; uprooted them like grass and rushed on after his supposed-to-be conquerors, rolling the dikes, rolling the houses, rolling the people in the houses along with other timbers. (161–162)

The black laborers' cabins are not protected by the dike but were structurally a part of the dike's function of protecting white agricultural property. The "monstropolous" lake forces the man-made wall across its southern border to "mutter" as it remakes the dike into a "cosmic" "road crusher," as it turns one of industrialism's tools of land transformation (the dike) against itself (as a road-crusher). The "beast" breaks its chains and rushes in admonition at "his supposed-to-be conquerors"; that the lake "rolls" the "timbers" along with the dike, houses, and people, brings to mind the great log rolls of the timber industry when felled forests were moved to market. The "great big ole scoundrel beast," in whom "Nature" is "high," is, as Sam Watson predicted, "eat[ing] up all de folks outa de house and den eat[ing] de house." In sum, the hurricane is not the "beast" here. Instead, nature comes to seem beastly when subjected to extreme forms of human intervention.

Tea Cake figures out his mistake of extrapolating out from plantation authority to divine authority and of mistaking the former for the latter, too late. He pays for his mistake in a telling way. Remarkably, it is neither the hurricane nor the flood that directly does Tea Cake in. Instead, he and Janie participate in an animal contest, which Tea Cake loses. On the couple's way to Palm Beach, Janie is blown out over and drops into water; in the water, she beholds an odd animal duo, a docile cow swimming with a "massive built dog" "growling" (165) on her back; as Janie tries to grab onto the tail of the cow, she becomes embodied as an "alligator"; Tea Cake dives in to save Janie from the dog, at which point he becomes an "otter" (166). The mad dog-over-cow figure functions as a metonym of the plantation complex, with the patrollers' hounds keeping a servile work force in submission through terror. The two wild creatures, the otter and alligator, are pulled inexorably into the orbit of the plantation regime; Tea Cake/the otter is bitten by the mad dog and absorbs its poison, becoming a "strange thing" "full of blank ferocity" (182), even though, as Tea Cake says, "Ah didn't mean tuh take his hate" (167). In other words, though both Janie and Tea Cake are graced with a playful, risk-wise, bio-sentience, they are unable, living as they do within the plantation world of the drained Everglades (along with its race-based environmental hazards), to resist the slow-acting poisons of slavery's legacies. In particular, these legacies cloud Tea Cake's vernacular epistemology.

Recent critics have seen the hurricane as expressive of Hurston's (and of Janie's) unbottled rage.[8] Some have argued that Hurston invoked the hurricane as a Vodou or Pan-African figure to return people of African descent to their rightful "affirmative blackness" and to prohibit any further black collusion with white "cultural, racial, and economic supremacy" (Lamothe 174). I have been arguing for a different interpretation. First, it is not the hurricane-as-metaphor that concerns her as much as does the 1928 flood as historical human product. Inevitably, a historical episode assumes a symbolism within a fictional book's semiotic economy, but one must also recognize how the numerous factual details that Hurston included in her novel suggest that she wants to signify meaning *through* considerations of the historical 1928 flood itself. It is also crucial to note how Hurston identifies the flood's devastation as a result of anthropogenic disturbance. Second, Hurston is not so much reaffirming blackness as she is exploring the contradictions within the black folk epistemology. Though such a biotically aware epistemology derives from generations of rural African Americans acting as the "means" of anthropogenic disturbance and hence gaining an exceptional insight into the violent nature of nature's own disturbance regimes, African Americans living in these rural zones did not necessarily distinguish the difference between the consequences of physical and anthropogenic disturbance. Their lives seemed so risk-saturated, seemed a game in which opponents always played with loaded dice, that it was often too great a challenge for these subjects to recognize their own "means-consequence"; to see the consequences of their actions in experimenting with those regimes; to accept the cognitive potential of their situation. In the case of the Lake Okeechobee flood, Hurston used the visible and catastrophic consequences of a massive drainage scheme to dramatize how even bio-sentient people could fool themselves into *not* knowing about risk-regimes that they have helped to create. Third, the "God" whom Tea Cake, Janie, and Motor Boat watch is not a partisan God; rather, it is the God described by Sam Watson when he says, God "made nature and nature made everything else." Though it is a dynamic, contingent force larger still than "stubborn-standing space," it enacts, impartially, a flow of "means–consequence." Humans must take measure of this truth through "operative techniques."

* * *

Because people of African descent in the rural south and Caribbean rarely espoused a worldview based on steady-state equilibrium, they offered a significant reservoir of nature-experience and nature-conceptualization, produced in a region of intense disturbance regimes, which, in the latter-day moment of ecological modeling, appears to have been remarkably insightful. It was not Leopold's "stability of the system" as such but rather the complex interplay of individuals and populations in geographic and cultural motion that intrigued Hurston. Dewey, Boaz, and, still earlier, Darwin prepared her to perceive "means" at such a scale and in such dynamic motion and with such eventuality. Hurston makes important contributions to our own contemporary concerns regarding environmental agency and citizenship in a cosmos understood to be naturally discordant. Hurston shows how challenging it was for people to discover their own hand in anthropogenic disturbance in a world they saw as violently aleatory. They rarely perceived that they were part of introducing a new order of catastrophe when their own history as a people seemed one long drawn-out cataclysm. The goal, then as now, is to act as if one has some efficacy in the gamble.

NOTES

1. See, for example, Max Horkheimer and Theodor W. Adorno, *Dialectic of Enlightenment.*
2. See John Crowe Ransom, "Reconstructed but unregenerate," in *I'll Take My Stand: The South and the Agrarian Tradition by Twelve Southerners* (5, 14); Booker T. Washington, *Up From Slavery: An Autobiography* (53); Alain Locke, *The New Negro* (6).
3. See Anthony Dewahare, *Nationalism, Marxism, and African American Literature Between the Wars: A New Pandora's Box* on Alain Locke's siting of a nationalist race capital in Harlem, while also clinging to Romantic ideas of authentic folk origins (33–34); see also Houston A. Baker, Jr., *Modernism and the Harlem Renaissance*; on Hurston's distinctive siting of a rural, southern, even tropical, modernity, see Leif Sorensen, "Modernity on a Global Stage: Hurston's Alternative Modernism."
4. See Hugh P. McDonald, *John Dewey and Environmental Philosophy* (72–73).
5. Contemporary ecologists distinguish among "physical disturbances," such as fires, floods, droughts, wind storms, and hurricanes; "biogenic disturbances," such as the impacts of herbivorous insects, mammals and pathogens; and "anthropogenic disturbances," in the form of such human activities as logging, drainage of wetlands, clearing for farming, introduction of alien species, and chemical pollution. The first two can be advantageous to an ecosystem because they eventually promote diversity of species. Too much disturbance—and this can often be anthropogenic—can make it impossible for the ecosystem to recover through diversification (del Moral and Walker 9–11; "Background").
6. In "Spunk," the protagonist of that name "ride[s] the dangerous log-carriage that fed the singing, snarling, biting, circle-saw"; he is mangled to death by the saw and laid out on a sawdust pile (108).
7. Adam Gussow, in *Seems Like Murder Here: Southern Violence and the Blues Tradition*, does an excellent job analyzing how Tea Cake teaches Janie about the "releasing pleasures" of the violence of blues culture alive in "the muck" (255); I would add that it is not just the risks caused by culture emphasized here but those caused by humanly altered nature as well.
8. See, for example, Keith Cartwright, "'To Walk with the Storm': Oya as the Transformative 'I' of Zora Neale Hurston's Afro-Atlantic Callings"; Thomas Cassidy, "Janie's Rage: The Dog and the Storm in *Their Eyes Were Watching God*"; Rachel Stein, *Shifting the Ground: American Women Writers' Revisions of Nature, Gender, and Race*; Sarah Ford, "Hurston's *Their Eyes Were Watching God*"; Anna Lillios, "'The Monstropolous Beast': The Hurricane in Zora Neale Hurston's *Their Eyes Were Watching God.*"

2 Haitian Soil for the Citizen's Soul

Karen Salt

On January 12, 2010, a devastating earthquake swept through Port-au-Prince and surrounding cities and areas in Haiti, causing deaths in the hundreds of thousands and displacing more than a million people from their homes. Although the scale of the devastation reflects, in part, what sociologist Mimi Sheller describes as "recent geographies of state rescaling and urban restructuring" that "emphasize the historicity of social space, the polymorphism of geographies, the dynamic restructuring of scale, and the continuous remaking of state space and urban space under capitalism," this devastation is also a story about human vulnerability to a different kind of violence enacted over a wide variety of spaces and across time (Sheller, "Virtual Islands" 18).

This chapter will focus on how the earthquake revealed this vulnerability as the large influx of Haitians who had already fled their nutrient-depleted fields or mountains devoid of trees for cities such as Port-au-Prince found themselves squeezed onto increasingly unstable and unsecure temporary camps after the earthquake. Literary critic and American studies scholar, Rob Nixon, defines "slow violence" as a "violence that occurs gradually and out of sight, a violence of delayed destruction that is dispersed across time and space, an attritional violence that is typically not viewed as violence at all" (Nixon 2). Applying Nixon's argument to Haiti, it becomes clear that the "spectacle" of building collapse and dramatic rescue of survivors is quickly splashed around the world by the global media, but reports focusing on a "slow violence" that has been unfolding for hundreds of years and has been affecting Haiti's soil, land, and population since earliest imperial contact remain unreported.

But there is a way to reveal this long, slow, shadowed neglect: re-read the land. According to Mimi Sheller, who writes about "Arboreal Landscapes of Power and Resistance," land has been "one of the key sites of social struggle in postslavery societies" (207). Sheller notes that "social relations of power, resistance, and oppositional culture building are inscribed into living landscapes of farming, dwelling, and cultivation" that mark out or "proclaim use-rights, ownership, or the sacrality of particular places" onto regions, territories, and entities such as roads, trees, and even soil (207).

This chapter reads the web of meanings surrounding landscape and soil at a particular temporal moment in the Caribbean basin as it responds to the hemispheric turn in American studies and the ecological and developmental turn in Caribbean studies. It charts the changing power dynamics and political implications that lend Haitian soil legibility and translatability across national and racial lines. Employing a postcolonial edge to my ecocritical lens, I engage in what Nixon describes as Caribbean environmental studies—an area he notes is a "particularly fertile domain of interdisciplinary enquiry" (Nixon 262). This interdisciplinary American and Caribbean studies approach is particularly needed in order to trace out how racialisms live through and within the land and transform articulations of landscape into power hierarchies of possibilities and control that resound in the multiscalar relationships at play in postearthquake Haiti today.

Rather than treat all Caribbean space in this chapter, I limit myself to a specific time and place. I examine the ways that Haitian President Jean-Pierre Boyer (1818–1843) utilized Haiti's landscape in a tangled campaign to sell Haitian citizenship primarily to freeborn and emancipated African-American laborers. I detail Boyer's efforts to frame this citizenship and link its rights and riches to the Haitian soil and landscape by investigating a series of letters written by Boyer to agents in the U.S. and his government appointee who toured the country in the early to mid-1820s. These private letters, republished in the U.S. by a printer in New York in 1824, illuminate the ways that Boyer foregrounds the Haitian landscape as a textual—and material—entity of exchange among humans, nations, and economic agents. I note the ways that Boyer twines the landscape into a commodity of racialized citizenship that was then "sold" to Americans of African descent. Through an engagement with these texts, I translate the Haitian landscape from "a soup of signs," as Benítez-Rojo describes the Caribbean region, into an entity that is materially concrete (2).

What emerges from Boyer's project materially is what I describe as a racialized citizenship scheme. Although the exact date of the project's start is not clear, Boyer's letters hint at an origin in the early to mid-1820s. It would be a plan doomed from the start because Boyer's desires for profit and control would increasingly overshadow the language of belonging and citizenship at the core of the campaign. Fighting for control and power would not be new to this Haitian head of state, who rose to power in Haiti after the assassination of Jean-Jacques Dessalines (1806), the yellow fever death of Alexandre Pétion (1818), and the suicide of Henri Christophe (1820) removed the final leaders of the Haitian Revolution and the first political leaders of the young nation from power. Once installed as president of Haiti, Boyer would unite Haiti and the Dominican Republic into one island nation. Focused on recapturing the wealth that earned Saint-Domingue its nickname as France's "Pearl of the Antilles," Boyer would reach out to other nation-states in the circum-Atlantic and declare that the "Pearl" had now become the "Queen of the Antilles."

This power play would demand a significant amount of rhetorical flourish and persuasion.

In order to convince others of Haiti's might, Boyer would need to frame Haiti in such a way that other Atlantic states would be willing—and eager—to trade with and acknowledge the young nation. He had to engage, then, in a form of self-fashioning that would see the "self" enlarged to encompass not the political and economic arrival of one individual but an entire nation.[1] To do this, he would turn to the natural landscape of Haiti in order to sell Haiti as a viable and economically powerful Atlantic republic.

Boyer grappled with how to economically move the young, self-avowed black republic into global markets still fueled and formed by racialized Atlantic slave economies. Leading a nation isolated and disavowed in many ways, Boyer sought a way to make Haiti free and economically prosperous in an Atlantic world that had no precedent for according those states of being to black-led nation-states, not to mention black, citizenship-seeking individuals. President Boyer representing a nation—as opposed to a free black community within the U.S., such as Philadelphia or Boston—sought a path through this mine field that would include trade agreements in the middle of the night, a flurry of diplomatic maneuverings, and a test of the tethers of affiliation between like-minded citizens and nations that sought to ease Haiti's isolated position within the chaotic family of Atlantic nation-states.

Although seized on and expanded by Boyer into a racialized form of citizenship, the migration of people of African descent from the U.S. to Haiti in the 1820s was initially prompted not by black activists or abolitionists in the U.S., but by an agent of the American Colonization Society (ACS). I will have more to say about them below and their official response to Boyer's plan. For now, it is important to register that the high public visibility of this scheme in the U.S. press was perhaps due to its link—for a time—with this supposed humanitarian group. Founded in 1816, the ACS counted Francis Scott Key, Henry Clay, and Thomas Jefferson among its supporters. While its popularity would ebb and flow in the nineteenth century, there is no mistaking its reach into diverse pockets of American society, as it would gather slave holders, philanthropists, Christian moralists, abolitionists, and crafty politicians under the umbrella of an aide society that not so innocently sought to remove free-born African Americans and emancipated former slaves to lands far away from white Americans.[2] Racialized notions of freedom, belonging, and identity were not somehow exceptional conditions within the U.S. Haiti, too, would face internal and external racialisms that impacted other Atlantic nations' reception of and engagement with it in the nineteenth century. President Boyer would face these dilemmas, and more, by politically responding to and playing on U.S.-based notions of racial difference. This gamesmanship is, perhaps, most apparent in his decision to send Jonathan Granville, a mulatto, to represent Haiti and advertise his plan in the U.S.

Identified as Citizen J. Granville in Boyer's letters and in American newspapers, Granville—a highly cultured, French-educated Haitian statesman—toured U.S. cities on Boyer's behalf in order to entice potential migrators and investors to support the project. Granville would, in effect, broker this citizenship for Boyer in key American markets. I use the term "broker" as it has been conceptualized by contemporary critics interested in development, social change, and the ways that globalization processes affect local populations and notions of citizenship. It is my contention that this description aptly encompasses the type of marketing that Granville would perform on behalf of his country's political leader. According to social policy critics David Lewis and David Mosse, brokers operate "within the fragmented politics of the postcolonial state, where power is exercised both through formal bureaucratic logics and through a diverse range of 'supra-local' associations and networks, in which there is a flourishing of intermediate actors and organizations" (Lewis and Mosse 12). Citizen Granville would employ these same logics in selling this scheme within America to various abolitionist and philanthropic organizations, black intellectuals, activists, and capitalists as the answer to America's and Haiti's racial and economic needs.

Boyer, through his letter-writing and the brokering of his statesman, agent Granville, carried out his scheme through a process that we might today call "place-branding," a term coined by twenty-first-century marketing and development theorist Simon Anholt, that ties places, nations, territories, and other entities with their resources, people, reputations, and histories.[3] I apply the contemporary concept of place-branding to this nineteenth-century situation in order to fully contextualize what I see as Boyer's buying and selling of Haiti's image. It is my contention that what Anholt identifies by name is not a new phenomenon but rather a much older practice. Today, many places now seek to give themselves a persona that can be linked to products or concepts. Much like a corporate brand, place-brands have become the new "it" thing for countries as they invest in shaping, broadcasting, and selling their images to the wider world.

Although spaces can change their images, the process also works to turn artificially engineered places into reality, such as Atlantis, the grand island resort on Paradise Island in the Bahamas. These massive developments proliferate in parts of the Caribbean, becoming spaces that sociologist Mimi Sheller describes as "new virtual islands—amalgams of infrastructure, architecture, software" that are "unbundled from local communities, citizenries and publics, and repackaged as intensely capitalized destinations of untouched paradise" ("Virtual Islands" 20). Although Haiti, with its political instability and environmental crises, would seem vastly different than the pristine, palm tree-laden splendor of these manufactured island paradises, we only have to remember that disaster can engender its own sort of tourism, as well as entice capitalists to rebuild places in their own image. Many fear that postearthquake Haiti's fate resides between these two poles.

Twenty-first-century advertising and corporate brand guru Wally Olins makes just this point. Olins—a leading advocate of and professional advisor about nation branding—notes that "the truth of the matter is that nations have always tried to create and modulate their reputations in order to create domestic loyalties and coherence and promote their own power and influence in neighboring countries" (170). Olins differs from Anholt in that the former embraces the marketing aspects within nation or place-branding and offers his services to various nation-states in crafting a brand identity. Although I would distance myself from Olins's more corporate and wealth-oriented approach to nation or place-branding, I cannot help but agree with his assessment that "there is in reality nothing new about national branding, except the word 'brand' and the techniques that are now used, which derive from mainstream marketing and branding techniques" (170).

Anholt and Olins may come at this from different perspectives, but both accurately sense the timelessness of the act of place-branding and its dangerous power to re-present the human and non-human world in intangible ways. Anholt links these "ways" with the art of persuasion and what he optimistically describes as a nation's "truth." He notes that "political parties, governments, good causes, state bodies, even non-governmental organizations [. . .] understand that profound truth about human endeavor which marketers always knew: that being in possession of the truth is not enough. The truth must be sold" (Anholt, "Branding Places and Nations" 214). It is this critical issue that I sense within the racialized citizenship scheme of Boyer. He would, as I noted above, sell one image of Haiti—and its landscape—in order to market another that depended less on the environment but more on labor and crop production. Publicly, Haiti would be a black paradise; privately, it would be a black workstation. Fate, or rather the Atlantic nation-states' history of disavowal and containment of Haiti, forced this contrapuntal scheme into action—especially the actions of the U.S.

Before addressing in more detail how Boyer used space and race to economically sustain and environmentally manufacture Haitian citizens, it is helpful to describe the political conditions that led to his citizenship plan. Initially, Boyer tried to sell self-avowed black Haiti not as a black nation, but as a French one in an Atlantic world where he believed that the support of a European power could help open the door to Haiti's arrival as an autonomous player within Atlantic economic markets. To do this, Boyer would encourage diplomatic relations with France that benefitted both countries. But times had changed significantly in France by the 1820s. Although the French Revolution played a significant role in the formation of both Haiti's and France's republican beginnings, by the time Boyer came into power, France had altered its political orientation, finding itself once again under a monarch. This political change within France prompted a historical readjustment.

France's first order of business? A didactic re-memory lesson. Official French governmental documents began referring to Haiti as the French-controlled colony Saint-Domingue in an effort to change history. It would be this historical amnesia that would fuel rumors within the Atlantic that a French invasion of the former colony was imminent. Although never fully actualized, the rumors forced Haitian officials, like Boyer, to fortify the surrounding ports and the interior from attack.[4] Significant amounts of money would be spent to expand and prepare the military for the widely anticipated and feared invasion by France.

For strategic reasons, then, a transnational alliance with another Atlantic nation-state made sense in order to fight off the French entities circling the island. According to theologian and Caribbeanist David Nicholls, Boyer may have sensed that "foreign protection from one power might at least prevent arbitrary intervention" by another more dangerous power (Nicholls 65). The trick would be in controlling the terms. Before Boyer could control any negotiation with U.S. officials, he had to get their attention.

James Monroe—then president of the U.S.—would make the task of forging a Haitian–American alliance difficult, if not impossible. Having just finished with the Missouri Compromise (passed by Congress in 1820), Monroe would be disinclined to deal with Haiti. Although the tenets of the Monroe Doctrine (1823) would seem to imply that Haiti would be one of the many lands protected by the U.S. from European interference, Monroe and his administration asserted that Haiti was not included in this new policy. This view was apparent as early as June 1823, when, in a letter to Thomas Jefferson, Monroe acknowledges having received a formal application from St. Domingo (one of Haiti's former colonial names) for recognition but side steps responding, preferring instead to offer silence (Monroe 316–317). Monroe might have been able to control his administration's stance regarding Haiti, but he could not stop the rest of his citizens from taking a keen interest in the young nation.

The *Niles' Weekly Register*—a leading nationally circulating news magazine established by Hezekiah Niles in 1811 and committed to "fairness and balance in the editorial agenda"—reprinted a letter written by Haitian President Jean-Pierre Boyer to John Dodge, a Boston-area trader (Kovarik 366). The prefatory editorial remarks before the letter situate the importance of this moment for the reader. The editorial acknowledges that the people of Haiti are not fully comprehended by the U.S. but predicts that "the day, we trust, is not far distant when the United States will acknowledge their independence, with the full consent, not only of the philanthropist, but of the sagacious statesman" ("Letter" 391).

According to the editor of the *Niles' Weekly Register* (hereafter referred to as the *Register*), establishing an economic and military alliance in the West Indies with Haiti made strategic sense for a U.S. intent on enlarging its strategic share of the global market. Niles understood that this recognition also contained a more practical issue: spatial proximity. In another editorial in the *Register*, Niles suggests that rather than sending thousands of "colored people" to Africa while many more were born in America's slave states, the U.S. could send every single person of color to Haiti. "This republic," he argues, had enough space to "receive *all* the colored persons of the United States, bond or free, at once." In Niles's worldview, African Americans could provide the corporeal space through which an American and Haitian trade alliance could flourish ("The Free Blacks" 283).

Boyer, himself, makes this point even more plainly. In his letter to Dodge, he stresses that "it cannot be denied that Hayti is of great importance in the scale of commerce" ("Letter" 391). Alluding to Haiti's past as France's "Pearl of the Antilles," Boyer reminds his readers that by aligning with the independent nation of Haiti, the U.S. could participate in Haiti's projected future wealth without having to deal with France's imperial shadow. This alignment, though, would have to recognize Haiti's power within the Caribbean as, Boyer states, "the *Queen of the Antillee*" ("Letter" 391). Boyer warns that if the U.S. was not willing to hail the Queen, some other nation would. To all this, Monroe and his administration offered no response.

Disavowed by the U.S., Boyer would again turn to France and this time try to come up with an agreement that would not force the nation to reestablish its colonial relationship with its politically former imperial master. Successful in fighting off French imperialistic attempts, Boyer would be less successful in fighting off the economic colonialism that France ultimately offered in tandem with its recognition of Haitian independence. In 1825, the King of France, Charles X, publicly announced his infamous *Ordonnance,* in which Haiti agreed to pay 150 million *francs* to the French planters who lost "property" during the Haitian Revolution in exchange for France's official recognition of Haiti. This deal, although designed to ensure Haiti's entry into global markets, actually chained Haiti with debt. Not surprisingly, Haiti had to secure the money from an outside source as it did not have that kind of wealth in its coffers. French banks were only too willing to loan the money at exorbitant rates to Haiti. In the lead-up to this offer, Boyer—recognizing from earlier negotiations that if France could not get Haiti's land, then it would take Haiti's money—reached out to those tied to Haiti through the legacies of slavery, migration, and displacement—African Americans.[5] Boyer reached this audience in multiple ways: through letters to commercial agents, abolitionists, and their supporters; African Americans who migrated to Haiti and reported their stay to those at home; African-American newspapers; and, what I will focus on here, an unlikely alliance (however brief and tenuous) with agents of the ACS.

According to an early ACS pamphlet, the ACS dedicated itself to establishing "colonies, by voluntary contribution, on the western coast of Africa, and thus [restoring . . .] free people of color to their kindred and country; [. . . and encouraging and producing] an entire emancipation of that race from America" (*A Sketch of the Origin* 7). By the early 1820s, the ACS had founded a colony with the financial assistance of the U.S. government at Cape Mesurado on the coast of West Africa. Ravaged by disease and facing intense animosity from the local inhabitants, the colony—and the ACS—encountered increasing public opposition in America. Annoyed at the amassing difficulties in garnering support for African colonization, Loring Dewey—an ACS agent from New York—decided to explore a much closer colonization opportunity after a chance encounter with a Haitian citizen. In March 1824, Dewey sent a vague and misleading letter full of questions directly to Haitian President Jean-Pierre Boyer inquiring about the possibility of creating an ACS colony in Haiti. Boyer wasted no time in responding and turning what Dewey initially instigated as a potential ACS endeavor into an economic opportunity for Haiti.

None of this is apparent in Boyer's initial response to Dewey's letter. Boyer merely answers Dewey's questions—such as inquiries into education, the place of marriage within Haitian society, and the possibility of Haiti funding all or part of the emigrants' voyages to Haiti's shores. Eventually, he deals with the major issue: an ACS colony in Haiti. He replies that this "cannot be," but follows up this rejection with these important lines: "Those who come [to Haiti], being children of Africa, shall be Haytiens as soon as they put their feet upon the soil of Hayti: they will enjoy happiness, security, tranquility, such as we ourselves possess" (*Correspondence* 10).

This passage is significant. First, note the explicit insertion of Africa as the cultural link between African Americans and Haitians. While Boyer does not tie his own ancestry to Africa, he makes it clear that those Americans who are somehow identified as "children of Africa" immediately become Haitians on spatial contact with the nation's fecund soil. But this vague ecological transference raises more questions than it answers, such as, does the designation of "Haytien" come with limited privileges or full citizenship? If full citizenship is accorded—and this is what I believe Boyer would like to imply—then why the shifting pronouns toward the end of the phrase? Based on Boyer's word choices, it would seem that he believes these new Haitians would be inherently less Haitian than Haitians born within the nation.[6] No matter how much he may have rhetorically danced around the racial sameness of Haitians and African Americans, Boyer could not hide the fact that African Americans who came to Haiti through this citizenship scheme were merely a means to an end, allowing, through their colored bodies, the Haitian nation-state to obliterate the continuous push and pull that it experienced between the Atlantic nations' disavowal of it and desire to obtain it.

The above passage, though, contains an additional important line. Boyer notes that once African Americans placed their "feet upon the soil" of Haiti, the natural environment would respond specifically to them. According to Boyer, during this process, the Haitian soil magically conveys citizenship to "the children of Africa." In some manner, then, the soil racially recognizes persons of African descent. Yet this process describes more than just recognition of ancestral belonging and racial affiliation. The soil, in Boyer's imagination, erects a protective border between Haitian citizens and (white) foreign others, distinguishing between those that do and do not spatially belong within the nation. In essence, this protective mechanism grants the natural environment the ability to recognize those persons whose cultural and racial roots lie within Haiti.

This protection even extended to the economy. In Boyer's ecological imagination, the landscape constrains the ability of foreigners to touch Haitian soil and receive any current or future wealth from it. Rather than see in the Haitian landscape a land ripe for *anyone's* plundering, Boyer recasts Haiti as a place that evokes—quite literally through the soil's productive output—the social and political order that surrounds it. As such, Haitian soil heals the damaged souls of Africa's descendants who experienced restrictive and racist conditions within the white Atlantic world.

This should, ironically, sound familiar to Americanists who study the nineteenth century and who will sense within this racial and spatial rhetoric what American studies and literary critic Amy Kaplan sees as the link between Manifest Destiny and domestic discourse within the U.S., in which "spatial and gendered configurations are linked in complex ways that are dependent upon racialized notions of the foreign" ("Manifest Domesticity" 583). In Haiti, the foreigner is always *blanc*—even ones who would be categorized as black in their own countries. In making African Americans neither *blanc* nor foreign, Boyer allows them to be recognized by the soil—and the nation—as Haitian citizens.

But in doing this, Boyer casts the landscape as a mechanism that can distinguish each individual's cultural and/or racial connection to Africa. It can literally read human soles and detect each person's African soul. Through some secret and shadowy process, this racialized soil/soul duality transforms into Haitian citizenship. As fantastical as it sounds, Boyer is not the only one to sense the landscape's role in human political agency. Mimi Sheller calls this aspect of the environment a "living landscape" that carries within it knowledge about the "different textures of freedom as lived" by its human inhabitants ("Arboreal Landscapes" 215).

None of this racial particularism mattered to ACS agent Loring Dewey. He used this moment to cast himself as the liberator of African Americans *and* Haiti. He would activate this fantasy by initiating the printing of Boyer's letters in New York in 1824. The published letters made headlines across the U.S. *The North American Review* printed a review of this correspondence in 1825. The reviewer states:

> Nothing can be more fair and honorable, or indicate a better spirit, than the part which President Boyer has acted, respecting the emigration of our people of color to that country. He invited them first by a proclamation, offered them lands, citizenship, and all the privileges of native Haytians [. . . .] Whatever may be the motives of interest with which he is influenced, in wishing to increase the population of the

> island, and extend the growth of its agriculture and commerce, all his communications and all his actions prove that he has a higher motive; that he feels deeply for the condition of the colored people in this country, and that he is ready to make any reasonable sacrifice for their relief. ("Review" 204)

By casting aside any material consideration of why Boyer engages in the plan, the reviewer emphasizes the "higher motive" that guides Boyer's actions. Motivated, perhaps, by a celestial calling, Boyer offered Haiti's providentially chosen "black" land to the U.S.'s debased black people. Or so Boyer would like for his American audience to believe.

In his letters, Boyer pushes the religious rhetoric even further. He stresses that Haiti's soil would baptize African Americans anew and turn them into something beyond what they were before. He continues these ruminations in a letter to another U.S. philanthropic agent, Charles Collins. Here, Boyer ties Haiti's soil to cultivation, cultivation to citizenship, and citizenship to virtues. He states:

> What joy will it give hearts like yours, to see these scions of Africa, so abased in the United States, where they vegetate with no more utility to themselves than to the soil which nourishes them, transplanted to Hayti, where they will become no less useful than estimable, ennobling them in their own eyes, [where they] cannot fail to attach them to regular habits, and the acquisition of social virtues, and to render them worthy by their good conduct, to enjoy the benefits which their new country will bestow upon them! (*Correspondence* 16)

Boyer argues that once on Haitian soil, African Americans would finally transform into the moral citizens they were always meant to be.

Yet, coming to Haiti and stepping on the soil would not be enough to actually make one Haitian. According to Boyer, Haitianness had to be earned. And not just by the new arrivals engaging in certain types of "good conduct"—as implied in Boyer's letter to Collins. Boyer articulates just what African Americans would need to do for their citizenship in his instructions to Jonathan Granville—the Haitian agent charged with marketing African-American migration in the U.S.

In these instructions, Boyer turns away from the flourishes seen in his earlier exchange of letters with the agents. Casting aside the language of racio-spatial citizenship, Boyer gets down to business, outlining who Citizen Granville should associate himself with in the U.S., where specific numbers of African Americans should live in Haiti, and what commodities they should produce. In placing restrictive boundaries around mobility, rights, labor, and belonging, Boyer attempts to police the citizenship promised to the "new" Haitians by tying their habitation to certain plantations and their labor to the production of certain goods.

In essence, what Boyer suggests in his cold, practical calculations is that while the soil "reads" for the right codes of blackness through the soles of all those who step on Haiti's shores, it also enchains the "new" Haitians to a system of material production by implicitly yoking orderly labor with orderly made products and orderly made products with economic stability. By selling the soil as abundant, rich, and giving, Boyer attempts to hide—except to his own agent—the fact that only through cultivating, laboring, and tilling the soil to increase the government's coffers could these "new" Haitians become citizens. Although forced, in many ways, to entertain this plan through the political disavowals and desires of U.S. and French officials, Boyer's scheme would successfully lure upward of 13,000 African Americans to Haiti for purposes that were neither as innocent nor as egalitarian as they at first seem.[7] In exchange for migrating to Haiti, African Americans would obtain a Haitian citizenship through a scheme enchained by demands of labor or capital. Although rhetorically laced through with the power of the natural world, Boyer's scheme would have less to do with the land, in figurative terms, and more to do with the literal cultivation of the land.

As noted above, Boyer sold Haiti's landscape to multiple groups—most notably African-American laborers—as the answer to the U.S.'s and Haiti's economic and racial problems. He sought to alter, through this campaign, Haiti's geopolitical position in the Atlantic world by shifting its reputation—or place-brand—from one of violence to one of power. Although cloaked in the language of inclusion, this extension of political belonging would in actuality operate as a commodity that linked Haiti's revolution, its fecund soil, and the unmarred beauty of the young nation's natural world with the political rights for blacks that nestled at the heart of Haiti's emerging national ideals. In combining citizenship, racial belonging, profit, and a demand for laboring bodies, Boyer created a product that could be internationally packaged, marketed, and sold to disparate bodies—one form to potential new Haitian citizens and another to the global leaders and merchants interested in benefiting from the wealth that Haiti's soil (and its laborers) could generate. This environmentally manufactured sense of racial belonging, though, hid the undercurrent of labor and the goal of economic productivity that drove the entire enterprise. What seems like an expansive form of racial connectivity across territorial boundaries was in actuality a mechanism for enlarging Haiti's labor force and ensuring the cultivation of specific capital goods. In reality, Haitian citizenship was pretended to be given for altruistic reasons, when, in fact, what was exchanged for this citizenship was labor.

What I have offered here, then, is a brief examination of how a form of ecological citizenship was created and marketed as part of nineteenth-century Haitian place-branding. As compelling as this branding might be, it would not be the last time that Haiti's landscape would become entangled in attempts to sell Haiti to the highest bidder. Although Boyer's plan was a response to colonial and hemispheric pressures, Haitian officials today face similar difficulties trying to balance this question: How much is Haiti worth and to whom?

CONCLUSION

Reports differ as to what happened to Haiti's new citizens. Some, it seems, returned to the U.S., convinced that Haiti was vastly different from the landscape that Boyer described; others stayed. A complete accounting of the 13,000 migrants remains unfinished. As of this chapter, no detailed history has been presented that illuminates how these various individuals navigated the lived realities of this commoditized form of racialized citizenship in which cultivation—and order—remained such key components. It is possible, though, to speculate about their lives, especially if one reads another publication intended specifically for those entertaining migration to Haiti alongside Boyer's rhetoric.

Published in New York in 1824, *Information for the Free People of Colour, Who Are Inclined to Emigrate to Hayti* is not authored by Dewey or Boyer, but contains elements of both within its pages, most notably, in the descriptions of the landscape that the new citizens would cultivate—and in some instances—own. Rather than noting the ways that the new Haitians would benefit from an encounter with Haitian soil, the *Information* notes the landscape restrictions imposed on the citizens.

Instead of profiting from the soil's abundance, the *Information* states that the new transplants could only inhabit "uncultivated or neglected lands"—ones the pamphlet is at pains to stress are *not* synonymous with lands in the U.S. that were "wild and uncleared land." Instead of having an open invitation to settle anywhere, the new citizens were limited to experiencing the ecological abundance from lands that had been "deserted" (7). In essence, lands abandoned by former French and Creole planters. As this document notes, nature operated as a cipher for a citizenship in which the newly minted Haitian/African-American laborers and the Haitian peasant population remained the most vulnerable and least protected within society.

Boyer, though, is only one example of the entities who have engaged in brokering Haiti's image or natural resources in the last few centuries. In offering a close examination of one of these actors, I present critics engaged in searching for a deeper understanding of the role of the built and natural landscape in political processes, new sources for perusal, and a new way of re-reading "a wider spectrum of texts." The importance of the environment is not something new, but its import, as the cholera epidemic suggests, remains a critical component of Haiti's recovery.[8] As this examination of Haiti's landscape over two centuries suggests, more work needs to be done to trace the import of the environment in the Caribbean than merely creating more descriptions of the land. Influential Caribbean writer and cultural critic Edouard Glissant argues that "describing the landscape is not enough." According to him, "the individual, the community, [and] the land are inextricable in the process of creating history. Landscape is a character in this process" (Glissant 59). The trick is in how to read it. Caribbeanist and cultural critic Antonio Benítez-Rojo suggests that this is actually a call to re-read the Caribbean in order to reveal "its own textuality" (Benítez-Rojo 2). It is my contention that re-reading the landscape reorients the power games among persons, nations, communities, and entities, enabling old materials and new ones to speak the landscape—especially in places such as Haiti, in which slow violence has been perpetrated over a long period of time in often uncharted ways.

For Haiti's political and economic future to be different, the tangled practices of consumption, extraction, profit, and oppression must be critiqued and, perhaps, changed. What I am suggesting is that the rationale for Boyer's nineteenth-century scheme matters to our present moment. Nation-states, corporations, and politicians sell various truths about the lands around us. It is up to us as community members and global citizens to take on anthropologist Michel-Rolph Trouillot's challenge to track these power shifts and expose their roots (Trouillot xix).

NOTES

1. For more, see Rayford W. Logan's *The Diplomatic Relations of the United States with Haiti, 1776–1891* (Chapel Hill: The University of North Carolina Press, 1941), and David Nicholls's *From Dessalines to Duvalier: Race, Colour and National Independence in Haiti* (Cambridge: Cambridge University Press, 1979).
2. See P. J. Staudenraus's *The African Colonization Society 1816–1865* (New York: Columbia University Press, 1961) for an excellent recounting of the ACS.
3. For more, see Simon Anholt, "Editorial," *Place Branding and Public Diplomacy* 1.1 (2004): 4–11.
4. See Logan and Nicholls.
5. For more, see Chris Dixon's *African America and Haiti: Emigration and Black Nationalism in the Nineteenth Century* (Westport: Greenwood Press, 2000).
6. In his letters to Granville, Boyer states that "the constitution having established by the 44th article, that all individuals of African blood, who will appear in the Republic, shall, after a years [sic] residence, enjoy the civil and political rights and quality of a citizen" (*Correspondence* 21). As I briefly show here and in more depth in my book, these rights contained significant chains—if they were fully granted at all.
7. Also quoted by Chris Dixon, this figure is considered an estimate. For more, see Julie Winch, *A Gentleman of Color: The Life of James Forten* (Oxford: Oxford University Press, 2002), and Colin [Joan] Dayan, "A Few Stories About Haiti, or, Stigma Revisited," *Research in African Literatures* 35.2 (Summer 2004): 157–172.
8. See "Cholera." *Partners in Health.*

3 Intimate Cartographies

Navajo Ecological Citizenship, Soil Conservation, and Livestock Reduction

Traci Brynne Voyles

In 1928 the U.S. government began plans for a massive dam project on the Colorado River. The Boulder Dam (or, as it was later renamed, the Hoover Dam) would go on to supply energy and water to major population centers in the Southwest. In designing and building the dam, federal geologists with the U.S. Geological Survey began to worry that large amounts of silt deposited in the Colorado River from upriver soil runoff would quite literally muck up the works, causing major operational problems for the dam (White 250–251). These geologists traced what they thought were the origins of the problematic soil runoff to the Navajo Reservation,[1] where sheep, goat, cattle, and horse grazing was an integral part of the culture, history, and economic life of the Diné people.[2] Livestock raising had been promoted by the Bureau of Indian Affairs (BIA) for decades as a self-sustaining economic practice. However, Boulder Dam geologists and Indian Service (IS) employees concurred that sheep could be blamed for what they saw as an inordinate amount of soil erosion attributed to overgrazing. Calling the Reservation " 'Public Enemy No. 1' in causing the Colorado Silt problem," it seemed clear to federal employees that drastic action would need to be undertaken to solve the soil erosion problem on Navajo land (White 251). Navajos themselves were well aware of the problem; it was clear to many that the region was experiencing a drought, which, in the Navajos' long experience with this high arid ecosystem, was not uncommon. Rather than blaming the sheep, as the federal geologists, conservationists, and IS personnel did, many Navajos recognized that the problem was rooted in the boundedness of the reservation, restricting Navajo sheep to an area inappropriately small for a growing Diné population and their herds (Roessel 46; Weisiger, *Dreaming* xvi–xvii).

The federal government, however, saw the problem as stemming directly from overlarge Navajo sheep herds and, as a connected problem, from the population growth of Navajos themselves. What began as an attempt to protect the Boulder Dam from this "Public Enemy" quickly became the government's first attempt at soil erosion control, under the Soil Conservation Service (SCS) and the Navajo Soil Erosion Control Project, ultimately resulting in more than a decade of now notorious policies that forced the selling-off and slaughter of thousands of Navajo sheep, goats, horses, and cows. The ultimate failures of the soil conservation and livestock reduction policies have been well documented by historians.[3] Livestock reduction proved intensely painful for Navajos, who, like tribal chairman Sam Ahkeah, would remember stock reduction as "the most devastating experience in Navajo history since the imprisonment at Fort Sumner" (quoted in Iverson 23).[4] Less studied are the implications of the cartographic, agronomic, and sociological projects that were conducted by the SCS alongside livestock reduction. Under the Navajo Soil Erosion Control Project, Navajo land and people alike became the subjects of intense federal scrutiny.

Using primary source archival research, this chapter explores the period of soil erosion control on Diné land, arguing that federal conservation policies were attempts at rationalizing not only Navajo soil and stockherding, but also Navajo family life and gender politics. Soil conservation and its attendant cartographies can be been viewed, as James Scott puts it, as "a state's attempt to make a society legible" (2). Thus, the mapping project that the IS and SCS had undertaken placed an emphasis on producing knowledge about Navajo life, bodies, and lands. It also functioned as an attempted assimilation of Diné family, economic, and ecological practices. The racial logic that guided these erosion control policies and cartographic projects constructed the Navajos as being outside the bounds of normative ecological citizenship, which, at the time, revolved around what was considered "rational" resource use, conservationism, and land occupancy. As tools of normative ecological citizenship through rational resource use, the modern sciences wielded by the SCS purported to alone resolve the soil erosion problem. The SCS proceeded to make the Navajo people and land subject to intense scrutiny, as they mined for data that would constitute endless charts and graphs that all demanded increasing reform of Navajo life and ecological practices. As I argue, Navajos were not only excluded from normative ecological citizenship, but in fact became constitutive of it as both a test site for conservationism and a cautionary tale against what was termed their "maladjusted" relationships to the environment. However, in response to these experiences with the federal government during the 1930s and 1940s, Navajo environmentalist praxis, from the 1970s to the present, has increasingly placed the Navajos as leaders in local, U.S., and global environmental justice movements, as they have shaped their own self-determined notions of ecological citizenship.

THE "NAVAJO PROBLEM"

In 1941, ER Fryer, then General Superintendent of the Navajo Service, submitted a report to Commissioner of Indian Affairs John Collier that succinctly summed up the federal position on the "Navajo problem." Fryer writes,

> Early in the [Navajo Service] program, the underlying causes of maladjustment were clearly defined as:
>
> Overpopulation of the Navajo country;[5] correlative evils of excess numbers and poor distribution of livestock, severe overgrazing, unregulated forest and woodland use, inadequate farming system and underdevelopment of potential agricultural resources, and deterioration of social interrelationships, Indian leadership, economics, and health.[6]

Described here by Fryer as a nexus of "correlative evils" having to do not only with social but also with ecological and economic challenges, the "Navajo Problem" became a focus of federal Indian policy during the 1930s and 1940s. Many government and media observers went so far as to predict dire consequences, including the extinction of the Navajo people if the "problem" were not addressed aggressively by reducing Diné livestock, curtailing human population growth, and educating the Diné about federal ideas of "good" resource conservationism. These tactics were undertaken rather than accommodating the Navajos' need for a larger land base to support their growing population and herds. For years, the only weapon wielded by the federal government against soil erosion was to reduce herds, which, as the singular economic resource of many Diné families, was economically and culturally indispensable. This single-pronged strategy reduced Navajo livestock from about 1,270,000 sheep or "sheep equivalents" to the federally determined carrying capacity of the land. The result was a devastating 56% reduction of the Navajos' total number of livestock.

Throughout the period of stock reduction, Commissioner Collier, General Superintendent Fryer, and other IS personnel seemed unable or unwilling to understand differences in Diné and U.S. conceptions of stock ownership. The Service treated a flock as property, ignoring the extra-economic roles of sheep, goats, cows, and horses in Navajo life. As environmental historian Marsha Weisiger documents, Navajo women owned many of the sheep, and most of the goats that were "reduced" in the 1930s, which severely curtailed the political and economic power and independence of Diné women (*Dreaming* 80). The government defined a flock as the property of one head of household (almost always male) rather than as collectively owned among a number of family members, including and especially women, extended family members, and children. As Weisiger points out, Navajo "[w]omen . . . controlled the means of their own production: livestock and land" ("Gendered" 442). The federal agents in charge of overseeing stock reduction, however, did not appear to recognize these gendered patterns in stock ownership, nor did they seem to appreciate that Navajos might derive more value from their stock than mere economic gain.

These kinds of elisions, and Diné attempts to rectify them in order to mitigate the violence of federal policies, emerged at the outset of conversations about stock reduction. In a 1928 Tribal Council meeting in Leupp,

Arizona, then Assistant Commissioner on Indian Affairs EB Meritt and then Superintendent of the Santa Fe Indian School Chester Faris presented the Tribal Council with an early version of stock reduction that would require excess grazing fees for stock owners who had herds in excess of one thousand head of sheep, goats, cows, and horses.[7] In the meeting, Meritt framed this proposal not only as a promotion of fairness and justice but also of economic and infrastructural development.[8] He argues that these efforts will "increase the quality of all [Navajo] sheep," a nod to a federal sheep-breeding program at the Fort Wingate Sheep Laboratory that sought to replace the "scrubby" and "degenerate" Navajo sheep (the Navajo churra) with a more marketable "fine blooded" American breed (the Rambouillet) (Weisiger, *Dreaming* 192–194).[9]

The subsequent discussion about Meritt's proposal at the 1928 meeting illustrates the depth of white misunderstandings (deliberate or no) of Navajo sheep ownership and family forms, which led to increasingly unjust reduction policies. While Meritt continued to insist that each individual stockowner would be allowed one thousand head of sheep, the Council members tried in vain to explain to him the more nuanced problem of multiple Navajo owners of one herd, including owners who were women and children. One exchange, between Meritt and Little Silversmith of the Southern Navajo Agency, reveals the depth of this misunderstanding. Little Silversmith declares that "I am speaking for my tribe. I think they are in the same fix as I am. You see a bunch of sheep, they don't belong to this one man. Now with the number of sheep I have, I have to eat and feed my children." While Mr. Merrit tries to allay Silversmith's fears by speaking in the language of grazing fees:

> Each family, the husband and the wife and the minor children will be entitled to one thousand sheep without paying an excess grazing fee. If you have children who are grown, who are 21 years of age, and that child is living with you, that child would also be entitled to one thousand head of sheep. . . . Now that same rule would apply to every child above the age of twenty-one years, so you see that this proposed rule would apply to only the big sheep owners.[10]

In this exchange, Little Silversmith tries unsuccessfully to communicate to Meritt the issues that stock reduction would raise in his own Southern district, particularly the fact that from a Navajo perspective this reduction policy in this proposed form was essentially meaningless, as no individual (male) "head of household" owned the entire herd. As Weisiger points out, "[t]he fact that women really mattered in Diné society . . . never fully penetrated the consciousness" of the IS ("Gendered" 441). This evidence is compounded by the fact that Meritt was asking that the proposal be approved by the all-male Tribal Council; women were simply not consulted by the federal agents nor regarded as important political or economic actors. The details of this Council meeting reveal the extent to which the federal government refused to recognize the relationship of Navajos to their stock herds and gendered patterns of stock ownership. In the 1930s, this would become a matter of great personal, political, and economic crisis for Navajos, who tried to resist the mass slaughter of their sheep, goats, horses, and cows, and looked on in horror as the carcasses of their stock were rounded up, sold off, shot, and sometimes burned.[11]

The IS's foundational misunderstandings would remain engraved in federal policy. Federal discourses reduced the despair of Navajo women, witnessing the violent destruction of their herds, to female domestic concerns. As Office of Indian Affairs field representative FW LaRouche explained to Commissioner Collier, "[u]nder present conditions [a Navajo woman] fears the loss of sheep because she does not know that other food can be acquired. She thinks that by taking the sheep, we are taking the food out of the mouths of her children."[12] Importantly, LaRouche couches these words in an argument for replacing the Navajos' livestock economy, which by the 1940s was a ghost of its former size, with *military* work. Drawing direct comparisons to the ideals of white heteronormative gender relations in wage-based economies, LaRouche writes that if Navajo men were to work in military industries, "[t]he wife could always buy food for herself and her family; she could always be sure some money would be available for future needs."[13] In further explanation of women's angst during and after stock reduction, LaRouche blames Navajo men's presumed economic impotency. He writes, "[the women] would rather keep their sheep because they do not believe they can depend on the earnings of their men, and experience seems to justify skepticism."[14]

While ignorance of Navajo gender roles played a significant role in stock reduction policy, the larger project of solving the "problem" involved even more violent elisions of domesticity, family forms, and reproduction. In the eyes of federal conservationists, it was not just livestock overpopulation that was to blame, but Navajo people as well. In the 1930s, long-held federal impressions of Navajo overpopulation of their "inadequate" land base were folded into policy discourses. An increase in the size of the reservation to accommodate Navajos and their herds was seen as a political impossibility, due in no small part to a noisy campaign made by white stockmen who ran their herds in the region to the east of the reservation proper.[15] An emerging discourse framed the Navajo as irrationally hyper-reproductive even in the face of scarce resources:

> The Navajo Indians [are] the largest tribe of Indians in the United States, increasing from 10,000 in 1868 to approximately 45,000 in 1938, a phenomenal increase in seventy years despite the poverty of their arid land. (Jones et al. vii)[16]

John Collier himself listed the constituent parts of the Navajo problem as "rapid deterioration of land, forage, and forest resources from overgrazing," "*increase of population to a point at which extraordinary effort is necessary to sustain living*," and "lack of knowledge on the part of many of the Navajos as to the seriousness of their situation" (see Pollock, *Navajo Policies and Program* 61).[17] In short, federal discourse about the Navajo problem concluded that "[m]ost of today's difficulties" result from the fact that population "is increasing faster than economic development of the resources of the tribe."[18] Concern over Diné population growth reflects larger tendencies in U.S. conservationist and environmentalist discourse to problematically link the growth of populations of color to environmental decline. This is particularly notable for twentieth-century Native American population growth, as population *decimation* in the previous four centuries wreaked havoc on Native nations throughout the Americas.

As part of SCS and IS attempts to map out the contours of the Navajo problem, sociologists and social workers were deployed to the reservation to collect data on Navajo social life, including family life and domestic practices.[19] One social worker, Ruby Tomlinson, paints a gloomy portrait of Diné family life:

> No homes were found to be sanitary and about 28 per cent were rated as fair in appearance for Navajo hogans. They still cling to the typical windowless, one room hogan constructed of poles and mud. Improvements in construction and in the way a few homes were kept were found to exist among a few families.[20]

Tomlinson implicitly links these domestic conditions to "illicit" sexuality and disease, noting that "[c]ourt records show that arrests over a period of two years were predominantly for social disorders," including "giving venereal disease" and "adultery and illicit cohabitation."[21] The author notes, "there probably would have been more arrests, if there had been more adequate law and order personnel."[22] She bleakly concludes that at "least 50 per cent of the families are burdened with extra dependents. Many of these families are large and poor. Homes are inadequate and unsanitary. The medicine man is still popular, diseases are widespread, and the death rate of children is high."[23]

These kinds of damning domestic reports were part of a larger national context of social and racial management through the private sphere, including far-reaching policies that sought to control domesticity and reproduction. These policies were both qualitatively and thematically linked to the then-dominant brand of Progressive era conservationism (Spiro 92–96; see also Park and Pellow, Chapter 12, this volume). The U.S. conservation movement was sparked in first decade of the twentieth century by the work of Gifford Pinchot and grew in strength and capacity through the 1930s. Conservationism is often juxtaposed against the environmental preservationism promoted by Pinchot's contemporary, John Muir, who advocated the preservation of wilderness in what he presumed was its pure form: untouched by "man," including Natives, who, Muir argued, had "no right place in the wilderness" (Kosek 156). "Wilderness," according to this view, is a discursive framework that forecloses the possibility of indigenous claims to territory and privileges the wilderness experiences of the "mythical 'first white man' " who encounters the virgin terrain of the wild New World (Adamson, *American Indian* 55). This discourse materialized in policy when, as environmental historian William Cronon notes, Natives were removed by force from legally protected "wilderness" areas, such as Glacier National Park, as a direct result of preservationist-style environmentalism (15).

Pinchot's conservationism, on the other hand, advocated vociferously for "the use of the earth for the good of man" (Kosek 78). This "use of the earth" was manifested in subsequent conservationist policy through the application of new sciences, such as forestry and agronomy, for turning wilderness into something more resembling harvestable cropland. Conservationism, with its emphasis on "good management" of resources and populations alike, became institutionalized within the federal government as its primary framework for developing natural resources. As noted by Louis Warren, the twentieth century marked a time when "a consensus emerged, especially among the middle and upper classes, that both nature and society needed to be better managed" (180). With its emphasis on "seeing" landscapes and people alike "like a state," conservationism became an important arbiter of what was considered good ecological citizenship (Scott 1–3).

In this heady context of the rational management of resources and populations alike, the Navajo reservation was marked as an ideal first test site for the practice of soil conservation, which in turn became a major part of federal land policy throughout the twentieth century. John Collier recounts in his memoir that management of the Navajo reservation was "a movement to extend to every continent in the dawning realization that all mankind is facing the same crisis, growing from wastage of soil resource, that faced the Navajo tribe" (251). A 1936 report from the U.S. Department of Agriculture explained that the selection of the Navajo reservation was based on the fact that this area "was outstanding in its need for proper land management and would make an ideal demonstration area," and the Navajo tribe with its "rapidly increasing population was dependent for its livelihood on the productivity of the land.[24]

What made the Navajo reservation even more attractive for these experiments was the nature of the colonial relationship between the Diné and the federal government; that is, in the view of the government, "the entire area was Federally controlled, which permitted the establishment of a project through a working agreement between the Bureau of Indian Affairs and the [SCS]."[25]

This "project" also reveals how the soil itself seemed to become improperly unruly and problematically un-reproductive in the eyes of the SCS and the U.S. Geological Survey. It did not behave as expected or as required, and it did not follow the patterns of agricultural productivity that U.S. conservationists anticipated. One report finds Navajo land insufficient for several reasons: "[t]he low rainfall, steep slopes, lack of permanent streams, lack of water storing or spreading possibilities and the texture of the soil," all of which "renders all but a small portion of this land unadaptable to farming."[26] As a result, Diné peoples and land were subject to a veritable flood of federal experts, ranging from ecologists, conservationists, agronomists, and cartographers to social workers, anthropologists, and economists. Eighteen Soil Conservation Districts were parceled out of the larger reservation to study the effects of scientific range development practices, deployed in the interest of "understand[ing] thoroughly the conservation problem on range and pasture lands," and producing "a complete natural resource inventory" of the reservation.[27]

The process of mapping, charting, and inventorying was not limited to the land. Included in the SCS's mission was to "learn the manners, traditions, and customs of the Navajo and the environmental factors affecting them, with special reference to their economic needs, and their adaptability to improved methods of livestock management."[28] By the end of 1935, it was clear that the SCS was operating under a quite ambitious mandate: assimilating the Navajos into a more "civilized" relationship with their land base. A 1935 report laments the fact that white men were not brought in to do SCS work, which "would have immediately simplified the work on the Reservation"; however, the Service consoled itself that at least employing Navajos for its projects would begin the long process of the Navajos "adjusting themselves to standards of accuracy and precision which have no relation to the Navajo background."[29] Indeed, the SCS saw itself as facilitating a kind of benevolent assimilation into good conservationism—in other words, an assimilation into what the SCS considered "good ecological citizenship." Their project, as they saw it, "should be the building in as many Navajos as possible, men, women, and children, and certainly in every man on the payroll, be he Navajo or white, a sympathetic understanding of the approach to the land use problem."[30] Building this new "point of view" and an understanding of the gravity of soil erosion would be the SCS's larger, quite ambitious goal.

Although lip service is sometimes paid to the need to educate whites as well as Indians, it is quite clear that the "Navajo problem" remained a *Navajo* problem. A school for Indian SCS employees was opened at Fort Wingate in 1934, which provided training in "topographical mapping, handling and laying out of construction work, and in developing in selected students an understanding of the Navajo land problem in general."[31] In its efforts, however, the SCS did not ignore the many Diné who were not in their employ. The Service dabbled in a number of educational programs for the larger Navajo public, including one that enrolled 12th-graders in a unit called "How to Restore and Keep the Land in Condition to Support the

Navajo People," in which the students were required to do fieldwork and make speeches about soil erosion and good conservation practices. Moreover, the SCS took their message to day schools and other reservation centers with an interactive exhibit.

In this way, the SCS undertook to assimilate the Navajo public into the federal "point of view." In a 1950 memo to "All Soil and Moisture Conservation Employees," Evan L. Flory, then-Chief of the BIA Branch of Soil Conservation, wrote a call-to-action under the subject "WANTED: Zeal and fire that will not falter or tire":

> I cannot refrain from passing on to you the lift I got on my last field trip from an Indian farmer on a brushy, rocky, steep, small mountain farm. . . . His pastures were weedy, brushy, and of low carrying capacity . . . and then, within the past two years, something happened. He was sparked by the zeal and enthusiasm of an understanding soil conservationist who has his hands in the earth. This Indian's eyes had a light in them that had never been there even as a youth because he was making a tired old farm live. He and the farm were being vitalized together.[32]

Flory describes a pastoral utopia, brought about by zeal and fire. Notably, the politics of family life are absent from this report. "Understanding soil conservationists" are the "something," the necessary catalyst that brings the "struggling" Native out of the reproductive incapacity of his soil and his dysfunctional ecological practices into his new (individualist and ruggedly masculine) rural idyll. Thus, the modern promise of soil conservationism and agricultural science is not merely one of developing the land, but of developing in individual men the ideology and practice of rationalizing their own landscapes.

Flory goes on to describe how whites might benefit from Native closeness to "nature" and enthusiasm for conservationism. The "Indian lives closer to nature. . . . Few realize that what he seeks in these chants and dances is to become a part of nature, rather than view it as something apart like most of the whites do." White "tillers," in contrast, should also live "close enough to the land" and with their superior zeal and fire make "knowledge an effective tool in the hands of the tiller of the soil, to use his hands in harmony with nature."[33] Here, the confluence of two kinds of cultivation, of "Indians" as Native agriculturalists and of whites who are more "in harmony with nature" (or what we might call better ecological citizens), reveals the ideological underpinnings of Collier-era Indian and conservation policies. Collier himself, an avowed liberal, felt he stood in opposition to prior federal Indian policies of forced assimilation into white language and culture, but the policies during his tenure merely translated into new forms of the old assimilationist ideology. Given this, Flory concludes the memo with a reminder about the particular mission of soil conservationists: "Remember, we are not succeeding in conservation until a folk knowledge, a behavior, or cultural pattern of conservation, is firmly fixed. When the Indians in your area practice conservation from habit, then they have attained full stature as farmers and citizens."[34]

Flory and the "liberal" assimilationist vein of conservation and IS work, under the leadership of John Collier, differed strikingly from more conservative views of Indian policy. In a 1946 report summarizing the past decade and a half of stock reduction and soil conservation efforts on the part of the federal government, Randolph C. Downes and Elizabeth Clark stake out the anti-Collier position of federal policymakers. They write that in 1931–1932,

> There had been a very dry summer and the Navajo stock were in pretty bad shape. Then came a long, hard winter and hundreds of thousands of Navajo stock—as well as Navajo Indians—were faced with starvation. Perhaps this was Nature's way of helping to "solve" the Navajo problem. If the "natural" course of events had been allowed to proceed several hundred thousand Navajo sheep, goats and horses would have died and many thousands of Navajo Indians forced to migrate or make-shift in some desperate way. The effect of such a process would have been harsh but it would have made the Navajos themselves conscious of the realities of the "Navajo situation," i.e. of the overstocked and over-populated condition of their country.[35]

Unlike Flory's understanding of the role of nature for the Diné, for Downes and Clark, nature is decidedly not on the side of the "Indians"; what would be natural, in fact, would be their extinction. For Flory, however, nature is part and parcel of Indianness itself, and the white man's burden is to help the Native marry "his" intrinsic affinity with the natural world to white strategies for economic progress.

What is clear is that the failure of the soil conservation project seemed destined to be blamed on the Navajos and their land, which would never respond to the range development plans laid out by the conservationists. In a 1946 report, in which the Diné are called "America's Minority Problem No. 1," echoing their designation as "Public Enemy No. 1" a decade earlier, the Navajo problem is summed up as the fault, primarily, of the land itself, which is described as "a barren wasteland" and "so desolate that a handful of white men could use it . . . only for scattered and part-time grazing."[36] This report marks an important transition in the federal approach by duly noting that the average family income more than doubled from 1940 to 1944 as a direct result of military work in the Navajo economy. At that point, federal stock reduction programs had achieved the desired reduction of livestock: in 1946, thirteen years after the program's official inception, the Navajo range was home to 449,000 sheep—110,000 less than the original reduction goal. Without herds to tend to, and recovering from the experience of livestock slaughters and brutal treatment by federal employees,

Navajos had been forced into war work off the reservation. When uranium was discovered on and near Navajo land, mining jobs were seen as good work by Navajos because they could remain close to home.

By the 1950s, the federal government had limited its plans for Indian policy in general to just two options: termination of the federal relationship to tribes and Pinchot-style conservation of tribal resources. In the eyes of these federal actors, having deemed Navajo land worthless for agriculture or sustainable stockraising, but rich in mineral resources, the Diné were primed for both options. The BIA began considering industry proposals to locate a variety of factories on reservation land, as well as to offer financial incentives for Diné to move to far away cities under the relocation plan of 1954. This can be seen in the 1949 report by authors Randolph Downes and Elizabeth Clark, who ultimately recommend escalation of oil and mineral surveys on the reservation.[37]

CONCLUSIONS: GLOBAL CHANGE, LOCAL IMPACT

Today, rusted Soil Conservation District signs still stand on road shoulders throughout the Southwest, hinting at the legacy of erosion control efforts that took place throughout the twentieth century. For Diné, the most longstanding legacies of the conservation policy revolve around massive economic changes that followed the conservation period. These changes were wrought most spectacularly through livestock reduction but more subtly through federal convictions that Navajos would have to enter a wage, rather than a subsistence, economy. To a large extent, this transformation of Navajo economies took place through military work, particularly during World War II, work on the railroad, and coal and uranium mining. After their experience with stock reduction in the 1930s and subsequent experiences with resource extraction-based industries, Diné environmental justice, social justice, and indigenous sovereignty organizations have become central to mitigating and confronting the impacts of just these kinds of federally or industry-backed environmentally destructive activities on the Navajo Nation. Today, the Diné actively participate in developing environmental justice frameworks and praxis that have revolutionized environmentalist politics in the U.S. and globally.

For example, in 1979, Navajos together with a coalition with other New Mexico indigenous activists, as well as white and Chicana/o activists, organized a three-day occupation of Mount Taylor to protect the mountain from renewed uranium mining. In 1988, Navajo activists successfully blocked the siting of a toxic waste incinerator in Dilkon, Arizona. In 1990, Navajos hosted a national meeting of a coalition of indigenous organizations and activists that went on to become the Indigenous Environmental Network, an organization with powerful influence worldwide. Several longstanding organizations, such as Eastern Navajo Diné Against Uranium Mining, the

Dooda (No) Desert Rock Committee, and Diné Citizens Against Ruining Our Environment, have made considerable progress in preventing new environmental incursions by mining industries on and near Diné land. The work of organizations like these, and the legacy of Navajo environmental activism, lends support to a Navajo Tribal Council moratorium on uranium mining that has been in place since 2005. These organizations chart the ways in which the local and global are intimately intertwined in struggles over the environment, indigenous nations, and natural resources. This environmental justice political praxis is informed, in large part, by the environmental problems unleashed in the stock reduction period and the ways in which it targeted Navajo relationships to their land, their livestock, and each other. With a keen eye to the powerful local implications of global forces, these organizations implicitly construct a politically potent kind of self-determined ecological citizenship: one that is organized around and for indigenous sovereignty and recognizes the complex multiple origins of environmental crises, including and perhaps especially those that might otherwise be blamed on what is seen as too many people and too many sheep living on too dry a land.

NOTES

1. Although still in use throughout the first half of the twentieth century, "reservation" is no longer used formally to describe the lands of sovereign Native nations. In 1969, the Navajo Tribal Council formally adopted the name "Navajo Nation" (Iverson xxiv), which overlaps the four corners of Colorado, Arizona, New Mexico, and Utah and sits within four mountains sacred to the Navajo: Tsisnaajinii or Blanca Peak, Tsoodził or Mount Taylor, Dook'o'oosłííd or the San Francisco Peaks, and Dibé Ntsaa or Mount Hesperus.
2. Diné people have been called the "Navajo" by the U.S., following a Spanish adaptation of a word borrowed from the nearby Pueblo tribes meaning "cultivated fields." I alternate between "Diné" and "Navajo," as do other scholars of Diné history (Denetdale 10).
3. Parman, 1976, Iverson, 1981, Iverson and Roessel (2002), White, 1983, Weisiger, 2007, Weisiger, 2011.
4. Sam Ahkeah served as the Navajo Tribal Council chairman from 1946 to 1954.
5. Emphasis in original.
6. Fryer, E. R. Letter to John Collier. November 17, 1941. MSS 517 BC, box 10, folder 5. Collection of William Zimmerman, Jr. Papers, Center for Southwest Research, University of New Mexico.
7. Goats and sheep counted for one head of stock; each cow or horse counted for four or five head. "Navajo Tribal Council Meeting Minutes—Leupp, AZ, November 1928," box 4, folder 28, p. 46. Robert W. Young Papers, Center for Southwest Research, University Libraries, University of New Mexico.
8. While in this speech Meritt repeatedly struck a populist chord, arguing for stock reduction especially for owners of big herds so that the smaller owners could have "justice," he was careful to praise these big herd owners as "shrewd business men," "leaders," and "good examples." No doubt this

vacillation was partly due to the presence of the influential Chee Dodge, the biggest of big herd owners, with whom Meritt was disagreeing.

9. The Navajo churra, as Weisiger explains, was in reality much better adapted to Navajo uses of sheep as well as to environmental conditions on the reservation; the Rambouillet "could not keep up with the long-legged, fast walking churras and goats, and Diné women found the fine, short-stapled wool, which was both greasy and kinky, unsuitable for spinning and hand-weaving" (Weisiger *Dreaming*, 193).
10. "Navajo Tribal Council Meeting Minutes—Leupp, AZ, November 1928," box 4, folder 28, p. 46. Robert W. Young Papers, Center for Southwest Research, University Libraries, University of New Mexico.
11. For Navajo accounts of this period, including Diné resistance to reduction, see Roessel (1974).
12. LaRouche, F. W. Letter to John Collier. January 13, 1943, box 10, folder 11. William Zimmerman, Jr. Papers, Center for Southwest Research, University Libraries, University of New Mexico.
13. Ibid.
14. Ibid.
15. These men helped defeat the Navajo-New Mexico Boundary Bill, which would have added critically needed acreage to the eastern portion of the reservation.
16. In the 1930s, Navajo women primarily used non-Western techniques of contraception, mostly derived from medicinal plants and herbs as well as long periods of breastfeeding, as a natural technique for birth-spacing (Shepardson 167). The Indian Health Service (IHS) was not formed until 1955 and thus was not a source of birth planning services for Diné women at this time. By the late 1970s, the IHS overused tubal sterilization rather than other, reversible contraception technologies, sterilizing as many as 25% of Native women of childbearing age (Lawrence 400).
17. Emphasis added.
18. Ricketts, Orval, and John McPhee, "The Navajo Indians in a Changing World," 1941, box 2, folder 18. Robert W. Young Papers, Center for Southwest Research, University Libraries, University of New Mexico.
19. In one Soil Conservation Service report under the heading "Fact Finding," the need for "a study of human groups and institutions through their functions and interrelationships," including studies of the "[d]omestic economy of household groups—housing, diet, clothing as a basis for intelligent handling of these basic problems affecting human welfare," was posed. See Soil Conservation Service, "Annual report for the year ending June 30, 1935," box 7, folder 16. U.S. Soil Conservation Service Region Eight Records, Center for Southwest Research, University Libraries, University of New Mexico.
20. Tomlinson, Ruby, "A Study of the Social and Economic Status of One Hundred Navajo Families," Navajo Service, Window Rock, AZ, February 1944, box 10, folder 5, p. 30. William Zimmerman, Jr. Papers, Center for Southwest Research, University Libraries, University of New Mexico.
21. Ibid.
22. Ibid.
23. Ibid.
24. Soil Conservation Service, "Annual report for the year ending June 30, 1936," box 7, folder 56. U.S. Soil Conservation Service Region Eight Records, Center for Southwest Research, University Libraries, University of New Mexico.
25. Ibid.
26. Soil Conservation Service, "United States Soil Conservation Service Report, 1938," box 12, folder 60. U.S. Soil Conservation Service Region Eight

Records, Center for Southwest Research, University Libraries, University of New Mexico.

27. Ibid.
28. See "Fact Finding," Soil Conservation Service, "Annual report for the year ending June 30, 1935," box 7, folder 16. U.S. Soil Conservation Service Region Eight Records, Center for Southwest Research, University Libraries, University of New Mexico.
29. Ibid., 174.
30. Ibid.,176.
31. Ibid., 178.
32. Flory, Evan L., "Memo to All Soil and Moisture Conservation Employees," box 2, folder 1. William Zimmerman, Jr. Papers, Center for Southwest Research, University Libraries, University of New Mexico.
33. Ibid.
34. Ibid.
35. Downes, Randolph C., and Elizabeth Clark, "Navajo Report," 1946, box 2, folder 19. Robert W. Young Papers, Center for Southwest Research, University Libraries, University of New Mexico.
36. Ibid.
37. Ibid.

4 Getting Back to an Imagined Nature

The Mannahatta Project and Environmental Justice

Jeffrey Myers

Environmentally themed publishers such as Sierra Club Books and the National Geographic Society have a long tradition of producing lavish coffee-table books that combine lush nature photography with natural history prose in celebration of places like national parks and other scenic wilderness landscapes. In addition to their aesthetic and educational purposes, such publications have the obvious agenda of calling attention to the uniqueness and beauty of wilderness areas in the hope of persuading the reader of the conservationist message that these areas should be preserved in an unspoiled state. A recent publication is a unique variation on this theme: in 2009, Wildlife Conservation Society scientist Eric W. Sanderson produced *Mannahatta: A Natural History of New York City*, the culmination of a ten-year research project in which he and fellow researchers reconstructed the ecology of New York City as it was when Henry Hudson sailed into New York Harbor in 1609. Along with the book, an interactive website and an exhibit at the Museum of the City of New York together made up what Sanderson and the Wildlife Conservation Society called the "the Mannahatta Project," which was featured prominently in the September 2009 issue of *National Geographic*. The book, the website, and the magazine article feature photographs of present-day Manhattan juxtaposed with "visualizations" by Markley Boyer, illustrations of the island as it might have appeared four hundred years ago—when, the website claims, "the concrete jungle of New York City was . . . a vast deciduous forest, home to bears, wolves, songbirds, and salamanders, with clear, clean waters jumping with fish"—an ecosystem with "biodiversity [that] rivaled that of national parks like Yellowstone, Yosemite, and the Great Smoky Mountains!" After chapters that catalogue, narrate, and describe the physical ecology, the plant life, the wildlife, and the indigenous people of Manhattan island circa 1609, the book ends with a vision of the island in 2409, four hundred years in the future, when—inspired and informed by the knowledge of "the green heart" of the island—New York City will be a sustainable urban civilization of green-roofed buildings powered by renewable energy, a populace moved about by streetcars and bicycles, and local agriculture in New Jersey, in Staten Island, even in the Bronx, Brooklyn, and Queens.

In terms of environmental sustainability—even environmental justice—there is much that is potentially salutary about the Mannahatta Project. The project's visual nature powerfully brings home to the reader the scale of what Sanderson calls "the human footprint in urban areas" (31–33). I believe Sanderson is right to think that a new respect and appreciation for the underlying ecosystem of New York City might help urban residents imagine a greener city, as well as appreciate the environmental benefits that accrue from nearby forests, waterways, and marshes in the city's environs. If the human future is largely an urban future, as Sanderson rightly points out, the project helps the reader to imagine North America's iconic urban location as a natural space; the last chapter's emphasis on long-term sustainability speaks directly to the issue of climate change. On a more local scale, although Sanderson could be more explicit about environmental justice issues in the current city environment, the closing chapter's emphasis on urban quality of life—a greener, more sustainable city—at least potentially addresses longstanding urban environmental injustices, whereby less affluent people in general and people of color in particular are disproportionately harmed by problems such as waste dumps and power plants while having less access to benefits such as parks and open space.[1]

One of the website's notable features is an interactive graphic that allows the user to "turn back time": by moving the cursor horizontally along a time line from 2009 to 1609, a satellite photograph of the present-day Manhattan of skyscrapers and avenues is peeled back to uncover the forested Manhattan of 1609. But in so forcefully visualizing the Manhattan landscape of 1609 as a wilderness paradise, the book and website obscure and elide as much as they reveal. Just as the literary celebrations of the National Parks on which *Mannahatta* is based often erased the peoples—including American Indians and poor whites—who were in some cases physically removed to create the parks, so too does the Mannahatta Project play down the presence of the original Lenape inhabitants of Manhattan. Likewise, this digital replacement of the "concrete jungle" with the "original ecology" of the island effectively substitutes the "biodiversity" of the imagined wilderness of four hundred years ago for the real human diversity of New York City today, and thus participates in an unfortunate strand of American cultural history in which immigrants and people of color have been represented as incapable of appreciating America's natural beauty, at best—or at worst, of being detrimental to the conservation of our natural resources. Tellingly, the imagined green spaces and local farms that surround the imagined urban core of "Mannahatta" in 2409 are located in what are some of today's most ethnically, racially, and economically diverse neighborhoods of Brooklyn, Queens, and the Bronx. Thus, the ambiguous and loaded title "Mannahatta Project"—which I take is meant to invoke a green, sustainable antithesis of the Manhattan Project—takes on potentially troubling overtones. At its best, *Mannahatta* asks us to imagine how the natural world links us all, regardless of nationality or economic status, by our dependence on clean air, good soil, and open space. But at the same time, the entire project, however unintentionally, encodes the anti-urban bias of the mainstream environmental movement, with all of that movement's past inattention to environmental racism as well as its racial, ethnic, and class exclusivity. If the project wishes to help envision a sustainable urban future, it must show greater awareness of how low-income communities of color have been marginalized and greater sensitivity to differing cultural responses to the natural world.[2]

Environmental historian William Cronon, in his highly influential article "The Trouble with Wilderness; or, Getting Back to the Wrong Nature," points out that the idea of wilderness as a pristine environment uncontaminated by humanity is a social construction—that such wilderness spaces are as much artifacts of human intervention as any urban landscape (69). Indeed, he points out that such spaces have never really existed as we have come to imagine them—that they are really only a romantic "myth of the wilderness as 'virgin,' uninhabited land" that depends on scientifically inaccurate notions of a static balance of nature and that downplays the impact of Native American inhabitants as active managers of their environment (79). In reconstructing Manhattan's "original ecology," in the words of the website, Sanderson's Mannahatta Project participates in the perpetuation of such a myth. The near-fetishization of the date "September 12, 1609," the lush, almost Edenic "visualizations," and the purple prose of the website cited above perpetuate the notion that Manhattan island was a static, unchanging wilderness paradise of balance and harmony, after which all later, anthropogenic changes in the ecosystem are seen as corruptions of the pure and original state. Cronon points out that any such notion of an "original" landscape is a fiction—and a reading of the text of *Mannahatta* itself shows that Sanderson knows all of this. To be fair, Sanderson devotes one of seven chapters of the book to the Lenape inhabitants and ascribes a number of landscape features of Manhattan in 1609 to their agency. And the scientific research that went into reconstructing the landscape of 1609 is painstakingly thorough and clearly explained, so there is little reason to doubt Sanderson's fascinating account of the flora, fauna, and topography of the island before European settlement.

But in many ways the visual material in the Mannahatta Project is at odds with the language of the text: a large part of the project's impact, particularly as it was represented on the website and in magazines such as *National Geographic*—but also quite prominently by the book's visualizations—clearly depends on the wilderness nostalgia Cronon debunks. Such a myth betrays an anti-urban bias that was long characteristic of the mainstream environmental movement and traditional nature writing, which extolled a pastoral tradition that valued the rural over the urban, the American West over the East Coast (Bennett, "From Wide Open Spaces" 31–35), and the environmental concerns of affluent whites over those of the poor and people of color. The project's most striking visual motif is the repeated juxtaposition of an aerial (or occasionally street-level) photograph of present-day New York with a visualization of the same site as it purportedly would have appeared four hundred years ago. The locations chosen are almost invariably sectors of the city with the highest concentration of skyscrapers and traffic, emphasizing the stereotyped notion of the city as crowded, artificial, and inorganic. By contrast, the visualizations of the same spots four hundred years ago appear almost impossibly tranquil and pristine. But this presents a false dichotomy that is anti-urban on its face. Modern New York, even present-day Manhattan, is not all concrete, glass, and steel. Nowhere do the photographs of modern New York in *Mannahatta* include the parks and tree-lined streets that grace the city today. Nor do they portray the greenmarkets, playgrounds, street performers, bodegas, and neighborhood cafes that would emphasize the city's vital human ecology. Thus, a tension emerges within the text between human diversity and biodiversity, as if the former inevitably takes the place of the latter.

A pair of images of Times Square, for instance, taken from *National Geographic* and featuring an illustration by Boyer juxtaposed with a modern photograph, exemplifies how the Mannahatta Project encodes this anti-urban bias. The illustration of Times Square circa 1609, which Sanderson's research has discovered was a red maple swamp, features a beaver perched on its lodge and nearby a fully antlered bull elk standing by the water, its body in profile and his face looking directly at the viewer. Soft light filters through the trees in a way that is reminiscent of a Bierstadt landscape of Yosemite Valley. Its modern corollary, while by no means unaesthetic, depicts Times Square as a blur of moving cars and people. *National Geographic*'s caption for this pairing of images leaves little doubt about how to interpret them: "Long before it became a symbol of Manhattan's hectic pace, [Times Square] was once a quieter place" (P. Miller 124). Thus, a familiar kind of binary is set up, with the "quieter" wilderness of 1609 privileged over the "hectic" present-day Times Square. That the binary is heavy-handed and obvious only underscores the degree to which the traditional environmental trope of the pristine wilderness over the degraded urban landscape is in play. The moving blur of people and traffic elides the human diversity that is one of the city's signature strengths, even as it suggests that the vast human presence is responsible for the lack of biodiversity that Manhattan once had.

Just as the importance of human diversity of modern Manhattan is downplayed, so too is its actual biodiversity underrepresented. Nearly all of the visualizations of "Mannahatta" in 1609 include flocks of birds winging across the skies, as a symbol of what the book asks us to imagine was the abundant wildlife of a prelapsarian Manhattan—while none of the accompanying modern-day photographs of the corresponding scenes do. Yet, this is a deliberate and manipulative oversight. From the red-tailed hawk Pale Male and his various mates, to the peregrine falcons that inhabit downtown skyscrapers, to the countless flocks of pigeons that are preyed on by the falcons, wild bird life is a conspicuous feature of present-day New York ecology. Indeed anyone who watched Capt. Chesley Sullenberger land his Airbus 320 on the Hudson River knows just how plentiful are wild birds in the Manhattan sky. Their conspicuous absence in the photographs—contrasted with their ubiquity in the 1609 visualizations—shows the degree to which the Mannahatta Project stacks the deck toward a view of the city as a "concrete jungle." As Ivan Grabovac notes elsewhere (Chapter 8, this volume), immigrants—particularly Italian Americans—at the turn of the last century were widely (and spuriously) blamed by some in the early conservation movement for their supposed role in the disappearance of migratory birds, at a time when "wildlife preservation and immigration restriction emerged as two sides of the same coin" (120). Immigrants were not only blamed for the birds' disappearance, but they were viewed as not having an adequate appreciation for wildlife in a worldview that linked, as Grabovac explains, "wildlife abundance and white racial purity" (122). The disappearance of New York's actual biodiversity in the Mannahatta visualizations replicates this trope on a contemporary basis.

Transparently, use of the term "concrete jungle" on the Manhattan Project website is clearly meant to appeal to a traditional (and an antiquated) environmentalist trope of cities as inorganic, degraded, and corrupt, especially as the "concrete jungle" of today is posited as the opposite of the "original" ecosystem, the "vast deciduous forest" that once covered the island. Indeed, this notion of cities as corrupt, inorganic opposites of a more pure, pastoral landscape goes back to the nation's founding: Thomas Jefferson likened "the mobs of great cities" to "sores . . . of the human body," whereas the countryside was God's "peculiar deposit for substantial and genuine virtue" (165). Further, terms such as "concrete jungle" or "urban jungle" (used in the *National Geographic* article) elicit visions of crime and urban decay, stereotypically associated with the urban poor and people of color. Sanderson, who came from "suburban Northern California" to take a position at the Wildlife Conservation Society (the organization that runs the Bronx Zoo) (16), confesses that his own initial unease with New York's urbanity was the basis for his desire to re-imagine Manhattan as natural space, writing in *Mannahatta*, "When I came to New York, I didn't know what to make of the place—so many people going in so many different directions—and so I started pulling in my own direction back toward nature" (138). Note that he posits "nature" here as the polar opposite of urbanity—indeed, even of humanity. As Cronon points out, such is "the central paradox [of] wilderness," which "embodies a dualistic vision in which the human is entirely outside the natural" (80). His oblique reference here to New York's crowded diversity, along with a few other passing references to the legendary "brash" and assertive qualities of New Yorkers, carry a faint, but I believe recognizable, ethnic and racial resonance. As Michael Bennett points out, "a new generation of whites who had been taught not to believe, or at least to vocalize, racist stereotypes simply transposed those stereotypes onto the deteriorating inner city, whose inhabitants just happened to be overwhelmingly people of color" ("Manufacturing the Ghetto" 174). However unintentional, this invocation of the "concrete jungle" has implications for the inclusiveness of Sanderson's *Mannahatta* vision.

Where the indigenous Lenape inhabitants are present, in the book more so than the website, there is tension between the desire to acknowledge the importance of the Lenape presence and the desire to present the island as a once pristine wilderness. However, Sanderson devotes a full chapter to the Lenape, stressing his main topic of their impact on the ecology of Manhattan island, but also with a narrative of their cultural and social practices as well as an important acknowledgment of their continuing presence in Oklahoma and other places in the Midwest. In places, he quite explicitly elucidates their role as ecological planners and thinkers, noting that "the Lenape created the Mannahatta they desired through horticulture and fire"—an important acknowledgement of the human cultural presence in North America and an antidote to noble savage myth-making (119). But here again the prominent and powerful visual material is at odds with the text. In the visualizations, where the human presence is registered at all, it is usually represented as one or two columns of smoke emerging from deep in the forest and often at a distance. Although there are portraits, historical and modern, of Lenape people, not one of the visualizations in the book portrays actual people. Were people present in the visualizations, such imagery would potentially support the places in the text where the Lenape are depicted as cultural and ecological agents. However, as it stands, the lonely columns of smoke and the lack of human subjects in the visualizations convey a noble savage myth of American Indians that goes hand in hand with the whole project's wilderness nostalgia. In his descriptions of Lenape life ways, Sanderson describes how in one typical settlement, "pots of porridge or stew bubbled continuously over low fires, one for each family"; meanwhile, "outside there would be another fire burning, another pot stewing" and, nearby, "they heated rocks over fires, then dropped in baskets of water" to create sweat lodges that "all the Lenape enjoyed" (116–117). That would be a lot of fires, and one would expect the visualizations to reflect that. Instead of the one or two single columns of smoke in the distance the book portrays, one might have expected the visualizations to show a Manhattan of 1609 covered in a haze of smoke—but then, that would belie the myth of the pristine wilderness that is at the heart of *Mannahatta*.

Partly this stems from Sanderson's secondary research, which claims that Manhattan was only home to between two hundred and 1,200 Lenape Indians (113). The truth of these claims is hard to dispute, but Sanderson's settling on a low-end count of six hundred in summer and two hundred in winter is startling, as is his own, original conclusion that only 12% of Manhattan was even "moderately suitable" for human habitation (111). Alternative claims that there were as many as eighty settlements in what became the five boroughs—and "as many as 15,000 inhabitants"—would seem to debunk the view of Mannahatta as a largely unpopulated wilderness in 1609 (Burrows and Wallace 5). Even Sanderson notes seventeen sites on a map in the text (107)—a far cry from the two lonely columns of smoke that are the visual signature of the native presence in the visualizations. Attempts to calculate the pre-contact indigenous population of the Americas have long been fraught with controversy: some have argued that there has been, for ideological reasons, a longstanding historical tendency to undercount the pre-Columbian population of North America by as much as a factor of ten—since a low count would both mitigate European culpability for reduced populations of American Indians as well as justify the appropriation of what would appear to be thinly populated—or even uninhabited—landscapes. Also, by selectively focusing here on only the Manhattan Lenape, rather than thinking about the presence of "perhaps another thirty to fifty thousand in the adjacent parts of New Jersey, Connecticut, Westchester County, and Long Island" (Burrows and Wallace 5), Sanderson elides the presence of a Native American civilization in 1609 of what became the present-day New York area, to which those Lenape who lived on Manhattan would have been connected. Thus, whether there were only two hundred Lenape on Manhattan island is hard to dispute, but it is certainly a notion that fits conveniently into longstanding myths of the Native American population as low-impact hunter-gatherers not really having significant claims to the North American wilderness spaces desired by Euro-Americans.[3]

Indeed, Sanderson confusingly presents conflicting evidence on the scale of the human presence on "Mannahatta," so that not only is the text at odds with the visual material but in places is even at odds with itself. On the one hand, he tells us that the Lenape were landscape managers who had a significant impact on the landscape through their use of fire to improve conditions for horticulture and game, a people for whom maize was so important that two of the native legends he cites in the chapter recount the divine gift of corn. The one dramatic visualization, in fact, that registers the Lenape presence strongly is one of a large, human-induced fire burning the Harlem Plains (though here, too, there are no actual human beings pictured). However, he presents evidence that the role of horticulture was relatively minor, referring to the Lenape several times in the chapter as primarily "hunters and gatherers" (106, 117), with a "mobile lifestyle" (112) that downplays notions of Indian sovereignty and reifies the noble savage myth. Again and again, the visualizations throughout the project (with this one exception in the book where fire is depicted) support this downplaying of the human presence by representing the island of Manhattan and the surrounding areas as a pristine wilderness, in some images sparsely inhabited—and in others completely empty of human habitation or even influence. But, such a representation runs counter to what historians have long known about the northeastern North American forest, that the clearing of land by fire was widespread before European colonization. As Stephen Pyne writes,

"The virgin forest was not encountered in the sixteenth and seventeenth centuries; it was invented in the late eighteenth and early nineteenth centuries. For this condition Indian fire practices were largely responsible" (46).

Thus, if, as an archaeologist whom Sanderson cites says, "We know nothing about 1609. We *can* know nothing" (104), then the portrait of the Lenape in 1609 is as much as anything else an act of imagination. The ambiguity of the evidence about the Lenape surely would justify Sanderson, illustrator Boyer, and others who had a hand in the project in visualizing a far more robust human presence with dozens of settlements, trails, dwellings, and fields of corn, squash, and beans. Again, there are photographs of modern reproductions of a wigwam and a small patch of corn, but in the book's most striking visual feature—the artist-rendered visualizations—these are all absent. A similar choice is the omission of the brutal circumstances that accompanied the Lenape diaspora, beyond a vague reference to their forcible removal in the caption under the photograph of a modern Lenape woman, Norma Thompson Dean, in Oklahoma (134). Nor is there mention of contemporary Native groups in the metropolitan area—the Shinnecock Nation of Long Island, for instance, who finally received federal recognition as this chapter was being written; or the Ramapough Lenape Nation of northern New Jersey, who to this day struggle to gain acceptance of their native identity and who have for decades suffered the effects of a toxic waste dump from the former Ford Motors Mahwah plant. In the latter case, the elision of a modern-day people in the New York metropolitan area who claim Lenape descent—a people who are the victims of a contemporary, rather than historical, environmental injustice—is indicative of the project's blind spots.

In and of itself, this downplaying of the Lenape presence would be significant in terms of historical claims of injustice toward American Indians, not to mention present legal claims such as those of the Shinnecock or Ramapough Lenape. But what gives it even more urgency is the degree to which it evokes the myth of the pristine, uninhabited wilderness on which much of the traditional environmental movement is based—and a myth that is inextricable from that movement's traditional racial and ethnic exclusivity. Sierra Club founder and environmental icon John Muir, a full-page picture of whom graces nearly the exact middle of *Mannahatta*, was perhaps the foremost promoter of this vision. Sanderson evokes the presence of Muir ostensibly to introduce the concept of what he calls the "Muir web," which I will discuss below, but also plainly because Muir is such a powerful advocate for the idea of a pristine and sacred natural world that was uncontaminated by humankind. The language on the Mannahatta Project website that I quote above ("a vast deciduous forest") has its roots in the nature writing that Muir popularized more than a century ago. But as historians Kevin DeLuca and Anne Demo have shown, Muir's vision of pristine wilderness not only "certainly forbids inhabitants" (553) but is "interlaced with the values of whiteness" (550). Indeed the formation of several national parks from Yellowstone to the Smoky Mountains—names directly invoked on the Mannahatta Project website—were accomplished only by the removal of American Indians, poor whites, and others who inconveniently resided there.[4] Muir's championing of the parks in his 1901 *Our National Parks* quite explicitly participates in this rhetoric, dismissing any claims of American Indian sovereignty in favor of spaces for the white middle class—"tired, nerve-shaken, over-civilized people"—to get "in touch with the nerves of Mother Earth" (721). By invoking Muir and Muir-like wilderness rhetoric, Sanderson links the Mannahatta Project quite clearly to a mainstream environmental movement that has traditionally privileged white cultural responses to the natural world over those of people of color and valued the environmental concerns of the affluent over those of the less affluent.

When one thinks of the final chapter of the book, "Mannahatta 2409," with its local farms located in modern African-American, Latino, and multiethnic neighborhoods in the outer boroughs—Bedford-Stuyvesant and Flatbush in Brooklyn and Jackson Heights in Queens are bucolic countryside in the imagined satellite photo of the future while Manhattan is still densely populated urban space—one is entitled to ask how such a transformation would take place. Not that Sanderson proposes any plan to get to this point. But it's worth pointing out that large-scale, centrally planned, and destructive transformations of ethnic neighborhoods have a precedent in New York, such as during the tenure of "master-builder" Robert Moses in the mid-twentieth century. Even earlier, the construction of Central Park was seen by its boosters as "an essentially middle-class gesture," Adam Sweeting has argued, "one that coincided with the aspirations of that class" (106). It was thought then, according to Sweeting, that the less affluent citizens of the city (and, by implication, immigrants and people of color) "would not know how to behave themselves in parklike settings" (98), showing the longstanding tradition of associating pastoral and "unspoiled" nature with whiteness that goes back at least to Jefferson.[5] Such a tradition has implications for citizenship and a sense of belonging when considering *Mannahatta*'s vision of a bucolic future New York. If part of the purpose of *Mannahatta* is to inspire city planning around a major restructuring of New York's architecture, infrastructure, open space, and neighborhood development, it is worth considering whether such a green transformation will tend to benefit affluent whites and Manhattan residents at the expense of the less affluent people of color and residents of the outer boroughs, as previous transformations of the city have. As Andrew Ross argues, "the green wave has to lift all boats" (246), adding that "if these [urban sustainability] practices are not directed by and toward principles of equity, they will almost certainly end up reinforcing patterns of eco-apartheid" (250).

Just a few pages prior to the Muir photograph, there is a full-spread visualization of the entirety of Manhattan island as the book would like the reader to imagine it in 1609. The largest of all the visualizations—appearing without an accompanying image of present-day Manhattan as the other illustrations do—this illustration portrays Manhattan as a pristine, uninhabited wilderness: the few columns of smoke that elsewhere at least allude to a human presence are here dispensed with altogether, and the entire region, including parts of New Jersey and Long Island, is presented as an unpeopled landscape of forests, marshes, and streams. In his *New York Times* review of *Mannahatta*, Robert Sullivan somewhat cheekily notes that this two-page illustration of Mannahatta "feels a little like a centerfold" (BR 13). Indeed, Lydia Millet compares the representation of the natural world in calendars and coffee-table books with pornography, arguing that "these props of mainstream environmentalism serve as surrogates for real engagement with wilderness, the way porn models serve as surrogates for real women"—adding that "at best they elicit a regretful nostalgia for a never-known past of unspoiled landscapes" (148).[6] As an eco-pornographic fantasy of a "virgin" wilderness, this illustration imagines Manhattan not as a country already peopled by American Indians with their own sense of history and agency but as a passive site available to be claimed—"the fresh, green breast of the New World" (Sanderson himself includes the Fitzgerald quote as an epigraph), however seemingly benign that claiming may be (9).

I don't want to lean on this point too heavily here: to be fair, Sanderson at points does extol the "human diversity" of New York (138); and clearly many multiethnic neighborhood groups in New York and other cities have taken leadership roles themselves in transforming the green character of their neighborhoods on their own cultural terms in ways that are entirely complementary with Sanderson's vision. But when he refers to New York's "largely affluent and educated population" as conducive to a green transformation, or envisions some of its most racially and ethnically diverse neighborhoods reverting to farmland, or imagines a Manhattanite of the future "fly-fishing" in a restored stream, he leaves the project open to questions of whether, as with the writings of John Muir, it is not "interlaced with the values of whiteness." Sanderson's vision of New York City four hundred years hence is meant as a scientifically informed conceptualization of a sustainable society that would potentially benefit all of the city's residents—and it is a compelling and valid one at that—but it needs to be acknowledged how many of the elements of his vision depend on ecological values that have been used in the past to justify the confiscation of lands belonging to groups marginalized by affluent white society and to the uneven distribution of environmental benefits such as parks and open space along the same lines.

In many ways, the placement of John Muir at the center—literally and figuratively—of *Mannahatta* signals the book's and the entire research project's greatest strength and greatest potential weakness in terms of its implications for urban environmental justice. Sanderson invokes Muir in the first place ostensibly to introduce the concept of the "Muir web," an ecological phenomenon where all organisms—and indeed even non-organic landscape features—are connected to a myriad of other species. But this ecological phenomenon is not universally called a Muir web by scientists, so the mention of Muir is in this sense gratuitous. (One would have hoped that if a bearded, avuncular nineteenth-century naturalist had to be invoked as the spirit of the book, at least it would have been New Yorker John Burroughs, who knew the city well and even wrote natural history essays on the Bronx, rather than the Californian Muir.) And yet the ecological connectivity among individuals, as well as the dependence those individuals have on a healthy environment in the Muir paradigm, is potentially beneficial in terms of environmental justice. Sanderson makes the connection between ecological diversity, which is healthy for an ecosystem, and human diversity, which is contemporary New York's greatest strength, stating that, "like the Muir web we both *depend on* and *are depended on* through our affiliations in groups." But even here he undercuts his point slightly by suggesting that this likeness to "nature" is metaphorical. Human diversity and biodiversity meet in the dependence of all human beings, regardless of race, class, or ethnicity, on a healthy environment.

The Mannahatta Project has the potential to transform the way that people imagine the city in positive ways. Sanderson's insistence that urban people need contact with nature echoes and underscores the urban environmental justice movement's call for less localized pollution and more access to open space for less-affluent and multi-ethnic urban residents; his scientific recognition that an increasingly urban society is compatible with an environmentally sustainable future supports the views of many urban environmental justice advocates. But in its nostalgia for wilderness, the traditional cause of a mainstream environmental movement that has historically detached itself from environmental problems that affect the poor and people of color, the Mannahatta Project as it was originally envisioned raises questions. Ross, again, demonstrates how the "life boat ethics" of Garret Hardin and some other early environmentalists have been used to justify what Ross calls "heavily guarded resource islands," where environmental benefits accrue to wealthy nations and to the wealthy within nations (242). He argues that attempting to build a sustainable urban economy by appealing mainly to the affluent demographic of the mainstream environmental movement "will end up doing little more than adding a green gloss to patterns of chronic inequality" (240). From community gardens, to a partially restored estuary, to a beaver and alewives re-inhabiting a cleaner Bronx River, New York is indeed already beginning to make a remarkable ecological transformation. But as environmental benefits continue to accrue to urban residents from imaginative projects such as the Mannahatta Project, it is worth keeping an eye on for whom they are accruing. Imaginative visions of the urban environmental future, in New York and elsewhere, must include all citizens in their sense of ecological belonging.

NOTES

1. The prevalence and seriousness of the problems of environmental injustice and environmental racism are well documented. See, for example, the many books edited by Robert D. Bullard, such as *The Quest for Environmental Justice*. For a discussion of environmental justice issues in New York in particular, see Julie Sze, *Noxious New York*. Sze highlights the degree to which class, and even more so race, have correlated with exposure to pollution from power plants and garbage transfer stations, resulting in alarmingly high rates of asthma. She also chronicles the decades-long struggle for environmental justice by activists in the affected communities. Andrew Ross's *Bird on Fire*, although taking the city of Phoenix as its focus, has wide applicability to discussions of how future urban sustainability can and must be achieved in ways that build on social equity.
2. In recent months, the Mannahatta Project website has been taken down and replaced with a new project, the "Welikia Project" (Lenape for "my good home"), which aims to bring the same research about the "original ecology" of Brooklyn, Queens, Staten Island, and the Bronx to those boroughs that the original project brought to Manhattan. By retitling the project, the directors appear to have anticipated some of the criticism that I will be developing here about the Mannahatta Project being oriented toward the more affluent sections of the city and containing an environmental aesthetic that may not appeal across all of the city's ethnic groups. Further, the new site removes some of the more problematic language—such as referring to contemporary New York City as "the concrete jungle"—which, as I will discuss, the original site contained. But the Welikia Project does not appear to have generated anything like the publicity that the original Mannahatta Project did, and at this writing, the website has not been developed with anything like the same capabilities of the original. This broadening of focus to include the larger metropolitan area is a welcome development and enhances the many worthwhile aspects of the project. However, given the prominence of the initial book and website, along with the accompanying media attention, I believe the criticisms that I develop of the original project around notions of ecological citizenship and belonging are still relevant.
3. The history of population estimates for North American Indians before 1492 is fraught with controversy, ranging from a low of 900,000 by Alfred Kroeber in the 1930s to a high of 18 million by Henry Dobyns in the 1960s. A helpful summary of the controversy can be found in Mann (92–96).
4. See Spence, *Dispossessing the Wilderness*, for a full treatment of the topic of Indian removal in the making of the national parks.
5. In recent years, a number of critics have made a compelling case for the way in which the idea of wilderness and nature prized by the mainstream environmental movement is hegemonic toward people of color, as well as women and gays and lesbians. See, for example, Evans, "'Nature' and Environmental Justice."
6. See also Knighton, "Ecoporn and the Manipulation of Desire."

5 The Oil Desert

Michael Ziser

> They were making the desert bloom as the rose and fulfilling the buried desire of every western American among them.
>
> —Wallace Stegner, *Discovery! The Search for Arabian Oil*[1]

In the autumn of 2009, renowned Canadian photographer Edward Burtynsky issued a collection of oil-related images culled from work he had produced over the previous dozen years. *Burtynsky: Oil*, an expression of what the artist describes in his preface as an "oil epiphany"—his sudden recognition of the ubiquity of oil and its infrastructure in the modern world—focuses on the massive manmade landscapes created wherever petroleum is extracted, processed, consumed, and disposed of, demonstrating in a powerful way the costs of humankind's 150-year love affair with liquid fossil fuels. In a worldwide canvass, Burtynsky's anthology presents the geographical extent and environmental penetration of the oil economy in all of its major phases: the production fields of Belridge, California ("Oil Fields #19ab"); the refineries of New Brunswick, Canada ("Oil Refineries #18"); the freeway interchanges of Los Angeles ("Highway #1"); the suburbs of North Las Vegas ("Suburbs #1"); the racetracks of Bonneville, Utah ("Bonneville #3"); the post-industrial ruins of Detroit and Baku ("Packard Plant #1" and "SOCAR Oil Fields #10"); and the auto and airplane junkyards of Tucson, Arizona ("Auto Wreckers #1" and "AMARC #5").[2]

Beyond their connection to oil, however, these images share a second important characteristic: almost all of them (and the majority of the ninety-seven plates in the book) are set in immediately recognizable desert locales distinguished by their relative aridity, lack of vegetation, and overall horizontality. Burtynsky's work, which has attracted significant attention from environmental humanists for its reworking of the sublime visual aesthetic pioneered in nineteenth-century American landscape painting, thus also serves to silently index a common but rarely remarked association of the contemporary petroscape with the desert environment. This chapter is an attempt to articulate the extent and significance of that widespread material and symbolic linkage, the "oil desert," arguing that full understandings of both oil culture and the modern desert depend crucially on recognizing their close intertwinement in the public imagination since the late nineteenth century. Contemporary discussions of the environmental effects of oil or the fate of desert ecosystems, particularly in the developed world, often unconsciously draw on a specifiable set of interconnected historical oil-desert discourses that limit what can and cannot be easily said about each subject. In an age of intensified geopolitical and environmental impacts from oil exploration and extraction, these discourses shape the futures being imagined for desert petroscapes in the West and elsewhere in the world. The first step in breaking the grip of fossil fuels on our cultural imaginary and our desert ecosystems is to anatomize and historicize the mechanisms by which they have become naturalized elements in our images and narratives.

The iconic image of the petroleum age—an oil derrick or pumpjack standing defiantly against a desolate desert background—is rooted in both geological necessity and specific human histories. Although recoverable oil can and does collect in a variety of geologic landscapes, it has a special affinity for deserts. To understand why this should be so, we will need to briefly consider the basics of petroleum geology. Unlike coal, which forms mainly from the breakdown of terrestrial plants, oil comes from the chemical conversion of tiny water-borne organisms, primarily plankton (diatoms, foraminifera, and radiolaria), whose corpses collect in innumerable layers at the bottom of oceans and large seas (Pohl 521–578).[3] If the water is low in oxygen because of bacterial activity and the absence of oxygen-rich currents from elsewhere (or because of a global anoxic event), the bodies of these creatures will not decompose as they would at the surface but will rather metamorphose into a compound mixture called kerogen. As additional layers of dead organic material are laid down over this kerogen, the combination of increased pressure and temperature may induce a further series of chemical reactions that ultimately results in crude oil. A major prerequisite of petrogenesis is thus a long, uninterrupted period of sedimentation in hypoxic conditions, a process associated with broad expanses of water covering a flat seafloor. For this crude oil to be recoverable by human beings, however, a further set of events must occur to ensure that the fluid will collect into reservoirs large enough to make drilling economically worthwhile. A relatively impermeable layer of shale, composed of small particles, must form above a layer of reservoir rock (usually sandstone composed of larger granules) in such a way that the crude oil becomes trapped and unable to run up and off. When the sealing rock is deformed by seismic, tectonic, or plutonic forces, a relatively large "pouch" of source rock may form in which large quantities of crude collect, often under pressure that can help drive the crude to the surface when drilled. Too much geological disruption, of the kind associated with mountain formation or volcanic activity, and the holding capacity of the sealing layer will be compromised, allowing the oil to migrate in ways that render it unrecoverable. Thus, at both the formation and entrapment phases, nature inclines toward a relatively undisrupted former seabed—a plain—as the likeliest landscape in which to find economic deposits of oil. Drilling rigs are rarely seen in the high mountains.

Of course, the natural processes involved are so complex and various—and the timeframes so long—that many exceptions exist to the general rule of oil's natural affinity for deserts. The beginning of the oil age in the U.S., to take but one prominent counterexample, is usually dated from the drilling of the Drake Well in Titusville, Pennsylvania, in the hilly and wet northwestern section of the state, and until 1904, the most productive oil region in the U.S. was a place not usually thought of as a desert, the Appalachian Basin. But by the twentieth-century heyday of oil, additional natural and historical factors converged to reinforce the desert association that had been partially established by geologic processes. Deserts are plains whose aridity usually translates into sparse or absent vegetation, a circumstance that made early large-scale geological exploration, which was based on careful field-mapping of exposed rock strata, a much easier task in deserts than in more topologically varied and verdant terrain, where bedrock might be protected from weathering and prying eyes under yards of organic soil and duff. Because deserts in the nineteenth and early twentieth centuries did not support sprawling agricultural settlement, large swaths of it were not privately owned and were therefore available for cheap leases from the federal government. No large settlements and few competing land uses meant minimal potential for conflict between locals and drillers over the environmentally disruptive practices of oil extraction, which then as now included the appropriation of large amounts of water, the fouling of surface and artesian water sources, soil pollution, and the range of social disruptions occasioned by the mostly male boomtowns that sprang up and wilted with every viable gusher. Furthermore, the technology and infrastructure needed to secure oil was similar to that traditionally required in the desert to bore wells for drinking water, crop irrigation, and salt production, avoiding a potential bottleneck in technology and skilled labor that might have slowed the exploration and development of the larger fields. For these reasons, the major U.S. oilfields between the turn of the century through the second World War—in the southern San Joaquin Valley of California, the Gulf Coast of East Texas, and Permian Basin in West Texas—were all located in desert locales. The proximity of these locales to the twentieth-century visual culture industry meant that the public profile of the oil-desert complex was amplified even further.

Turning our attention beyond the U.S. at the turn of the twentieth century, we can see the oil-desert phenomenon repeated in a variety of key locales, in particular the great deserts of the Arabian peninsula. The iconic Bedouin oil sheik has been a stock figure in the cultural imagination since at least the 1970s, when oil from the Middle East became the dominant input into world petroleum markets. And while dwindling stocks of "easy oil" in the contemporary moment mean that oil rigs can now be found in virtually every environment, from deep-sea beds to mountain jungles to Arctic plains, these newer petroscapes are often reminiscent in visual profile and imagistic association of the dry and desolate territories where the predominant cultural meanings of oil were first established.

On the consumption side, the oil-desert connection has been just as powerful. The most widely experienced forms of oil consumption—the combustion-driven automobile—found desert spaces convenient for road testing, racing, and the setting of speed records. Relatively free of inclines and obstacles that would require twists and turns in the road, deserts allowed the space-annihilating promise of automobility its freest, purest, and fastest expression. From the 1910s on, the great salt pan at the Bonneville Salt Flats in Utah has been the premier venue for land speed records, recently joined by the alkali flats of the Blackrock Desert in the neighboring state of Nevada. The image of the flat desert expanse thus both indexed and symbolized the growing conviction that the power of modern industrial culture was constrained only by its own internal limitations and not by the climatic and geographical conditions that were presumed to restrict civilizations in the eighteenth century. The overlapping road-trip and outlaw film genres (*Badlands*, *The Road Warrior*, and *Thelma and Louise*) have reinforced the connection among the automobile, the desert landscape, and a host of cultural associations constellated around liberation, danger, and self-reliance. In a more widespread and concrete sense, automobiles and sprawling road networks (and oil-powered locomotives) were the *sine qua non* for much of the twentieth-century Anglo settlement of the desert southwest. Tucson, Las Vegas, Dallas, and other major southwestern cities all prominently bear the stamp of oil and automobile culture.[4] More recently, nearly 40 years of imperial military engagements in desert oilscapes—often prepped for at military installations and bombing ranges in the desert U.S. southwest—have sealed the oil-desert association with blood and ash.[5]

These natural and economic conditions make the oil-desert complex possible, but their elaboration in cultural productions is what gives the oil desert a portable ideational and ideological form. Here a more fine-grained historical account of the desert petroscape is called for, an account that must begin with the arid American West. Literary historian Nicolas Witschi has argued convincingly that the American West's strong association with literary realism in the late nineteenth century was conditioned not by its grand expanses of uncivilized nature (the domain of the cowboy and the homesteader) but by its role as a major provider of raw material resources for eastern and midwestern industry. It was through this understanding of the western states as industrial extraction colonies that writers from Bret Harte and Mark Twain to Mary Austin and Raymond Chandler grounded their claims to tough-minded realism.[6] The year Witschi singles out as the key transitional moment in Western American literary history, 1902, was marked by the demise of the mining camp and the rise of the cowboy as the gauge of the authentic in western writing, a shift consolidated with the death of Bret Harte (and his tales of the gold mines) and the publication of Owen Wister's paradigmatic cowboy novel, *The Virginian* (Witschi 88). Though Witschi mentions oil as one of the key extracted resources, his choice of literary texts obliges him to focus on the transition from hardrock mining to large agribusiness rather than on the persistence of mineral extraction in the form of the oil industry. Notably, the moment he identifies as the end of the extraction era was in fact the real beginning of the ascendance of oil as the underlying driver of the national economy, for it was during the last years of the nineteenth century and the first decade of the twentieth century that automobile production on a large scale began in the U.S. (Kimes). Kate Chopin, writing at the turn of the twentieth century, pointed out that the association between these changes was more than simple coincidence: "The West of today is no longer the West of Bret Harte. Mining camps are not so very far from the police station, and the bucking bronco is colliding with the automobile."

Although Witschi's miner-to-cowboy chronology would seem to contradict Chopin's cowboy-to-automobile one, together they accurately sketch the peculiar history of representations of the western U.S. As a matter of historical development, Chopin is right to see the succession of ranching by wildcatting as the major driver of the southwestern economy at the turn of the century. But at the level of cultural representation, the cowboy did usurp the miner as the dominant western figure. Thus, the western literary tradition identified by Witschi did not really abandon Harte's mineral realism at the beginning of the century, when the significance of mineral extraction was on the cusp of massive and rapid growth. Neither, with a few exceptions I will discuss below, did it simply shift its setting from the mining camp to the oil field. Instead, these western American writers continued to reflect the status of the arid west as an energy colony, albeit in a disguise provided by the burgeoning tradition of cowboy literature and film. The twentieth-century tradition of the Western is thus not simply one of archaism and nostalgia for a bygone economic mode, but a representational vehicle for the new petroleum age. The rugged individualism demonstrated by the cowboy as he crosses great distances in the desert southwest is in many respects a costume drama whose real subject matter is the rise of the automobile cities of the oil desert in the first half of the twentieth century. Oil production and consumption—closely tied to the desert landscape—has a widespread occulted presence in the ranching and farming literature of the era. The established culture of western cattle ranching, with its particular social structures and folkways, was grafted onto an entirely different kind of economic base, coloring the oil industry in a way that remained significant throughout the twentieth century.

This legerdemain became especially pervasive after the discoveries of massive reserves in the Permian Basin of Texas crowned oil as the preferred fuel of the future. Among the more arresting instances of oil culture disguising itself as ranching can be found in the image of the Texas oilman, be it a real-life figure such as Glenn McCarthy or the fictional characters like J. R. Ewing that they inspired. In the many unpublished or self-published memoirs of the era, wildcatting, cowboying, and homesteading were blended into a single phenomenon, and the popular novels and films that were based on such memoirs—Edna Ferber's novel *Giant*, for example—began to shape the narrative of oil and populate its image bank with ten-gallon hats and cowboy boots.

Even western writers like Wallace Stegner, who was inclined to be suspicious of the get-rich-quick mythos of the American West, could be drawn in by this conjunction of cowboys and drillers. Stegner, fresh from the publication of his well-received history of John Wesley Powell's explorations of the Colorado River basin and on his way to becoming a spokesman for a mature (if still Eurocentric) vision of development of the arid west, accepted a commission in 1955 from oil giant Saudi Aramco to write a popular account of "the pioneers of Arabian oil." The peculiar result, *Discovery!: The Search for Arabian Oil*, unites the deserts of the Great Basin and those surrounding the great Saudi oilfields through images of ranching culture. As a historian of U.S.–Saudi relations describes the book, Stegner "begins with the ritual howling wilderness, where history is set in motion by the coming of a civilizing agency, in this case pipelines and oil pumps, and ends with the moment of the frontier's passing" (Vitalis 408). (The final chapter is indeed titled "The Frontier Closes.") That passing takes the form of the domestication of the quarters set aside for the employees of Standard Oil, notably through irrigation and gardening projects that culminate in a scheme to import and breed desert-hardy cattle for ranching purposes. As Stegner writes, the local herdsman responsible for driving the cattle over a thousand miles of desert from Yemen "had done something that might elicit the respect of the men who made the drives up from Texas that stocked America's northern plains" (212). Even when oil development took place in locales that had their own traditions, recent and ancient, within which to frame the novelty of petroleum exploration, a particular western American story—itself of suspect historicity—often became the template.

For a brief window of time before World War II, this peculiar transposition of ranching and drilling in the oil desert was the subject of direct literary treatment, nowhere more remarkably than in Mary Austin's 1917 novel, *The Ford*. Infrequently read even by Austin aficionados, *The Ford* fictionally stages resource conflict in the western U.S. with an intensity that rivals Frank Norris's *The Octopus* and reveals its author's somewhat surprising immersion in the shift to the petroleum economy. The title refers primarily to a small river crossing in the fictionalized Owens River watershed that is the setting of much of the novel's action, but also—crucially—to the automobile that finally frees the female protagonist to pursue her vision for herself and her region as a highly mobile real estate agent. The very name of that character—Anne Brent—conjures combustion: *brent* was the most common past-tense form of *burn* up until the sixteenth century. As has often been remarked since the first reviews, the novel has a notably schizophrenic structure, albeit one that accurately reflects the counterintuitive substitutions of agriculture for oil sketched above.[7] The first half concerns the disruption to the existing ranching economy introduced by oilmen who are drawn to the geology of the valley and its oil seeps. The seemingly easier and more remunerative existence of the oilfields leads the Brent family to abandon the agropastoralist life that had supported them, spiritually if not quite materially, up until that point. *The Ford*, in its first volume, promises to be one of the most significant novels about the social dimensions of early California oil culture. The oil industry established and led by the paternalistic local businessman "Old Man" Rickart turns out to be limited and short-lived, however, and after an extensive narrative build-up that culminates in a fist-fight between representatives of two local factions and an accidental fall into a petroleum tank, the momentum shifts away from the oil story and toward an alternative vision of regional development. This vision involves vanquishing the desert itself through local development of water resources, a goal that requires an additional round of political conflict among the original native inhabitants of Tierra Longa, the more recent Anglo ranchers, the small farmers hoping to irrigate the valley, municipal interests seeking to divert the river to supply the needs of San Francisco (Austin's twist on the real history of Los Angeles's annexation of the Owens River), and, finally, real estate brokers selling bits of the California Dream to eastern immigrants.

In giving preference to an irrigated smallholder agricultural future for the California desert, Austin was following in a long line of earlier Anglo writers on the southwest, from Charles Nordhoff to John Wesley Powell to William Ellsworth Smythe. All of these writers spoke of well-distributed water as the magical ingredient that would make the desert bloom into an economic and social paradise. (Smythe in particular touted the kind of cooperative investments in local irrigation infrastructure that Austin's novel ultimately appears to advocate.) What is unusual about Austin's treatment of what historian Mark Fiege terms "irrigated Eden," however, is the degree to which she renders explicit a connection between water and oil that is less easily discerned in the work of her precursors. Consider a piece of eloquence from a chapter of Smythe's called "Irrigation is a Miracle":

> No consideration of the subject can be appreciative when it starts with the narrow view that irrigation is merely an adjunct to agriculture. It is a social and industrial factor, in a much broader sense. It not only makes it possible for a civilization to rise and flourish in the midst of desolate wastes; it shapes and colors that civilization after its own peculiar design. It is not merely the life-blood of the field, but the source of institutions. (42)

While Smythe's language bears clear signs of the pressure of the hyperbolic oil rhetoric of the era, Austin's novel clinches the association and makes clear that she sees irrigation as the true deliverer of oil's promised bounty.

The grand underground reservoir on the Brent ranch that was wrongly thought to hold petroleum in the mad scramble described in the first half of the book turns out to have an even more valuable application in the second, where the locals speculate about its utility as a storage site for irrigation water. And yet the oil does not recede into the background: in the closing pages of the novel, Old Man Rickart reveals that the Brent property does in fact contain oil, albeit in a different quarter than the earlier prospectors supposed, and he advises Anne to keep it undeveloped until there is a railroad in the vicinity to bring it to market and to serve as a direct consumer. Oil and water may not mix, but both can bring out the "sleeping potentiality . . . of the home, the field, the orchard, and the workshop" from the isolated and economically marginal lands of the desert (Smythe 176).

Not all of the early instances of the oil desert are disguised in this fashion. A key text for assessing the canonization of the oil desert as a cultural phenomenon is John James McLaurin's *Sketches in Crude Oil*, a manic anecdotal survey of the American oil industry from its earliest days through the end of the nineteenth century. First published in 1896, McLaurin produced new editions in 1898 and 1902. The third edition (1902) contains an appendix related to new exploration, particularly at Spindletop in southeastern Texas (struck in 1901), and it is here that oil begins to take on its recognizably modern identity. Elsewhere in the country, where coal was abundant, oil was most frequently used for lubrication (as grease) and illumination (as kerosene). But the territory around the Spindletop strike was exceedingly coal-poor, and the relative abundance of oil encouraged its use as a substitute industrial fuel, especially for transportation. Both the Southern Pacific and the Atchison, Topeka, and Santa Fe Railroads, the dominant carriers in the American Southwest (with lines from Chicago to St. Louis, Dallas, Houston/Galveston, Denver, Salt Lake City, Albuquerque, and Los Angeles/San Diego), were the first major rail companies to convert their boilers from coal to oil (sourced in Texas and southern California), establishing a major new source of industrial demand that would soon become the most important market for the producers. In addition, the Spindletop oil lay near an excellent shipping harbor, Port Arthur, which made its transport to distant national and international markets cheaper and easier. Earlier wells had to rely on pipelines and local markets, but Texas oil was shipped to a variety of coastal cities and quickly became a recognized commodity across the rest of the U.S. And Spindletop was not without its spectacular elements, which ensured even broader attention from the readers of national and foreign newspapers and journals. As McLaurin narrated it:

> Last year Texas, an empire in area and resources, astounded mankind by a display of subterranean wealth none had deemed possible. . . . The tools had punctured a hard capping of rock at eleven-hundred-and-sixty feet, on Thursday forenoon, January tenth, 1901. Precisely at 10:30 o'clock on that memorable day the pent-up gas cut loose with

> terrific force. Water, sand, rocks, oil and joints of casing were hurled into space and scattered hundreds of feet, tearing the top of the derrick to pieces in their lofty flight. Drenched and bruised from head to foot, a man up the derrick had the toughest job of his life climbing down to safety. Not a moment's warning of the eruption was given. The gas simply let go and the greatest oil-well on earth burst into existence with appalling suddenness and majesty. (459–460)

The gushers at the site are still a matter of legend, with dozens of jets of crude blasting into the sky 100 yards or more and pooling in massive lakes of oil. When one of these oil lakes caught fire, the result was a conflagration that drew even larger crowds of spectators and journalists (Figure 5.1).

The human drama was no less a source of entertainment. The ferocious and disorganized competition, speculation, and fraud that had marked the early industry in Pennsylvania was in Texas raised to a fever pitch, breathlessly narrated and illustrated by a press that by then had developed a conventionalized rhetoric of Gilded Age fortune and folly. National newspapers like the *New York Times* covered the stories of tricks and backstabbing among the motley crew of independent drillers and large oil concerns, keeping its readership posted on mergers and divisions among the players. Its first story after the initial news of the gusher concerned the astonishing good fortune of J. N. Page, a "hard-working man" of Georgetown, Texas, who in 1899 purchased fifteen acres in the center of Spindletop for $200 and then resold them at the height of the speculative frenzy for $665,000, a 3,325-fold return ("One Texas Oil Fortune"). Through such extensive media exposure, "Spindletop leaped into fame at a single bound. . . . The waste of scanty herbage, too poor to be fenced with barbed wire, acquired extraordinary interest" (McLaurin 462).

The unexpected, unexampled wealth that rained down on these desert oilmen was often described in terms that drew on Old Testament precedents about the unmerited and enigmatic visitation of both curses and blessings. On the curses side, there are classic plagues on the Israelites (of locusts, sandstorms, frogs, etc.) as they wander in the deserts of Egypt described in *Exodus* 7–12. On the blessings side of the ledger is the "raining down of bread" on the grumbling Israelites wandering in the desert (*Exodus* 16) as well as lesser-known miracles such as the widow's (vegetable) oil (2Ki 4:4–7). The general motif of bounty found in the key New Testament miracles—the draught of fishes from the sea of Gallilee (John 21:1–14), the feeding "in a desert place" of the five thousand with the two fishes and five loaves of bread (Matthew 14:13–21), and so on—likewise supplied American chroniclers of the first oil booms with a template on which to construct their stories of the far more material fortunes made almost from nothing in the midst of a desert.

Like the physical compound to which it refers, oil discourse is the result of millennia of cultural depositions, accumulations, compressions, and

Figure 5.1 The Lucas Gusher, 1901. Reproduced courtesy of The University of Texas at Arlington Library Special Collections.

conversions. In particular, it owes a deep debt to the words and images circulated in the twentieth century that link it with the sacred wastelands of the desert southwest and the desert kingdoms of the Arabian peninsula. The postwar period in the U.S. is filled with televisual, filmic, and literary elaborations of the oil-desert associations identified above, from the Okie oil tycoons featured in *The Beverly Hillbillies* (Henning 1962–1971) to the carbon-starved apocalypse of *Mad Max 2: The Road Warrior* (Miller 1981), and the fable of primitive accumulation in *There Will Be Blood* (Anderson 2007). For many of those privileged with the power to direct energy and military policy, it is difficult to think about oil in the absence of its associated biblical, imperial, and apocalyptic baggage, a discursive nexus with all too real consequences for the oil-rich desert societies of the western U.S., the Middle East, Central Asia, and Africa. Similarly, the conception of the desert as the venue for massively destructive existential contests over resources—and as the natural resting place for the toxic byproducts of modernity—leaves little room for older understandings of it as a life-giving homeland. As the global movement to decarbonize the world's energy systems advances, these naturalized histories will continually be brought to the surface. Perhaps with enough cultural and technological effort they can be combusted in the engines of a new paradigm, one that sees in the deep past more than an expendable accumulation and in the future more than a forsaken dumping ground for the consequences of present wealth.

NOTES

1. Stegner's work, drafted in 1956, was first suppressed by his patrons and then serialized in redacted form from 1968 to 1970 in the Aramco house journal, *Saudi Aramco World*, a digitized archive of which is available at: http://www.saudiaramcoworld.com/issue/196801/discovery.the.story.of.aramco.then-chapter.1.contact.htm. The original manuscript, provisionally titled *American Discovery: The Beginnings of Saudi Arabian Oil*, has never been published and is housed with the Wallace Earle Stegner Papers collection at the University of Utah library.
2. The images included in the book can also be viewed on the artist's website. For a recent stock-taking of Burtynsky's work alongside that of other contemporary photographers, see Szeman and Whiteman.
3. The anti-global-warming crusade of conservatives in the U.S. has led some to contest even this well-settled theory of the biogenic origin of petroleum. For details of this pseudo-controversy, see Glasby.
4. Several excellent recent studies have been conducted of the oil-fueled growth of the twentieth-century modern metropolis, most notably Duany, Plater-Zyberk, and Speck. The special affinity of the sprawling petropolis with the desert until recently has been overshadowed by urban environmental histories that stress water as the key resource governing growth in southwestern cities. But see Axelrod and Ross for illuminating discussions of Los Angeles and Phoenix, respectively, as fossil-fueled postwar boomtowns.
5. Perhaps the most visually impressive instance of this is Herzog's *Lektionen in Finsternis*, a nightmarish tour of the burning oilfields in Kuwait and southern Iraq after the first Gulf War. On the abuses of the desert by the military, see Adamson 8–9, 21; and Solnit.
6. See also Robbins 1–5.
7. See, for instance, the unsigned review in *The North American Review* (July 1917) 132–135.

6 Japanese Roots in American Soil

National Belonging in David Mas Masumoto's *Harvest Son* and Jeanne Wakatsuki Houston's *The Legend of Fire Horse Woman*

Sarah D. Wald

Landscape representations offer a rich and underexamined source to explore race,citizenship, and nation in narratives about Japanese American internment. During World War II, the U.S. government forced more than 110,000 Japanese Americans into "relocation centers" across the inner-mountain U.S. West. Two-thirds of these internees were U.S. citizens while the remaining internees were Issei, or first-generation immigrants, whom the federal government deemed racially ineligible for citizenship. In using racial identity as grounds for suspected national disloyalty, the government blurred the line between racial and national identity. Works written in the decades following internment, like Monica Sone's *Nisei Daughter* and John Okada's *No-No Boy,* depict characters struggling with their knowledge that society and government dictated "it wasn't alright to be Japanese and American" (Okada 91). In contrast, more recent works by David Mas Masumoto and Jeanne Wakatsuki Houston refute the assumption that a rejection of Japanese identity is required for the formation of an acceptable Japanese American identity. There is no fundamental contrast developed between Japanese and American cultures in Masumoto's nonfiction essay collection *Harvest Son: Planting Roots in American Soil* or Houston's novel *The Legend of Fire Horse Woman.* Instead, Masumoto and Houston assert the possibilities of a Japanese American identity with roots in Japan.[1] In both works, it is the characters' relationship to the land that suggests the compatibility between Japanese cultural identity and U.S. national identity.

Masumoto's and Houston's exploration of national and racial identity through landscape representations reinforces the usefulness of ecocriticism for analysis of Asian American literature. As Robert T. Hayashi contends in "Beyond Walden Pond: Asian American Literature and the Limits of Ecocriticism," few critics have examined Asian American literature from an ecocritical perspective. To do so requires adjusting ecocritical paradigms by expanding what constitutes nature and the environment in literary texts.

As my readings of *Harvest Son* and *Fire Horse Woman* suggest, expanding ecocriticism reveals the significance of Asian American claims to the U.S. landscape in the context of exclusion from that landscape.[2]

Depictions of Japanese Americans as legitimate land holders and legitimate members of the nation found in the work of Masumoto and Houston also contribute to an emerging exploration of internment's significance in post-redress Japanese American literature. As Alice Yang Murray argues in *Historical Memories of the Japanese American Internment and the Struggle for Redress*, the redress campaign of the 1970s and 1980s renegotiated the public memory of internment. Following a series of public hearings in the early 1980s, this campaign achieved a major victory when Congress passed the Civil Liberties Act of 1988 providing a formal apology and $20,000 in monetary compensation to each living internment camp survivor. Murray shows that different organizations involved in the campaign entered a struggle over the public memory of internment that activated various narratives. As John Beck contends in *Dirty Wars: Landscape, Power, and Waste in Western American Literature*, post-redress literary narratives participate in the public debate over internment's legacy (82). As I will show, Masumoto and Houston enter this struggle to "redress" the history of internment by disrupting an exclusive racially constituted national belonging in their construction of an inclusive ecological belonging rooted in relationship to place. Masumoto's use of agrarianism and Houston's claims to indigeneity offer forms of ecological citizenship defined outside of and in opposition to U.S. legal citizenship's racial logic. Through representations of Japanese American interactions with nature, they contest the racialized nationalism manifest in many representations of Western U.S. landscapes by suggesting cross-national and cross-racial solidarities forged through shared relationships to the earth.

AN AMERICAN FARMING COMMUNITY WITH JAPANESE ROOTS

David Mas Masumoto is a prolific writer and public speaker, comparable to Wendell Berry for his pastoral themes and commitment to farming communities. He grows organic peaches on a small farm near Fresno, California. Here I focus on *Harvest Son*, a collection of non-fiction autobiographical essays, in which Masumoto most extensively discusses his family's internment experiences. Rather than a linear narrative, Masumoto offers a patchwork of memories from which the narrator, his family, and his community emerge. He discusses his childhood, college years, post-college visit to Japan, courtship with his wife, and role as a community historian, but always in relationship to Masumoto's familial legacy—a legacy embedded within his family's history in Japan.

Harvest Son captures a fluidity of national identity not always available in earlier Japanese American texts. Masumoto's visit to Japan, for example, contrasts starkly with the narrator Kazuko's visit to Japan in Sone's *Nisei Daughter.* Sone's work, written in the early Cold War, deconstructs a biological reading of race to assert the primacy of national culture in determining identity. Consequently, while her memoir affirms the possibility of a Japanese American identity, it painstakingly distinguishes between Japanese American and Japanese national identities. Her text asserts that cultural difference trumps what might be perceived as racial difference. Thus, Kazuko's visit to Japan is in a chapter titled, "We Meet Real Japanese." Masumoto, writing in a period with far greater understanding of race's social, not biological, origins has little interest in the question of racial affiliation. His memoir is not invested in countering a reading of his characters' relationship to Japan as one of biological authenticity. While Sone emphasizes the strangeness of Japanese rituals, describing them as "all so new and strange" (92), Masumoto suggests their familiarity: "I knew this ritual from my childhood" (100–101). Masumoto consistently compares the individuals he meets in Japan with his own beloved grandfathers. He explains, "This man, like Baachan, had spent a lifetime in the fields" (80). Moreover, as this passage suggests, the commonality between Japanese and Japanese American that Masumoto most often mentions is their shared relationship to the land. Although his insufficient Japanese language skills prevent direct communication with the rural farmers he meets, they were still able to "speak the language of family and farms" (85). Masumoto disrupts nationalist narratives that contrast Japan and the U.S. by emphasizing a shared agrarianism focused on family and community.

For Masumoto, farming supersedes nationality. The commonality he highlights is the universality of the rural farm family. He notes, "Perhaps the lesson was that I was part of a chain of Masumotos who were only commoners, peasants who had worked the land for generations, dirtying our hands and enriching the earth" (112). Masumoto's investment in Japanese peasant farmers dilutes the nationalism that one might otherwise read in his American agrarian narrative. Masumoto's characters are connected not by their common national character but by their common working relationship to the land. Repeatedly Masumoto reminds us that farm labor connects men across language barriers. This is the case with his interactions with Japanese relatives as well as the relationships his grandfathers established with other immigrant farmers. It is also the case with the Mexican immigrants who Masumoto hires. He writes, "They may or may not speak English or be American citizens. It makes little difference. We are joined by the bond of working the land (186)."[3] Just as farming connects Masumoto to relatives in other lands, agrarian labor connects today's immigrant farm workers to his own grandfather's experiences. This is a narrative not of nationality but of a shared knowledge of nature through labor.[4]

Masumoto's determination to demonstrate the similarity between the ways that Japanese peasants and his Japanese American relatives relate to the land contradicts the nationalism inscribed in earlier Japanese American representations of farming. The American farmer has become an iconic nationalist figure, in part from the cultural legacies of Thomas Jefferson's claim that the self-reliant farmer was the ideal citizen as well as historian Frederick Jackson Turner's frontier thesis. Japanese Americans were excluded from this cultural narrative as the U.S. government and anti-Asian organizations depicted them as unable to assimilate and thus unable to become U.S. citizens. As Colleen Lye details in *America's Asia: Racial Formation and American Literature, 1893–1945*, novels, newspaper articles, and political tracts depicted Japanese American farmers as a threat to white U.S. farmers and the U.S. as a nation. Since Japanese Americans were presumed unable to be "Americanized" by farming the land, they threatened to "Orientalize" American pastoral landscapes. Organizations like the Associated Farmers stoked anti-Japanese fears suggesting that Japanese American farmers posed a military threat from Japan.

Japanese Americans responded to such racist cultural constructions by writing themselves into the American agrarian fantasy as Jeffersonian farmers. Pre-internment Japanese American narratives of farming in California frequently emphasized western pioneering roots. Historian Eiichiro Azuma, in *Between Two Empires: Race, History and Transnationalism in Japanese American*, contends that pre-internment descriptions of Issei as pioneers successfully negotiated between two national ideologies. According to Azuma, the Issei pioneer thesis successfully drew on both the U.S. frontier thesis and a Japanese discourse of overseas development that held certain similarities to manifest destiny. Issei historians in the pre-internment period developed a narrative about Japanese farmers that incorporated Japanese Americans as participants in manifest destiny even as they drew on the ideologies that might confirm Japan's threat as an imperial power.

Masumoto echoes these earlier narratives in his emphasis on the pioneer roots of Japanese American farmers. He explains, "I think of pioneers when they first migrated into this valley. Men and animals labored in tandem to turn the virgin flatlands into lush fields. My grandfathers worked behind mules and horses, opening the earth for the first time with plow and scraper, claiming the land from the wild, not as explores but settlers who came to stay and live" (31). Yet Masumoto disrupts the exceptionalism of the American farm narratives by highlighting the similarity between rural Japanese and rural Californian landscapes. As Masumoto rides a train into Kyusho, he describes:

> The rice fields with their miles of dikes and hundreds of irregular shapes stretched on both sides of the tracks, they created a design in the land, a pattern of family farms etched into the valley floor over the course of generations. [. . .] As you near Fresno, family farms with their small

> vineyards and orchards multiply and dominate the landscape. [. . .] Both in California and Japan, these family farms are as varied as their owners. (80)

Masumoto incorporates Japanese immigrants into an American agrarian myth. Yet in connecting the rural farm families in Japan and the U.S., he challenges an exceptionalist reading of the U.S. landscape. Nothing in his narrative suggests the embrace of the Japanese expansionism or entrepreneurship that Azuma finds in the original Issei pioneer thesis. However, it must be acknowledged that Masumoto's embrace of a pioneer narrative for Japanese Americans fails to address Native American land rights, thus naturalizing the relationship between Japanese Americans and the American landscape and erasing the existence of groups that held prior claim to that land.

John Beck's work helps to explain why Japanese American writers such as Masumoto might embrace new versions of the Issei pioneer thesis. Beck argues that "coerced pioneering" operated as justification for internment, requiring the symbolic or literal death of the patriarch but allowing "the rest of the family. . . . to remake themselves as Americans" (99). According to Beck, neither "Japanese nor American, the Issei patriarch remains the exception that enables the construction of Japanese American identity in his absence" (99). Masumoto's work details the abjection of the Issei patriarch, echoing the narrative that Beck identifies in texts from Houston's *Farewell to Manzanar* (1974) to Rizzuto's *Why She Left Us (2000).* Masumoto depicts his grandfather post-internment as weak, helpless, and displaced by the son. He explains, "Dad managed to persuade a farmer to prune some of the vines by piecework and hid Jiichan in the interior rows of the vineyard where he could snip and prune at his own pace. Jiichan was proud of his son and contented with the work. He understood and accepted the circumstances—his destiny would now be determined by his children" (233). The reconstitution of the Masumoto family occurs as the son hides the patriarch from view. The post-internment return to American agrarianism occurs on the condition of patriarchal displacement.

However, in contrast to the texts Beck examines, Masumoto's storytelling works to bring Jiichan (grandfather) back into view. His narrative offers its own strategy of redress through recognition. He uses story-telling to "value the old" and return the vanquished to their rightful role in the community (236). His stories reconstitute a forgotten history. He states, "My family's history grows by gradual accrual—story by story gathered year by year" (219). This accruing history ensures that the grandfathers are remembered as the patriarchs. Although the memoir is titled *Harvest Son*, it is as a grandson that Masumoto repeatedly identifies himself. He explains, "Neither Jiichan Masumoto nor Jiichan Suigmoto planted my peach orchards, but they left behind the seeds of hard work that have sprouted and thrive today" (239). Masumoto establishes his legacy built not from the destruction that internment wrought on his grandfathers but from their hard work and pre-internment experience as farmers. He restores the continuity between pre- and post-internment life as one method to ensure his grandfathers' presence in the family history.

THE NATIVE ORIGINS OF JAPANESE AMERICANS

Instead of portraying Japanese Americans as immigrant farmers, Jeanne Wakatsuki Houston's *Fire Horse Woman* addresses the similarity of Japanese American and Native American experiences of displacement. The novel celebrates the characters' Japanese origins but also links these characters, racially, romantically, and politically, to Native Americans. Unfortunately, in doing so, Houston's novel conveys a problematic racial essentialism that is expressed in the characters' spiritual relationship to the Manzanar landscape, a landscape that remains haunted by its native past.

Fire Horse Woman follows three generations of women who are interned at the Manzanar Relocation Camp at the edge of the Sierra Nevada mountains in California's Owens Valley. Sayo immigrated from Japan as a picture bride. Her daughter Hana is trapped in a loveless arranged marriage. Hana's sexuality is awakened through an affair with an orphan named Shimmy, whom she meets at Manzanar. A significant portion of the novel details Hana's twelve-year-old daughter Terri's crush on a soldier named Billy. Alternating chapters return to the turn of the twentieth century, describing Sayo's romance with a Native American named Cloud who she believes was killed in the 1906 San Francisco earthquake. The novel's ending reveals that Cloud is Hana's father. Unbeknownst to Sayo, he was not killed during the earthquake but imprisoned fighting for his people's land. Cloud and Sayo reunite when his tribe, recognizing the similarity of the Native American and Japanese American experiences, performs the ghost dance at the internment camp. In the novel's concluding pages, Cloud sneaks Sayo out of camp disguised as a Native American.

Houston's depiction of Manzanar echoes other descriptions of internment camps, such as the swirling dust, the ominous presence of watch towers, and the border of barbed wire. Houston's desert, however, is distinct from other representations of internment landscapes because Manzanar is haunted. She describes a "foreign land, this glaring, naked expanse of sand surrounded by barbed wire and rattlesnakes and Indian ghosts" (16). Unlike Masumoto, who fails to acknowledge the dispossession of Native Americans from their territories, Houston's novel sets Manzanar on ancient Indian burial grounds (37, 40). As Sayo explains, "It's no wonder their spirits are appearing. We will be seeing lots of ghosts" (37). These ghosts serve as a reminder of past injustices. As Elena Tajima Creef explains in *Imaging Japanese America: The Visual Construction of Citizenship, Nation, and the Body*, internment narratives rarely reveal that the majority of camps were established on or near reservations (138). Houston's novel breaks from this tradition. She establishes the land as Paiute in the prologue, explaining, "The Owens Valley Paiutes, driven out long before the Los Angeles Water District stole the river's water, were now scattered throughout the nation" (1). The novel's ghosts suggest forgotten histories made manifest in the present. This includes both the "white settlers who took the land from the Indians" and Hana and Terri who are influenced by Native blood they do not know they carry (326). By foregrounding forgotten legacies, Houston promotes an anti-racist multiracial coalition politics. Yet Houston's portrayal of Paiute ghosts is also problematic as she relies on an ecological Indian trope and depicts spiritual traditions inherited genetically and expressed through the land. While Houston describes the internment camp as unjust; she represents the natural landscape of Manzanar and the Native American spirituality that pervades it as healing for the characters. Each of the three main characters experiences a rebirth or transformation while interned: Sayo is reunited with her lost love, Hana finds love for the first time, and Teri meets her future husband. The power of the Manzanar landscape to enact these changes comes through the characters' Native ancestry.

The characters' connection to an indigenous past finds expression in the pool and cave that Billy, Terri's soldier crush, allows her to visit outside of the camp's barbed wire fence. When Billy first tells her of the pool, he explains, "It's really a magic place. They say the Indians went there for healing" (80). Similarly, when Terri tells Sayo about the cave, she exclaims, "I think we discovered a holy place" (206). Teri knows the cave is holy because "there are bones, and old Indian stuff there" (206). Houston establishes the sacred power of both the cave and pool through their connection to Native Americans. She draws on an image of Native Americans as mystical. More explicitly, Teri's experience of the desert is expressed through her experience with Indian ghosts. The first ghost Terri meets "speaks a language she has never heard but, strangely, understands" (35). He recognizes her as a blood relation, "someone of my own tribe," even as she remains ignorant of her heritage (35). The sacred spaces, the oases in the novel, are also directly linked to Native Americans. The wind at the pond speaks "a language similar to the one the handsome brave spoke that night in the Horimoto compound" (83). The pond, a place where Native Americans previously went for healing purposes, now offers rejuvenation for Sayo's female descendents.

However, the Native healing that Houston depicts unfortunately builds off a New Age self-discovery and self-healing mantra that relies more on Western conceptions of individual redemption than engagement with Paiute beliefs.[5] As Shari Huhndorf explains in *Going Native: Indians in the American Cultural Imagination*, "the fixation of self-discovery and self-healing articulate the very Western ideology of bourgeois individualism" (163). The experience of "Going Native" heals the characters even as the text suggests that such characters' access to this healing comes from either loving a Native American or being partially Native American. Such a proposition is disturbing both for its implication that cultural knowledge and religious beliefs are transmuted biologically and for the stereotypical New Age representation of indigenous spirituality.

For Sayo, Hana, and Terri, the spiritual healing that the native land and Native American ghosts offer emerges through romance narratives and marriage plots. The "holy" and "sacred" space of the cave leads the three female characters to romantic fulfillment. Hana experiences this most directly as she consummates her affair in the cave. This sexual encounter signifies a personal transformation, a belated coming-of-age. Houston conveys Hana's rebirth through her straightening spine. As Hana stands straighter, she develops a backbone in her relationship to her husband and a sexual awakening as she commences her affair. Hana's turning point occurs when she heads with Sayo to the cave. Doing so requires she cross under the barbed wire lining the camp. Houston explains, "For Hana the thin barbed wire had represented more than a boundary imposed by the military. . . . Contained within, she could accept its limits, remain unchallenged to break the barrier between herself and the open space of her soul" (221–222). When Hana crosses that boundary, she finds not only a place of romance but a new relationship to herself. Like Terri, this transformation occurs in the nexus between the sacred space of the cave and her native blood. Right before Hana and Shimmy make love, she glances in her mother's mirror, left in the cave. Reflected back at her is "an image of herself, bronze-colored with long black braids" (252). In the moment in which Hana is most true to herself, she sees herself as an Indian. The self that Hana finds, Houston implies, is a Native American self. The landscape around Manzanar heralds this clichéd discovery of the Indian within Hana, Terri, and Sayo.

The cave also offers Teri and Sayo a specific salve by reuniting them with Billy and Cloud, respectively. Sayo instructs Terri to leave a memento from Billy in the cave if she wants to hear from him. This act eases Terri's heartache: "She realizes it no longer hurts to think about him" (211). She subsequently receives a letter that almost matches the high expectations her months of fantasies have produced: "And now he asked for her forgiveness, just as she had imagined he might" (296). Sayo similarly leaves the mirror given to her by Cloud in the cave. While the mirror shows Hana her emerging self, the Indian version of herself, Sayo's mirror reveals to her Cloud's return. After she leaves the mirror as an offering, "her great love return[s] from the dead!" (318). He appears in the camp with a group of Native American dancers, who perform the ghost dance as form of subversive entertainment. Because this plot development is rather unbelievable, Houston leaves open the possibility that Sayo has in fact reunited with Cloud in death, not life. Reunited, they are young again, dancing and "breathing life into their souls left wounded so many years" (324–325). Houston describes Sayo's experience as a type of freedom: "She is Free! Free again to begin and end another life" (324–325).To be free in the world of the novel is to be restored and renewed. Manzanar heals each of its three female protagonists, linking this healing to romantic love, consolidated through a romanticized relationship to Native American spirituality embodied in the landscape. Significantly, by locating these places of rejuvenation and restoration outside of the barbed wire and repeatedly referencing that the characters need to crawl under the fence to reach the pool and cave, Houston establishes that the sacred landscape of the Sierra Nevada, not the internment camp, is responsible for the characters' personal fulfillment. The landscape Houston depicts and her characters' relationship to it is "not American. [but] Indian" (237). Thus, the origin story for Japanese American identity Houston captures replaces U.S. national identity with a hybrid of Japanese and indigenous origins.

In *Fire Horse Woman*, the characters' newfound Native identities give them special insight into Native American culture. Sayo somehow knows how to harness the power of the cave while her ability to masquerade as an Indian in the novel's closing affirms her status as honorary Native American. Terri's relationship with the Indian ghost hinges on her hidden ancestry as she mysteriously understands the language the ghost speaks (35). Hana sees herself in a new way when she recognizes herself as Indian: "She feels a strength never before felt. Instead of the tall, gangly outsider she thought she was, she is a cross between two bloods, a hybrid person with a soul both Japanese and Indian" (313).[6] The relationship between Native Americans and Japanese Americans is realized through Hana's "hybrid" body and consolidated through her spiritual and sexual awakening in the camp (319).

All of this suggests a problematic biological understanding of race. Houston repeatedly emphasizes physical identity as a stand-in for her characters' indigenous heritage. When Hana first learns of her father's identity, her first thoughts are of appearances: "She understands her skin's amber tones, the high-bridged nose, eagle-wing eyebrows. My God! She is half-Indian" (310). Her newfound Indian identity is reduced to her facial features, a pattern repeated when Terri enters the room: "Hana looks at her with new eyes. She sees the tawny skin, long limbs, high cheekbones" (313). Houston's emphasis on the characters' physical features is particularly troublesome given a history in which Native Americans needed to prove their Indian identities to government officials and were suspect if they did not look Indian enough (Allen 176). Houston's text both appropriates indigeneity in order to claim a contemporary Japanese American relationship rooted in the land and lays claim to this indigenous identity by emphasizing genetics and appearances in ways that reify biological race and echo the problematic attempts of the federal government to delineate indigenous identity.

In depicting Sayo and Cloud's romance, moreover, Houston goes beyond casting solidarity between Native Americans and Japanese Americans based on shared oppression. She argues for cultural affinities based on genetic similarities between Native Americans and Japanese Americans. Houston explains that Cloud "found an affinity with the Japanese and Chinese—not only because of the common prejudice directed against them all, but for the comfort he felt in their presences, as if they shared a deeper connection than simply being outcasts" (154). Sayo and Cloud discover many shared beliefs, including, "There are spirits in everything" (124). Houston also writes that Japanese Americans "looked Indian" (2) because "some genetic particle of the blood running through their veins may have coursed through those of Mongolian nomads who, eons ago, crossed the Aleutians from Asia and later migrated down the frozen tundra to the lush North American continent" (2). This emphasizes the similarity of appearances based on transmuted "genetic particle(s)" and further reveals a problematic biological understanding of race at work in the novel.

It is important to distinguish Houston's emphasis on physical similarity and cultural identity transmuted genetically from the controversy surrounding Kiowa novelist N. Scott Momaday's concept of "blood memory." As Chadwick Allen explains, Native American authors and activists have long resisted the federal government's attempts to define who is and who is not Indian through blood quantum, asserting their right to determine indigenous identities. This ability to control group membership has significant material stakes, including access to land, fisheries, and other resources (Allen 9). Allen argues that Momaday's notion of "blood memory" evokes a narrative process that incorporates racial identity, memory, and imagination through which collective identity is reproduced and the individual sees him or herself in relation to the group's past, present, and future (Allen 181). Houston's characters Terri and Hana do not engage in this narrative practice. Their indigenous identities are passive; they are inherited in a way the federal government would recognize but Momaday might not. Houston's use of racialized heredity as a marker for the characters' ability to access Indian identity opens itself to the same criticism that Gerald Vizenor directs toward Momaday for characters that evoke a "static Indian identity based on an idealized Indian past" (Allen 192). While Houston's embrace of Hana's "hybrid" identity seems to speak to Allen's call vis-à-vis his reading of Vizenor for more fluid categories of identity, Houston undercuts such a move by rooting this hybridity in biological rather than cultural mixing.

While Allen justifies the strategic use of "blood memory" narratives in works by indigenous authors as an act of resistance, an attempt to "liberate indigenous minority identities from definitions of authenticity imposed by dominant settler cultures" (Allen 16), Houston's novel evokes a highly problematic "authentic" relationship to Indian spirituality given legitimacy through heredity. By claiming a genetic, cultural, and spiritual similarity between Japanese American and Native American characters, Houston uses inherited identities to offer Japanese immigrants the legitimacy and "authenticity" of a Native American relationship to the land. While Masumoto draws on an agrarian ethos to affirm Japanese Americans' belonging to the nation, Houston makes her claim to national belonging by hinting that Japanese Americans may be, at the root, Native American. This is an act of appropriation and romanticization that Philip Deloria has termed "playing Indian."

As Deloria contends, Indian costumes and masks participate in a search for American identity via a reinterpretation of Indianness. The ambiguity at the heart of American identity lies in the dual desire to displace aboriginal inhabitants to claim the land and to naturalize American identities by claiming affinity with indigenous inhabitants (Deloria 5). While Houston applauds the struggles of Native Americans to retain their land, she ultimately displaces them as the Native American characters occur in the novel primarily as ghosts, suggesting an Indian past appropriated by a Japanese American present. The characters have access to warnings from Indian ghosts and the restorative power of the landscape not only because of their Native American heritage and the supposed genetic and spiritual similarity of Asian immigrants to Native Americans, but also from Sayo's romantic ties to Cloud. Loving an Indian becomes a substitute for being an Indian. Indeed, Sayo becomes the one character to don Native dress as she escapes from Manzanar with Cloud (323). In these ways, Houston's Japanese American characters participate in the very practice of "playing Indian" that Deloria critiques.

The cultural logic of such a narrative refuses the complexity of Native American relationships to the land and ignores contemporary Native American existence by viewing Native American culture as a fallen Eden never to be regained. It homogenizes Native Americans and links them to the past. As Joni Adamson argues in *American Indian Literature, Environmental Justice, and Ecocriticism: The Middle Place*, it invokes a series of dichotomies, "strict categories such as *traditional* and *modern*, *authentic* and *unauthentic*, *primitive* and *civilized*, and *natural* and *cultural*," which make no sense within the constructions of much contemporary Native writings (158). The sacred relationships to nature that Houston's characters gain through their inherited indigeneity suggest the very notions of authenticity that Adamson critiques. It suggests an essentialized internal identity in which Native blood allows access to indigenous knowledge and the sacred power of the land.

Yet, it must also be noted that Houston makes substantive attempts to bring specificity to her rendering of Native Americans. She establishes that her Native characters are Owens Valley Paiutes, the indigenous inhabitants of the land where the Manzanar Relocation Camp was situated, instead of using simply the homogenizing "Indian" label. The struggles over water that Houston references are historically accurate. Houston's article "Crossing Boundaries" suggests her research process incorporated a problematic blend of romanticized fantasy and fact finding. Of particular note is an encounter with Richard, a Native docent at Manzanar. As Houston sits with him in a café, she explains that the presence of "a full-blooded Indian . . . swept [her] back to childhood fantasies" (177). Her narration of the conversation suggests the discussion was mediated by her own romanticized vision of indigenous authenticity; she imagines Richard as "a modern-day Indian guide tracking a path through a forgotten wilderness" (178). She tells him of a scene she has already written "in which a teenager girl interned at Manzanar has a vision of a granite obelisk transforming into an Indian warrior" (178). She asks him, "Is that vision believable in the Indian sense?" (178). In this instance, she allows Richard to speak for all Indians. She seeks and receives validation for a scene she "made up" (178). Houston's dedication to incorporating the Native history of the Manzanar landscape is laudable and, as stated previously, unique among internment narratives. Yet, her incorporation of "made up" instances and romanticization of indigenous identities mark her efforts as ultimately unsettling and unsatisfactory.

Houston's engagement with settler colonialism is similarly unsatisfactory. On the one hand, her recognition of the Native history of internment landscapes is significant in that it disrupts a more dominant immigrant narrative in Asian American fiction that fails to grapple fully with the U.S. as a settler nation. By revealing the history of conquest and colonization, Houston's novel laudably disputes the U.S.'s legitimacy as a gate-keeper of the nation. Yet, Houston offers a Japanese American version of the U.S. literary plot where white (in this case, Japanese American) characters gain access to Native American wisdom through their romances with Native land and Native peoples. Even as Houston strives to construct an identity rooted in the landscape that is Indian and Japanese rather than American, she subscribes to the trope of playing Indian that has long been central to the formation of American identity. The complexity in Houston's novel lies in its ability to both appropriate and disrupt the U.S. wilderness plot by using female Japanese American internees as her protagonists.

THE ROUTES AND THE ROOTS

While Houston rewrites the typical wilderness plot of U.S. literature, Masumoto complicates the Jeffersonian agrarian myth. By writing Japanese Americans into California's farming history, Masumoto asserts the legitimacy of Japanese American claims to California farm land. Yet, in suggesting the similarity between a Japanese American relationship to the land in California and a Japanese relationship to the land in his family's village in Japan, Masumoto questions the essentialism of U.S. agrarianism. He disputes the uniqueness of the independent American farmer. Ultimately, both Masumoto and Houston rewrite the relationship between Japanese Americans and the internment landscape to assert the Japanese origins of a post-redress Japanese American identity. Masumoto and Houston root this Japanese American identity in a new understanding of the American landscape. They suggest a relationship between Japanese American characters and the U.S. West defined outside of a primarily nationalist context. *Fire Horse Woman* and *Harvest Son* offer ecological citizenship not only as an alternative to racially constituted nationalism, but also as a foundation for U.S. multiracial solidarity and for transnational and transcultural relations. Yet such a vision is undercut by Houston's romanticized vision of indigeneity and Masumoto's romanticized vision of global agrarianism. Houston and Masumoto offer visions of belonging to the land that are both productive and problematic.

The forms of ecological citizenship that Masumoto and Houston envision echo in some ways the emphasis on routes over roots that Ursula K. Heise calls for in *Sense of Place and Sense of Planet*. Heise critiques much American environmental writing for romanticizing place-based identities and failing to see that an identity rooted in the land is as socially constructed and historically contingent as social identities like race, gender, and nation. She exposes the faulty logic at work in the claim that an investment in the local will necessarily lead to sustainable behavior. She calls instead for a project of eco-cosmopolitanism that goes "beyond the aforementioned 'ethic of proximity' so as to investigate by what means individuals and groups in specific cultural contexts have succeeded in envisioning themselves in similarly concrete fashion as part of the global biosphere" (62). Houston and Masumoto circumvent the claim to a natural national identity to depict, instead, alternative "imagined communities" based around shared histories of migration, oppression, and relation to the land (a relationship based in labor in the case of Masumoto and a shared spiritual relationship in Houston's novel).

For both Masumoto's narrator and Houston's protagonists, dwelling in the land provides access to long histories of migration, even as those histories are romanticized. Houston connects "Mongolian nomads who, eons ago, cross the Aluetians from Asia" to the immigration patterns of nineteenth-century Japanese immigrants (2). Masumoto connects his Japanese ancestors who worked the land in California to his relatives who continue to work the land without leaving Japan. He invests in the similarity between his own relationship to the farm and that of his Mexican workers, viewing both as connected by shared labor if not language. Unfortunately, the ways that Masumoto and Houston envision themselves as part of the global community are far more romanticized than the deep histories of place that each also offers as the basis for a connection among migrant groups. As *Fire Horse Woman* and *Harvest Son* reveal, routes can be as problematic a basis for identity as roots.

In each text, the most productive possibilities for alliances emerge through an engagement with the long history of particular places. Masumoto and Houston use the appearance of ghosts and the depiction of haunted landscapes to access the history of these particular locales. As Masumoto explains, "I take for granted my family's history. I never had to dream of a Masumoto farm; no land or property was ever taken away from me. I've never gone to sleep hungry. Yet my family's ghosts walk with me and whisper about a legacy" (235). The legacy that Masumoto inherits is the social and historical context of his own family history as well as the land itself on which "the ghosts of families who have worked this land" can be felt (149). In Houston's novel, Terri's frequent encounters with Indian ghosts convey the history of conquest and colonization as well as Terri's own secret family history. Avery Gordon, in *Ghostly Matters*, urges us to take ghosts seriously, describing haunting as "one of the most important places where meaning—comprehension—and force intersect" (194). Ghosts suggest the materialization of abstract relations of power and historically produced social conditions. As Gordon explains, "To be haunted is to be tied to historical and social effects" and to understand "not only 'their' story, the old story of the past, but how we are in this story, even now, even if we do not want to be" (190). The ghosts that haunt Masumoto's and Houston's landscape urge the characters as well as readers to consider the long history of places and the multiple ways that each locale is connected to the histories of other places.

Masumoto's and Houston's texts reveal the power, possibilities, and dangers of engaging simultaneously with routes and roots. While the global and the local are both at risk for romanticization, the long histories of places provide a means to excavate the historical dynamics through which contemporary social relations emerge. Landscape representations in post-redress internment narratives provide access to a rich and complex web of meanings attached to race, nation, and nature.

NOTES

1. Such a reading is consistent with Comer's argument that post-1970s U.S. West landscapes no longer "lend themselves so handily to the maintenance of the nationalist empire" (6).
2. Here, I am referring in part to California's Alien Land Laws, first passed in 1913 and strengthened in 1920, which aimed to prevent Japanese immigrants from owning farm land. All western states on the continent except Colorado eventually passed some version of the Alien Land Law. See Daniels (15–17) and Walz (416).
3. Masumoto's imagined commonality with the workers in his fields is quite romanticized. He grapples with this relationship in several of his books, acknowledging but never quite escaping the paternalism that shapes his interactions with the workers.
4. On the class dynamics of knowing nature through labor, see White (177).
5. For a discussion of Paiute beliefs, see Varner, *The Owen's Valley Paiute*.
6. Hana is never given any information about Cloud's heritage other than that he is Indian. His Paiute identity goes unstated.

Part II

Border Ecologies

7 Our Nations and All Our Relations

Environmental Ethics in William S. Yellow Robe, Jr.'s *The Council*

John Gamber

The scene opens on a lone Indian, tribal nation or community unknown (and frankly irrelevant), dressed in buckskins, his head adorned with a single upright feather, paddling a canoe through a woodland stream. The farther he paddles, the more polluted the waters become: paper appears floating in front of his watercraft, then more garbage; soon he emerges in an industrial waterway with barges, cranes, refineries, and smokestacks in the dark, foreboding background.[1] The lone Indian (Indians are always alone, right? He might even be the last of his tribe) beaches his canoe on the littered shore, looking forlornly (Indians are always forlorn, right?) about him, as a baritone voice cues: "Some people have a deep, abiding respect for the natural beauty that was once this country." The camera pans to the stone-faced man, his hair in braids, a bone choker around his neck. Cut to the nearby freeway, and a white hand casually tossing a trash-filled bag from a moving car, as the voice continues, "And some people don't." The bag lands at the Indian's feet, bursting with the remains of a fast-food meal; french fries spill over his moccasins and leggings. But our stoic Indian takes no personal affront to someone throwing garbage at him. We pan into the Indian's face as the voice informs us, "People start pollution. People can stop it." The camera close pans farther as we see a single tear falling from the Indian's right eye.

A tension exists in Native American Studies between challenging the ecological Indian stereotype portrayed here and recognizing widespread Native cultural values of ecological community. The "Crying Indian" Keep America Beautiful ad (1971) did not create this stereotype, but it did a hell of a job in propagating it. Plenty of work has been done to question whether such a respect is universal in Indian cultures. Of these, Shepard Krech III's *The Ecological Indian* is certainly the most famous and widely cited example. Krech points to the 1970s as the dawn of the Ecological Indian. However, Annette Kolodny, in her study of Penobscot writer Joseph Nicolar's 1893 *The Life and Traditions of the Red Man*, finds a much earlier example of Native ecological citizenship. Kolodny argues:

> Nicolar shaped all the components of what Krech would later call the Ecological Indian. In so doing, however, Nicolar conceptualized a

> challenge far more radical than anything Krech hints at. In effect, Nicolar constructed two very different orientations to living in the world: the white man's stubborn, greedy, and exploitive commitment to power and possession as opposed to the Native peoples' sharing communality and intimate interdependence with the world and its creatures. The two orientations are fundamentally incompatible. (15–16).

Likewise, Jace Weaver explains:

> One strain of this stereotype of Natives as "environmental perfectionists" holds that they did not *use* the land, existing on it in some ecological stasis box and leaving no tracks or traces of their presence. This seemingly affirmative, if highly romantic, vision in reality contributes to the exploitation of Natives and their land. It denies Indian personhood and erases Natives from the landscape where they lived for countless generations before the advent of European invaders. (*Defending* 4)[2]

For Weaver, the ecological Indian stereotype is not only inaccurate (Indian people not only used but actively and consciously shaped the landscapes of the Americas through widespread agriculture among other things), it is also condescending and detrimental to Native presence in the Americas. Moreover, assuming a single, universal environmental worldview in all Indian cultures in America represents a remarkable oversimplification, especially when one looks at the entire span of Native presence throughout the two continents, which goes back tens of thousands of years, if not to the very dawn of time itself. Many relatively recent findings suggest that humans were in the Americas far longer than the 13,000 years (a temporality that corresponds to the land bridge hypothesis) that many people are taught. Archeologist Al Goodyear's findings, for example, point to continuous human habitation dating back some 50,000 years ("University of South Carolina").

Lindsay Claire Smith notes a correlation between representations of Native people in U.S. literature with "the wilderness landscape and its associations with pre-lapsarian innocence and quintessential American possibility" (1). The unspoiled landscape of the Americas serves throughout these representations as the site of a nostalgic past that, of course, never was.[3] In fact, the Crying Indian's narrative draws on a discursive tradition that dates back beyond the founding of the U.S. as a nation. European colonizing nations relied heavily, if not absolutely, on the myth that the Americas were virgin territory. If the Americas were *terra nullius* (land belonging to no one), they could be claimed by Europeans, especially under the legalized theft brought by the Doctrine of Discovery, which worked by erasing indigenous land claims at the time of contact. This doctrine, which Patrick Wolfe notes, is "misleadingly referred to . . . in the singular," though it is in fact a complex of European conquest discourses, grows largely out of papal bulls issued in the fifteenth century, granting Portugal and Spain the rights to conquer newly found lands (390). However, these Vatican-originated documents have continued to have profound effects on indigenous versus settler-colonial land claims throughout the Americas, and in the U.S. in particular.[4] Vine Deloria, Jr. explains, "Every legal doctrine that today separates and distinguishes American Indians from other Americans traces its conceptual roots back to the Doctrine of Discovery and the subsequent moral and legal rights and responsibilities of the United States with respect to Indians" (2). While this legal discourse of discovery may date back centuries, it nonetheless continues to shape the material realities of Native nations throughout the Americas.[5]

The occupation of the Americas under the legalistic auspices of the Doctrine of Discovery marks a particular loss for Indian people because of indigenous bonds to space and place. Native American cultures, traditions, and artistic creations abound with representations of ecological communities between humans and the rest of the world—if not the entirety of the universe. This chapter examines one such representation: Assiniboine (also known as Hohe, Nakota, or Stone Sioux) dramatist William S. Yellow Robe, Jr.'s 1990 play, *The Council*.[6] In light of this volume's focus on ecological citizenship, I address what might be termed an ideology of nation-as-ecological-community as a living environmental praxis for the contemporary moment in Yellow Robe's play.[7] This chapter discusses some of the dangers of the environmental Indian stereotype, the reality of pervasive Indian environmentalisms, and some of the specific issues of tribal nationalism present in contemporary American Indian communities and Native American Studies. I focus primarily on Native American frameworks within what has become the United States—a settler colonial nation itself containing more than 550 Native nations. Within the discourse of tribal nationhood, citizenship is a critical trope. However, the tribal nation, Yellow Robe's text suggests, is merely one mode of crafting citizenship, be it Native American, indigenous, or otherwise. *The Council* offers an alternate conception of nation that challenges (if not utterly refuses) isolationism in the form of the territorial or settler-colonial nation-state, tribal nation, pan-Indian coalition, or racial nation. Likewise, eschewing a dichotomous relationship between Native Americans and Europeans, for example, it at no point casts any population as environmental saviors or destroyers. Instead, it places all of humanity within a single nation bound together in an ecological community with all life. *The Council* serves to remind all of humanity that we have a tendency to forget about our ecological citizenship. Indeed, Yellow Robe's play never identifies Indian people at all within its narrative and goes so far as to name Man, a mythic and perhaps metonymic construction, as the cause of dramatic disorder and unsustainability. While Yellow Robe's work has to this point been remarkably understudied, it offers important insights.

The Council begins in the present, with a father and his two children encountering a whale that has beached itself. However, the beach or coastline on which this occurs remains unidentified, rendering this setting as a potentially global mythic present. The family attempts to determine what it can do to help the creature, to coax it back into the sea. The next scene moves into the mythical past and the dawn of human existence. A group of animals, the play's eponymous Council—comprised of Orca, Condor, Wolf, Tiger, Panda, Walrus, and Lizard—discuss humanity's role in the world and whether they should allow this relatively new species to continue to exist (where humans or any species came from is never made express—other than that they come "from the earth") (77). Wolf and Tiger wish to destroy humans, but Panda reminds them that it is not the Council's place to destroy a species. Walrus takes a wait-and-see approach, hoping that humans will "go away. Pass on" the way Lizard's relations the dinosaurs did (though the dinosaurs' *biological* descendents might also include Condor if viewed from the position of evolutionary theory) (77). They agree not to hunt people to extinction (their extinction still seems likely considering Man's thin skin, lack of claws, and frankly poor hunting skills). From this moment humans are recognized as potential members of the Council, but also as not yet fully matured. The animals teach people to hunt, to swim, and to fish. Orca is chosen to represent Man in the Council until he learns enough to speak for himself. Orca vows to teach Man, "We are all different, but we must live together as one" (79). In short, humanity is granted provisional, if not domestic dependent, nationhood. However, humans quickly begin to overstep their bounds, especially as they harness the use of tools and fire. They lose sight of the traditional ways of the council, most notably the one that states, "Kill only to hunt or to protect" (82).

Of course, we must first note in an examination of this play from a tribally specific Assiniboine and more broadly Native American perspective that two of these species—Panda (*Ailuropoda melanoleuca*) and Tiger (*Panthera tigris*)—are not endemic to the Americas.[8] Moreover, Orca (*Orcinus orca*) and Walrus (*Odobenus rosmarus*), while occasionally American species, are hardly members of the land-locked Assiniboine local community (now largely in northern Montana in the U.S. and southern Alberta and Saskatchewan in Canada). Rather, Yellow Robe's text understands ecological national communities from across the globe (pandas and tigers are from Asia, wolves [*Canis lupus*] inhabit much of the northern hemisphere, condors [genera *Vultur* and *Gymnogyps*] inhabit relatively small sections of North and South America—they are unrelated to the so-called old world vultures [subfamily *Aegypiinae*], including buzzards, eagles, hawks, and kites, which reside on every continent except Antarctica and Oceania—lizards [order *Squamata*] are present on every continent but Antarctica, orcas range the entire world but generally prefer coastal settings, and walruses range primarily in the seas of the Arctic circle). All of the lands of the earth are represented by these species, as are the seas. Notably, terrestrial Africa and Australia have none of the charismatic megafauna often related to their environmentalist efforts (e.g., elephants, lions, wallabies)—though the World Wildlife Fund's mascot, the Panda, is present. The geographic ranges of these characters present some critical complications to considering *The Council* within a single tribal perspective. This complication challenges recent trends in Native American literary criticism toward artistic and intellectual tribal nationalism.

NATIONALISM, TRIBAL AND OTHERWISE

Within Native American Studies, particularly Native American literary studies, nationalism takes on a specific tenor. A nationalist approach has come to the fore within such studies, especially as put forward by figures including Craig Womack, Jace Weaver, Robert Warrior, Elizabeth Cook-Lynn, and Simon Ortiz. As Weaver, Womack, and Warrior assert in their *American Indian Literary Nationalism*, "Nationalism is a term on a short list, one that also includes sovereignty, culture, self-determination, experience, and history, that is central to understanding the relationship between the creative expression of Native American literature and the social and historical realities that such expression embodies" (xv). Nonetheless, no single definition for such a nationalist approach exists. I offer Craig Womack's *Red on Red* as one clear example. In that text, Womack lays out a primary purpose for his approach: to encourage "tribal people to talk about literature" in the hopes that "tribes, and tribal members, will have an increasingly important role in evaluating tribal literatures" (1). Such an approach "arises out of a conviction that Native literature, and the criticism that surrounds it, needs to see more attention devoted to tribally specific concerns" (1). This short version of one approach to tribal literary nationalism serves as a good jumping off point. Womack's thesis, one shared by literary nationalists, is that interpretation of tribal literatures has been overly controlled by people outside the tribal communities that created them, and that should change. Moreover, instead of seeing tribal literatures as growing out of or responding to white-authored literatures, critics should work to understand the tribal narratives (written, filmic, oral, etc.) out of which those literatures grow. While some would argue that Native literature must always be understood as entirely hybridized, altered by contact with European and Euro-American literatures, among others,[9] nationalists would assert that tribal cultures have been interacting with outsiders for millennia, and the adaptation of outside tools, words, lifeways, religions, foods, or what have you is simply part of the ever-evolving moving targets that mark all cultures. So, Creek writers, as applies to Womack's Creek-centered text, who adopt English as a mode of communication are not assimilating to English and English language literature so much as making English a Creek linguistic tool.

Despite calls for greater nationalism from literary critics, there are challenges in reading *The Council* from a tribally specific perspective beyond the globally set species that comprise its cast. Yellow Robe's text is not and does not pretend to be some sacred articulation of Assiniboine (or any) tribal religion or a pan-Indian creed or faith. I would argue that it is heavily influenced by indigenous conceptions of ecological community and tribal nations, but it nonetheless represents a contemporary reimagination of that community, contemporary nation-states, and tribal nation constructions. This is not to say that *The Council* reads as a universalizing narrative but, as is true of many Native stories, serves as one story of human relationships with other species that need not trump any other in its details. As David Treuer advises readers of Native American fiction (which he somewhat hyperbolically argues does not exist), "It is important to remember that we are entering textual fantasies here, not a sweat lodge" (Treuer 6).[10] *The Council* is not a sacred Assiniboine story, not an ancient rite of tribal spirituality. Nonetheless, it does embody a textual fantasy of indigenous environmentalism or understanding of ecological communities writ global. Yellow Robe's play does not fit within a tribal nationalism paradigm, though it clearly revolves around issues of nationhood and citizenship.

Still, I would argue that *The Council* does extend a Native American (or possibly more broadly indigenous) environmentalism to the planet as a whole, extending the concept of the nation to a global perspective—a literal and literary worldview. After all, many Indian and indigenous people[11] and communities do feel deep bonds to the earth, other species, or ecological communities of which they recognize themselves as parts. These bonds frequently take the form of reciprocal, pragmatic, and familial relationalities. Vine Deloria notes, "The land use philosophy of Indians is so utterly simple that it seems stupid to repeat it: man must live with other forms of life on the land and not destroy it" (189). However, the "land use" of which Deloria writes is not only pragmatic. He asserts, "People used to laugh at the Indian respect for smaller animals. Indians called them little brother" (186). Along these lines, Yellow Robe's play draws a correlation between the nations of animals with more familially defined clans. During one calamity, as all the nations are scattering, Wolf instructs Man, "Hurry! Stay with your clan. You will survive this if you stay with your clan" (101). Clans mark a basic unit of innumerable Indian families and communities—often based on common descent from a totemic being. Native people have identified kinship relations with the other-than-human for millennia. Winona LaDuke (Anishinaabe) continues Deloria's pragmatic land use but also explains the role of the non-human in educational, communal, and familially based roles. She explains in *All Our Relations*:

> Native American teachings describe the relations all around—animals, fish, trees, and rocks—as our brothers, sisters, uncles, and grandpas. Our relations to each other, our prayers whispered across generations to our relatives, are what bind our cultures together. . . . These relations are honored in ceremony, song, story, and life that keep relations

> close. . . . These are our older relatives—the ones who came before and taught us how to live. Their obliteration by dams, guns, and bounties is an immense loss to Native families and cultures. (2)

We see in these discussions a description of Native land relationships based on kinship, education, *and* support. Indeed, LaDuke endeavors to foster practices of such a worldview in her environmentalist work as founding director of the White Earth Land Recovery Project, which strives, among other things, to "facilitate the recovery of the original land base of the *White Earth Indian Reservation* while preserving and restoring traditional practices of sound land stewardship" (White Earth). Her work is national within the U.S. as well as inter- and transnational between tribal and federal nations. As co-founder of Honor the Earth, LaDuke works with international organizations, non-governmental organizations, and indigenous and non-indigenous alliances. Many Indian communities identify certain environmentalist values as part of their core and traditional beliefs, and whether those recognitions are products of recent adaptations and absorption is irrelevant to me. Since tradition is always in process, always becoming something new by remembering lessons of the past, there is nothing untraditional about any of this.

The Council establishes nations existing in deep ecological and ethical interrelationality with and to one another. When we return to the beached whales in the final scene, we understand their reasons for coming ashore. One whale explains, "I am Ice Traveler of the Orca Nation. We can live together as one in the circle of life. The people of my nation will try to get on land and find those who are willing to work together as one. Live as one" (123). To some degree, Yellow Robe's play explains why whales beach themselves, a question to which there remains no clear answer. Whales come to speak with us, risking their lives that we might understand our position in a global citizenry of life. Within this play, despite the ills of humanity, Man literally follows Ice Traveler's lead. The stage directions narrate, "*She beaches herself. Man follows her*" (123). Man responds by attempting to get her back into the water: "Help me, Ice Traveler. I can't do this by myself. Please. Someone, anyone, we can't do this by ourselves. We need help from anyone who will give it. Please. I am Man, one of the nation of Man. We need your help" (124). Nation takes the form of species rather than legal mandate, while Man's call, placed within the context of a staged play, serves as an appeal to the audience to reclaim their ecological citizenship.[12] Man needs help to save Ice Traveler, to return her to the sea (help that must come from both Ice Traveler and the other humans); he also needs help from the humans to recognize their commitments to other species as members of a global community. In this recognition of broad communities, we are forced to recognize the self in the other, to come to terms with the fact that destructive acts are not only cast outward but also always inward. We are likewise inclined to understand that nationalistic separatism—a belief that national boundaries should not be crossed, permeated, and penetrated—is difficult to defend.

National markers in the other-than-human world run throughout Yellow Robe's play, imagining nationhood as a far-from-human construct. The creature-characters in *The Council* invoke a widespread Native tradition of introducing themselves by name, position, and nation: "Panda Bear, Talker of the Panda Bear nation and all their relations" (80). The summoning of all one's relations is familiar to many who recognize the reference to the Lakota phrase *Mitakuye Oyasin*, a prayer or blessing often translated as "all my relations," to which LaDuke's aforementioned book title alludes (the closely related Nakota phrase has a similar meaning—as does the Dakota *Mitakuyapi Owas'in*). This utterance, as well as the play's holding of Council, can be read to place it within an Assiniboine-specific tribal structure; it also invokes the recognition of the community of the speaker that includes the human and the other-than-human, including biotic and geologic elements, beings, and forces.

It is critical to note the English word *nation* has been applied to "The animal kingdom, the world of animals" since at least the fourteenth century (OED). Extending nationhood and citizenship to other-than-human creatures is not solely a Native practice. But, it is also important to note that the Panda Bear nation (in which Panda and Bear are capitalized but nation is not) has relations beyond the nation, references to whom are included with the conjunction "and." The nation here is extended beyond kin and marks only one method of community formation. Yellow Robe's commentary places nationhood as an important political, ideological, and sovereign collectivity, but not exclusive of other kinds of belonging. Indeed, the belonging emphasized again and again within this play is to a community of international, interspecies, and truly global life.

Of course, the term "nation" is fraught with a history that places its definition outside of the commonplace understanding as a synonym of country or state. Benedict Anderson points out, "Nation, nationality, nationalism—all have proved notoriously difficult to define, let alone to analyze" (3). No single definition of what comprises a nation seems to fit every collectivity that is commonly considered, let alone considers itself to be a nation. Fenton and May point out that definitions based on size (whether geographic or population), sovereignty, shared ancestry or ethnicity, shared belief or custom, external recognition, or race, do not fit for all nations (1–2). Anderson most famously demonstrates that nations are "imagined communities," which, despite not existing as absolute, noumenal, a priori, or essential entities, nonetheless remain materially profoundly significant social facts. Michael Billig further notes that these imagined communities reinforce themselves through "a whole complex of beliefs, assumptions, habits, representations and practices," which he terms (borrowing from Hannah Arendt) "banal nationalism" (6). Walker Connor, however, does offer a concrete definition of nationalism and nation. He asserts, "nation connotes a group of people who believe they are ancestrally related" (xi), while nationalism "connotes identification with and loyalty to one's nation as just defined. It does *not* refer to loyalty to one's country" (xi). Connor offers, to avoid such confusions, "ethnonationalism" as a substitute or synonym for "nationalism," feeling this new term is necessary in part because the definition of nationalism is "unfortunately" seldom used in its "pristine sense" (xi). Subsequent theorists of ethnonationalism challenge Connor's absolutism (cf. Fenton and May). Nonetheless, we see how tribal nationalism fits, no matter one's perspective, within Connor's ethnonationalism. However, it is absolutely critical to recall that in demanding the recognition of Indian nations, we are emphasizing tribal sovereign rights and calling for those rights to be recognized internationally. Niezen explains:

> There is strong resistance among indigenous leaders to the terms "minority" and "ethnic group" applied to indigenous peoples, but these leaders make prominent use of the symbols of nationhood and from a broad view share some of the basic premises of ethnic and state nationalism. Some of these are the felt need to belong to a group with common territory, traditions, laws, language, spirituality, and social institutions. (200)

With the definition of nation so debated in scholarly circles, it is difficult to describe indigenous U.S. nationhood in any clear-cut way. The primary definition of nation according to the OED is "A people or group of peoples; a political state." This definition includes both Connor's pristine and the more "corrupted" common usage of a political or legal state—we can think of the nations recognized by United Nations (UN) as an example of the latter. A tension exists within the international community as symbolized by the UN relating to indigenous nations. Fenton and May note:

> the UN remains wary of bestowing the word "nation"—or its equivalent in legal terms, "peoples"—on indigenous groups. . . . The reason for such concerns, from both established nation-states and supranational bodies, is simple enough. The status of nation carries with it the corollary, or at least possibility of claims to self-determination, claims that would be potentially disruptive to the larger states within which national minorities and indigenous peoples are encapsulated. (5)

Countries like the U.S. stand to lose power, wealth, and territory by honoring their treaties and recognizing the sovereignty of Native nations. Niezen notes:

> the actions and objectives of indigenous peoples are often seen as contradictory, above all as contradicting the goals of state sovereignty and constitutional uniformity. The paradoxes of indigenous rights in some

> ways also run contrary to the realized aims of the civil rights movement and the antiracism of decolonization. Distinct indigenous rights go beyond rights based upon individual equality. (17)

Nonetheless, the U.S. finally endorsed the (non-binding) UN Declaration on the Rights of Indigenous Peoples in December 2010.

We must also note that this nation-based approach to indigenous recognition likewise presents countless pitfalls. We must ask, for example, who exactly gets to determine nation status for indigenous groups? Frequently, the answer to this question is the colonial nations that have worked to marginalize, if not eliminate, their indigenous populations. Many communities within the U.S. cannot satisfy settler-colonial governmental conditions for gaining federal recognition. Many eastern and southern states in the U.S. house no federally recognized tribes. Moreover, during the termination period, from the end of World War II to the mid-1960s, the U.S. eliminated its relationship with 109 tribes and bands. We must also bear in mind the tribal nations that have been crossed by U.S. federal borders, groups like the Tohono O'odham of southern Arizona in the U.S. and Northern Sonora in Mexico. These nations have been divided;, their access to their lands, communities, and families regulated; and their lands militarized.

Nonetheless, the above OED entry points to Native peoples fulfilling the primary definition of nationhood. The subheading for this entry defines a nation as a "large aggregate of communities and individuals united by factors such as common descent, language, culture, history, or occupation of the same territory, so as to form a distinct people." It goes on to explain that it "now also" means "such a people forming a political state." Thus, we see the evolution of nation from a people to a political entity. Nation, after all, shares the same root (from Latin *nasci*, to be born, as in nascent) as the word native, a person born of a specific place or status (consider the relation to the word nativity). Moreover, the word nation has been applied to Native people of the Americas in English since at least 1650 and quite commonly and consistently since then (OED).

However, the understanding of Native nations in the U.S. as such has been eroded both by whitestream cultural erasure of Indian people and communities and by legal constrictions for centuries.[13] As Deloria points out, "when the idea of Indian tribes as nations is voiced, many Americans laugh at the pretension, convinced that Indians have some primitive delusion of grandeur that has certainly been erased by history" (1). However, as Niezen asserts, "Indigenism is a transnational phenomenon, and as such it represents a process some might see as corrosive of nation-state authority and stability. In fact, indigenous organizations are a form of transnational solidarity invading the institutional space of states from two directions, both internationally and locally" (198). Indigenous populations are mobilizing around the world, working both within and without the framing conceptions of the nation.

ECOLOGICAL TRANSNATIONALISM

The Council, from its early scenes, challenges human exceptionalism in terms of both separation and superiority. The first scene (after the prologue) opens with several animals taunting Man because he can't fly. Instead, he is invited to Council on the back of Condor, who, Eagle notes, is "the strongest of all of us" (74). In this instant, the eagle, with which the U.S. among other nations often relates itself, defers to the bird of carrion. Eagles, known for being adept hunters, are lesser in strength to this scavenger (though eagles commonly partake in carrion). This pairing is also critical in an examination of indigeneity across the Americas. As Angelique EagleWoman asserts:

> In the reclaiming of tribal sovereignty during the 1970s, Central, South, and North American indigenous peoples engaged in many efforts to rebuild the sense of community that existed prior to the settlement of Europeans in the Western Hemisphere. The symbol for North American indigenous peoples has been the eagle, while the condor has stood for those from Central and South America. In recent years, U.S. policy regarding its border with Mexico has had the effect, whether or not intentional, of separating the eagle and the condor. (2008 33)

In this instance, Man covets Condor's ability to fly and begins to pluck his feathers in hopes of learning this skill. However, as he does so, Condor begins "having problems flying" (Yellow Robe 75). This is Man's first act of egotistical self-destruction. In pulling out the feathers of the bird on which he is flying, he increases the likelihood that Condor will fall from the sky, taking Man down with him. Man fails to understand the basic interdependence taught to us by ecology, as he fails to realize that Condor's flight equates to his own safe passage. But this is not the last such act by Man; immediately afterward, he leaps off Condor's back and goes "splat" (76). Condor here stands synecdochically for the earth itself. Just as humanity travels through space on the earth, Man travels through the sky on Condor. Man hopes to fly like Condor, to possess the powers of the rest of the world around him, and perhaps there is nothing wrong with that. But, in hoping to shape reality to his whims, Man begins to harm the living entity on which he travels, which leads not only to the destruction of that entity but, as it carries and sustains him, of himself.

Things take a troubling turn in the fifth scene when Man introduces a new term to the world, including a form of nationhood that emphasizes separatism. He explains to the council, "we, 'my' nation, are 'human beings,' and you are just beings—'animals.'" The other nations are no longer seen as relations but relegated to an inferior and subjugated position in a national hierarchy. Yellow Robe's drama posits the intellectual or philosophical differentiation between humanity and the rest of the life of the planet, our erstwhile recognized relations, as the dawn of an era that leads to ecological calamity. Soon thereafter, while demonstrating fire to the Council (a thing about which they have known for "many seasons"), he creates an inferno that spreads and threatens all living things. Wolf asserts, "This is more of his irresponsibility" (102). Man seems incapable of acting as a full member of the council of life; his nation fails to recognize its responsibilities to others. After this point, Tiger declares that Man should now be hunted. The correlation between Man opposing himself to all other life—distinguishing between himself and nature—and loosing a fire on the world is hardly coincidence.

Yellow Robe structures his drama to examine nationhood from multiple perspectives, including the tendency to structure the nation as a legalistic system. To counter the ways of the Council, another Man introduces something new to the world: "laws." "The first law is, Man can kill for food, to protect, to secure his property, and when he feels the urge. Second, all animals are beneath Man and should obey and serve Man. Third, Man has the right to use the trees, waters, air, and ground to enrich life for himself and his family. And finally, Man has the right to enter any territory or home that belongs to an animal and make it his property" (111). The legal system that man creates for his own purposes, which privileges him, his pleasure, and his convenience above all else may remind the reader or viewer, especially within the broadly indigenous context of this play, of the purely self-referential and cyclical legal justifications of settler colonialisms, including the Doctrine of Discovery.

The epilogue returns to the whales that have beached themselves, carrying on a conversation with Joey and Michelle, the two children from the Prologue. They speak to the three whales while their father goes for help. The whales explain, "We are looking for someone who will sit and hold a council with us. Those who will listen and help. There are others from other nations in this world who are having a hard time, and they don't know how to ask for help" (125–126). Yellow Robe's play imagines a kind of ecological UN in which nations "having a hard time" can hold council with others. We can likewise think here of global coalitions of indigenous populations, many of which are led by organizations in the global South. And while we might find the anthropocentric turn here troubling, we should also remember that the human species remains globally quite successful—for the time being. The children respond, "We'll do it. We'll hold the council with you. We can help you. I am Michelle." "I am Joey." "We are from the nation of Man" (126). It is important to note in this instance that it is a female who speaks first, as opposed to Man and Woman earlier in the text—in whose case Man repeatedly insists on speaking for Woman.[14] The lesson also serves that children represent hope for the future in terms of environmental sustainability. The stage directions continue: "*Father and another man enter. Michelle and Joey cross to them and bring them near the whales. Blackout*" (126). Children serve as leaders here, guiding adults. As is often the case, the environmentalist message of *The Council* targets young people. This has been one successful strategy of environmentalist movements—engaging and involving children and young people who will continue their ecological communities and who are often more receptive than their predecessors. While there is a troubling emphasis on biological procreative reproduction here, including a heteronormative undercurrent with one boy and one girl and their father (though an absent backstory might complicate this), there is also an emphasis on *cultural* reproduction of ecological community. A message is communicated from the whales to the children; the children pass it on to a human community.

Yellow Robe's play refuses portrayals of U.S. indigenous people, nations, or communities as idealized environmental saviors, positing instead that all people are members of a flawed community. In this play, Man and Woman, as well as Michelle and Joey, are without ethnic or racial signification (apart from speaking in English). Just as there is no single White perspective on humanity's place within our ecosystems, it cannot be said that indigenous people share any single environmental ethic. Yellow Robe's work fits within a broad matrix of Indian but also global environmentalisms, which emphasize human interdependence, responsibility, and community with the species with which we share the earth. *The Council*'s movement between the mythical past and the present simultaneously grounds human membership in this wider community as a diachronic genealogy and a synchronic imperative. We are charged with understanding our place as one species among many and with reforming the cultures in which we belong from assuming a human exceptionalism that promises to continue the ecological destruction of our present era.

NOTES

1. I generally challenge the use of the term "polluted," which presupposes a prior purity before things became tainted. I use it self-consciously here to demonstrate that this advertisement works under flawed assumptions.
2. For more on romanticism in representations of Indian people, see Paul Chaat Smith (13–27).
3. After all, what better image of a better past that never was than a Sicilian-American actor pretending to be Cherokee in the Crying Indian ad?
4. See *Johnson v. McIntosh* (1823) and *Cherokee v. Georgia* (1831), two thirds of the infamous Marshall Trilogy that continue to serve as precedence in federal law regarding Native peoples.
5. Recently, indigenous groups have made use of legal instruments such as the UN Declaration on the Rights of Indigenous Peoples to counter these long-standing colonial legal devices to secure both civil and human rights for indigenous groups.
6. I use the term "Assiniboine" because Yellow Robe prefers it in his writing.
7. I argue Yellow Robe's construction of the nation reimagines all currently existing nations (be they Native nations or federal nation-states) as a possible future for constructions of political and ecological community.
8. I am assuming Panda represents the giant and not the red panda.

9. These critics are generally lumped together as the cosmopolitans and include Arnold Krupat and Elvira Pulitano in particular. Krupat is especially critical of Womack's literary nationalism, as well as Elizabeth Cook-Lynn's. In their stead, he prefers his model of Native cosmopolitanism: "The cosmopolitan critic [. . .] can agree with Womack in believing that criticism of Native literatures 'should be a study of the *primary* culture that produces them,' without, however, sharing his separatist conclusion that studying the effect of the meeting between that 'primary culture' and other cultures is of little concern" (20). Nationalism is seen from the outside, then, as an exclusionary and, if I may, intellectually endogamous endeavor. However, that supposed endogamy counters the inclusive nature of Womack's vision of Creek identity. Shari Huhndorf offers the term "transnationalism" to refer "to alliances among tribes and the social structures and practices that transcend their boundaries, as well as processes on a global scale such as colonialism and capitalism" (2009 2). Instead of focusing primarily on non-Native influences, Huhndorf asserts that we can examine intertribal movements and extend those into the contemporary moment to understand colonialism within that framework. We must further note that the positions held by these scholars are not fixed or static but subject to change and adaptation. Within the intellectually fertile soils of these debates, we recognize the ways authors from various camps engage in respectful dialogue with one another, from Pulitano's and Womack's recent collaborations to Warrior's discussion and support of elements of Huhndorf's critiques (Presidential Address).

   It would also be interesting to compare this cosmopolitan discourse with Ursula Heise's eco-cosmopolitanism, a discussion that is, unfortunately (and even ironically), disallowed by issues of space here.
10. Treuer challenges the connections drawn between Native people and Native literature, suggesting that the constraints of representation of real communities challenge the possibilities of literature being read as fiction. He asserts, "The presence of myth and language [in much of Native fiction] suggests an intense emotional longing for culture, but they are not culture" (199).
11. The tensions between these terms, "Indian" and "indigenous," are fraught. I doubt any definition for indigeneity could survive application to all who define themselves as such any more than all nations fit any definition of the term "nation." However, a global movement of indigenous peoples is afoot, "challenging state notions of citizenship, national culture, and individual rights; and, internationally, striving not only for equality within states . . . but also for a greater measure of self-determination, recognition of indigenous peoples's status as distinct societies with rights of self-governance and control of land and resources that derive, in turn, from their status as original peoples" (Niezen xv–xvi). I am grateful to Joni Adamson for prompting this clarification.
12. We are reminded of Gary Nabhan's recent work on food justice, in which he writes about such concepts as Salmon Nation and Bison Nation to refer to regions of North America that would become more ecologically diverse and healthy for all life were they patterned less on contemporary monoculture and more on historically sustained and sustainable bioregional models.
13. Sociologist Claude Denis coined the term "whitestream" to describe hegemonic European societies in his study of Coast Salish cultural change in *We Are Not You: First Nations and Canadian Modernity*.
14. Earlier in the play, Woman successfully hunts and fishes while Man bumbles, ruins her plans, scares her game, but nonetheless assumes a dominant position in relation to her. We note that many indigenous organizations are led by women, as are a large percentage of environmental justice movements.

8 Preserving the Great White North

Migratory Birds, Italian Immigrants, and the Making of Ecological Citizenship Across the U.S.–Canada Border, 1900–1924

Ivan Grabovac

In a 1908 letter to Earl Grey, the Governor General of Canada, U.S. president Theodore Roosevelt recognized what we would now call the "transnational" implications of the conservation and preservation movements: "It is evident that natural resources are not limited by the boundary lines which separate nations, and that the need for conserving them upon this continent is as wide as the area upon which they exist" (qtd. in Dorsey 4). In particular, the migration of birds across the U.S.–Canada border became an ecological driving force behind the emergence of new forms of sovereignty in both countries, but especially in the U.S., on which I focus domestically and in relation to its northern neighbor.

Lauren Berlant observes that, "U.S. citizenship has always involved tensions between federal and state systems." In fact, "for most of U.S. history, state citizenship had priority" (38). During the twentieth century, argues historian Louis S. Warren, "what was local became national" as state and federal governments "assumed powers over human relations with the land that were once within the purview of local communities" (1997: 10–11). But the trajectory that Warren describes is incomplete. Roosevelt's discourse suggests that control over certain fugitive resources, i.e. resources difficult or impossible to partition (Hackett 59), assumed not only a national but also transnational character. At a crucial moment, in order to wrest control over migrating birds away from not only local communities but also the states, who claimed to hold wildlife in trust for their citizens, the U.S. government sought Canada's help. I am referring to the 1916 Migratory Bird Treaty between the U.S. and Great Britain, representing the Dominion of Canada (hereafter the Migratory Bird Treaty with Canada or, as it was called in Canada, the Migratory Birds Convention Act). This treaty was both a product of the historical tensions Berlant identifies between state and national citizenship in the U.S. and simultaneously marked the emergence of a kind of "ecological citizenship," a term I use to refer to a distinct form of what she calls "global citizenship," which is based on "linkages among people on a transnational or global scale" (38).

These transnational linkages were ecological in that migrating birds freely crossed the U.S.–Canada border, requiring cooperation between the two nations if they were to be preserved. But the reasons for each nation's cooperation with the other differed. Canadians such as C. Gordon Hewitt were concerned about the plight of migrating birds during the time that they were in U.S. territory, where protective laws or their enforcement were more lax. His U.S. counterparts, in contrast, sought the treaty primarily for domestic reasons having to do with the constitutional balance of power between state and federal governments. Under the U.S. Constitution, treaty-making is an exclusively federal power. By means of an international treaty, the U.S. government sought a constitutional leg up over states such as Missouri, which claimed jurisdiction over migrating birds and other wildlife in their territories. The paradoxical consequence was that, in order for control over migrating birds to become *national*, it had to become, at once, *transnational*.

These transnational linkages were also racial, based on migrations of different racialized groups of people. The Migratory Bird Treaty was negotiated in the context of nativism in the U.S. (English-speaking Canada produced its own complementary version of nativism), which Peter Schrag glosses as the impulse to define who or what counts as truly American "through disdain of alien people or influences" (6). This was a powerful impulse throughout U.S. history but reached a crescendo between the 1880s and 1920s, when millions of "non-traditional" immigrants from Southern and Eastern Europe began arriving in America (Dinnerstein and Reimers 56–88). In particular, writes Warren of the U.S., "it is difficult to overstate the degree to which conservationists despised Italians for killing songbirds and insectivorous birds" (1997: 25–26). The former were valued primarily for aesthetic and spiritual reasons, the latter as "helpers" of the American farmer in the war against insect pests.

The reasons that Italian immigrants hunted birds and other small animals foreground the economic and cultural differences between Italian immigrant hunters and the native-born sportsmen-preservationists who sought to restrict their activities and ultimately to restrict their immigration. In *Hungering for America*, Hasia R. Diner argues that "food, its scarcity in Italy and knowledge of its availability in America, underlay the emigration" (47). In large part, this was owing to the availability of relatively well-paid work in America, which allowed poor Italian immigrants to re-create the foodways of wealthier Italians back home. Diner also suggests, however, that some poor immigrants returned to more traditional foodways or persisted in foodways that had become illegal in modern Italy but were either permitted or on the cusp of illegality in the U.S., including certain kinds of hunting and foraging.

In 1922, John B. Burnham, the president of the American Game Protective Association, was quoted in the *New York Times* claiming that Italian immigrant laborers in New York State "killed and ate anything.

Woodchuck stews were one of their delights. They also killed and ate owls, hawks, crows and seagulls. I don't think there is any bird or animal that they would not eat." Claiming further that "such birds are never killed by Americans," who possess a native "instinct" to preserve them, Burnham both celebrates a New York law denying "aliens the right to carry firearms" and deplores the laxness of the City Clerk's office, which continues to issue licenses to foreigners ("Aliens Play Havoc With Song-Birds" 35). As Warren notes about Italian immigrants in rural Hillsville, Pennsylvania, "their taste in wildlife—songbirds and groundhogs—must have struck American-born locals as bizarre," leading in part to the passage of that state's 1909 Alien Gun Law. As I go on to argue, these state-level gun laws seeking to control immigrant hunting practices anticipated subsequent federal legislation restricting immigration, culminating in the Johnson-Reed Act of 1924.

On the one hand, then, my argument foregrounds the importance of what Kornel Chang terms "transnational white solidarity" across the U.S.-Canada border (671). Leading sportsmen-preservationists such as Theodore Roosevelt, Madison Grant, and, especially, William T. Hornaday, whose 1913 *Our Vanishing Wild-Life* was the bible of the nativist discourse of preservation, represented a distinctly racial form of nativism, the belief that true Americans are descended from "Nordic" or Northwestern European stock. According to Grant's *The Passing the Great Race*, Nordics originated around the shores of the North Sea and constituted an extended, globally dispersed family whose blood ties ran deeper than national differences. Although living in another country, white, English-speaking Canadians were not regarded as truly alien by U.S. nativists such as Grant. Paradoxically, they were deemed more American than non-Nordic immigrants to the U.S. or African Americans. Like the birds they sought to preserve, moreover, U.S. nativists such as Hornaday considered it a privilege of whiteness to cross the U.S.–Canada border freely, cooperating with their racial kin on the other side. They imagined that only they could appreciate nature aesthetically and spiritually and hence preserve it from the environmental threats posed by other races.

In contrast, these other races were deemed aliens not only racially but also ecologically, and their ability to enter the U.S. from either overseas or across the land border with Canada was put under political pressure. "It is striking," Schrag observes, linking today's struggles over immigration to historical events, "how many immigration restrictionists came, and still come, from a Progressive or conservationist background" (6). This illustrates how notions of "ecological citizenship," based on the trans-border migrations of birds and a transnational concept of the Nordic race, constituted an important early context of the Migratory Bird Treaty and some of the earliest iterations of what Park and Pellow (Chapter 12, this volume) term "nativist environmentalism."[1] I further suggest that this race-based notion of ecological citizenship helped pave the way for the Johnson-Reed Act of 1924, which sought to exclude or restrict members of non-Nordic races from entering the U.S. Although Canada did not pass similar legislation, the enforcement of racial quotas on immigration to the U.S. across the northern land border required Canadian cooperation, as I go on to discuss.

In the U.S. in the first quarter of the twentieth century, wildlife preservation and immigration restriction emerged as two sides of the same coin. Concerns about *Our Vanishing Wild-Life* (Hornaday's title) dovetailed with concerns about *The Passing of the Great Race*, the title of Grant's 1916 popularization of racial anthropology. Even as the U.S.–Canada border remained "soft" for Nordics—and migrating birds—it became "harder" for certain groups of human migrants, whom preservationists in both countries, but especially the U.S., regarded as threats to wildlife abundance.

THE GREAT WHITE NORTH

In *The Passing of the Great Race*, the first edition of which was published the same year as the Migratory Bird Treaty, U.S. author Madison Grant argues for the primacy of racial above other categories of identity, including nationality and language: "Modern anthropology has demonstrated that racial lines are not only absolutely independent of both national and linguistic groupings but that in many cases these racial lines cut through them at sharp angles" (xv). It is misleading to think of Grant's nativism as a race-based U.S. nationalism. It is instead a kind of transnationalism. In a remarkable aside, he confesses that, "personally the writer believes that the finest and purest type of Nordic community outside of Europe will develop" not in the U.S. but "in northwest Canada" (73), which is to North America what Scandinavia is to Europe, truly the Great White North.

Grant emphasizes Canada's racial makeup. Not only in the West but also in "upper Canada," the province of Ontario, "as in the United States up to the Civil War, the white population was purely Nordic" (72). He argues, however, that after the Civil War, Canada and the U.S. went separate ways. While Canada largely remained the Great White North, the U.S. increasingly became the epicenter of a racial and ecological struggle of global proportions.[2] Grant is concerned not only about Italian but also other non-Nordic immigrants and African Americans. He raises the specter of "the passing of the great race" from this part of North America, which dovetails with concerns about what Nordics imagined as "our" vanishing wildlife—its simultaneous destruction by non-Nordic races.

The production of Nordic decline and wildlife decline—or, conversely, the fight to preserve the Nordic race and "our" wildlife—as two sides of the same coin prompted U.S. nativist preservationists to idealize Canada. On the one hand, argues Mark Simpson, citing William T. Hornaday's *Campfires in the Canadian Rockies*, Canada became a shining beacon to Nordics south of the border as a signifier of "wildlife abundance while

'America' tend[ed] to name wildlife poverty" (70). As the Audubon Society activist John C. Phillips wrote at the time, "There was a hazy kind of faith in the existence far north of our borders of a sort of mysterious duck and snipe factory which could turn out the required supply practically forever" (5). On the other hand, Hornaday imagined the U.S. as "a land now rapidly filling up with Italians" (*Our Vanishing Wild-Life* 94), who not only threatened the nation's racial purity but also endangered its wildlife.

Italians and Italian immigrants were singled out by nativist preservationists such as Grant, Hornaday, and Francis H. Herrick, cited below, first because of their race. According to Joseph J. Cosco, southern Italians, especially, were imagined as "constitut[ing] a branch so far removed from the Anglo family tree" as to be considered scarcely European, rather "less than white, with something of the Oriental or black" about them (63–64).

Second, Italians and Italian immigrants were singled out because of their feelings and practices toward nature (especially birds), which were understood in racial terms. "Made to be taken and destroyed" is the phrase Herrick, writing in the Audubon Society's journal, *Bird-Lore*, uses to express

> the general attitude of Italians toward the wild life of their country, and this ancient verdict upon birds was no doubt shared by many of the Mediterranean peoples. The Italians do not feel those sentiments of friendship and affection for the song-birds of the country, so common in England and Germany, as well as in most parts of America. (196)

Herrick is writing about Italian hunters in the context of bird migration between northern and southern Europe. What seems especially to provoke his ire is less that the Italians kill their own birds and more that they kill migratory birds from northern Europe, who winter in the south. Migratory birds give Nordics a powerful stake in what "Mediterraneans" are doing in their own countries, transforming local practices into transnational concerns. " 'How to protect our migratory birds,' thus becomes a difficult problem in Europe . . . for one may well ask, 'Of what use is it to protect the wild birds of England and Germany for the Italians to kill in their own country, or for Greeks, Latins and Arabs to destroy in the Nile valley, and other parts of the Levant?' " (Herrick 198–199).

In the North American context, the same transnational logic informed the Migratory Bird Treaty between the U.S. and Canada. In his 1921*Conservation of the Wild Life of Canada*, C. Gordon Hewitt argues, "Even with the strictest enforcement of protective laws Canadians would have been unable to prevent the continued decrease of migratory birds unless the requisite protection were given to such birds during the time that they are in United States territory" (265–266). Unlike his U.S. counterpart Hornaday, however, Hewitt does not racialize his concern with the plight of migratory birds in the U.S. or imagine the U.S. as, to Canada, what Italy is to Northern Europe. Without denying that, as historians such as Tina Loo have argued, in "Canada as elsewhere, the battle to save animals, birds, and fish amounted at times to class and race warfare" (40–41), it remains true that, comparatively speaking, bird preservation dovetailed with racial anxiety primarily in the United States. Hewitt's *Conservation of the Wild Life of Canada* contains nothing like the entire chapters that Hornaday devotes to "The Slaughter of Song Birds by Italians" and "The Destruction of Song Birds by Southern Negroes and Poor Whites" in *Our Vanishing Wild-Life*.

Hornaday was a taxidermist, the director of the New York Zoological Society's Bronx Zoo (Madison Grant was its secretary), and an associate member of the Boone and Crockett Club (Grant was its co-founder with Theodore Roosevelt), an elite society of sport hunters simultaneously active in wildlife preservation. In 1905, he went on a big game hunting expedition to southeastern British Columbia with his friend John M. Phillips, the game commissioner of Pennsylvania, an account published the following year as *Campfires in the Canadian Rockies*. This text provides a remarkable glimpse of how U.S.-based nativist preservationists imagined Canada.

"At Gateway," Hornaday writes, describing his party's crossing of the 49th parallel, "we had the pleasure of seeing the mythical International Boundary, and standing astride it. It lies across the railway-platform, and is painted white" (*Campfires* 7). Crossing the border—more precisely, "standing astride it," one foot in Canada, the other in the U.S., whose essential unity is represented as the integrity of the transnational white body—gives Hornaday a jolt of "pleasure." He does not slip or "sneak" across the border—like a "Hindoo" or an Italian, as he subsequently imagined in *Our Vanishing Wild-Life* (334)—but boldly positions his body so as to underscore that he is free to cross it at will.

The appeal of Canada to Hornaday as a land of wildlife abundance and white racial purity is challenged as soon as his party arrives in the coal mining town of Fernie, however. "It reminds one of the fatalistic Italian peasant villages on the slopes of Vesuvius" (*Campfires* 10–12), he writes suggestively, a reference not only to its topography and the risk of natural (or industrial) disaster but also, more obliquely, the fact that most of the coal miners are Italian immigrants. Yet this is the only allusion to their presence, an obliquity that may be explained by the fact that, unlike his later polemic, *Our Vanishing Wild-Life*, which foregrounds the Italian threat, *Campfires in the Canadian Rockies* is the account of what is supposed to be a "vacation" in which Hornaday and Phillips remain committed to the ideal of a pristine Canadian "wilderness" set apart not only from the coal mines but also the men who labor there. "We dread the day of the ranch, the road, the railway, and the coal-mine," he writes, "anywhere near the Elk and the Bull Rivers," where he and Phillips went hunting. "We left behind us all those 'improvements' on the face of nature, and went far beyond the last tin can of civilization" (*Campfires* vi–vii).

By 1911, however, out of a population of 5,000, some 1,200 Italian immigrants were living in Fernie, according to Paul Magocsi (793). In Canada, too, Magocsi writes, "During the early part of the twentieth century, imperialist English-Canadian nationalism and nativism placed Italians on the long list of non-preferred immigrants from beyond the borders of the desired areas of Britain, the United States, and northwestern Europe" (823). Hornaday implicitly registers Fernie's Italian miners and other immigrants as a social and environmental problem whose solution is American or American-style control on Canadian soil. This is suggested, again rather obliquely, by his account of the hotel where his party stayed, which was owned by a fellow American. This man "tamed the bar-room when he assumed control of the hotel, and has since ruled it with a hand of steel in a velvet glove," with the result that although "twenty-four nationalities are represented in that little town, [. . .] the place is quiet and peaceful to the point of dullness" (*Campfires* 11–12). Taking their cue from the American hotelier, Hornaday and Phillips "strongly recommend" to their Canadian hosts, the members of the Fernie District Game Protective Association, "that immediate steps be taken by the provincial parliament to permanently set aside, as a game preserve, the country between the Bull and Elk Rivers," and that existing game laws be made more restrictive. For "whoever aids in preserving from extinction the grand game of British Columbia renders good service to two countries" (*Campfires* 9).

Hornaday's call for a warden to police this game preserve, to be appointed by the B.C. legislature, and his notion that whoever fills this role would serve not just the province, and not just Canada, but Canada and the U.S., is anticipatory. For even as his text may itself be said to perform "good service to two countries," it registers that in Canada in 1905, as in the U.S., game laws and bag limits actually fall within the jurisdiction of provincial and state governments, respectively. What needs to be explained is how power subsequently shifts, through the vector not of large game animals such as the mountain sheep Hornaday and Phillips hunted but migrating birds, from the local to the transnational scale.

THE MIGRATORY BIRD TREATY OF 1916

According to the English common law transferred to the American colonies, wild animals (*ferae naturae*) were *nullius bonis*, the property of no one, and hence common property. The 1896 U.S. Supreme Court decision of *Geer v. Connecticut* understood this to mean that individual states held wildlife in trust for their citizens. They could determine how citizens could reduce game to private property, for example, by killing and taking possession of it (Tober 146–150, 167; Lofgren 84). *Geer v. Connecticut* became the cornerstone of the so-called state ownership doctrine.

From an ecological perspective, however, the problem was that game procured legally in one state could be sold in a neighboring state even if the latter had a closed season. Because it was practically impossible to tell where the game originated, the tougher laws of the bordering state were thus effectively undermined (Bean 10–17). Indeed, hunting pressure could intensify. In his 1934 history of migratory bird protection in North America, John C. Phillips, an Audubon Society activist, Boone and Crockett member, and chairman of the American Game Association (not to be confused with John M. Phillips, Hornaday's hunting companion in Canada), described a once seemingly "hopeless" situation where "each state wanted to get all the game it could on the general theory that if it did not, some neighboring state would get more than its fair share" (6).

Extending the state ownership doctrine, the Lacey Act of 1900 tried to solve this problem by drawing on federal constitutional authority to regulate interstate commerce. It transferred ownership of game from one state to another as it was shipped across state lines. Hence, game procured legally in one state could not be sold in a neighboring state if the latter had a closed season because, on crossing the state line, it became subject to the latter's game laws. Whereas the Lacey Act was originally understood as a reinforcement of state laws, however, by introducing a competing regulator, the federal government, it actually opened the door to federal control of wildlife whose self-propelled migrations crossed state lines (Tober 159, 162; Bean 17–19). Hornaday called it the "first move ever made for federal protection of game birds" (*Thirty Years War* 161).

It was at this critical juncture between state and federal control that Hornaday's *Our Vanishing Wild-Life* located itself. The text was part of a campaign to secure passage of the Weeks-McLean Migratory Bird Act of 1913, the precursor of the Treaty of 1916, which declared, "All . . . migratory game and insectivorous birds which in their southern and northern migrations pass through or do not remain permanently the entire year within the borders of any State or Territory, shall hereafter be deemed to be within the custody and protection of the Government of the United States."[3] Madison Grant edited Hornaday's manuscript and raised $10,000 to print 13,000 copies and distribute them, accompanied by a cover letter, to legislators and influential persons across the U.S., including every member of Congress (Spiro 190–191). His commitment to Hornaday's project was not only environmental but also racial. As if to foreground the racial themes of his book, Hornaday also distributed 10,000 copies of a circular titled "Slaughter of Useful Birds: A Grave Emergency," including what he described as "a picture of two glass jars containing 'the dead bodies of 43 valuable insectivorous birds that were taken from two Italians in October, 1905, in the suburbs of New York City, by field agents of the New York Zoological Society.' " He boasted that this circular and *Our Vanishing Wild-Life* were instrumental in generating support for the bill in Congress and the press. "The book," wrote the bill's co-sponsor, Senator McLean of Connecticut, to the New York Zoological Society, "arrived just in the nick of time, and it put a fourteen-inch hole through the hull of the enemy from side to side" (qtd. in Hornaday, *Thirty Years War* 163–164). According to Phillips, these enemies were principally market hunters, as well as what he called "sportsmen (so-called), who wanted to continue the practice of spring shooting, and legislators who believed honestly, or otherwise, that legislation on this subject was unconstitutional" because according to *Geer v. Connecticut* wildlife was the property of the states (9). The latter included Senator Reed of Missouri, who attacked McLean and the supporters of his bill as "Hornadays of legislation," mere "mouthpieces" of the "eminent gentleman" and his clique of wealthy sportsmen-preservationists in New York.[4]

The Migratory Bird Act was signed into law in 1913, but the constitutional objections raised by Reed and others did not go away. Federal district courts in Kansas and Arkansas upheld the doctrine of state ownership of wildlife as the case worked its way up to the U.S. Supreme Court. Preservationists were not confident they would prevail. It was at this point that Senator Elihu Root, also a Boone and Crockett member, proposed an ingenious strategy to circumvent the opposition of states' rights advocates. He reasoned that the U.S. Constitution gives the federal government the exclusive power to make treaties with foreign countries. Moreover, according to Article VI, "All Treaties made, or which shall be made, under the Authority of the United States, shall be the Supreme Law of the Land."[5]Accordingly, if the provisions of the embattled Migratory Bird Act were incorporated into an international agreement, this migratory bird *treaty* could, in Phillips' words, "supercede" state regulatory power pursuant to Article VI, rendering the "constitutionality" of the original Act "an academic question" (12–13). Indeed, after the passage of the Migratory Bird Treaty's implementing legislation in 1918, the Supreme Court never ruled on the constitutionality of the original Weeks-McLean law (Bean 19–20).

Root's original proposal only called on the president to negotiate a treaty with one of the U.S.'s continental neighbors. The question arises as to why the U.S. decided to negotiate with Canada first instead of Mexico.[6] Kurkpatrick Dorsey contends, "Conservationists dreamed of spreading their laws wherever American birds migrated, but imposing their ideals on other cultures would be very difficult." The implication is that this difficulty would be minimized in the case of Canada because, albeit a different nation, Canada was not considered an altogether different "culture." The U.S. and Canada "had an ease of communication that few countries could match," which included but went considerably beyond the fact that the relevant players on both sides of the border spoke English (197–198). On the Canadian side, Hewitt concurred. Noting the difficulty of securing "international protection of birds in Europe" because of "a considerable diversity of interests and opinion"—what Francis Herrick, cited previously, reduced to differences between Nordic and Mediterranean races—he claimed that "many of these difficulties do not exist in North America," meaning "the

United States and Canada," where "there is an ever-growing sentiment in favor of preserving what is left of our former wealth of wild life" (270).

Dorsey argues that, although many preservationists wanted to preserve birds for what he terms "sentimental" reasons, however, they finally had to compromise their core feelings and beliefs and make the case on more utilitarian and economic grounds: birds as a food source (game birds) and as "insectivorous" friends of the American farmer. These were the terms finally privileged in the Migratory Bird Treaty. But he also repeatedly underscores that what made the Treaty possible in the first place was the deep "cultural" affinity or kinship between the U.S. and Canada. What this suggests is that the Migratory Bird Treaty did not banish sentimental, aesthetic, and spiritual arguments for preservation. Rather a kind of ecological citizenship, which cohered around the belief that only Nordic whites, on both sides of the U.S.–Canada border, could truly appreciate nature aesthetically and spiritually and hence preserve it, emerged as what Dorsey calls the Treaty's underlying "cultural" condition of possibility. This notion of ecological citizenship not only bound whites to nature, then, but also to each other. Whiteness was not only an identity shared by preservationists on both sides of the border but also a form of attachment. This affective bond made it easier to preserve birds that, migrating between the U.S. and Canada, reinforced the feeling of "brotherhood" among sportsmen.

The U.S. government sought a treaty with Canada, finally, not mainly to preserve birds in Canada—"Unlike Mexico," according to Dorsey, "Canada had bird protection laws that were already better than most of those in the United States" (197)—but to overcome domestic opposition to the production of a U.S. national wildlife commons. Phillips recounts a dramatic meeting in Ottawa between Senator John Burnham and Sir Martin Burrell, the Dominion Minister of Agriculture, in which the former pleaded "the necessity of the treaty, in order to preserve the law" (i.e., the U.S. Weeks-McLean Migratory Bird Act), which was "thought . . . unconstitutional," and which, if it came before the U.S. Supreme Court, he feared would result in an "unfavorable" decision (18). When the Treaty was finally signed, Hornaday wrote to U.S. president Wilson, calling it "the greatest victory ever achieved for the birds of this continent, or any other continent" (qtd. in Dorsey 214).

On April 19, 1920, the constitutionality of federal control over migratory birds was decided by the U.S. Supreme Court in *Missouri v. Holland*. The attorney general of Missouri (Senator Reed's constituency) had intentionally violated the Migratory Bird Treaty with Canada by hunting ducks out of season. He was arrested by a federal game warden named Ray Holland and sued (joined by Kansas as *amicus curiae*), citing the doctrine of state ownership of wildlife upheld by *Geer v. Connecticut*. But the U.S. Supreme Court ruled that "wild birds are not in the possession of anyone, and possession is the beginning of ownership. The whole foundation of the state's rights is the presence within their jurisdiction of birds that yesterday had not arrived, to-morrow may be in another state, and in a week a thousand miles away." Moreover, the court ruled that while migratory birds constitute "a national interest of very nearly the first magnitude," they "can be protected only by national action in concert with that of another power. . . . But for the treaty . . . there soon might be no birds for any powers to deal with."[7]According to Michael J. Bean, *Missouri v. Holland* was "a watershed in the development of [national] wildlife law. Nearly every subsequent case in which state authority was asserted in conflict with a federal mandate has been settled in favor of the federal government" (qtd. in Spiro 206). In a similar Canadian case, the Supreme Court of Prince Edward Island cited Holmes's ruling in a 1920 decision that the Dominion government, not the province, had jurisdiction over migratory birds (Green 224).[8]

THE JOHNSON-REED IMMIGRATION ACT OF 1924

"Let every state and province in America look out sharply for the bird-killing foreigner," writes Hornaday in *Our Vanishing Wild-Life*, joining the U.S. states and Canadian provinces in a common anti-immigrant crusade, "for sooner or later, he will surely attack your wild life. . . . The Italians are spreading, spreading, spreading. Meet them at the threshold with drastic laws, thoroughly enforced; for no half way measures will answer" (102). Once again, Hornaday's text is anticipatory. For while wildlife preservation laws specifically targeting Italian immigrants had already been passed by a number of U.S. states, his call to "meet them at the threshold with drastic laws" is also implicitly a call for immigration restriction. This culminated in the Johnson-Reed Act of 1924. Although Canada produced no similar legislation, it became complicit with U.S. racial quotas on immigration as a consequence of the Canadian Agreement of 1894, to be discussed.

At the state level, Hornaday cites a New York law requiring aliens to buy a hunting license costing $20, which he claims "has saved a million (perhaps) of our birds." But the model he holds up to the rest of the country is Pennsylvania's 1909 Alien Gun Law, which banned outright "the ownership or possession of guns of any kind by aliens" under the assumption that such ownership or possession constitutes *prima facie* the intention to slaughter wildlife (103; Warren 21–47).[9] This law was upheld by the U.S. Supreme Court in the 1914 decision of *Patsone v. Pennsylvania*. An unnaturalized Italian immigrant, who was not even hunting, had been convicted and fined for the possession of a shotgun on his own property. He challenged the constitutionality of the statute under the equal protection clause, claiming he had been discriminated against. But the Supreme Court ruled in the state's favor. Justice Oliver Wendell Holmes, who subsequently wrote the decision upholding the Migratory Bird Treaty with Canada in *Missouri v. Holland*, concluded that "a state may classify with reference to the evil to be prevented, and that if the class discriminated against is or reasonably might be considered to define those from whom the evil mainly is to be feared, it properly may be picked out." In short, "it is not enough to invalidate the law that others may do the same thing and go unpunished, if, as a matter of fact, it is found that the danger is characteristic of the class named."[10]

Hornaday and other nativist preservationists ultimately viewed anti-immigrant laws as ineffective at the state level, however. Instead of dealing with undesirable immigrants after they had already entered the U.S., it would be more effective to restrict them from entering the country in the first place. This could only be achieved at the federal level.

In a chapter titled "Introduced Species that Have Become Pests," Hornaday links the control of ecological aliens to the control of racial aliens. "The man who successfully transplants or 'introduces' into a new habitat any persistent species of living thing, assumes a very grave responsibility," he writes (330). This is because the alien population can explode, upsetting the ecological balance delicately maintained by "native" species. Hornaday cites the example of the so-called Indian mongoose: "Every country that now is without the mongoose will do well to shut and guard diligently all the doors by which it might be introduced" (333). He praises the Agriculture Department for prohibiting its importation under the Lacey Act.

The Lacey Act of 1900, to reiterate, was the first federal wildlife statute, whose unforeseen consequences with respect to the emergence of a national wildlife commons I discussed in relation to the Migratory Bird Act of 1913 and 1916 Treaty with Canada. Its more immediate consequence, however, was to empower the Secretary of Agriculture, advised by a board including Hornaday and a number of other sportsmen-preservationists, to bar the importation of foreign species deemed injurious to the U.S.

But the Lacey Act was ineffective. "In spite of the vigilance of our custom house officers, every now and then a Hindoo from some foreign vessel sneaks into the country with a pet mongoose (and they do make great pets!) inside his shirt, or in the bottom of a bag of clothing" (334). The implication is that it is impossible to enforce the Lacey Act, which bars the Indian mongoose, without simultaneously barring the Indian. Building on the Chinese Exclusion Act of 1882 and the so-called Gentlemen's Agreement with Japan of 1907, in 1917, Congress passed the Asiatic Barred Zone Act, which restricted immigration to the U.S. from most of eastern Asia and the Middle East, including India.

Hornaday's principal target, I wish to suggest, is not the Indian, then, who was already on the cusp of illegality, but the Italian, whose immigration to the U.S. remained unchecked. Italians are "pouring into America in a steady stream," he warns. "Wherever they settle, their tendency is to root out the native American and take his place and his income. Toward wild life the Italian laborer is a human mongoose. Give him power to act and he will quickly exterminate every wild thing that wears feathers or hair" (101). The rhetorical slippage is noteworthy. Whereas the "Hindoo" sneaked into America with a *pet* mongoose, the Italian immigrant *is* a mongoose. Hornaday's rhetoric culminates by producing the racial and ecological alien as one and the same.

The Emergency Quota Act of 1921 and the Johnson-Reed Act of 1924 greatly restricted, but did not completely exclude, Italians from immigrating to the U.S. Mae M. Ngai describes the latter as the first "comprehensive" immigration law in the U.S., which incorporated the exclusion of Asians with new restrictions on European immigration. Both diverging from and converging with the ideology of racial nativism espoused by men like Hornaday and Grant, it "deemed all Europeans" to be white even as it "classified" them "as nationalities and assigned quotas in a hierarchy of desirability," which favored Northern over Southern and Eastern Europeans (7). I suggest that Hornaday anticipates this legislation as the missing complement of the Lacey Act.

The Johnson-Reed Act assigned no numerical quotas on immigration from Canada and Mexico, however, although these countries were not treated equally. As Ngai notes, "the enforcement provisions of restriction—notably visa requirements and border-control policies—profoundly affected Mexicans," generating an "emergent Mexican 'race problem' " in the 1920s (7). By contrast, Marian L. Smith cites the "magical difference between the northern and southern borders" (128–129). In the nineteenth century, Canada was a "natural migration route" not only for birds but also Northern Europeans en route to the northern midwestern states. By the 1880s, however, this Nordic migration "swelled with immigrants from elsewhere in Europe" seeking "to avoid a growing number of barriers or inconveniences at U.S. ports of entry." It was not until then, when these groups "threatened to defeat the United States' implementation of a national immigration policy, that any effort was made to control this traffic" (128–129). In other words, as with national protection of migratory birds, the U.S. could not successfully implement a national immigration policy without Canadian cooperation. The result was the Canadian Agreement of 1894, under whose provisions signatory Canadian transportation companies "agreed not to land immigrants destined for the United States at *Canadian* ports of entry unless the immigrants were admissible under U.S. law" and even went so far as to permit U.S. immigration officials to be stationed on Canadian soil (128–129; see also Ramirez 42–43). By contrast, writes Claudia Sadowski-Smith, "Mexico's government was not interested in supporting U.S. enforcement of Chinese exclusion," or subsequent European national origins quotas (787–788). I suggest that an additional context for the 1916 Migratory Bird Treaty with Canada, then, was the history of cooperation on *immigration* matters going back to the Canadian Agreement of 1894.

The co-sponsor of the 1924 Immigration Act, Senator Albert Johnson, was a protégé of Madison Grant, whose views figured prominently in the Congressional debates around this legislation. But the link between racial nativism and wildlife preservation, made most forcefully by Grant's friend and ally Hornaday, was also a subtext of these debates. "I would like to say to the Members," argued Johnson in Congress, "that a restrictive immigration act is as truly a conservation measure as any dealing with natural resources."[11]

I want to conclude by citing Hornaday's "Code of Ethics" for sportsmen in *Our Vanishing Wild-Life*, which includes this succinct early twentieth-century U.S. formulation of ecological citizenship: "No man can be a good citizen and also be a slaughterer of game or fishes beyond the narrow limits compatible with high-class sportsmanship" and "A game-butcher or market hunter is an undesirable citizen, and should be treated as such" (384–385). Hornaday and other racial nativists believed that only Nordics in the U.S. and Canada could fit into this definition of the good ecological citizen because only they could appreciate nature aesthetically and spiritually, and hence preserve it. The Italian immigrant was produced as at once a racial and an ecological alien, a "human mongoose." Although Hewitt's *Conservation of the Wild Life of Canada* does not explicitly target Italian or other immigrant groups, its reproduction of Hornaday's code, which Hewitt urges "every Canadian sportsman to promote," is effectively complicit with this nativist understanding of ecological citizenship (298–299).

NOTES

1. See also Sadowski-Smith's (Chapter 10, this volume) comparison of contemporary U.S. enforcement of its borders with Canada and Mexico.
2. Citing Italian official statistics, Bruno Ramirez notes that Italian "emigration to Canada was the proverbial drop in the bucket" compared with Italian emigration to the U.S. (2001: 155).
3. 62nd Congress, 3rd Session, Chapter 145 (1913), 847.
4. 53th Cong. Rec.10682–99 (July 10, 1916).
5. U.S. Const. art. VI.
6. Mexico agreed to a migratory bird treaty in 1936 (Dorsey 196).
7. *Missouri v. Holland*, 252 U.S. 416 (1920).
8. The legal status of wildlife in Canada was not exactly the same as in the U.S., however. Tina Loo argues that, albeit influenced by developments in the U.S., "in Canada wildlife was not transformed from a 'local commons' " into "one national commons" but rather "several centralized ones whose regulation was not entirely 'delocalized' " (16). Yet migratory birds, she notes, were an important exception, "expos[ing] the shortcomings of local and even national measures and the benefits of international cooperation" (85).
9. Alien Gun Law, No. 261, 1909 Pa Laws 466.
10. *Patsone v. Pennsylvania*, 232 U.S. 138, 144 (1914).
11. 65th Cong. Rec. 5648 (April 5, 1924).

9 Boundaries of Violence
Water, Gender, and Development in Context

Julie Sze

INTRODUCTION

Despite tendencies in the U.S. and other industrialized nations to render invisible power relations in the access and delivery of water through large-scale technological systems, the politics of water are literally made concrete by the border wall on the U.S.–Mexico border (specifically between San Diego in southern California and Tijuana, Mexico). As supporters of the U.S. border patrol describe the wall on a website (emphasis added):

> It lays there in the dark like a sinuous black python. . . . It crawls from the surf of the azure blue Pacific Ocean, up the glistening white beach and then on to the east—over the rolling hills and toward the high mountain peaks at the southern extremity of California's Sierra Nevada mountains. It is all that stands between the *health, beauty and wealth* of America and the *drug inspired violence* of Mexico.[1]

The wall juts out twenty yards into the ocean, a reminder that even in the vast and beautiful ocean, political borders, psychic threats, and cultural fears about violence and political chaos overwhelming "America" loom large. However, the "health, beauty and wealth" of the U.S. depend in part on its disproportionate use of natural resources and labor exploitation both at home and abroad (and made abundantly clear at the borderlands where that home and abroad meet). The expansion of corporate-driven "free trade," decreased state regulation of corporate power, and the increased movement of goods for profit are accompanied by a strict policing of people and growing social, cultural, and environmental violence.[2]

This chapter examines cultural and literary representations of women and water in diverse geographic locales, specifically the U.S. borders with Canada and Mexico and the Central Valley region of California. I analyze Kem Nunn's *Tijuana Straits* (2004), Linda Hogan's *Solar Storms* (1995), as well as cultural representations (such as on-line photo exhibits) of contemporary water and environmental justice activism in the Central Valley to examine how conflicts over water and pollution are gendered in the context of globalization and human rights. Through a close reading of these texts in their social, political, and historical contexts, I argue that water functions as a metaphor for environmental and justice issues and their racialized and gendered dimensions in North America. Water landscapes and the struggles over water provide the backdrop for the novels because of the unique properties of water and environmental pollution to cross boundaries. In crossing political boundaries, water symbolizes the contested politics and the geographic and cultural spaces between nations and communities that hold vastly unequal power. Water also represents complex forms of violence as a result of large-scale economic development and the cultural changes this development ushers in, on the one hand, and persistent underdevelopment in the Central Valley context and their gendered effects, on the other hand. The impacts of environmental, bodily, and cultural violence resulting from development and transnationalism hit Mexican and Native women on the border as well as in the Central Valley in a gendered fashion (Kearney). These range from the literal "interzone" of pregnancy, where toxic exposures damage growing fetuses in *Tijuana Straits* and in high rates of miscarriages and birth defects in the Central Valley, to the dynamic between the past and the present and the intergenerational effects of individual, familial, and community violence depicted in *Solar Storms*.

WATER AND ECONOMIC DEVELOPMENT AT THE U.S. BORDERS

Much contemporary political concern is centered on the U.S.–Mexico border in the context of post-9/11 fears of terrorism. The dominant political discourse is about "strengthening" the borders as a technological and militarized space.[3] The unique properties of natural resources—specifically, water—points to the absurdity of this militarization since ecosystems cross borders (70% of the Tijuana River watershed is in Mexico while 30% is located in the U.S.). Pollution crosses political boundaries, and borders *exacerbate* pollution because environmental management is divided (Herzog). The San Diego/Tijuana region is intimately connected by air pollution and water quality (Nada and Kiy). Corporate expansion after the North American Free Trade Agreement (NAFTA) increased population *and* pollution.

The Tijuana River forms the geographic landscape for *Tijuana Straits* (Nunn). The novel opens with Sam Fahey, a former surfer and drug runner rescuing Magdalena Rivera, a young Mexican activist escaping hired guns out to silence her. As Fahey rescues Magdalena, "[o]ff-shore, a number of dolphins were at play among the waves, primordial shapes suspended in translucent faces—such were the wonders of the Tijuana River Valley, where sights and sounds all but obliterated from the southern half of the state might yet be found—God's script, written among the detritus of two countries" (Nunn 17). The physical beauty and the political "detritus" in the Valley exist alongside one another, standing for interpersonal and national relationships in the novel, with water representing this explosive cocktail of beauty and danger.

This unpredictable dynamic of water is evident in Magdalena's escape. Throwing herself in the water is what allows her to evade the hitmen. She is filled with a primordial terror of waves and drowning:

> the current took her at once, stronger than any man. . . . The huge fence loomed above her, repository of crosses, the names of the dead—the infamous fence. In Las Playas they died among its narrow pilings on a regular basis, pinned there like so many exotic insects by the powerful current that swept the beach, the currents she had failed to consider. And she had seen how it would be, drowned at the border like one more clueless pilgrim, within shouting distance of the river that had taken her mother. . . . She would drown, she concluded, in the land of the free. Whereupon a big wave broke directly on top of her, taking her wind, driving her down. She thrashed in the darkness, in the terrible creeping cold, till death was something she could taste, and in the end, she gave herself to it. (Nunn 37)

The river that had "taken" Magdelena's mother is a reference to the 1980 flood that affected 20,000 residents in an area along the Tijuana River in the flood plain known as Cartolandia (Bath; Bustamante). Cartolandia (so-called because the housing was made of cardboard) was targeted by the Mexican government because of its poverty, lack of adequate housing and services, and burgeoning population. The government promoted the piping of the river, the building of a flood control channel, and evictions. Twenty residents died, and another 200 were rumored missing, never to be found, when the river burst its banks after heavy rains and a release of water from the Rodríguez Dam (Manson). The novel includes Magdalena's mother and grandmother among the victims (Nunn 23).

For Magdalena, water symbolizes the waves of national and international economic development and cross-border political corruption that took her family, at the same time that it delivers her from certain death. The target of her activism is a smelting and battery recycling plant in Tijuana owned by a U.S. businessman. Residents near the plant reported skin ulcers, respiratory ailments, and birth defects, and several children had died as a result. This fictional case is drawn from an actual dispute over an abandoned lead smelter brought to attention by a cross-border activist group and presented before an international organization created by Canada, Mexico, and the U.S.[4] One compelling account of the activism against this lead smelting campaign in Tijuana can be found in *Maquilapolis: City of Factories*, which highlights the women activists fighting trans-border environmental and occupational pollution (Funari, De La Torre, and Grupo Factor X).

Water, floods, and cross-border development conflicts also form the backdrop for *Solar Storms* (Hogan). Centered on Angela Jensen, a troubled Native American teenager, the novel chronicles her return to Adam's Rib on the boundary waters of Canada and Minnesota. Sent away as a young child, physically disfigured from her mother's abuse, she returns unmoored and unfamiliar with her indigenous roots and practices. She reunites with her great-grandmother (Agnes Iron), great-great-grandmother (Dora-Rouge), and a woman called Bush, who, although not a blood relation, raised Angela's mother. The four women go on a quest to their northern homelands, canoeing through the waters, in an attempt to heal their personal, familial, and cultural wounds. As Angela describes her return, "I was like Agnes had said: Water going back to itself. I was water falling into a lake and these women were that lake" (Hogan 55).

Angela finds home and safety in family and through learning indigenous cultural practices. That healing is soon threatened by a hydroelectric dam project, drawn from the James Bay hydroelectric project. Specifically, the novel references the 1986 announcement of the "Great Whale Project," which called for the damming and diversions of five rivers that would flood Cree and Inuit land along the Great Whale River in northern Quebec. The power generated was intended for export to the U.S. and southern Quebec. Cree opposition led to Chief Matthew Coon Come's 1990 canoe trip down the Hudson River into New York City. Protests were a major factor in New York State's 1992 withdrawal from a purchasing agreement showing the power of transnational social movements in this component of the overall project (Webester).

Damage from the flooded waters is a key concern in *Solar Storms*, specifically the environmental impacts on land and animals. Angela ponders the *cultural* meanings for the Cree. During one meeting where environmental organizers meet, she drifts off:

> As I sat thinking about the million dollar dreams of officials, governments and businesses, thinking about the lengths to which they would go, my mind drifted off to water, to wetness itself, and how I'd wanted so often to hold my breath and remain inside the water that springs from the earth and rains down from the sky. Perhaps it would tell me, speak to me, show me a way around these troubles. Water, I knew, had its own needs, its own speaking and desires. (Hogan 279)

Water has its own properties, manifesting into springs and rains, representing age-old relations with the natural world and playing a crucial role in indigenous practices and epistemologies. But, as Angela realizes, for "officials, governments and businesses" focused on economic development with little concern for the environmental, cultural and social costs, the dam's meaning is very different. Thus, Angela ponders a radio powered by newly acquired energy:

> a darkness of words and ideas, wants and desires . . . part of the fast-moving darkness was the desire of those who wanted to conquer the land, the water, the rivers that kept running away from them. It was their desire to guide the waters, narrow them down into the thin black electrical wires that traversed the world. They wanted to control water, the rise and fall of it, the direction of its ancient life. They wanted its power. (Hogan 268)

In seeking to harness "power" in the water (and to export it to the U.S. as a commodity through "black wires"), the dam threatens not only to flood hunting lands, disturbing animals, plants, landscapes, and peoples, it also disrupts natural cycles and seasons, and ways of knowing and being in the world based on indigenous cultural and social values.

Power also has a dual meaning, in the literal units of energy, as well as the metaphoric. Here, sociologist Jill Harrison's description of "raw power" is illustrative. In *Pesticide Drift and the Pursuit of Environmental Justice*, she examines pesticide drift activism, policy and science, and the seeming paradox of how poisoning become both "pervasive" and "invisible." She opens with one of the high-profile cases in Earlimart, a small farmworker town, where more than 170 Spanish-speaking residents vomited, couldn't breathe, had burning eyes and lungs, and experienced dizziness. The emergency response personnel didn't speak Spanish and brought the most ill residents to the school, stripped them publicly, and sprayed them with hoses. Later, an investigation revealed that a cloud of metam sodium, a soil fumigant that is a known carcinogen, was to blame. She shows how the pesticide industry and the environmental regulatory state tells a particular "story" about incidents like Earlimart as both *accidental* and *exceptional*. Harrison's argument is that pesticide drift details how the workings of "raw power" shift the burden of pesticide pollution to the bodies of the most marginalized and vulnerable residents (1). Although she is discussing pesticides, her theoretical articulation of "raw power" and the *normalization* of environmental abuse on the most vulnerable populations are extremely relevant to the stories of the individuals and communities flooded in both novels and in the Central Valley context.

BORDER VIOLENCE, INTERZONES, AND GENDER

Just as water and environmental pollution does not respect political borders, pollution does not respect bodily borders between mother and child. Developing fetuses are particularly vulnerable to toxic exposures. The placenta is like an interzone, or an "in-between" space, similar to a border region between beings and nations (Loustaunau and Sanchez-Bane). The interdependence of mother and child is what makes pollution and its impact on fetuses so devastating (Steingraber). Toxic and occupational exposures often manifest themselves as reproductive problems, disproportionately affecting low-income women of color concentrated in dangerous manufacturing environments (Pellow and Park).

The southern border is a site of excessive violence and danger. Crossing the border is dangerous due to geographically specific risks such as drowning in oceans and rivers and heat deaths in the desert (Eschbach, Hagan, and Rodriguez; Donato and Patterson). Gendered violence ranges from rape (so common that female border crossers take birth control to avoid pregnancy from it), to the murder of factory girls that acts as a back story in *Tijuana Straits* (echoing the mass murder of female factory workers in the Mexican city of Ciudad Juarez). This violence is also gendered through the presumptive "villain" of the novel, who is also a "victim" of economic development. Armando Santoya, the hitman hired to kill Magdalena, used to be a maquila employee who worked as an assemblyman with toxic solvents. The factory was where he met Reina (another economic migrant for the rural hinterlands) who bore their child, born with a deadly tumor. Their child was born where an "entire wing of the hospital" was filled with "children with anencephaly, that is, children born without brains, the children of factory workers" (Nunn 91). Although these plot devices are drawn from the Texas border region (anecephaly clusters in Brownsville/Matamoros and the murders at Ciudad Juarez), the politics that shape toxic exposures, labor exploitation, and gendered social relationships are also common in Tijuana.

Armando's turn to violence is inextricably linked to the toxic environment he faced as a maquila worker. As a result of his despair at his son's death, he becomes violent toward Reina, who escapes to a safe house sponsored by a women's organization for which Magdalena volunteers. Thus, Armando feels special rage toward Magdalena when he is hired to kill her. In their last encounter, Magdalena attempts to reason with Armando, discussing the poisons in his blood "that would carry him away present even at the moment of his conception, in the blood of the parents, and that blood tainted like the very water at Armando's feet" (Nunn 272). She argues that his blood is like the polluted water in the Tijuana River, connecting their familial tragedies with that of their country, with its blood "sucked dry." His son and her mother were "taken by the same agents of avarice and greed" (Nunn 273).

The intergenerational, gendered, and bodily violence in *Solar Storms* is simultaneously literal, symbolic, and cultural. On their voyage, the four women encounter towns that had been resettled by the government from their ancestral lands. As Dora-Rouge describes, "the people were in pain . . . she would never have recognized their puffy faces and empty eyes, their unkempt, hollow appearance. It was a murder of the soul that was taking place there. Murder with no consequences to the killers" (Hogan 226). The cultural violence and disconnection from the land and rituals explain the larger stakes of the dam:

> The devastation and the ruin that had fallen over the land fell over the people, too. Most were too broken to fight the building of the dams, the moving of the waters, and that perhaps had been the intention all along. But I could see Dora-Rouge thinking, wondering: how do conquered people get back their lives? She and others knew the protest against the dams and river diversions was their only hope. Those who protested were the ones who could still believe they might survive as a people. (Hogan 226)

Thus, Angela understands that the maternal abuse she suffered was a result of pain and violence—not just as individual acts, but a result of complex cultural and intergenerational wounds directed at Native peoples, of which the dam is the most recent incarnation. Thus, she understands that anti-dam activism is how "broken" communities can reclaim their identity and dignity.

WOMEN, WATER, AND ACTIVISM IN THE CENTRAL VALLEY

The dynamic that Angela comes to understand—that the terrible environmental and social abuses directed at her community are paradoxically a source of renewal and activism—is echoed by real-life stories of female environmental justice activists in the Central Valley. As sociologist Jill Harrison notes, the Central Valley region in California is particularly vulnerable to environmental pollution as a result of its agricultural development as the most productive agricultural region in the world—as a site of "high value" agriculture (in the case of pesticides, the region is 2% of farmland but 25% of the nation's pesticide application, and 90% of the pesticides there are vulnerable to pesticide drift often with disastrous health consequences for local communities). This agricultural run-off is one major source of water pollution in the region.

The Central Valley is also the home of a large concentration of new prisons, despite a steadily falling crime rate in California. These conditions are a result, as geographer Ruth Gilmore argues in *Golden Gulag: Prisons, Surplus, Crisis, and Opposition in Globalizing California*, of a spatialized and racialized response to political and social crisis in California. The social and environmental conditions of the Central Valley (highest rates of air pollution in the country, high risks from water contamination, carceral landscapes, high poverty and residential foreclosure rates, low educational attainment) are not accidental but rather, structural. These social and environmental ills of the Central Valley and the activism against these problems are the focus of recent research (Perkins) and public outreach projects.

Specifically, the project is titled, 25 Stories from the Central Valley. 25 Stories is a public, on-line campus/community collaborative research and outreach project that highlights the photos and narratives of female environmental justice activists in the region.[5]

Water, its pollution, and the health impacts on vulnerable populations are one major theme in 25 Stories. Particularly, the photo of the gleaming California Aqueduct and the caption explaining the paradox of water pollution in small farmworker communities point to another expression of Harrison's "raw power" using water pollution as the example (see Figure 9.1).

In these communities, the drinking water is contaminated by agricultural run-off, particularly nitrates, and race and social factors are related to higher rates of exposure (Balazs et al.). The contaminated tap water samples from Visalia tested positive for nitrates from both fertilizers and mega-dairy cow manure (Figure 9.2). In addition, groundwater water in these samples also contains Dibromochloropropane, a pesticide banned in 1977. Thus, in some low-income communities in the Southern San Joaquin Valley, all of their household consumption must be purchased. Another photo from 25 Stories shows Sandra Meraz, a local community water activist, purchasing water because her water is contaminated (in her situation, by arsenic). She led the fight to get a new water system for her community. Meraz, who is Native American and Latina, is the first woman of color to have a seat on the Central Valley Water Quality Control Board (see Figure

Figure 9.1 Photo of the California Aqueduct. Credit: Tracy Perkins.

Figure 9.2 Tap water samples taken around Visalia.Credit: Tracy Perkins.

Figure 9.3 Photo of Sandra Meraz. Credit: Tracy Perkins.

9.3).[6] As in the example of pesticide drift, the most vulnerable populations to polluted water are also the most exposed to pollution.

Sandra Meraz is part of a vibrant network of Latina activists and advocates working on water justice issues in the Central Valley. Susana De Anda and Laurel Firestone are co-directors of the Community Water Center based in Visalia, who argue that, "Clean drinking water is a human right, not a privilege."[7] One description of their organization describes the "life and death" urgency of their work by describing the existing conditions of their physical landscape: "Tulare, in the San Joaquin Valley, is one of the most productive dairy and agricultural counties in the country. While publicly funded systems pipe crystalline Northern California river water to farms there, decades of intensive fertilizer and pesticide use and run-off from animal factories have so contaminated the groundwater that hundreds of thousands of residents are being poisoned by their tap water."[8] The profile continues by explaining, "Susana DeAnda is determined to change that," detailing her family's journey from Mexico to California and her own journey to major in environmental studies and work in the field of environmental advocacy. She explains that, for her, environmentalism was connected to: "my uncles, all farm workers, with leathered skin. . . . I realized that the yellow planes that flew over us at recess were spraying poison or pesticide drift" (see Figure 9.4).[9]

As an organizer for the Rural Poverty Water Project at the Center on Race, Poverty, and the Environment, De Anda traveled to low-income, unincorporated communities where she and her colleague, Firestone, "saw horrific evidence of the health consequences of drinking water with high concentrations of nitrates, arsenic and other toxins." They began organizing leaders to start La Asociación de Gente Unida por el Agua (AGUA), a coalition of 17 communities and seven nonprofits (De Anda notes that many of AGUA leaders are women).[10] Through her work at the Community

Figure 9.4 Photo of Susana De Anda, National Drinking Water week event in Seville, CA, May 4, 2010. Credit: Bear Guerra.

Water Center, she hopes to identify and *change* existing social and environmental conditions: "Families who had buried too many stillborn infants and who drove long distances to purchase bottled water they could ill afford rather than drink black tap water that smelled like sewage, were galvanized into action. They raised their voices at public hearings, won seats on local water boards and secured legislation that directed $2-million to a pilot project for water quality and wastewater treatment for disadvantaged communities only in the Tulare Lake Basin."[11] The environmental pollution and their impacts on women and their families echoes the heart-breaking stories recounted by Numm and Hogan.

CONCLUSION

Faced with complex forms of violence as a result of transnationalism and economic development, Magdalena and Angela, and the Central Valley environmental justice activists like Sandra Meraz and Susana De Anda, recognize the dangers that water and water projects represent to their communities and their intergenerational impacts. But water simultaneously stands for a powerfully benevolent response and reaction to these same political and environmental problems. Angela's people are from the "world of water." In the *Solar Storms*, the dam ceases as a result of Native mobilization, and Angela's pain is ultimately eased through the love she discovers. In *Tijuana Straits*, Armando's turn to drugs and violence to numb the pain and loss of his family is contrasted with Magdalena's activism to avenge her mother and grandmother's deaths from floods and the continued problems of top-down economic and corporate development. She is saved by Fahey's kindness, who in the last scene fashions a human chain with border crossers that enables them to collectively survive the wave that sweeps Armando out to sea. This collective strength enables survival in the face of forces that can swat down the individual.

In the novels I examine, gender and globalization, the politics of transnationalism, and the power of water are represented through lyrical language and compelling narratives. In creating complex characters and stories, the novels represent the human costs of the intense levels of violence of development and transnationalism emanating from the U.S. and how these shape the lives of Mexican and Native women at the borderlands. At the same time, within these novels and echoed by the women water justice activists, the "victims" of the pollution re-imagine, interpret, and represent the culture and politics of transnational environmental and justice claims and offer a powerful antidote to the dominant political discourse on iron-clad national borders and unimpeded free trade in the contemporary U.S.

The "raw power" of pollution, like racism, is met alongside community resistance to these forces. Gilmore defines racism as the state-sanctioned or extralegal production and exploitation of group-differentiated vulnerability to premature death. Like Wilson's notion of "slow death" in discussing climate change, or in Harrison's example of pesticide drift, the persistent patterns of water contamination and destruction are not accidental but instead endemic and embedded in systems of exploitation, heightened in an era of neoliberalism. Neoliberalism idealizes market and capital, and consumer subjectivities over that of communitarian notions of belonging or justice.

Thus, in this context, the activism of the women in the novels and in the Central Valley become particularly significant, and sharing their stories a powerful attempt to correct the "flood" of neoliberalism in a world where global warming and water shortages loom large. The work of activists like Meraz, De Anda, and the border activists is to *de-normalize* existing environmental and social conditions of injustice and pollution and to bend power from the raw power of exploitation, environmental, and otherwise into new social and material realities.

NOTES

1. This particular quote, along with music alternating between the patriotic and the threatening, was accessed at http://www.usborderpatrol.com/borderframe1301.htm, on December 16, 2006, at a website called the "US Border Patrol," maintained by "supporters of the United States Border Patrol." This specific quote and music have since been taken down, although the site's ideology remains the same. Specifically, the site argues that, "On horseback, and on land, sea, and air, the United States Border Patrol defends America" (accessed June 15, 2007). This website is not a source of objective information on the U.S.–Mexico border in general or on the wall in particular. The implication that the wall is a single entity stretching to the Sierra Nevada Mountains is not factually accurate. But this website effectively illustrates particularly insidious cultural discourses of fear and anxiety around globalization and immigration at the moment when the border wall is being debated in Congress. The border wall is actually a series of discontinuous barriers built as part of three larger "Operations" to "control illegal immigration." These are: Operation Gatekeeper in California, Operation Hold-the-Line in Texas, and Operation Safeguard in Arizona. These barriers are located in the urban sections of the border, the areas that have been the location of the greatest number of illegal crossings in the past, including San Diego, California, Nogales, Arizona, and El Paso, Texas. In September 2006, Congress approved the "Secure Fence Act," which authorizes 700 new miles of fence on the U.S.–Mexico border. President George Bush signed the Act into law in October 2006. The law calls for a double set of steel walls with floodlights, surveillance cameras, and motion detectors along one-third of the U.S.–Mexican border.
2. Numerous studies have documented this gap between the promises made by "free trade agreements" such as the North American Free Trade Agreement (NAFTA) and its actual effects. One such report (Environmental Health Coalition 2004) provides statistics on pollution rates and health issues along the border, specifically in the San Diego/Tijuana region. One other issue that critics of U.S. immigrant policy point to is that, in general, the U.S. does not enforce employer sanctions against those who hire undocumented people.

3. The Department of Homeland Security awarded Boeing a contract for the Secure Border Initiative to handle technology upgrades for border control, including increased manned aerial vehicles and next-generation detection technology. Boeing relies on adapting military technology and proposed 1,800 towers equipped with cameras and sensors (Porteus 2006). In May 2006, President Bush proposed sending National Guard to police the Southern border.
4. The Commission for Environmental Cooperation (CEC) was established to address regional environmental concerns, prevent potential trade and environmental conflicts, and promote the enforcement of environmental complementing NAFTA's environmental provisions (see "CEC Home Page" 2007).
5. I worked with Perkins as a faculty advisor to the 25 Stories From the Central Valley project. For a full list of community partners and funders (including the American Studies Association), see http://twentyfive.ucdavis.edu/
6. For a historical analysis of the origins of environmental discrimination in California water, an overview of water governance in California (who controls and regulates water and what the barriers to implementing environmental justice are in water governance), and an overview of the water-related injustices communities struggle with on a daily basis, see *Thirsty for Justice: A People's Blueprint for California Water*, retrievable at http://www.ejcw.org/our_work/blueprint.html
7. See the profile of Susana de Anda, retrievable at "Fellows: The Petra Foundation," http://www.petrafoundation.org/fellows/Susana_DeAnda/index.html
8. Ibid.
9. Ibid.
10. Personal conversation, May 16, 2012.
11. See the profile of Susana de Anda, retrievable at http://www.petrafoundation.org/fellows/Susana_DeAnda/index.html

10 U.S. Border Ecologies, Environmental Criticism, and Transnational American Studies

Claudia Sadowski-Smith

In June 2010, top Republican members of the U.S. House Natural Resources Committee sponsored a bill that would exempt the Border Patrol from environmental regulations protecting public lands along the U.S. borders with Mexico and Canada. A significant percentage of U.S. border areas are made up of public lands and waterways. Lands administered by the Department of Interior (DOI) cover over 700 miles or nearly half the U.S.–Mexico border area and almost 600 miles or 10% of the U.S.–Canada boundary ("Marijuana and Methamphetamine Trafficking" n. pag.).[1] The National Forest Service supervises an additional 24 million acres within fifty miles of the U.S. borders with Mexico and Canada. The 5,000-mile U.S.–Canada boundary runs through several wilderness areas, twelve national parks, and four Indian reserves. The 2,000-mile U.S.–Mexico border traverses national parks, reservation lands, wildlife refuges, wilderness areas, and other environmentally sensitive areas. Like the United States, the governments of Canada and Mexico have imbued boundary land with environmental significance by placing it under national or provincial/municipal stewardship. In combination with reserves in the municipality of Sonora, Mexico, for example, public Arizona borderlands form one of the largest networks of protected areas in North America (Flesch et al. 172).

The proposed House legislation posits that environmental regulations prohibiting motorized vehicles, road construction, and the installation of surveillance structures on public lands prevent adequate border enforcement. Such a lack of oversight, the bill alleges, enabled the 2010 killing of U.S. rancher Robert Krentz, who is believed to have been slain by someone crossing through the 2,300-acre San Bernadino National Wildlife Refuge, which straddles the Arizona–Sonora border. The bill employs this incident to propose a shift in control over public border lands from the DOI and the National Forest Service to the Department of Homeland Security (DHS)—just as Arizona Republicans have used Krentz's murder to pass Senate Bill 1070, which makes it a state crime to fail to apply for or carry immigration documentation.

Despite the focus on the Arizona portion of the U.S. southwestern border and its alleged connection to undocumented immigration, the new bill also addresses the U.S.–Canada boundary. It points out that, in comparison to the U.S.–Mexico border, where some environmental laws were suspended in the mid-2000s to speed up fence construction, similar legislation has remained intact at the U.S.–Canada. border. The bill claims, for example, that prohibitions of motorized vehicles in areas inhabited by the endangered grizzly bear make it harder for the Border Patrol to do its job (Lengell n. pag.).

The inclusion of the northern border into debates coupling border enforcement with concerns for the environment highlights the need to treat the two U.S. border areas *explicitly* as boundary ecologies. Such a focus brings together environmental and U.S. American studies approaches, which have recently internationalized along somewhat divergent trajectories. U.S. American studies have moved beyond their original focus on the U.S. nation-state into hemispheric and transnational perspectives, to which the analysis of the U.S.–Mexico border has been central.[2] The hemispheric perspective explores historical and contemporary connections among events, people, communities, and geographies in the Americas, while transnational work is less centered on a specific geography and emphasizes how non-U.S. cultural forms, events, or processes impact or are related to the United States. Often this work focuses on diasporic connections between U.S. ethnic and racial groups in the U.S. and their areas of geographies of origin.[3] At the same time, environmental criticism has moved beyond its emphasis on cultural productions from the United States and Britain to also include Asian and diasporic postcolonial representations.[4] While environmental criticism originally privileged the preservation of rural and wild spaces, what Lawrence Buell has called newer "sociocentric approaches" foreground public health issues, such as pollution, workplace safety, and waste disposal, while also highlighting the inequities of environmental benefits and hazards, especially with regard to racialized populations.[5]

The U.S.–Canada border has so far been largely absent from U.S. American and critical environmental studies.[6] In contrast to the U.S.–Mexico boundary, the U.S.–Canada border has experienced delayed and more limited enforcement and has been associated with the threat of terrorism rather than undocumented immigration. Because of a strong focus on place in environmental studies, inquiries into the U.S.–Canada border ecology have focused on the local and regional levels and often do not resonate along the length of the boundary.[7] In the absence of a well-defined scholarly approach to U.S.–Canada border ecologies, I will turn to *Border Songs* (2009), a recent novel by Jim Lynch. The novel imaginatively inserts the U.S.–Canada border into debates about the effects of border enforcement, immigration, and drug smuggling on public lands that have so far been limited to the U.S.–Mexico boundary.

In its emphasis on the northern boundary, the novel highlights connections among two concerns that have remained largely separate in emerging work on the ecological consequences of U.S.–Mexico border enforcement. In addition to advocating fewer environmental regulations, pro-enforcement rhetoric has characterized increases in human activity on public borderlands, such as migration and smuggling, as a major reason for ecological degradation. These discourses have ignored the selective enforcement of particular locations along the southern border as the central factor that has shifted human activity to environmentally sensitive areas protected as public lands. In contrast, anti-enforcement discourses have largely backgrounded the ecological impact of migration and smuggling so as not to weaken the political emphasis on immigrant rights and activism. *Border Songs* combines an attention to the ecological effects of intensified U.S.-Canada border militarization after 9/11 with a focus on the consequences of growing human activity along protected portions of the ecosystem as a result of this enforcement. In thus bringing together concerns for public lands with those for borderlanders, *Border Songs* challenges currently dominant pro-enforcement debates that pit the environment against border crossers by either advocating for the suspension of environmental legislation or emphasizing the environmental cost of increased human activity on public border lands.

A reading of the novel also helps develop a comparative approach to two non-contiguous border geographies that have been similarly transformed by enforcement policies of the U.S. state in response to transnational human activity. Such a focus contributes to current attempts in environmental studies to reconceptualize how the local and regional are impacted by translocal forces, while also reminding U.S. American studies practitioners of the importance of place and place-attachment for hemispheric and transnational theories. An analysis of the novel further helps transcend divisions between the older preservationism and the newer socioeconomic ecological focus in environmental studies. In their contribution, Lisa Sun-Hee Park and David Naguib Pellow (Chapter 12, this volume) show how the older preservationism was intrinsically linked to nativist efforts for immigration restrictions. Similar to the contemporary anti-immigrant rhetoric that faults migrants for the environmental degradation of border ecologies, environmental preservationist of the twentieth century identified immigrants as the main cause for growing urban pollution and the destruction of wild places. *Border Songs* models a concern for intersections among the environment and its human users that should inform studies of and activism against the transformations of border spaces through U.S. enforcement efforts. The resulting perspective would bring together the voices of U.S. American studies scholars who are becoming increasingly involved in social movements, such as immigrant right activism, with those of many environmental activists and organizations that have already moved beyond the older connection between preservationism and anti-immigrant sentiments and toward struggles against border militarization and immigration restrictions.

BORDER ENFORCEMENT AND BORDER ECOLOGIES

Set on the border between Washington State and the province of British Columbia, Jim Lynch's *Border Songs* articulates a local view on recent U.S.–Canada border developments. While reviews of the novel have described *Border Songs* as a fictionalized account of the effects of increased U.S.–Canada border enforcement on border residents, they have failed to appreciate the novel's ecological focus.[8] *Border Songs*' protagonist Brandon Vanderkool is a newly minted Border Patrol officer in the dairy farming community of Whatcom County, Washington. Here the national boundary separates Boundary Road, where the Vanderkool dairy farm is located, from Zero Avenue, a rural highway 12 feet away in British Columbia, where Vanderkools' closest neighbors, the Rousseaus, live.

A high-functioning autistic (and modeled after Temple Grandin), Brandon spends his time patrolling the border by counting birds, building structures from natural elements, and observing the landscape. The novel explores Brandon's sense that enforcement and heightened smuggling have contributed to the ongoing destruction of the local border landscape, which includes four nationally protected areas and seven state parks. These human activities are disturbing a transnational ecosystem already plagued by environmental degradation, including air and water pollution from population growth and from industry, especially mining and farming.

Unlike the highly militarized U.S.–Mexico border, Whatcom County's 120 miles of border are "nothing more than a drainage ditch" (Lynch 4). First *systematically* re-enforced with 10-foot-high chain-link fence in the 1970s, U.S.–Mexico border militarization accelerated throughout the 1990s with the construction of triple-layered fencing (Dunn 38). Many of these installations are concrete-filled steel posts or sheet metal with small openings that are associated with cleared vegetation, graded roads, and floodlights. Other sections consist of vehicle barriers that are often coupled with barbed-wire fences (Flesch et al. 172). In contrast, the part of the U.S.–Canada boundary fictionalized in *Border Songs* has remained "less momentous than a state line, less delineated than the average cul-de-sac" (Lynch 91).

But *Border Songs* highlights other forms of enforcement along this boundary, including a growth in Border Patrol officers and virtual fencing, and the novel focuses on Brandon's relationship with the border ecosystem he patrols. Brandon joined the Border Patrol in the early 2000s, at a time when the agency was not only recruiting new agents but also transferring hundreds of agents and Customs Service personnel from the U.S.–Mexico border to the northern U.S. boundary (B. Miller n. pag.). Following the September 1, 2001, terrorist attacks on the United States, the number of agents stationed at the U.S.–Canada border tripled (Andreas 456). In contrast to the majority of agents who were transferred from the U.S.–Mexico border, however, Brandon has lived all his life along the U.S.–Canada border, a place where "[t]he soil, the weather, the scams, the drugs—everything's different" from the southern boundary (Lynch 27). Brandon joined the Border Patrol because "his father had forced him off the dairy [so he would start his own life] and nobody else was hiring" (Lynch 8). Two of the area's key industries—farming and cross-border tourism—are in severe decline. Cross-border tourism has diminished as a direct result of the increased enforcement of urban border crossing points that lead many residents, including Brandon's father, dairy farmer Norm Vanderkool, to avoid crossing the border. High-potency marijuana that is grown in hydroponic indoor gardens and then smuggled across the border has become British Columbia's largest agricultural export (Andreas 456). As *Border Songs* reports, the growth of this industry has also initiated "a curious construction boom" that has turned dairy farms into new cul-de-sacs and trophy homes on both sides of the border (Lynch 5).

In addition to the surge in the growth and illicit cross-border distribution of marijuana, dairy farms have become raspberry fields worked by undocumented Mexican immigrants, who circumvent immigration law by flying to Vancouver, British Columbia, and then crossing the border on foot. An increasing number of border residents, many of them dairy farmers who, like Brandon's father, are struggling financially, have also become involved in human and drug trafficking. Farmers and their families are caught smuggling marijuana and undocumented immigrants across the border or, alternatively, taking bribes from cartels in return for letting them use trafficking corridors through their properties.

Unlike concerns about undocumented immigration—and more recently drug trafficking—that have dominated popular narratives about the U.S.-Mexico border, association with terrorist activity (and to a much lesser extent with marijuana smuggling) has provided the strongest ammunition for U.S.–Canada enforcement. Long touted as the "world's longest undefended border," in the aftermath of 9/11, the U.S.–Canada boundary became redefined into yet another potential threat to the United States, porous to the influx of Middle Eastern terrorists and illegal goods. The fictionalized Whatcom Country's Border Patrol Chief exemplifies the conflation of terrorism and drug smuggling when he insists that "most of the bud is run by organized crime. And there's also evidence that terrorist cells in Canada are getting into the business to raise money, which of course means the war on drugs has, in fact, become the war on terror" (Lynch 122). In the novel, Brandon stops a 29-year-old border crosser with marijuana, a map of Seattle, several IDs, and a substance similar to nitroglycerin. Even when the suspect eventually turns out to be a middle-class U.S. American citizen, the incident provides further ammunition for the oft-repeated belief in the connection between terrorism and the U.S.–Canada boundary that has culminated in tougher border security.

This fictionalized incident hints at persisting assertions that the 19 terrorists involved in the 2001 attacks entered the United States through Canada, even though all of them arrived in the United States legally on tourist, business, and student visas. The link between the U.S.–Canada border and terrorism originates in the late 1990s, when the Palestinian Gazi Ibrahim Abu Mezer was stopped at crossings in Whatcom County (the fictionalized setting of *Border Songs*), the last time six months before his arrest in New York where he was plotting to blow up the subway system (Norton n. pag.).[9] In December 1999, the Algerian Ahmed Ressam was captured at the nearby crossing of Port Angeles, Washington, with explosives designed to blow up the Los Angeles International Airport and other targets during the Millennium Celebrations. Ressam later admitted that he had been trained in camps connected to Osama Bin Laden's network. Even though the 9/11 terrorist attacks were not connected to the U.S.–Canada border, they initiated a new phase of what Peter Andreas has called the "Mexicanization" of the U.S.–Canada border, including closings of crossing points, the intensification of searches at ports of entry, and the installation of internal border checkpoints similar to those along the U.S.–Mexico border. These types of border enforcement put an end to efforts for the creation of a common "open and seamless border" between Canada and the United States in the early years of the twenty-first century (Walker A1).

Despite the official anti-terrorism rhetoric, the fictionalized Border Patrol agents in *Border Songs* know that their work mainly consists of "[s]topping people from getting work or-God forbid!—getting high" (68) and "helping Canuck drug dealers jack their prices by driving up the value of their merchandise" (69). In fact, as a result of the massive injection of resources and staff to guard against terrorists crossing the U.S.–Canada border, the Border Patrol has mostly caught undocumented immigrants and thus created a backlog of court cases and a flurry of protest from the public about random highway stops and bus or train inspections ("Heightened" n. pag.). In roving patrols or surprise checkpoints on buses, trains, and highways located up to 100 miles of the actual border, even those foreign visitors who can document their legal status have been detained and sometimes imprisoned in detention centers for up to three weeks (Woodard n. pag.).

The novel shows that, similar to the U.S.–Mexico border, the activities of human and drug traffickers have moved to rural and wilderness areas as a result of stepped-up enforcement at official checkpoints near cities, such as the second busiest U.S.–Canada border crossing, which is located at the Peace Arch Park between Blaine, Washington, and Surrey, British Columbia. As it focused on the most popular crossing points near urban areas in California and Texas, selective enforcement at the U.S.–Mexico border attempted to transform remaining areas, such as the desert along the Arizona-Sonora, into buffer sites whose perilous nature would deter undocumented human movement (Reyes et al. n. pag.). But rather than preventing immigration, human activity shifted to the state of Arizona and to environmentally sensitive areas protected as public lands. Increased human activity in this ecosystem has contributed to its degradation. But pro-enforcement interests have ignored increased and selective border enforcement as the main reason behind the shift in human activity to protected areas and instead focused on increased human movement and smuggling in these locations as the main contributors to ecological damage. In the late 1990s, Joni Adamson already reported on the effects of diverted human activity on Arizona ranchers. They were suddenly faced with damaged fences, broken water tanks, and scattered refuse left behind by migrants. The repair of fences, the collection of trash, and the disposal of dead livestock put severe financial strain on the ranchers and took their attention from other essential tasks (Adamson, 2002, 222). In the early 2000s, the ranchers' observations about the ecological and economic consequences of diverted human movement have been taken to new levels. The website of a nativist group called "Desert Invasions" asserts that migrants and smugglers litter the land with garbage, clothing, and human waste; that migrants and smugglers create new foot paths "the width of roads" that erode hill side vegetation; and that smugglers' vehicle traffic causes motor oil and fuel to leak into streams and endangered species habitat.[10] Sarah Jaquette Ray has shown that this "green anti-immigrant rhetoric" draws on historical connections between earlier efforts to maintain U.S. American identity and wilderness preservation that dominated mainstream environmentalism, efforts that deny how the U.S.–Mexico border landscape was first cleared of indigenous and later Mexican populations to become "wilderness" (14–15).[11] As both Grabovac (Chapter 8, this volume) and Park and Pellow (Chapter 12, this volume) discuss, at the turn of the twentieth century, environmental preservationists identified immigrants from eastern Europe, Italy, China, and Japan, among others, as the primary cause for the rise in urban pollution and the destruction of wilderness areas. Tensions also arose between members of the upper classes who hunted for sport and trophies, while many European immigrants hunted for food sources.

While today's green anti-immigrant rhetoric no longer comes from environmental groups, it is not limited to one website or to conservative politicians. Secretary of Homeland Security Janet Napolitano has similarly argued in favor of border enforcement so as to stem the flow of millions of undocumented crossers who over the past decade have supposedly ruined some once-pristine lands with piles of trash, vehicle tracks, and contaminated water (Dinan n. pag.).The focus on the ecological damage caused by trafficked migrants and drugs has also been extended to characterize humanitarian efforts by a Tucson-based group called No More Deaths to leave clean drinking water for Arizona-Sonora border crossers in response to the staggering surge in immigrant deaths, which have far surpassed the number of casualties recorded in the mid-1980s from drowning (mostly in the Río Grande) or from homicide and auto-pedestrian accidents in the late 1980s (Eschbach et al. 11–12, 14).[12]

Border Songs shows similar processes at work along the U.S.–Canada border, where the diversion of human and drug trafficking to protected portions is already damaging boundary ecologies. Smugglers have forged new routes through the waters of Boundary Bay (probably a fictionalized representation of the protected Birch Bay), through swamps, and across the ridges of the Cascade foothills, by, for example, packaging their contraband into hollowed-out tree stumps that are then placed into the boundary waters. The novel also addresses how the production and trade in drugs destroy vegetation, contaminate waterways, and disrupt wildlife. Smugglers in the novel excavate a wide swath of land near the border into which they place a gutted school bus where they grow marijuana. In addition, smugglers retrofit empty or rental houses into indoor growing laboratories. While the novel does not show this, marijuana growers also often clear timber and ground cover to prepare large cultivation areas. Pesticides used to protect the crops poison native wildlife and foliage. Furthermore, hired workers who live in camps near grow sites typically leave behind trash and human waste ("Marijuana and Methamphetamine Trafficking" n. pag.). Because he notices even subtle changes in the border ecosystem as a result of human activity, Brandon becomes what the other agents call a "shit magnet." He intercepts several shipments of marijuana and even handguns, and he apprehends a record number of undocumented crossers who come from everywhere in the world, including the Philippines, Cambodia, Romania, Mexico, Iran, Sri Lanka, Venezuela, Morocco, France, Algeria, and China. At the end of the novel, Brandon even stumbles on a ninety-yard border tunnel connecting Zero Avenue to Boundary Road, which is a thinly veiled reference to the 2005 discovery of a 360-foot drug smuggling tunnel between British Columbia and Washington ("Tunnel Discovered" n. pag.).[13]

While the novel highlights the shift in trafficking to rural and protected areas after the enforcement of urban crossings points, it also shows that the implementation of tougher border security has harmed the boundary ecology in ways so far discussed only with respect to the southern land border where several environmental regulations were waived to speed up border enforcement. Under the 2005 Real ID Act, then Secretary of Homeland Security Michael Chertoff suspended in their entirety 37 federal laws and all state, local, and tribal laws, including the Coastal Zone Management Act, the National Environmental Policy Act, the Endangered Species Act, the Migratory Bird Treaty Act, the Clean Water Act, the Clean Air Act, and the National Historic Preservation Act.[14] The 2010 report of the Good Neighbor Environmental Board (GNEB), which has advised the U.S. president and Congress on environmental and infrastructure practices since its creation in 1992, found that the erection of border walls has caused increased flooding; led to changes in soil characteristics and soil erosion;

contributed to gene isolation and the eventual depopulation of migratory species; and participated in the loss of or damage to wilderness areas, sensitive habits, species, and cultural resources. In Arizona, in particular, border militarization has exacerbated seasonal flooding on both sides of the border; accelerated erosion on the Organ Pipe Cactus National Monument; destroyed Native American burials on Tohono O'odham ancestral lands in southern Arizona; fragmented critical wildlife corridors for jaguars, black bears, coatimundi, and other species; and damaged the desert habitats of several bird species, including an endangered quail. The cross-border movement of bighorn sheep, necessary to prevent the isolation of some populations on the Arizona side, has also been threatened. In New Mexico's Playa Valley, border walls have blocked the movement of one of the last wild herds of bison, whose range straddles the U.S.–Mexico border. In Texas, border structures in the Lower Rio Grande Valley National Wildlife Refuge have fragmented habitat critical for the survival of the endangered ocelots. Because so few are left in the United States, they must have access to mates in Mexico to avoid inbreeding, gene isolation, and eventual extinction. In California, 53 acres of rare coastal wildlife habitat were lost to fencing construction in the Border Field State Park and the Otay Mountain Wilderness in southern California now contains roads and fences in areas that previously only boasted natural vegetation on steep mountain slopes.[15]

While the 2005 Secure Fence Act only provided for the installation of fencing along the U.S.–Mexico border, it also allowed the building of 330 miles of *virtual* fencing along *both* U.S. boundaries. This multibillion dollar mix of networked cameras, radar, heat, and motion detectors and communications gear technology is known as SBInet (Caldwell n. pag.). By 2007, nine 98-foot towers equipped with cameras, sensors, radar, and other surveillance systems were erected along the Arizona-Sonora border. The project was considered the prototype for hundreds of such towers along both U.S. land borders. *Border Songs* fictionalizes threats to the U.S.–Canada border ecology from the construction of this "virtual" fence, which consists of sensors and motion-detecting video cameras and is enhanced by the activity of surveillance drones, helicopters, and boats. The novel here references the 2002 installation of a $50 million surveillance system consisting of cameras mounted on 50-foot metal poles and sensors placed on farmland and fields thought to be the most frequented smuggling routes (well before the arrival of plans for SBInet) (Shaw n. pag.). As along the U.S.–Mexico border where the camera-mounted towers first appeared, these structures not only threaten the free passage of wildlife, but the traffic associated with their maintenance also has negative ecological consequences. While the findings of environmental organizations and the GNEB highlight how an enforced U.S.–Mexico border threatens the migration of mammals, along the northern boundary, the protection of migratory birds has received the most attention.[16]

Cameras mounted to the towers also raise fears about the invasion of privacy because they can capture images up to four miles away. In the fictionalized Border Patrol headquarters of *Border Songs*, Brandon can thus observe the day-to-day activities of border residents. As "[m]ost vehicles cruising the northern line after dusk were now green-and-whites [and] unmanned military aircraft's cameras could read a cereal box from fifteen thousand feet" (Lynch 208), complaints about the Border Patrol hassling local residents increase. The Vanderkools' Canadian neighbor Norm Rosseau, a retired political science professor at the University of British Columbia, even goes so far as to shoot out one of the cameras. And when Brandon's father Norm develops a blood clot that almost kills him, his condition is widely interpreted as a response to Border Patrol allegations of his involvement with drug traffickers. When the allegations turn out to be wrong, the farming community comes to believe that "[t]he increased security is killing us" (Lynch 266–267). The hysteria created by the Border Patrol Chief Patera eventually backfires. Patera had earlier employed the all-present threat of terrorism to warn against possible attacks on the region's dairy farming industry. The deaths of cows at several farms coupled with the discovery of a suspicious package at a Girl Scouts reunion at the Peace Arch Park border crossing led Patera to suspect a concerted terrorist attack. But when all of these events turn out to have no relation to terrorism, Border Patrol agents are transferred back to the U.S.–Mexico border. The border cameras, which had consistently malfunctioned at higher temperatures, are also turned off. Economic changes finally deal the death knell to enforcement efforts. The ascent of the Canadian dollar meant that "raspberry fields were put to bed, illegal farm workers returned to their homelands and fair-weather residents abandoned their toy ranches. Customs interrogations softened, too, and the few remaining agents grew increasingly reluctant to confront anybody, especially after the immigration-detention centers maxed out" (Lynch 275). The new enforcement policy includes capturing and releasing undocumented immigrants rather than confining them to overcrowded detention centers, thus further stressing the underfunded U.S. immigration system. As *Border Songs* informs us, "the rising Canadian dollar had accomplished what the drug czar and Border Patrol and police forces couldn't" (Lynch 276).

After Brandon Vanderkool quietly resigns from the Border Patrol to take care of the family dairy while his father recuperates, calls for border enforcement reemerge as "incumbents and particularly desperate challengers form northern states were demanding an immediate and renewed commitment to border security" during an election season (Lynch 286). These resurging discourses about the porosity of the U.S.–Canada border include demands for the further growth in Border Patrol personnel and the installation of virtual fencing. In fact, in 2009, the year of the novel's publication, plans for the expansion of virtual fencing along the northern U.S. boundary reemerged. The U.S. DHS announced a $30 million "Northern

Border Initiative" as a first step toward a more extensive monitoring system modeled after the one at the U.S.–Mexico boundary (Frank n. pag.). The government awarded the project to Boeing Co., the same company that had been responsible for constructing the pilot 53 miles of virtual U.S.–Mexico fencing. Right after its completion in March 2010, Homeland Security Secretary Janet Napolitano announced the suspension of the project, and it was cancelled in January 2011 (Kelly n. pag.). Not only was the project riddled with technical problems, but Boeing was also accused of overspending after the government had already invested $1 billion (Preston n. pag.).

Despite these problems, Boing is currently constructing virtual fencing along the northern border; eleven towers are being installed in Detroit and five in Buffalo, New York, to help monitor water traffic along Lake St. Clair and the Niagara River (Ramirez and Krupa n. pag.). In late 2010, Customs and Border Protection announced the preparation of four environmental impact statements to assess the effects of further enforcement at the U.S.-Canada boundary ("CBS Seeks" n. pag.).

CONCLUSION

Even though enforcement at the U.S.–Canada border has taken place primarily under the guise of anti-terrorist measures rather than anti-immigrant sentiment and has not been taken to the same level of intensity, the similarities in the ecological effects of militarization along both boundaries are striking. These parallels question the notion that the trafficking of immigrants and drugs is the main cause of environmental destruction along public border lands. They also problematize the idea that ecological issues can be addressed through immigration controls that configure migrants into scapegoats while failing to examine the environmental consequences of border enforcement strategies. Parallels among the two borders call attention to the effects of federal policy on both the environment *and* crossers. Such a focus may help overcome the divisions between two seemingly separate approaches to environmentalism: attention to the preservation of wilderness and endangered species (promoted by groups such as Defenders of Wildlife, which are active along the U.S.–Mexico border), on the one hand, and a socioeconomic focus on border populations. These two approaches need to merge. Environmental groups like Defenders of Wildlife have pioneered such a symbiosis by moving beyond the earlier association of environmental activism with anti-immigration sentiment to become strong opponents of border enforcement because it directly affects border ecologies and wildlife and goes hand in hand with the passage of immigration restrictions and the ongoing criminalization of human movement. The Sierra Club has also worked against border militarization. Some members of No More Deaths, like Daniel Millis, who was accused of leaving water bottles in the desert, have ties to this organization.

As fictionalized in *Border Songs*, renewed attempts at enforcing the U.S.–Canada border continue to ignore the recommendations of the GNEB to address the ecological damage that enforcement has already caused at the U.S.–Mexico border. The Board's proposals include bringing border enforcement into compliance with the National Environmental Policy Act and other environmental, historic, and archeological preservation laws; allowing for adequate environmental review, public participation, and scientific analysis into the design and implementation of security; and exploring technology that reduces the physical footprint of interdiction activities. The report also tacitly points to a reversal in Obama's policies. On the campaign trail, then senator Obama promised that he would change Bush-era policies in favor of a "better approach," such as deploying more border guards and installing better surveillance technologies. But after taking office, the Obama administration has left intact provisions of the 2005 Real ID Act that waive environmental, public health, and cultural heritage laws. Some environmental activists have said that even if these waivers were revoked now, the environmental damage may already be irreversible. As one activist puts it, "I don't know how you go back and undo it" (Reese n. pag.).

Even the DHS, which is in charge of the Border Patrol, has admitted that border walls have had negative effects on border ecosystems. In Environmental Stewardship Plans prepared ahead of construction, the DHS identified the purchase of equivalent replacement lands to make up for the many thousands of acres of land separated by newly built walls. In 2008 and 2009, the U.S. Congress even allocated some mitigation funds. The proposed legislation by the House's Natural Resources Committee with which I began this chapter, however, not only aims to weaken existing environmental regulations of federal lands, it also objects to the payment of such mitigation funds. Politicians have repeatedly called the funds "extortion" and have worked to keep them from reaching the Department of the Interior (Berger n. pag.). While not a single acre of replacement land has been bought, the DHS has addressed only a small portion of the damage wrought by border enforcement. The "Border Fence Monitoring and Mitigation Project" includes "reasonable mitigation measures" to compensate for the damage or loss of animal and plant habitat and cultural areas, including modifying fencing to curb flooding and to accommodate threatened and endangered species by restoring their habitats or acquiring new habitats ("Destroying" n. pag.).

In the face of U.S. government efforts to continue border enforcement that has consistently harmed border ecologies while failing to curb human and drug trafficking, the Canadian government has also moved away from its independent position on international issues, including environmental and border concerns. It has done so to comply with pressure from the United States to create a smoother interface between the two trade and security partners (Konrad 246). Thus, efforts for environmental protection continue to be hampered by U.S. dominance over its neighbors that extends to boundary issues and the environmental effects of border enforcement. As Joseph Nevins and Timothy Dunn have put it, the politics of border enforcement has "illustrate[d] the deeply impoverished nature of what passes for debate on immigration and national boundaries in the United States, a debate that is largely reduced to narrow matters of law, order, and security" (Nevins and Dunn 25). This debate has also and equally occurred at the expense of protected U.S. boundary ecologies.

NOTES

1. If one includes the water and land portions of the Alaska/British Columbia and Yukon boundaries, the portion of public land along the U.S.–Canada border may be high as 25%. Victor Konrad, private email, February 21, 2011.
2. On the importance of scholarship about the U.S.–Mexico border for transnational and hemispheric perspectives in U.S. American Studies, see Amy Kaplan and Donald Pease; Carolyn Porter; Priscilla Wald; Paul Jay "The Myth"; and John Carlos Rowe.
3. For a more in-detail analysis of hemispheric (inter-) American studies perspectives, see Claudia Sadowski-Smith and Claire F. Fox. For examples of inter-American work, see Anna Brickhouse, *Transamerican Literary Relations;* Kirsten Silva Gruez, *Ambassadors of Culture;* and José David Saldívar, *Border Matters* and *The Dialectics of Our America.* For some of the most recent examples of transnational work, see, for example, Juanita Heredia; Paul Jay, *Global Matters*; and Shari M. Huhndorf.
4. Other terminology for the field includes ecocriticism, literary-environmental studies, literary ecology, literary environmentalism, postcolonial ecocriticism, or green cultural studies.
5. For an overview of recent developments in environmental literary studies, see Lawrence Buell (2011b).
6. In literary studies, exceptions include Rachel Adams, *Continental Divides: The Remapping of North America,* and Russell Brown, "The Written Line."
7. Amy Lauren Lovecraft has argued that the regional focus is the result of the federal governments devolving many of their responsibilities for the cross-border environment to states, provinces, and municipalities."
8. See, for example, Ron Charles and Phillip Meyer.
9. As Dee Norton reports, at the time of Mezer's apprehension, Canada's immigration policies were blamed for the alleged U.S. entry of terrorists from Canada. Mezer was caught three times, released, and sent back to Canada; the third time he was released pending a deportation hearing, which he did not attend. Instead, he turned up six months later in New York, where police arrested him in a plot to bomb subways. He was convicted of conspiracy and sentenced to life in prison.
10. For the website of the organization Desert Invasion, see http://www.desert-invasion.us/reports/hull_border_env_damage.html
11. John Tanton, an active member in the National Audubon Society, the Sierra Club, and other environmental groups, for example, was instrumental in creating a network of anti-immigrant groups in the late 1970s, including the Federation for American Immigration Reform (FAIR) and Numbers USA, which have worked closely with members of Congress (mostly Republicans)

to put in place strong border controls. Most recently, Kris Kobach, a lawyer with ties to FAIR, has helped draft Arizona's Senate Bill 1070.

12. On the numbers of border deaths, see Eschbach et al. 11–12, 14. Eight deaths alone have occurred on the Buenos Aires National Wildlife Refuge or on directly adjacent land since 2008, but this tragedy has been overshadowed by the more intense focus on the unfortunate murder of *one* U.S. rancher, Krentz, in the proximity of another protected portion of the Arizona-Sonora border. In 2008, a U.S. Magistrate in Tucson found Daniel Millis of No More Deaths and a member of the Sierra Club guilty of the charge of littering in the Buenos Aires National Wildlife Refuge. But two years later, a federal appeals court reversed the decision, stating the term "garbage" as used in Millis' conviction was "sufficiently ambiguous" ("Court Tosses Conviction").
13. In his article on the novel, Albert Braz, however, points out that drugs, firearms, alcohol, and undocumented people also flow in the other direction of the border, which is not fictionalized in *Border Songs* (Braz 198).
14. In 2007, Secretary Chertoff again waived several regulations, including the Endangered Species Act and a host of other federal laws, to allow for construction of border fencing through Arizona's San Pedro Riparian National Monument and the Barry M. Goldwater Range, home to the endangered Sonoran Pronghorn. Fencing was also erected in the Organ Pipe Cactus National Monument and in the Cabeza Prieta National Monument, which house rare birds such as the Cactus Ferruginous Pygmy Owl and the Thick-billed Parrot. In 2008, the administration evoked the Real ID Act one more time to allow the construction of another approximately 500 miles of border fence.
15. The June 2010 "Letter to President Barack Obama" by the Good Neighbor Environmental Board (GNEB) is available at http://www.epa.gov/Border2012/news/13thGnebEnglishFinal.pdf. See also Stephen Ceasar.
16. Konrad writes that conservationists and governments have attempted to extend the migratory bird protections to other migratory species, such as the Caribou that crosses the Alaska–Yukon border and the Monarch butterfly, which migrates to Mexico where it is threatened by illegal logging destroying their winter nesting grounds. Another growing ecological problem is the disposal of waste across the U.S.–Canada border, especially the significant increase in hazardous waste from the United States to the provinces Ontario and Quebec after the curtailment of on-site inspections and fines (225, 238).

11 Climate Justice and Trans-Pacific Indigenous Feminisms

Hsinya Huang

This chapter explores the connections between indigenous feminisms and climate justice by examining indigenous women's works in the context of environmental and trans-Pacific histories. It centralizes the role of gender and indigeneity to challenge the customary ways that Euro-American scholarship imagines basic concepts such as place and agency by drawing on three indigenous authors with links across the Pacific. The chapter goes beyond the U.S. and its readily identifiable, cultural anxiety about the geopolitical rise of China to examine how indigenous women in the U.S. and Taiwan experience exclusion, marginalization, and forced displacement directly related to climate change and environmental racism. It analyzes how writing and art can contribute to change and gesture toward common ideas of resistance that reflect Andrew Ross's argument, quoted in the Introduction to this volume, that "common resources" cannot be walled off only for the rich and privileged but must be equitably shared if we hope to create an ecologically fair world for all the planet's citizens.[1] Focusing indigenous women's experiences produced on the U.S.-Mexico border and in Asian/Austronesian villages in Taiwan, this chapter examines how indigenous communities are engaging the trans-indigenous Pacific politically and culturally as they create their homes as sites of contestation and contingency or as imaginative/other spaces that register an "ecoglobalist affect." This phrase, coined by Lawrence Buell, means an emotionally laden preoccupation with a near-at-hand physical environment defined by gender and racial relationships where there is an "imagined inextricable linage between that specific site and a context of planetary reach" (Buell, "Ecoglobalist Affects" 232). In their respective communities, Margo Tamez (Lipan Apache) on the U.S.-Mexico border, Rimuy Aki (Austronesian/Atayal) and Liglav Awu (Austronesian/Paiwan) in Taiwan configure off-center relations to the U.S. or to Han-dominant China.[2] Dispossessed and displaced by waves of nation-building and confined into physical, racial, and economic spaces, these authors ask questions about how indigenous women restructure opportunities for deep alliance building among their clans and other indigenous groups around the world. They also raise significant questions about how gender and indigeneity matter in the formation of climate justice and about how narrative forms can combine indigenous women's life stories and environmental histories in ways that illustrates a justice-oriented trans-Pacific indigenous feminist response to global climate change.

Emerging from the environmental justice movement, the movement for climate justice calls for the fair treatment of all people and freedom from discrimination by the systems that create climate change and perpetuate structural discrimination against indigenous or ethnic minority groups in policies and projects that address or fail to address climate change. It seeks the fair treatment and meaningful involvement of all people regardless of race, color, sex, national origin, or income with respect to the development, implementation, and enforcement of environmental laws, regulations, and policies related to climate change.[3] While colonialism and profit-driven corporate globalization create cultures of exclusion, dispossession, and scarcity, in recent years, there has been an emergent counter political movement from the grassroots for sustainability with a significant focus on climate justice. This grassroots reaction entails a vision for dissolving and alleviating the unequal burdens of environmental damage due to the creation of policies and projects that ensure the right of all people to live, work, play, and pray in safe and healthy environments. It therefore recasts many environmental issues, which are not only concerned with resource use or pollution but also equality, justice, and human rights.[4] These issues are also ethical ones with planetary implications. If, as Gayatri Chakravorty Spivak puts it, "to be human is to be intended toward the other" (73), the predominant quality that defines humanity is our obligation and responsibility toward the other, an other that Spivak defines in planetary terms. She writes, "When I invoke the planet, I think of the effort required to figure the (im)possibility of this underived intuition" (72). In further defining what she means by "planetary," Spivak speaks of an "other" that involves millions of people who experience and see the earth as a family as well as communities consisting of beings and humans of all colors, beliefs, and classes, and transcending physical, cultural, and national boundaries. In her view, therefore, the planet is viewed as a commons instead of private property.

Lawrence Buell also raises the centrality of a planetary-level ethics for environmental criticism. Buell refers to the writings of Michel Foucault and Jacques Derrida, who have contributed to the relegitimization of "ethics talk" (Buell, "What We Talk About When We Talk About Ethics" 2). The former, through his "revaluation of the category of the self, conceiving of care of the self as an ethical project" (ibid. 2) and the latter, by engaging in a fruitful dialogue with Emmanuel Levinas who "has awakened us [to a conception of] an unlimited responsibility that exceeds and precedes my freedom" (Buell, "Introduction: In Pursuit of Ethics" 9).[5] Given that nature is a complex web of interconnected systems, ethics is about the order of how all beings are relevant in the functioning of planetary systems. For instance, climate change is not just a change of weather patterns over a certain period of time or a change in the distribution of weather events with respect to an average temperature. Climate systems involve a complex web of interconnected events. It is this fact of interconnectedness that can make the challenge of climate change feel so overwhelming and disorienting. Thus, when we talk about "justice," we would not be talking simply about how specific environmental policies, events, and outcomes affect local minority communities or how these communities might be targeted for the placement of polluting industries and factories but rather how these groups are part of an entire planetary system. "Justice" would require that they not be disowned and deprived of collective biological, cultural, and ecological heritage in the "commons" or victimized by (environmental) colonialism and/or corporate globalization.

Recognizing their obligations and responsibilities toward not only the members of their own tribal groups but all inhabitants of a planet damaged by climate change, three indigenous writers, Margo Tamez, Rimuy Aki, and Liglav Awu, create their narratives and poetry in the context of a changing climate and other linked social and environmental issues. Margo Tamez is a Lipan-Jumano Apache poet, scholar, and internationally recognized activist who grew up on the Texas-Mexico border in Brownsville, Texas. She has worked with the Apache, Ak-Chin O'odham, and Mexican indigenous-ethnic groups that pass through central Arizona where they hope to find employment in agriculture. While working on her master's degree in Fine Arts in Phoenix, Arizona, and living in rural Maricopa County, she often saw undocumented migrants from south of the U.S. border and smelled the chemicals being sprayed on the fields by corporate agricultural businesses. She learned that the migrants she was seeing were exposed to toxins while working in the fields. She writes,

> Working on and with this land, indigenous to the Ak-Chin, O'odham, Maricopa peoples, and in an all-encompassing cosmic climate that is simultaneously hard as leather and fragile as webs, has *grieved* me as I have seen, smelled, tasted and touched the impacts of toxic behaviors and practices that have wounded the land and the people in interconnected ways. (*Daughter* 191; italics added)

Tamez speaks of ongoing grievances over the impact of climate change and "toxic behaviors and practices" on the lands surrounding her Maricopa home, and she asserts that indigenous people have long been the victims of unjust history and colonialism. Tamez grieves while experiencing a sense of violation and loss of traditional land ethics: border militarization and the criminalization of migration violates the traditional worldview of interconnectedness shared by the O'odham people indigenous to central Arizona. Several years later, when earning a doctorate in women and gender studies and American Studies, Tamez joined her mother, Eloisa Garcia Tamez, to build a movement to resist the border fence that the U.S. proposed building across lands owned by the Tamez family and straddling the

U.S.-Mexico boundary. She has also taken the issue of the border wall to international forums and to the courts of the U.S.[6] In these actions, she is calling for full recognition of human rights for indigenous people who are protected by international legal instruments, including the UN Declaration on the Rights of Indigenous Peoples. These transnational organizing experiences have triggered her ethical response to environmental degradation and intensified her sense of responsibility to indigenous groups on the U.S.-Mexico border, including those tribes that are not treaty-recognized within the U.S. Today, she is working with "regional, national, and transnational indigenous groups and nonindigenous others who are committed to anticolonial, antiviolence praxis" (Adamson 14).[7]

In her poetry, written while still living in Arizona, Tamez addresses the notion of a "commons" as she discusses how seeing the conditions in which migrants live causes her to want to share resources:

> I wanted to learn how to grow enough food without the use of chemicals, or dangerous toxins, to feed my family and the Indigenous North American migrant workers, who came to me asking for help, sustenance, prayers, meals, water and hope *every winter as they came to stay in this harsh country through the summer harvests in the monoculture corporate-run farms in the vicinity.* Some of them stayed and lived either on my land, or close by, until mid-August, returning cyclically [and] . . . often walking the whole way from their homes in Caborca, Sonora, Mexico, across *one of the fiercest climates a human-being can encounter in North America.* (*Daughter* 191–192; italics added)

Ironically, the migrant workers moving back and forth across the U.S.-Mexico borderlands rarely benefit from their own hard labor. They make a living by working for the monocultural corporate-run farms and by contributing to the summer harvests, and yet they are victims of the harsh desert extremes. In this passage, Tamez deploys Maricopa County as a geo-cultural space where agribusiness exerts an impact on the environment. "One of the fiercest climates" is not simply physical but metaphorical. Here, Tamez depicts how large-scale, corporate-run, export-oriented farming in Maricopa County results in landlessness, hunger, and food insecurity for migrant workers. That she provides shelters to migrant workers bespeaks her active agency and ethical practice in attempting to redress the devastating impacts of corporate globalization on people, communities, and the environment.

Indeed, as a former field worker herself who was exposed to toxic contamination as a young girl in Texas, Tamez became involved in the U.S. Environmental Justice movement as a young woman. This work later inspired her to work with indigenous women all along the U.S.-Mexico border to call attention to the links among toxins in the water, air and food that lead to miscarriage and birth defects, and toxic ideologies that lead to social injustices. In her second chapbook of poetry, *Raven Eye*, she writes about living in Maricopa as a young mother. There, she experienced toxin-related illnesses and suffered multiple miscarriages. She buries "her miscarried young / Who never had a chance against DDT and poisoned wells" (*Raven Eye* 68). In a still unpublished book of poetry and prose titled *The Daughter of Lightning*, she includes an autobiographical narrative titled "Grave of Babies." In this memoir, she describes "a graveyard of fetuses with names painted carefully in glittering colors on old plywood and some manzanita" (*Daughter* 139).[8] In a poem titled "Last Message to My Father," she confesses: "I could never tell [my father] about the deaths of my children. The disaster of agriculture in the desert. The contamination in our flesh. The wretchedness of burying their curdled bodies" (*Daughter* 142). Tamez was linking the chemicals she is exposed to as a young girl in Texas to her miscarriages in Maricopa County. Her poetry in both *Raven Eye* and her first chapbook, *Naked Wanting*, also links her own toxin-induced miscarriages with those of other women living all along the length of the border. Tamez points out that the damage inflicted by herbicides comes back to haunt women at the level of human reproduction. In another poem, she makes the issue of environmental toxicity even more explicit: a Lipan/ Jumano mother migrates to an agricultural community where "Factory-farmed cows / Rot and antibiotics and growth hormones, / Seeping into the ground flowing underground northerly / Up through the aquifer's / Veins into the wells through everyone's bodies" (*Daughter* 56). Tamez yearns for justice and survival, as she senses "the chemical cocktail seeping into our air ducts" (*Daughter* 135). Tamez speaks as someone who has experienced first-hand how the body can be restructured by environmental toxins in the air, water, soil, and food.

The traditional territory of Tamez's Lipan Apache forebears includes present-day Texas, New Mexico, Colorado, and the northern Mexican states of Chihuahua, Nuevo León, Coahuila, and Tamaulipas. Tamez's tribal community has been split on both sides of the U.S.-Mexico border since 1752, when the Spanish forged the *camino militar* (military road) along the Rio Grande to protect their northern boundaries against French, British, and U.S.-American invasion. This road later became the International Boundary between the U.S. and Mexico, and today it is policed by agents of the U.S. Border Patrol. The history of the Tamez family showcases that of other indigenous inhabitants on the border, who live under the threat of dispossession by powerful nation-states or natural disasters such as hurricanes, which have been a part of Apache life in the Lower Rio Grande Valley for hundreds of years. The predicaments facing Tamez and her community, including border militarization, the seizure of their land for the border fence, and climate change, propel her to engage in activism to address the wrongs inflicted on her people. With her mother, she cofounded Lipan Apache Women Defense, which has grown into an international alliance of indigenous groups, university working groups, and human rights groups across the length of Texas, New Mexico, and Arizona. Tamez describes the joint venture of Lipan Apache Women as "an intensely fought battle for self-determination and autonomy of indigenous women's societies and the renewal of a long historical pattern of Lipan Apache women facing down an empire on the grounds of indigenous rights" ("Restoring" 559). On numerous occasions, mother and daughter have attended public meetings and added their own testimonies to those of their community members, the Lipan Apache people, who are aboriginal land title holders to territories of South Texas, the Rio Grande River, and into northern Mexico.[9] Tamez also writes a blog to disseminate information about what is happening in her community. In one blog entry, "Hurricane Dolly—Human Rights and U.S. Fraud, Waste and Abuse—FEMA and DHS Cause Further Harm Against Indigenous People," she explains that, currently in South Texas, because of the effect of climate change, many

> communities are undergoing great losses and tragedy, including loss of homes, livelihoods, livestock, crops, and . . . in this ongoing devastation . . . physical, psychological, emotional and spiritual needs are being neglected [while] the nation-states [move] to protect their corporate investments—hotels, resorts, oil platforms, airforce jets and planes, and other 'vital' assets of the United States and its companies.[10]

Here Tamez calls attention to a grossly deficient response to humanitarian needs while the nation-state is quick to defend a matrix of national and colonial domination working in complicity with global/international capitalism. In the aftermath of Hurricane Dolly, which blew into the Lower Rio Grande Valley in July 2008 and caused massive flooding and displacement of some of the poorest indigenous peoples in the hemisphere, Tamez and her mother signed "The Anchorage Declaration," which was drawn up at the Indigenous Peoples' Global Summit on Climate Change in April 2009. This illustrates how they are joining with other indigenous peoples in the Americas who are deeply alarmed by accelerating climate devastation as they experience "disproportionate adverse impacts on their cultures, human and environmental health, human rights, well-being, traditional livelihoods, food systems and food sovereignty, local infrastructure, economic viability, and [their] very survival as Indigenous Peoples."[11] This summit brought the Inuit of the Pacific and the Lipan of the U.S.-Mexico border together to insist that the rights of indigenous peoples "must be fully respected in all decision-making processes and activities related to climate change."[12] Hence, Tamez's group is linking itself to other groups with trans-Pacific ties that are leading efforts to partner with other groups experiencing similar conditions and finding common cause on global issues that affect their communities.

Indeed, in her writings, Tamez's metaphors turn to weather extremes and climate change. These weather disturbances, which Tamez experiences as "frightening," later became a catalyst for survival and solidarity. In *The Daughter of Lightening*, Tamez describes the relationship of the Lipan Apache and her mother, Eloisa Garcia Tamez, to storms and to knowledge of the increasing ferociousness of these storms.

> *[Eloisa's] family resided a mile from the mighty Rio Grande and only the levy protected [them] from its path should it overflow. . . . [A]ll the family members would gather for days in the home which was considered the most stable to survive the torment and also to be together during this frightful experience. [Eloisa's] grandmother would come to [her] to perform a ritual, which in the minds of the all the family gathered, was key to breaking the torment.* (120; italics original)

In traditional Lipan Apache communities, relationships become mobilized and consolidated as threats and disturbances link family members together in the "home which was considered the most stable." One of the fiercest incidents in the family's memory took place in the 1930s when Eloisa's grandmother took her out into the raging winds of a hurricane. The grandmother raised a butcher knife to the sky and made the sign of the cross in the four directions upward to the sky and then in the direction of the darkest of clouds. The granddaughter then was instructed to repeat the sign of the cross and pray. This ceremony broke the force of the wind and kept the family safe, and this was the day that Eloisa Tamez became a "daughter of lightning," the signature figure of Margo Tamez's memoir *The Daughter of Lightning*, who is the one chosen to inherit the rituals of their Lipan Apache grandmothers. The foremothers, then, teach Lipan daughters to fiercely face adverse climates.

These significant connections of the Tamez family to the sky, winds, and lightning open avenues for contemporary Lipan Apache women to enter pan-tribal and pan-global alliances as they face both a changing climate and increasing militarization of their homelands. In response to the construction of the border wall and to natural disasters such as Hurricane Dolly, Lipan Women's Defense mobilized numerous community empowerment projects aimed at building capacity to respond to forced federal land condemnations and community displacement. The Lipan are matrilineal, matrifocal, and matrilocal, and their relationships often involve a strong intergenerational female linkage that generates spiritual strength and healing (Tamez, "Restoring" 560). Building on this strength, Tamez explains, the Lipan are facing land dispossession, forced displacement, and communicable diseases directly related to flooding and climate change, and they are building alliances with other groups around the world that are also facing "catastrophes that indigenous women have been experiencing en masse" ("Restoring" 562). In her article, "Restoring Lipan Apache Women's Laws, Lands, and Strength in El Calaboz Ranchería at the Texas-Mexico Border," Tamez traces the historical disruption of Lipan women's livelihood and intrinsic relationship to fragmented and disfigured identities, ruptured cultures, and ecological destruction. Lipan women, who live in the poorest county in the U.S., have managed to build social and cultural networks and indigenous feminist alliances that are not based on victimhood but activist resistance. In forming the Lipan Apache Women Defense and linking it to groups such as the Inuit peoples who signed the Anchorage Declaration, Tamez and her mother are forging innovative models for trans-Pacific feminisms and human rights activism in other places around the world.

There is no word for feminism in many indigenous languages. The English word *feminism*, the Spanish *feminismo*, or the Chinese phrase 女性主義 (nyu-xieng-zhu-yi) are not terms used in everyday conversation among indigenous family, clans, and communities doing anti-violence work. However, the three indigenous poets analyzed in this chapter, by the perspectives and principles of their matrilineal and matrilocal culture, legitimately exercise a central social-economic-political role as key influencers, shapers, and implanters of decisions affecting governance as well as keepers and transmitters of traditional tribal values, cultures, and everyday practices. As Tamez's work documents, indigenous women often take the lead in life-threatening, climate-related situations or struggles against the military and economic global superpowers.

Like the Lipan women, the *Vuvu*, meaning "Grandmothers" (in the Paiwan langauge), of Taiwan are providing for their communities the structures needed to restore and strengthen collective-rights movements that are disrupting or halting national and global forces that are becoming pervasive in their home territories. Growing out of desires to "witness" that are similar to Tamez's, Rimuy Aki and Liglav Awu, two prominent indigenous women writers in Taiwan, write about environmental crises and the resistance of indigenous women to assaults on their cultures. Rimuy Aki is from the Atayal tribal group, and Liglav Awu is from the Paiwan tribal group. Taiwanese aborigines are part of the Austronesian-speaking peoples who originated in Taiwan and then spread across Oceania and Southeast Asia. Fourteen tribes in Taiwan were recognized in 1996 by the Council of Aboriginal Affairs, a ministry-level organization charged with carrying out coordination and planning of indigenous affairs.[13] Though official recognition marked a milestone in Taiwanese history, providing consistent and progressive formulation and execution of indigenous policies and coordinating planning for the full-scale development of indigenous society has been slow. For this reason, activist movements of indigenous groups who are working for self-reliance and self-determination have been emerging in Taiwan.

Like Tamez, both Liglav Awu and Rimuy Aki grieve the loss of traditional lands, values, and beliefs, and both authors delineate the significance of female linkages in resistance movements. Both stress the value of story-telling in a time of danger and crisis. Like Tamez, both rely on the strength of their foremothers for rootedness and follow a similar trajectory in their activism and alliances. In her *Mulidan—Tribal Notebook*, Liglav witnesses the devastation of a Paiwan sacred mountain by the construction of a national highway, which she experiences as a deep cut through her tribe's spirituality. She writes,

> Scholars and experts, who don't know about the importance of the Da-wu Mountain to Paiwan people, made the wrong decision to build South Across-Island Highway without serious [social and environmental] assessment. Such a decision exposed the tyranny and corruption of the national regime. If the South Across-Island Highway is to be constructed, all kinds of devastating machines (such as the backhoe) will cut and dig not only the lands in the Dawu Mountain but also the life and soul of the Paiwan people. (243)[14]

The Da-wu Mountain, which was formerly included in Paiwan traditional territory and cultivated as a "commons" for their material sustenance, is now the route through which the South Across-Island Highway cuts. In order to contextualize her response to the highway, Liglav also writes about the contact of the indigenous in Taiwan with colonial powers and colonization. Major Han Chinese migration to Taiwan began in the seventeenth century. While the island was a colony of Japan from 1895 to 1945, after World War II, the military regime from the Chinese mainland became the centralized government. Their policies encouraged assimilation and removal of the aborigines so that lands could be cleared for new immigrants arriving from China. This history has become a traumatic memory for Liglav's people and other indigenous groups on the island. Contemporary encroachment into indigenous lands has continued to inflict pain and long-lasting harms on the tribes and their environment. In 1972, a highway built by the Han people cut across the mountains for corporate profits, leisure, and tourism. Liglav examines the exploitation and manipulation of her tribal home base in terms of the environmental and cultural ills that the highway has caused. She focuses on how the Taiwan government, in complicity with corporations, brings in huge machines and root plows and allows them to denude communal lands of natural vegetation.

These activities have been blamed for the devastating effects catalyzed by the 2009 Typhoon Morakot, a Category 1 hurricane on the Saffir–Simpson Hurricane Scale. The storm wrought catastrophic damage in the mountain villages, leaving 461 people dead and 192 others missing. It produced copious amounts of rainfall and triggered enormous mudslides and severe flooding. One mudslide buried the entire village of Xiaolin, killing an estimated 400 indigenous people. The South Across-Island Highway was destroyed completely. In this case, the construction of a highway almost certainly exacerbated the loss of life catalyzed by Typhoon Morakot. This illustrates why, as Priscilla Wald argues in her 2011 American Studies Association Presidential Address, our understandings of "natural disasters" should be challenged by our growing understanding of the ways in which structural violence and institutional racism can complicate extreme weather events. As Wald points out, the disproportionate "effects of, for instance, hurricanes or pandemics on different populations—by income level, race, gender, sex, or another marker—manifest underlying inequities" (191). While people in the urban areas of southern Taiwan remained largely unaffected, the tragedy that happened among the indigenous peoples of Taiwan who were not consulted on the construction of the highway was a consequence of such structural inequalities.

Novelist Rimuy Aki also addresses the environmental crisis caused by Typhoon Morakot. Her 2010 novella, *The Homeland of the Mountain Sakura*, maps the route of an Atayal family's migration from the central mountains of Taiwan to the south and then return in the 1960s to reestablish their ties to the tribal group. Typhoon Morakot is the subtext beneath the telling of the migratory history of the Atayal people, which engenders a tension between inconsolable despair resulting from colonial oppression and faith in the traditional concept of *gaga*. *Gaga* is the "natural order of things in the universe," which represents ancient teachings the Atayal people pass down from one generation to the next. While the growing climate change crisis results in numerous deaths and environmental refugees from indigenous communities, a rapid disappearance of indigenous rituals, beliefs, values, and spirituality alerts the author to a crisis of another kind. Aki translates this devastating reality into fiction:

> Surprisingly, the torrential rain at night transformed the tiny creek into a rolling river flooded with mud and stones, which scoured a passage into the mountains and cut it into two halves. What's worse, there was no hope for them to get away by wading across the muddy river, which flooded over the banks. (176)

Aki depicts how the family faces violent storms in the 1960s with despair. While fierce weather has been a common experience for mountain people in Taiwan, the mudslides and flooding in the novella anticipate the disastrous outcome of Typhoon Morakat in 2009, the year before the novel was published. Aki's story pivots around this 1960s migration from the northern mountain village of Skalu to the southern village of Namasia, which is located in Sanming County, literally meaning "County of Three Peoples." After Taiwan "recovered" from Japanese colonization in 1945, the new military Han Chinese government optimistically envisioned a democratic nation "of the people," "by the people," and "for the people." While "recovery" ("kuang fu" in Chinese) indicates the end of one imperialist conquest, for the Atayal, it is also the beginning of another regime, which continues to force broad cultural assimilation and political and social changes.

By telling a migratory indigenous story, Aki offers a counter-narrative to romanticized nationalistic discourse about "three peoples" (Japanese,

Han, and indigenous). She inserts numerous references to tribal foodways, names of traditional herbs, ceremonies and rituals, and insights and stories about the sky, environment, and land while tribal people face political and social acculturation, climate change, and natural disaster. The novella presents a search for the "recovery" of Atayal values and beliefs. Additionally, by pivoting around an Atyal woman named Yawai's everyday life, Aki recuperates a distinct tradition of Atayal female significance. Yawai is the key decision maker of her people, and she is also productive and reproductive. Her three sons inherit her wisdom, experiences, foodways, stories, and, most importantly, knowledge of Atayal ancestors and tribal genealogy. Aki illustrates how modern Atayal preserve their culture even while in diaspora.

Aki's writing is completed in the midst of fierce weather extremes, which she describes in the preface. She recalls the grief she experiences when she hears news about the people who gave her the Atayal stories featured in her novella: "Namasia, where I did my fieldwork in February 2009 was hit badly by Typhoon Morakot. Mountains, rivers and the indigenous homelands were destroyed and can hardly be recovered at present" (7). Echoing the author's lament in the foreword to Aki's novella, Paelabang danapan, the Minister of Indigenous Peoples in Taiwan (himself from the Puyuma tribe), speaks of how he was also saddened by the consequences of the typhoon for the indigenous people who were killed. He writes, "Typhoon Morakot impelled our tribal people to once again migrate. . . . However, this migration was not the adventurous migration of one family in the 1960's as depicted in Aki's narrative but rather the collective and involuntary removal of the entire tribe from their traditional village" (7). He describes archeological research in numerous Taiwan aborigines' old villages, which have proven that in the years before Japanese occupation, indigenous tribes stood the test of natural disasters thanks to the wisdom of elders who could predict when the people should migrate ahead of a typhoon. However, after colonization, "top-down" Japanese administration disrupted the migratory practices of the indigenous tribes. Paelabang danapan's point is that the relocation of the tribes after a typhoon involves not only spatial movement but also cultural, psychological, and historical displacement. Thus, Aki's novella represents a conscious effort to draw attention to the links among colonization, development, and climate change and to confront these global forces by recuperating indigenous women's cooking and weaving practices, preserving food sources and foodways, and, most importantly, maintaining and transmitting the values and beliefs of the ancient pact with nature in a time when the tribe is facing changes with both local and global consequences.

Aki addresses not only loss but gain. While the frame story is organized according to the time of "linear history" (i.e., history imposed by the colonists), tribal continuance and survival relies on "ceremonial history and time" or rather "monumental time," to borrow poststructuralist Julia Kristeva's terminology. Multiple modalities of time permeate Aki's narrative. Ceremonial/monumental time retains a sense of "cycles, gestations, the eternal recurrence of a biological rhythm which conforms to that of nature" (Kristeva 16) and whose regularity corresponds to what is experienced by tribal people as cosmic time and vertiginous visions. While these visions cut across the linear time frame, Atayal vocabulary disrupts the flow of Aki's Chinese writing. She retains not just her tribal language but the foodways embedded in that language, which, in time of crisis, hold together migratory communities. Atayal women gather *qarauw* (bamboo pieces) and *ziluk* (wild cherries) to prepare dishes; *maqaw* (mountain peppers) chicken soup and *cimmya* (salted bacon), which illustrate different means of production and consumption of meat, rich with cultural meanings; and *tgwil tayal* (mountain cucumber) is especially appealing for migrant aborigines as it is "big, juicy and handy" (Aki 68). Aki depicts a modest life of subsistence practiced by women who take care of both the family and the social (cultural) body in the face of crisis and danger as "state-owned forestry encroached on [their] ancestral *gyunam* (hunting ground)" and "*gaga* was broken and scattered" (82–83). While the bonds that tie all living things, human and non-human, into an interconnected web were once widely understood, these beliefs and practices have nearly been lost. However, women's gatherings and cooking in contemporary times provides a material basis for return to *gaga*, the traditional way of gathering and cooking. These sections of the novella demonstrate that Aki prizes ecologically sustainable management of indigenous foods and resources in accordance with *gaga* and is urging readers to practice self-sufficiency as the community faces drastic changes. By taking back the food system, she illustrates how the Atayal are resisting oppression and structural inequality and forging new routes to indigenous "roots."

While Aki begot the "root" (the protagonist Yawai's son named *Garmil*, literally meaning "root") in migrancy and returns to her roots by retrieving *gaga*, Liglav Awu traverses Taiwan to uncover the forgotten memories of many indigenous groups. She implies that assimilation of indigenous groups can be resisted through walking. In her creative nonfiction, *Vuvu with a Red Mouth*, Liglav represents her prayer, education, and healing for Mother Earth through a walking journey that illustrates the teachings of *Vuvu* (Grandmothers), which serve to combat the unprecedented destruction of the earth and of indigenous ways of life. Liglav lays out the prospect of indigenous alliances by claiming the common oppression of indigenous peoples as she travels from the northeastern Atayal village to the southern Bunun tribe, the Mayasvi and the Tabylas villages, and then to the east coast, where the Truku tribe is protesting against Asia Cement Corporate.[15] She also goes to the International Indian Tribal Council (I.I.T.C.) held in Venetie Indian Reserve, Alaska, where she works to consolidate international connections through articulating common experiences of removal and violence against indigenous peoples. In her narrative, she employs metaphors of extreme weather conditions that trigger patho-physiological reactions of grievance: she writes that she experiences an "incredible penetrating coldness" in Alaska as she hears the stories of contemporary corporate intrusion into an Artic village as well as those of the Trail of Tears and Wounded-Knee Massacre (Liglav, *Vuvu with a Red Mouth* 29–50).

While Liglav experiences pain as she learns more about the histories of trans-Pacific indigenous peoples, she finds healing in her return to her village. Two chapters in *Vuvu with a Red Mouth*, one in the middle and one at the end, feature her return to the local community and link her international fieldwork among other indigenous groups to her work with her own people. Her return coincides with the important Paiwan ceremonies of Malavek and Masulu[16] and renews her contact with *Vuvu*, Grandmother A-gan, and *I-nag*, Mother Mulidan. As a woman and a mixed-blood with a Han Chinese father and a Paiwan mother, Liglav craves a sense of belonging to counter the sexual, racial, and cultural othering she has experienced over the course of her life. She regains her power when she rediscovers and recognizes her maternal Paiwan linage. In her reconnection with the tribal female community, she identifies the values of living as an indigenous woman. The matrilineal Liglav household headed by *Vuvu* manifests tribal sovereignty and empowers her. As *Vuvu* puts it, "I have the right to decide on my own life. [. . .] Each has her way of singing and way of living; I sing this way and my song will continue" (Liglav, *Vuvu with a Red Mouth* 123). *Vuvu*'s characteristic red mouth marks her link with orality. By singing/chanting, *Vuvu* retrieves ancient stories and brings the family into contact with ancestral/divine sprits. One of these stories is about lightning:

> Legend has it that during summer afternoon, Salugajav (god of lightning) would be meeting with his beloved Salaiumuk (goddess of lightning) and in flaming body language, they related to each other their admiration and amour. The flame of love sparked lightning, shining on the Da-wu mountains. Currently, my tribal fellows in Aumagan Monalit might not have realized how the world had been deteriorated. (Ibid. 92–93)

Reminiscent of Tamez's "Daughter of Lightning," Liglav's "lightning people" gather at the home considered the most stable for surviving the torment. The legend provides a shield of strength and activates and sustains affection and relation among the tribal community. The Chinese phrase "fen-yun-bian-se" (literally "wind and cloud changed their colors" while the world was deteriorated) implies disastrous changes in the imagery of weather disturbances. However, after a diasporic journey, the female self emerges as an ethnic subject, embodied in the communal context of the suffering of others in "the world" and their efforts to achieve collective justice. While *Vuvu*'s stories offer the means of regaining a spiritual equilibrium, Liglav's narratives bear eloquent witness to the ways her walking journey bespeaks the indigenous (female) subject's ethical response to contemporary social and environmental injustice by nation-states and neoliberal development. Through walking, Liglav retrieves an "imagined inextricable linage between [a] specific site and a context of planetary reach" (Buell, "Ecoglobalist Affects" 252). Precisely because the global commons are taken away from indigenous peoples for the benefit of a wealthy minority or nation-state elites, the underprivileged and the earth suffer from the ill consequences of a "deteriorating" world.

Liglav's narratives are to be read as a collective voice of Taiwanese indigenous women (Paiwan, Atyayal, Amis, Bunun, Tsou, Rukai, Puyuma, Saisiyat, Tao, Thao, Kavalan, Truku, Sakizya, Sediq, etc.). They are representative of emerging trans-Pacific indigenous women's coalitions. Liglav and Aki, together with Tamez, tell stories about the survival of indigenous women as distinct peoples. Each author speaks of her resistance and survival by narrating stories about local lived experiences with migrant workers, mothers, women, and activists across the U.S.-Mexico border or in Taiwan. Each cultivates innovative collective responses and takes on ethical responsibilities for other human and non-human beings.

Theorizing "Indigenous Feminisms," Margo Tamez contends that we must pay heed to "the work of indigenous women, [. . .] which emerged from the daughters and granddaughters of the indigenous multitudes, who were invisible in plain sight" ("Restoring" 564). In responding to climate change, Tamez's, Liglav's, and Aki's narratives witness and acknowledge indigenous women's experiences and construct trans-Pacific indigenous feminisms as a forum where indigenous issues can be articulated and configured and the indigenous female subject emerges to communicate her message to communities of other dispossessed and displaced peoples. It is a project in process and progress, from which these writers/activists anticipate solidarity and affiliation with other indigenous peoples across the Pacific. These alliances displace national perspectives in favor of a Pacific Rim perspective that connects not only regions but bio-regions, connecting local and enlarged communities and environments. These writers are urging their readers to live with care and honor and to celebrate and share the planet as a commons in ways that are more ethical and just.

NOTES

1. See Andrew Ross, *Bird on Fire* and Adamson and Ruffin, "Introduction" this volume.
2. Han Chinese, the dominated ethnic group constituting 98% of the population in Taiwan, began migrating from mainland China to Taiwan in the seventeenth century. Chinese immigrants arriving after 1949 were referred to as "Waishenren" (meaning "people from foreign provinces"). Over the years, clashes among these immigrant ethnic groups over land, water, and cultural differences have resulted in major social and political disputes in Taiwan. In this chapter, the word "indigenous" is appropriated as a convenient tool for

articulating information about the status of indigenous Taiwanese tribes, whose histories and cultures have been hidden in successive waves of colonization in Taiwan.

3. Concerning existing and changing international environmental laws, regulations, and policies, see, for example, G. Miller 2003; Schlosberg 2007; Nixon 2011; Adamson 2012.
4. For environmental justice and human rights, refer to Boyle and Anderson 1998; Zarsky 2002; Tamez 2010.
5. For a detailed discussion on environmental justice and the problematics, ethics, and politics of environmental criticism, see Chapter 4 "The Ethics and Politics of Environmental Criticism" in Lawrence Buell's *The Future of Environmental Criticism*, 97–127.
6. In October 2008, Tamez testified at the Organization of American States Inter-American Commission on Human Rights (IACHR-OAS).
7. See Adamson, " '*¡Todos Somos Indios!*': Revolutionary Imagination, Alternative Modernity, and Transnational Organizing in the Work of Silko, Tamez and Anzaldúa."
8. Tamez's unpublished manuscript, *The Daughter of Lightning*, is cited with permission from the author.
9. For the history of Lipan title to aboriginal lands, see Tamez, "Restoring Lipan Apache Women's Laws," and Adamson, "' *¡Todos Somos Indios!*.'"
10. See "Hurricane Dolly—Human Rights and U.S. Fraud, Waste and Abuse—FEMA and DHS Cause Further Harm Against Indigenous People." Available at http://lipanapachecommunitydefense.blogspot.com/2008/07/genocide-in-south-texas-fraud-waste.html
11. See "The Anchorage Declaration." Available at http://unfccc.int/resource/docs/2009/smsn/ngo/168.pdf.
12. See "The Anchorage Declaration." I am indebted to Joni Adamson for her insightful comments on Margo Tamez's environmental activism. For more details on Lipan activism surrounding climate change, see Adamson, "' *¡Todos Somos Indios!*.'"
13. For details, see the official website of the Council of Aboriginal Affairs, Taiwan, at http://www.apc.gov.tw/portal/index.html?lang=en_US.
14. Both Liglav Awu and Rimuy Aki write in Chinese; English translations are mine.
15. In 1991, the government took away communal lands from Truku indigenes and designated Hoping Village to be the industrial area of Asia Cement Corporate. This action provoked indigenous protests for the next two decades. For details, see Kaji Cihung, "Truku People about Asia Cement Event."
16. Maleveq, the most significant Paiwan ceremony, is held every five years to commemorate their ancestors or gods, whereas Masaru is a ceremony that celebrates the harvest of rice.

Part III

Ecological Citizenship in Action

12 Roots of Nativist Environmentalism in America's Eden

Lisa Sun-Hee Park and David Naguib Pellow

Sitting high in the Rocky Mountains in Aspen, Colorado, is a Mecca for skiers, hikers, nature enthusiasts, environmentalists, European concert music lovers, and economic, political, and cultural elites from around the world. In 2000, we entered this exclusive vacation spot to investigate the recent passage of an anti-immigration resolution by the city council. On December 13, 1999, the City Council of Aspen unanimously passed a resolution petitioning the U.S. Congress and the president to create greater restrictions against both documented and undocumented immigration. The resolution called on the federal government to strengthen the U.S.–Mexico border and implement stronger legal barriers to immigration in order to preserve the economic, cultural, and ecological integrity of the nation and this exclusive city. Of particular interest to us was the strategic and pronounced role of environmentalism in arguing for greater restrictions against particular unwanted populations. This chapter focuses on the faulty logic of nativism, as expressed through anti-immigrant sentiment and policies.

We focus on Aspen as an "aspirational" space of great wealth and its accompanying and largely invisible pronounced inequality. Like many communities across the U.S., Aspen must deal with changing demographics, shifts in the global economy, and local environmental and land use pressures. And, like so many communities, immigration has taken central stage in these public struggles. From 2000 to 2009, we conducted archival research on the area's history, content analyses of contemporary letters to the editor in local newspapers, and interviews with 70 key players in the local debate concerning immigration, labor, and environmental policy. In this chapter, we provide a slice of our research findings and highlight the nativist (anti-immigrant) logic that runs through environmentalist arguments against low-wage immigrant Latino workers. We go behind the veneer of "green lifestyles" and consider the ecological impacts of wealthy communities and argue that such phenomena may have a much more profound harm on ecosystems than immigration and/or overpopulation.[1]

With the unanimous passage of Aspen's anti-immigrant resolution, City Council member Terry Paulson, a longtime immigration critic and self-avowed environmentalist, savored this victory. He received support and guidance from nationally prominent immigration control organizations such as the Carrying Capacity Network and the Center for Immigration Studies, who reportedly told him, "Other communities haven't had the courage to do so. . . . Because many current immigrants are members of minority groups in the [U.S.], attempts to limit immigration may be seen as racist" (qtd. in Heiman). Paulson wasted no time in calling for an expansion of the resolution beyond the city of Aspen. He announced his intention to launch a statewide campaign to "promote overpopulation awareness," and he declared, "If we address population and do something about it everything else will fall in line" (qtd. in Heiman). The Aspen City Council then successfully persuaded the county to follow its lead, and in March 2000, the Pitkin County commissioners voiced unanimous approval for a "population stabilization" resolution. Again, population control was articulated as fundamental to local environmental sustainability.

Located within the Roaring Fork Valley, more than 600 miles from the U.S.–Mexico border, Aspen is an exclusive resort town with an international reputation for high-end service and a stunning landscape of pristine mountains, all configured to welcome wealthy skiers in the winter and well-heeled nature lovers in the summer. Aspen's year-round residential population is just under 6,000, but in July and August, the number of people in town can reach nearly 30,000, when the various summer festivals are held. While skiing may be what Aspen is most famous for, the summer season in this year-round resort rivals the popularity of its winter activities. Like many communities in the U.S., Aspen depends on cheap immigrant labor to fuel its service economy.

The average price of a home here was around $4 million in 2007, and locals attend free seminars at the Aspen Institute on "how to pay no estate tax to the IRS." Homes in the trailer parks sell for $300,000 and up, and professionals like doctors, architects, and lawyers are among the residents there (Brady). One writer put it this way: "Aspen may be the only ski town that has become a verb. To Aspenize, in the eyes of those who live elsewhere, is to destroy a nice little ski town with conspicuous wealth, development and self-indulgence" (Clifford 33).

While 95% of the city's population is white, there are transnational elites who own a second, third, or fourth home here. Prince Bandar bin Sultan bin Abdul Aziz, for instance, obtained permission from the City Council to build a 56,000-square-foot home. Like many of Aspen's wealthiest denizens, this is just one of Prince Bandar's multiple homes. The ecological footprint involved in building and maintaining such a structure for someone who rarely visits Aspen is considerable.[2] Most elite jet setters with homes in the area spend little time here but often want their multimillion dollar domiciles ready for them whenever they arrive. Property managers in the area look after absentee homes that sit empty for 45 weeks out of the year. Yet the homes must stay heated in the winter so the pipes do not freeze, and their swimming pools, as a rule, are heated continuously for whenever the owners arrive (Conover 245).

At the same time, Aspen's reputation for environmentalism and New Age spirituality is highly regarded.[3] As the director of the Aspen Valley Community Foundation told us, "We have a ton of environmental non-profits in this small area" (Friedman). With a penchant for Eastern philosophies (and their Westernized derivatives), this area is a veritable theme park for people seeking spiritual rejuvenation through outdoor activities and access to motivational speakers, gurus, and spa treatments.

CONSTRUCTING IMMIGRATION AS AN ENVIRONMENTAL PROBLEM

The call of immigrants to its shores is one of America's most foundational stories. This narrative has served as a comforting cover for the realities of conquest, slavery, and imperialism, which are also fundamental to our nation's founding. Since at least the eighteenth century, every wave of people immigrating to the U.S. has confronted the antagonism of those who immigrated before. The result has been a cycle of nativism, perpetrated by the white Anglo Saxon Protestant community in particular and by successive groups of Euro-Americans in general (Feagin 14). Citing historian John Higham, Juan F. Perea writes that nativism is an "intense opposition to an internal minority on the grounds of its foreign (i.e., "un-American") connections" (Higham 4). Perea writes that, during periods of nativism, "democratic processes are turned against internal minorities deemed foreign or 'un-American,' resulting in discriminatory legislation and immigration restrictions" (1). These legislative maneuvers function to demarcate particular communities as marginal to the nation and undeserving of the privileges of citizenship. Nativist movements today are not fundamentally different from those of yesterday. The claims of threats to "quality of life," "American culture," and the anxiety over "limited resources" continue to animate and motivate these groups (Gottlieb 256).

U.S. environmental history does not just harbor strains of nativism here and there; rather, nativism is embedded throughout U.S. environmental history. Intrinsic to the triumphant immigration saga are the images of landscapes, with their majestic mountains, valleys, and great natural riches, "from sea to shining sea." But that glory is not without its problems. While many people who support the goals of ecological sustainability and an awareness of our ecological impacts are motivated by genuine concern for the planet, a dark side to such efforts also exists. Many efforts aimed at protecting the earth's finite resources are also deeply connected to the idea of controlling the world's population for the benefit of a powerful minority.

For instance, throughout the 1800s and into the 1920s, the conquest of Native lands and peoples was supported by U.S. federal law and several Supreme Court decisions that relied on the view that such actions were just and moral because of the inherent superiority of European American culture.[4] Native peoples were viewed as foreigners in their own land and were judged incompetent stewards of nature.[5] In the early twentieth century, many Euro-American elites turned their sights on newcomers and identified immigrants as a primary cause of ecological woes in the cities. Specifically, immigrants were blamed for the rise in urban pollution, when in fact these populations were associated with polluted spaces because they were forced to live and work in smoke-choked neighborhoods and occupationally hazardous factories and sweatshops (Gottlieb 21). In addition, prominent environmentalists in the early 1900s worked with the eugenics movement in the U.S., viewing immigrants and people of color as naturally inferior to Anglos and voicing approval of reproductive restrictions on these groups (Gottlieb and Dreier). In fact, noted preservationist and eugenicist Madison Grant collaborated with Margaret Sanger, the early U.S. women's movement leader and supporter of birth control technologies, on parallel agendas, revealing how gender and women's reproductive capacity underpin ideological battles over immigration and population growth.

Despite significant advances at the beginning of the twenty-first century, the power of racism continually presents itself in both environmentalist and nativist movements. At the 1987 Round River Rendezvous gathering of environmentalists, EarthFirst! (EF!) founder Dave Foreman and fellow EF! activist and author Edward Abbey insulted the peoples of Latin America and the Caribbean by describing them as backward and primitive (Panagioti 8–11). Abbey's 1988 book, *One Life at a Time, Please*, featured his favorite essay—"Immigration and Liberal Taboos." Abbey, who has inspired innumerable radical ecologists the world over, wrote in that essay, "It might be wise for us as American citizens to consider calling a halt to the mass influx of even more millions of hungry, ignorant, unskilled and culturally-morally-genetically impoverished people" (8).

Many possible explanations exist for the persistence of nativist environmentalism. Historically, nativist scholars, politicians, and activists in the U.S. have often harbored concerns about the prospect of "race suicide" that might result from either a lack of white population growth or from being "overrun" and outpaced reproductively by non-whites.[6] More recently, since the 2000 and 2010 censuses revealed several states as having "majority minority" populations, predictions that the U.S. will one day constitute a white minority has generated some anxiety. For the first time, almost half of the 100 largest cities in the U.S. are "majority minority" cities (Schmitt). Reports of these demographic shifts have produced fear and worry among native-born whites concerned that it is not just "their jobs" but now "their *country*" that is in danger of being taken over by foreigners. This anxiety is directed toward immigrants as whites and other citizens try to restrict access to education, health and social services, decent jobs, housing, and a broad range of environmental amenities. These are longstanding and continuing nativist concerns.

Because the U.S. electorate is so deeply divided on the issue of undocumented immigration, none of the recent federal proposals to address "the immigration problem" is finding traction with the majority. In addition, virtually none of the major proposals put forth in recent years addresses concerns over living wages or human, civil, and labor rights for immigrant workers who desire regularization. More recent manifestations of this conflict erupted in 2010 when the state of Arizona passed S.B. 1070 and again in 2011 in Alabama—both legislations obligated and empowered local law enforcement to profile and detain immigrants. Clearly, William Boelhower's notion of a planetary commons, in which the recognition of non-human and human belonging to local, national, global, and ecological communities is foundational, remains obscure (47). Instead, the political reality for many immigrants in the U.S. continues to persist within Garrett Hardin's increasingly shrinking "lifeboat."[7]

These longstanding concerns are now tinged with even greater consequences. The dangerous coupling of nativist *and* environmental movements—what we term "nativist environmentalism"—is today all the more potent because of what we now know. It is common knowledge that the planet's ecological systems are in peril and that the U.S. has contributed as much or more than any other nation to that crisis through its economic and military policies and through its consumption and production practices—independent of immigration flows into its borders.

Nativist Environmental Organizing in Aspen

In June 1999, an organization calling itself the Valley Alliance for Social and Environmental Responsibility formed.[8] The Alliance was spearheaded by two Aspenites who have been vocal nativist environmentalists for many years. Terry Paulson moved to Aspen in 1982 and has served on the City Council since 1993. He is an outdoor enthusiast who loves downhill skiing, has taught cross-country skiing for many years, and is a licensed paraglider pilot. Paulson was instrumental in getting the Population Stabilization resolution passed in the Aspen City Council and at the Pitkin County Commission. Mike McGarry is the other driving force behind the Alliance. He is a unique and boisterous man who lives in Aspen but works as a maintenance technician and custodian. In 1995, he filed a federal lawsuit charging that the Pitkin County government exercised bias in favor of people of color whom were hired for three different maintenance jobs instead of him. Challenging the county's affirmative action policy, McGarry (who is white) alleged that he had been the victim of "reverse discrimination," and he sued for what he claimed were lost wages. The case eventually made it to federal court, and he won a $50,000 settlement. He rightly took credit for being the impetus behind the county's elimination of its Equal Employment Opportunities policy. In 2001, McGarry joined the race for a city council seat (he lost), and as he filed his petition, he stated, "If elected I will make it part of my every decision to consider the greater geographic and demographic picture" (qtd. in Hooper, "Illegal"). Together, McGarry and Paulson have made immigration the number one villain of environmental sustainability in the Valley. And they have support from high places.

The same week that the Alliance was launched, former Colorado Governor Dick Lamm spoke at a Men's Club luncheon in Aspen, where he warned his audience about the social and environmental degradation—such as urban sprawl—that he declared results from continuing immigration into the U.S.[9] Lamm has a second home in Aspen and is adamant about wanting to protect Colorado's ecosystems from population growth and other threats. The former Governor considers Paulson and McGarry his colleagues and offered public support for their efforts. A Democrat, Lamm has been a long-time immigration critic. He became a populist environmental hero in Colorado in the 1970s when he stopped the Olympic Games from coming to the state on the grounds that it would produce an enormous negative ecological footprint. He has taken a stand on environmental issues ever since. He also resides firmly in the nativist camp. He is a board member of the Federation for American Immigration Reform (FAIR), a leading anti-immigration organization, and he has written extensively on immigration and population growth as ecological threats. He was one of the nativist candidates running for election to the Sierra Club Board of Directors during their internal crisis over immigration in 2004. Lamm attributes his passion for population and immigration politics to his experience in India during the 1960s—that trip profoundly impacted his thinking about growth. He recalled, "We came back from there really believing very strongly that the world ought to stabilize its population and so should the United States" (qtd. in Stiny A1).

In October 1999, Lamm delivered a keynote address at a conference in Aspen organized by the Alliance titled "The Myth of Sustainable Growth: Population, Immigration, Environmental Degradation." At the conference, Lamm proposed that the U.S. decrease legal immigration levels by 80%. Regarding this event, Mike McGarry declared, "Population is the No.1 factor in the encroachment of environmental degradation—immigration is the No. 1 factor contributing to population growth" (Stiny A1). All of this work laid the foundation for the passage of the December 1999 population stabilization resolution by the Aspen City Council. Lamm continued to work with the Alliance, using troubling metaphors to describe immigration's effect on the country, such as the following: "Cheap foreign workers are like heroin: they're addictions, you get hooked on them."[10]

The Valley Alliance for Social and Environmental Responsibility also counts outspoken nativist Republican Congressman Tom Tancredo among its supporters (Carroll). Tancredo is virulently anti-immigrant, Islamophobic, and pro-war.[11] He has repeatedly placed himself at the fringe of the Republican Party and has earned the respect of many racists across the country for his uncompromising stances on these issues. The Alliance is one of many nativist groups in the state of Colorado and in the Rocky Mountain Region that is well networked, a group that includes the Colorado Alliance for Immigration Reform (CAIR), a state affiliate of FAIR.[12] The Alliance has friends and supporters in Congress, at FAIR, NumbersUSA, and other nationally active and highly visible nativist groups.

At the Myth of Sustainable Growth Conference, many others spoke to a packed audience. Jonette Christian, the founder of Mainers for Immigration Reform, was one of them. She gave a speech at the conference that was well received and hit straight to the point from an unapologetic nativist perspective. Christian's presentation made two key nativist claims. The first is that the culture of the U.S. Anglo majority is superior to that of any other nation:

> Culture is fundamental in understanding poverty and high growth. Authoritarian cultures, not surprisingly produce authoritarian governments, and these nations are especially vulnerable to economic domination from outsiders. The ruling elites of Latin America have had little interest in protecting the welfare of their own people. But the problem lies within the culture. In Latin societies there is no code of conduct that calls for social responsibility or citizen activism outside of the family. It is not an accident that America has given the world the game plan for modern democracy and the example of a culture which continually works to improve itself.[13]

This deeply racist American exceptionalism runs through much of the rhetoric undergirding U.S. nativism. Dick Lamm seconded Christian's statement when he declared, "Our best course is to model sustainability for the rest of the world." Considering how much pollution and hazardous waste the U.S. government, military, and businesses produce and the enormous volume of ecological wealth these institutions consume, this idea is internally contradictory. The second major claim that Jonette Christian made is the nativist-populist argument that immigrants are, making life hard for working people in the U.S.:

> We are seeing increasing disparity between rich and poor, and massive immigration is largely responsible. . . . In other words, our current immigration policy is making it increasingly difficult for our most vulnerable populations—blacks, minorities, recent immigrants, and the poor to earn a living wage. . . . Do we have an obligation to protect the living standard of unskilled workers in this country, or are we going to require them to compete with third world wages? (Christian)

The vast class disparities that now rival the gilded age are blamed on working, poor immigrants who are believed to be responsible for bringing down wages. In this analysis, the wealthy escape any scrutiny.

In the last decade, the Valley Alliance has continued to gather support for its cause and found it in the form of nationally recognized and respected authors, activists, and foundations. Lester Brown, Chair of the Board of the World Watch Institute, attended a conference on sustainability in Aspen in 2004 and has frequently appeared at many events sponsored by nativist and population control organizations. Population has always been one of the key indicators of the global ecological crisis that World Watch has followed for many years. Brown spoke directly to many of the main concerns the Alliance shares with regard to the impact of population growth on ecosystems.[14] While we would not describe Brown as a nativist environmentalist, his emphasis on Malthusian theories of population growth lends credibility to this approach.[15]

Members of our research team had a chance to sit down with Alliance founders Terry Paulson and Mike McGarry. They spoke candidly and forthrightly. McGarry described the region's social problems in this way:

> Our problem is that we got this monster looming out just outside the city limits. A population monster. Because this thing's going to bury us all. . . . You know if you just conceptualize no growth in the sense that you don't need growth if you're a person, you have an infrastructure called your anatomy, your physiology. You're not built to be 6'5", 500lbs, you know? Herman Daly, our ecological economist, he would make the distinction between qualitative and quantitative development. You could continue to improve your body. But you don't necessarily have to grow the body. (Paulson and McGarry)

McGarry's analogy, like those used by many nativist environmentalists, draws on biological or "natural" models for much of its logic. On the sensitive subject of immigration, it becomes clear that, for many nativists, there are desirable and undesirable immigrants. We asked about the numerous Australians and Europeans we noticed in Aspen, working on the ski slopes and in swank restaurants. Referring to the town's iconic resort, Paulson stated, "The Ski company has been lobbying pretty heavily in the southern hemisphere to get people to come up here when their off-season is, so we get people from Queenstown, New Zealand, Australia, Argentina, Chile." McGarry added, "It's their summer experience, it's great, it's great for everybody." These immigrants are viewed ethnically as white. Unfortunately, for McGarry and Paulson, these immigrants are in short supply by comparison to people from Mexico and Central America.

McGarry and Paulson located the origins of the current immigration "crisis" in the Roaring Fork Valley in part to earlier European immigrants who liked to call in sick on days when the skiing was good. So, according to

Paulson, employers soon switched to recruiting non-European immigrants who had little interest in skiing and who would also work for less money. Terry Paulson recalled,

> I came here in '82. That time here, I thought I was in Sweden because there were a bunch of Swedes here (laughs). They were washing dishes, skiing, you know, whatever. I think there was a business concern here about finding workers that were reliable and wouldn't call in sick on powder days. I really think that's what started the whole move to look for a work force that wasn't interested in the sports that we enjoy.

McGarry picked up the story from there:

> The people washing dishes in the restaurants were more native people, people who have lived here, they were part of the Alpine culture too, they were skiers and backpackers and so forth. So we had a schedule that said whoever was there the longest, if they could find someone to replace them, they could go on out and go skiing on good days. So everyone adapted to the culture, so then we had people hired from out of the country because they were cheaper, they were not going to participate in the culture. They will work day and night no matter what. . . . So we get more and more dependent on these guys who will work for low wages. The employers rigged how all these things developed. (Paulson and McGarry)

Here we see populist anti-corporate rhetoric combined with a soft racism of permanent cultural difference between people from European versus non-European nations. Terry Paulson jumped in to say, "Also in terms of the cultural, I think Europeans in general have a sense of population and where they want their countries to be. Other parts of the world, I don't think have that same concept of overpopulation as Europeans" (Paulson and McGarry).

These two founders of the Valley Alliance for Social and Environmental Responsibility spoke about the strength of ecological ethics and policies in the Aspen area. They both embraced the recent thirtieth anniversary celebration of the Aspen Wilderness Workshop—a local environmental group—because, as Paulson claimed, the group's pressures on ski companies in the area resulted in the use of recycled materials and "a kind of diesel fuel that's more ecological" (Paulson and McGarry). McGarry proudly added, "I think that if we look at the big picture, Aspen is as environmentally-conscious and as conservation oriented and as aware as any town." Like other towns, Aspen requires positive "mitigations" to offset development that might be ecologically harmful. In other words, projects that are intended to improve local ecosystems when other efforts cause harm. However, in Aspen, these development practices have a distinctive flair. As

Terry Paulson explained, "For instance if someone wants to put in a heated driveway . . . so you don't have to shovel snow . . . he has to mitigate that somehow, he has to make small changes in his other plans." We queried, "Did you just say a heated driveway?" McGarry stepped in, "They're all over the place up here."

Both men reported disgust with the federal government's response to undocumented immigration from Mexico. When asked about the recent public fight over the INS's attempt to locate a detention facility in nearby Glenwood Springs, McGarry snorted,

> They don't come here. They don't do on-sight raids, the INS. That location down there was strictly to deal with the I-70 traffic, you know the vanloads. There's no INS in Aspen. They go on the record all the time and they couldn't be more apologetic, going on profusely about (in a whiny voice) "we're not here to mess with the local businesses, we're only here to stop the trafficking on I-70." It's an addiction. It's turned into just an addiction like heroin. Cheap foreign labor. That's all they see and it's all they invest in. That's the revenue. We need to cold turkey these guys. (Paulson and McGarry)

Near the end of the interview, two Latinas passed by us on the sidewalk, and Paulson and McGarry stopped talking while they walked by, glaring at them.

Backlash Against Immigrant Rights Groups

Not only did the Valley Alliance work to build nativist-environmentalist sentiment against immigrants in the Roaring Fork Valley, they have specifically set out to target organizations that provide support services and advocacy for these populations. This effort had an impact on the public perception of these organizations as undeserving and as an additional indicator of the alleged drain on resources caused by immigration.

One such target was Roaring Fork Legal Services (RFLS), which opened its offices in Aspen in 2001 with a $3,000 grant from that city. Created at the request of the local bar association, RFLS is a non-profit organization that offers legal advice to immigrants—regardless of citizenship—on civil matters including divorce, landlord-tenant disputes, welfare law, and immigration law. This public service is offered to those who otherwise are unable to afford an attorney. The news of this group's founding created an uproar among local nativists. During one city council meeting, Mike McGarry and a colleague of his—a woman who refused to give her name—lambasted the council for supporting the organization. They demanded that RFLS require proof of citizenship or residency for any Latino clients they serve. When Councilman Tony Hershey pointed out that asking someone from one ethnic group for identification would be racist and probably illegal,

McGarry snapped, "Don't even bring up that race crap with me" (qtd. in Harvey, "Issue").

When word spread about RFLS, many locals linked that organization to the mission of other groups in the Valley that advocate on behalf of immigrants. One particularly virulent letter to the *Aspen Times* called into question these organizations' tax-exempt status:

> Their defenders and heavily financed front organizations—Roaring Fork Legal Services, the Stepstone Center and Latinos Unidos, race-based organizations with racist, race-based ends—are beneficiaries of tax exempt status as 'educational' nonprofits, a status granted them by a United States government agency. Go figure. And yes, "criminals." People who invade our borders, against our law, forge and use forged documents to further their dishonest ends while they make up, hide behind and perpetuate the preposterous (and humorous) charge of racism, a stylistic tactic right out of Joseph McCarthy's playbook, are criminals, and their apologists are subversive, multicultural hypocrites. People, unless you want to be forced to eat the worm at the bottom of the bottle, wake up and smell the tequila. (Barber)[16]

Again, the language that some nativists use is overtly racist, yet they deny that racism. Instead, they claim reverse discrimination by stating that to acknowledge race at all is racist. This logical quagmire has the effect (if not intent) of stopping all conversation and consideration of racial inequality while perpetuating it.

During this time, a number of organizations were created across the Valley to meet some of the needs of the area's growing Latino immigrant population. Some of these organizations received government grants for their work. They include the Mountain Family Health Center, which offers subsidized healthcare to uninsured immigrant families. Catholic Charities of the Western Slope offers resources and advice to undocumented persons seeking citizenship. The activist-oriented Stepstone Center organizes around issues facing Latinos and the broader community to empower people at the grassroots level to confront corporate power, environmental injustices, and nativism. Additionally, the Aspen Valley Community Foundation developed a program for grants around issues facing working Latino families (Harrell). The fact that none of these groups distinguishes between documented and undocumented persons raised more than a few eyebrows among local immigration critics.

These groups' success at keeping a planned INS facility out of the Valley incensed many local Anglos, who let their feelings flow onto the written page. One Aspen resident wrote:

> OK, Latinos, you've scored a coup and stopped a legal action by the U.S. government. The INS can't camp in your back yard. Congrats.

> Now why don't you address the real reason the community and our government likes you as individuals, but refuses to accept you as a group. Last week there were two stories in the paper—two more Latinos were arrested for peddling cocaine, and a 14-year-old girl was taken to the hospital for cocaine overdose. You and your people have proven you have time to protest against our government. How about taking time to form Good Latinos Against Drugs, and protest against an activity we all know is evil? You got what you want, how about showing you care for someone other than yourselves? (Taylor)

The association of immigrants and people of color with crime and illegal drugs runs deep in the American psyche, nurtured by news media and film and music industries that push these images daily (Hall et al.; Bullock et al. 229). Immigrant workers, who are ubiquitous in the industries that fuel the resort community, are made out to be the cause of irreparable harm to the culture, security, and ecology of other people's vacation sites. These concerted attacks have destabilized virtually every non-profit organization that assists Latinos in the Roaring Fork Valley. The short tenure of these organizations and rapid turnover in employees serve as an obvious testament to the high level of burnout experienced by those who must combat these controlling, negative images of Latino immigrants in the U.S.[17]

CONCLUSION

The evidence presented here leads us to two conclusions. First, the mainstream environmental movement in the U.S. is largely unconcerned with racial justice. Nor has it shown much willingness to fight for even the broader—and less controversial—goal of social justice. This is not only because it has often traditionally been reserved for middle and upper class populations, but also because it has always been haunted—indeed fueled—by a strong thread of white supremacy and nativism.

The environmental movement's blind spots are unfortunate and tragic. Environmentalism could become a transformative force that embraces justice for all, given our shared global ecosystem. Instead, we have constructed political, economic, and social borders to protect only certain people's ecosystems and human communities. These borders are not only artificial, they are also the *source* of environmental devastation. The exclusive "protection" of the backyard of the privileged is absolutely dependent on the impoverishment of someone else's common space. The volume of resources required to maintain the heavenly experience of the very few in Aspen is profound. If environmentalists are truly committed to ecological sustainability, they must find ways of reducing ecological damage through an acknowledgment and alleviation of social inequality rather than fixating on immigrants and population control.

The second conclusion we draw is that nativist movements are also generally supported by a strong current of ideology that is not just about protecting one's economy, language, culture, or borders, but also about protecting the nation's land, air, and water: in other words, the environment. These issues are closely held together in nativist ideology. That is, nativist movements tend to be environmentalist in their outlook, which is why we see nativism and environmentalism as part of the same broad continuum of movements. In fact, environmentalism functions to convey a level of legitimacy for some nativists who may seek to smooth over their sharp racist inclinations. Nativist movements are not just anti-immigrant in their approach to the world; they are racist and generally white supremacist.[18] Thus, nativism does nothing but function as a disservice to environmentalism. Rather than bolstering their membership with restrictionist fear-mongers, environmentalism might act as the mass movement that it could be and separate from and condemn nativist ideology as fundamentally anti-environmental.

Most of the major environmental organizations in the U.S. have (or have had) programs or campaigns focused on population analysis. Among others, this list includes the Sierra Club, the National Wildlife Federation, and the Audubon Society. This interest in population control extends beyond environmental and nativist groups to federal government agencies, international development organizations, and global philanthropies. Many federal agencies and large foundations in the U.S. determined, decades ago, that population control is one of the pillars of national and corporate security. Since the early 1950s, the Ford Foundation, John Rockefeller III's Population Council, and other institutions began funding research at U.S. universities on the links between population and political stability. By the mid-1960s, U.S. international food aid programs became some of the key players in supporting family planning in the global South. By the 1990s, the U.S. Agency for International Development (USAID) became the world's largest funder of population control initiatives in the global South.[19] This was troubling for women's rights advocates around the world who recalled USAID's troubling history of sterilization policies.[20] Population control efforts have often used the notion of conserving the earth's resources as a vehicle for exerting influence over the world's low-income and global South populations. Therefore, population control as an ecological sustainability project is actually very much in tune with nativist ideology.

However, history shows us that early on there was a glimmer of hope that the U.S. environmental movement might have taken a different path. In the early twentieth century, social reformers who advocated on behalf of immigrants working in sweatshops and living in America's slums could also be viewed as environmental justice leaders. They were critical of the power relations that relegated economically and politically marginalized groups to hazardous living and working environments. These far-sighted public intellectuals and activists included Jane Addams, Florence Kelley, and Alice Hamilton. Together they challenged the social forces that threatened the public health status of European immigrant communities in Chicago and elsewhere, places where men, women, and children were forced to work long hours for low wages, where lead poisoning was a way of life, and where garbage dumps came with the neighborhood (Gottlieb and Dreier). The mainstream environmental movement made a choice *not* to cast its lot with this brand of activists, and the movement suffered greatly in its lack of capacity for melding social justice with ecological protection. We believe some in the movement might one day challenge their colleagues to remember Addams, Kelley, and Hamilton and embrace a different path.

NOTES

1. Some observers have noted that consumption by wealthy nations and communities is the major driving force behind our global ecological crises, while people in global South communities tend to consume and pollute far less. See Fred Pearce, "On World Population Day, Take Note: Population isn't the Problem."
2. The term "ecological footprint" is a measure of human demand or impact on the earth's ecosystems.
3. The city of Aspen received an environmental award from the U.S. EPA "that will make it the only municipality in the nation to be designated as one of the Best Workplaces for Commuters District." To qualify for the award, the city's employers must offer benefits to employees who commute, such as showers, lockers, monthly transit passes, and so on (Hooper, "EPA").
4. See *Johnson v. McIntosh* (1823), *Cherokee Nation v. Georgia* (1831), *Worcester v. Georgia* (1832), and *Lone Wolf v. Hitchcock* (1903).
5. This argument was perhaps best embodied in the Dawes Severalty Act of 1887, which forced Native Americans to move beyond collective and commons property arrangements to individual private property allocations. The Act also imposed Euro-American agricultural practices on these populations.
6. See David Roediger, *Working Toward Whiteness: How American's Immigrants Became White*. Recent articles and public statements regarding the 2010 census demonstrate this dynamic as well, concerning the increase in Latino women's fertility above the rate of non-Latino women (see "Minorities Will Soon be the Majority").
7. See Garrett Hardin, "The Case Against Helping the Poor."
8. An advertisement for the Alliance reads, "Are you curious, concerned or disturbed that your city and county resources and ski company efforts are going to further an artificial population growth in the Roaring Fork Valley? Are you curious, concerned or disturbed that massive, endless legal and illegal immigration are the principal causes of these developments?" (Harvey, "New Watchdog").
9. Lamm was Colorado governor from 1975 to 1987.
10. This comes from a presentation that Lamm gave at the Rural Resort Region conference. The title of his talk was "The Agonizing Dilemma of Immigration." He is now Director of the Center for Public Policy and Contemporary Issues at the University of Denver (Harvey, "Lamm").
11. In 2009, Tancredo lambasted Supreme Court Justice Sonia Sotomayor for her affiliation with the National Council of La Raza, which he called "nothing

more than a Latino KKK" (*CNN Live*). At the 2010 Tea Party Convention, he called for a return to literacy tests for voters in order to prevent the election of candidates like Barack Obama, whose ascendancy he blamed on the "cult of multiculturalism." He earlier argued that if the U.S. bombed holy Muslim sites in the Middle East, such a practice would deter Islamic extremists from attacking domestic U.S. targets ("Tancredo: If They Nuke Us, Bomb Mecca").

12. The CAIR website reads: "Advocating for the Rights of future generations of Americans." The website logo is fitting, in that it is simply a picture of a snow-capped mountain range, with no people and no evidence of human settlement whatsoever. This is a true preservationist approach to immigration and environmental policy (CAIRCO.org).
13. The Myth of Sustainable Growth Conference, at which this presentation was made, was sponsored by the Sopris Foundation, whose motto is "Creating Awareness of Population and Environmental Issues Worldwide." The similarities between Christian's speech here and EarthFirst! activist Edward Abbey's words at the 1987 Round River Rendez-vous are striking in terms of their contemptuous views of Latin American cultures.
14. Fifth Annual State of the World Conference, Aspen, Colorado, July 2004.
15. Brown spoke at a "Reinventing Malthus for the 21st Century" conference sponsored by Negative Population Growth and the Federation for American Immigration Reform (FAIR) in 1997. In his remarks that day, he said, "We have this infatuation with technology, which is understandable, whether it's exploring Mars or the internet and all the things one can do now in the telecommunications field. It's fascinating, it's exciting, but it doesn't solve the food problem. And it doesn't bring about the balance that we need between our continuously expanding numbers and the earth's resources, which have not changed very much since the time of Malthus."
16. This letter was written in response to the protest against the INS plans to build a detention facility in Carbondale. The author of the letter is from Aspen, Colorado. See also Mildred Baumli, "Bleeding Hearts," a letter that specifically targets the Stepstone Center, since, like the letter's author, it is based in Carbondale. Baumli writes, "As for the Stepstone Center it should be investigated for saying they are tax 'exempt.' "
17. A more detailed analysis of these organizations and their strategies are found in Park and Pellow's book, *The Slums of Aspen: Immigrants vs. the Environment in America's Eden*.
18. This includes movements such as the Proposition 187 mobilization, which was supported by many Latinos. People of color can work in the interest of white supremacy, so this "diversity" of support doesn't negate that fact (see Denise Ferreira Da Silva, *Toward a Global Idea of Race*; and George Lipsitz, *The Possessive Investment in Whiteness: How White People Profit from Identity Politics*).
19. See Betsy Hartmann, *Reproductive Rights and Wrongs*; and Betsy Hartmann, "Conserving Racism: The Greening of Hate at Home and Abroad."
20. In 1977, R. T. Ravenholt of USAID announced the agency's plan to sterilize a quarter of the world's women. He stated, "Population control is necessary to maintain the normal operation of U.S. commercial interests around the world" (qtd. in Wagman). See Andrea Smith, *Conquest: Sexual Violence and American Indian Genocide*.

13 Wielding Common Wealth in Washington, DC, and Eastern Kentucky

Creative Social Practice in Two Marginalized Communities

Kirsten Crase

> "Always ask of any proposed change or innovation: what will this do to our community? How will this affect our common wealth?"
>
> —Wendell Berry, "Conserving Communities"

Farmer and social critic Wendell Berry poses a core question that forms of environmentalism—from mainstream U.S. conservation to U.S. environmental justice movements to indigenous and global South movements—have long addressed ("Conserving Communities" 19). What will a given "change" or event mean for "our community?" The root of the word "community" is of course "common," as Berry suggests, and an ethic of connection and interdependence, of shared wealth, and of the need to care for that wealth collectively, remains at the center of most locally based environmental movements. As such, Berry's exhortation is a fitting starting point for an examination of locally oriented practices of ecological citizenship. By itself, however, it leaves "community" and "common wealth" unmoored from any situating attributes of scale or context. While the concepts' flexibility gives them their expressive and practical potential, it can also risk allowing them to sink beneath the weight of their own conceptual breadth and elasticity.

Here, I locate the foundational breadth as well as the situational specificity of Berry's exhortation as it is put into practice in two communities. I undertake a fine-grained analysis of "common wealth" in terms of how it is understood and employed by individuals in Washington, DC, and the Appalachian coalfields of eastern Kentucky. The areas of Washington, DC, and eastern Kentucky examined here differ dramatically in terms of their histories, geographies, and demographics, yet they share in experiencing longstanding race and class marginalization and increased vulnerability to environmental risk. It is for this reason that I examine these two seemingly dissimilar communities—one urban and one rural, one predominantly

African American and one predominantly white—in parallel. By constructing ethnographic sketches of individuals who live in these communities and by analyzing their efforts to deal with the overlapping effects of marginalization and environmental risk, I demonstrate how "common wealth" can be grounded, articulated, and even "wielded" through creative visions and practices of ecological citizenship.

MARGINALIZATION, ENVIRONMENTAL JUSTICE, AND CREATIVE SOCIAL PRACTICE

The two communities highlighted here differ in their locations, physical environments, histories, and resident identities. However, both communities have been marginalized structurally and discursively. Through mutually reinforcing processes of structural disinvestment and negative discursive stereotyping, the communities have been treated as if they were throwaway regions inhabited by dispensable populations. These communities have, over time, been marginalized due to lack of both economic and governmental investment in their social and infrastructural maintenance. "Disinvestment" can be characterized as the crippling of an already meager tax base by local and outside elites with little political will to enact policies that would benefit struggling residents. Disinvestment's damaging effects can be seen in everything from crumbling infrastructure to poor local schools to the criminalization of residents.

In terms of the ecological consequences of disinvestment, in marginalized urban areas, waste and pollutants are allowed to contaminate homes, neighborhoods, waterways, and the urban ecosystem as a whole; furthermore, the ecology of the built environment and the tangible elements of local memory are damaged or erased as homes and local gathering places are destroyed to make way for commercial development. In marginalized rural areas, contamination by pollutants also occurs, and extractive industries wreak havoc on local geography. Berry, who is himself a lifelong resident of Kentucky, where extractive industry is a prominent feature of the regional economy, discusses the kind of "structural violence" that occurs with extractive industry. He describes mining's ecological damage and the extent to which the philosophy of depletion and destruction has spread to other practices:

> Mining we have allowed to become an industrial war against the land and all its living communities, taking whatever is of most immediate value, and leaving in return ruins and poisons that are substantially worse than nothing. [. . .] we have allowed the economies of agriculture and forestry to mimic the economy of mining, [. . .] taking much temporary wealth and returning permanent ruin to the land and its natural and human communities. ("Simple Solutions" 56)

While Berry is primarily discussing rural communities here, his notion of "war against the land and all its living communities" applies equally well to urban communities whose "resources" are their potential real estate value and the presumed dispensability of their low-income, usually non-white residents. Furthermore, in marginalized urban and rural communities, social inequalities tend to dovetail with environmental inequalities. David Naguib Pellow and Robert J. Brulle describe the mutually reinforcing tendencies of these inequalities as follows:

> certain neighborhoods and regions of the United States are defined as "undesirable" not only because of the level of pollution in these places, but also because of the type of persons who occupy these spaces. "Bad" neighborhoods, for example, are as much about the type of ecological disamenities found in these areas as about the type of people found there. Hence, where we find social inequalities we also find environmental and health inequalities. (2)

In a more hopeful vein, however, environmental justice and its initiatives and movements also speak powerfully to Berry's notion of the common wealth, and in particular to my exploration here of what it means to "wield" common wealth—to understand our shared commons as not only a resource to protect but also as a tool for imagining our future.

Writing about the concept of place, Tim Cresswell suggests that place "provides the conditions of possibility for creative social practice" and "becomes an event rather than a secure ontological thing" (39). Indeed, when a strong, creative, and communal sense of place flourishes, the transition from idea to practice can become almost seamless, with practitioners embodying their commitment to place through their everyday actions. Active, creative, unbounded, and "unfinished" understandings of spatial concepts—whether place, home, environment, or commons—characterize the vision and practice of ecological citizenship in these communities, the "wielding" of common wealth. In melding these concepts together in innovative ways, residents demonstrate creative social practice that productively nurtures the wealth we hold in common as ecological citizens.

COMMUNITY SKETCHES

The urban Washington, DC, community I examine is the entire area located south of the U.S. Capitol and east of the Anacostia River, covering most of the city's southeast quadrant. Commonly referred to by non-residents as "Anacostia," this is actually a misnomer as Anacostia is only one of the community's several neighborhoods. For the sake of simplicity and in order to encompass the whole area, I refer to it here as "East Washington"[1]

After its official incorporation into the District of Columbia in 1871, East Washington housed increasing numbers of African Americans, as well as working-class whites (Hutchinson xxii–xxiii). Over the course of the twentieth century, as school desegregation and so-called urban renewal transformed the community, its population became predominantly African American and at the same time increasingly impoverished, isolated from the rest of the city, and neglected by both the federal and district governments. Affordable housing and residential dislocation have also been persistent issues, with low-income and public housing complexes having been razed as part of mid-twentieth-century urban renewal and freeway constructions projects as well as more recent restructuring of public housing programs. All of these dislocating and isolating processes have reinforced patterns of disinvestment in East Washington.

The neighborhoods east of the Anacostia have traditionally been viewed as a dangerous and unattractive back alley of the nation's capital. In the last decade, however, a new identity has emerged for this area, one that envisions it as the "last frontier" for development in Washington, DC (Meyer), and the site of a series of ambitious redevelopment plans featuring high-end housing and retail, continued razing of public housing, cleanup of the polluted Anacostia River, and construction of the new Department of Homeland Security headquarters.[2] These plans promise the community a new and improved image, but also the unspoken corollary that the most destitute residents will be neither welcome nor capable of affording housing in the neighborhood's revamped, gentrified version. Taking as a metaphor Berry's notion of the ethic of depletion associated with mining, we can consider this a kind of effort at emptying the community of its largely low-income, non-white residents, together with their "common wealth" of local knowledge and sense of place. It is this impending change that is galvanizing some residents of East Washington to formulate new ideas about their home community, about what it means to call this place home, and about how they might address the coming changes and thus develop unique local practices of ecological citizenship.

The rural eastern Kentucky community I examine is that of Letcher County, located in the middle of the central Appalachian mountain range. Before the arrival of railroads in the late nineteenth century and the subsequent development of the extractive industries of mining and timbering, small-scale subsistence agriculture dominated eastern Kentucky and the central Appalachian region. When industrial barons descended on the region, urging farmers to sell the mineral rights to their property without explaining the consequences of this transfer, the Appalachian region entered the era of modern industrialization and began its tumultuous relationship with coal. Conflicts over issues such as the rights of miners versus company operators, the coal industry's political power, and the siting of mining operations have rankled the community ever since. The coal industry' dominance has also led to a kind of monoculture that has entrenched poverty, isolation, poor education, and a variety of other social problems in the region (Eller 221–260; Williams 334–366). On more than one occasion, the coal industry has been deeply—and occasionally illegally—involved in local politics. Furthermore, a complex discourse of coal as the centerpiece of local heritage and identity has become interwoven with everyday life.

In the last decade, the tensions caused by the coal industry's stranglehold over the community have become even more intense with the advent of mountaintop removal mining. Mountaintop removal is an extremely destructive mining form in which the tops of mountains are dynamited off in order to access thin seams of coal. Preferred by the coal industry because of its efficiency in accessing coal more quickly and easily and its cost-effectiveness in requiring fewer workers, the negative impacts of mountaintop removal on surrounding communities are manifold. Impacts include severe scarring of the physical landscape; pollution of water sources; damage to plant and animal habitats; loss of mining jobs in already economically deprived communities; and damage to the built environment, cultural heritage, and livability of the area (Burns 118–140). In addition to these visible effects, more intangible consequences also take place at the discursive level of place and identity, accentuating divisions between residents and often forcing them to make painful choices between livelihood and human relationships (Burns 33–59). Looking again to Berry's philosophy of extractive industry, we might consider that the livelihood and health of the place itself, in addition to the coal, has begun to be depleted. It is the intensification of the coal industry's damaging effects that is galvanizing some Letcher County residents to formulate new ideas about their community, about what it means to call this place home, and about what it would mean to practice ecological citizenship in the face of their local environment's literal dislocation.

ETHNOGRAPHIC SKETCHES

In interviews with four individuals, two in Washington, DC, and two in eastern Kentucky, what begins to emerge is a glimpse into the myriad and sometimes contradictory ways in which "common wealth" is being wielded in each of these historically marginalized communities. Each interviewee differs in age, race, class, educational background, religion, and political identification. They share, however, a common commitment to nurturing their understanding of "common wealth" and to crafting productive forms of local ecological citizenship in response to major changes in their environment's structure and landscape. Significantly, their responses suggest that while marginalized communities such as these have often viewed environmentalism suspiciously as an elitist movement with little connection to their daily lives, attitudes may be beginning to shift. These four individuals, among others in their communities, are engaging in creative social practice and are acknowledging the value of an environmental "common wealth" of some fashion. Interviewees are also committed to addressing their community's severest forms of marginalization, even though their notions of marginalization often differ. Perhaps most usefully, they make diverse and creative use of place, home, and environment, utilizing these spatial concepts to both crystallize and complicate their visions of how to wield common wealth.

I begin my interview analysis by examining how "home" is articulated by two residents of East Washington, particularly in terms of how it relates to recent changes in the community's landscape and composition. Sharon[3] is a middle-aged, African-American, middle-class woman who has spent most of her life in East Washington. She is a social worker in a branch office of the Washington, DC, City Council located in Anacostia. When asked how she feels about her community and her employment there, Sharon explains, "I love this community, I really love it, and the people in it." She emphasizes that "most of my work has been on this side of the river, 'cause I want to give back to my community."[4]

For Sharon, the prospect of new development in her community presents a mixed bag of potential outcomes. On the one hand, like most residents, she recognizes the shortage of basic amenities. She also feels some pride that her community is, at last, being eyed for the kinds of investment and development that have brought amenities to other communities in the Washington area, saying, "I think we deserve the same conveniences that everybody else has." On the other hand, she worries that the perennial problems of displacement and gentrification will accentuate the hardships experienced by her community's impoverished residents. Discussing a colleague's efforts to convince her that gentrification would not negatively affect existing residents, Sharon says, "She tried to, she *tried* to convince us that it was just about new neighbors coming in. Well, it would be okay if new neighbors came in if some of us weren't being displaced, but it has yet to happen where folk are not being displaced." What Sharon is referring to is that several other Washington, DC, neighborhoods that were once like hers, with relatively low-income populations and large numbers of African Americans, have experienced intense gentrification in recent decades. With the redevelopment of U Street, Columbia Heights, and other neighborhoods, large swaths of low-income residents have been displaced through the conversion of rent-controlled units into expensive condominiums and through the skyrocketing of property tax rates for those few who owned homes.[5] Anticipating that low-income residents of her community will likely face a similar fate, Sharon concludes that development and gentrification as currently practiced present benefits for some residents and hardships for others, and that the dilemma has no easy reconciliation.

When initially asked about her community's environmental attitudes, Sharon responds that environmental issues are generally not a high priority for communities struggling with "social ills such as violence and unemployment and chronic disease." She explains further that policymakers and environmentalists don't often speak "plain folks' talk," which contributes to a sense of environmentalism as an elitist project. Instead of suggesting that struggling groups in her community have no concern for or experience with environmental issues, however, Sharon complicates the concept of the environment, broadening its parameters and placing it within the context of everyday life in a particular place, in this case the public housing projects of the 1980s, when she was beginning her social work career:

> For me, thinking of the environment is thinking about cleanliness, inside the home and outside of the home. And people were just angry, they were in despair. [. . .] And back in those days there were kids that were pumping gas for you [. . .] and that was before they had those nozzles to contain the fumes, and these are little bitty kids, [. . .] the kids would go pump gas because their mother didn't come home for a couple of days, because she's strung out on drugs somewhere, and there was no food in the house, so they had to go make money to eat.

In this excerpt, Sharon weaves together issues of poverty, despair, drug abuse, lack of employment, childhood hunger, and environmental hazards, all under the umbrella of environmental quality and well-being. "Home" as environmental well-being is at the center of her concept of ecological citizenship. This shows that she is thinking in terms of a kind of environmental common wealth that encircles home and community.

When discussing ways of cultivating and nurturing an ethic of common wealth and common good among community residents, Sharon suggests that metaphors of home, cleanliness, and well-being are most appropriate for two reasons. First, much of the environmental degradation that contributes to health problems originates inside the home as a direct result of poor maintenance of the community's multifamily dwellings. She explains that "the environment is [. . .] also the indoor environment. [. . .] I think it's really important because I find that a lot of chronic disease is attributed to our environment, and we don't recognize the significance of that."

The second reason Sharon suggests using metaphors of home, cleanliness, and well-being is that "they [community residents] understand what that means" in a practical sense and can participate in it in such a way as to see direct improvements in their own lives and the community. In the following excerpt, she explains how the developer of an affordable housing complex involved residents, some of whom were illiterate, in converting the complex into the first LEED-certified affordable housing property in Washington, DC (*Rebuilding*).

> They've got this geothermal heating thing under the buildings, but they took it a step further, and their residents have to take workshops on going green in their units. [. . .] They've got these little green stickers throughout their apartments that helps them to remember [energy-

> saving practices], cause they really got a kick out of it! They were anxious to do it because it seemed like fun to them. It's really quite fascinating how they [the developers] managed to do that, because they understood the audience that they were working with.

It is important to note that Sharon's discussion here glides over catchphrases such as "going green" without a careful consideration of what this actually means to residents, short of potentially "seem[ing] like fun to them." Nevertheless, her enthusiasm for this project and what it accomplished for residents was palpable; she saw it as creating home spaces that were more conducive to health and well-being.

For Sharon, ecological citizenship is intimately tied up in providing for the basic needs of all community members so that issues such as poverty, disease, drug abuse, illiteracy, and unemployment do not define people's lives. It's about building a participatory framework that reempowers residents, recognizes them and energizes them as citizens, and makes them more committed to their community's well-being and preservation, particularly when outside commercial forces work to destabilize and displace that community. Sharon's vision of *wielding* common wealth is ultimately about *strengthening* community—helping provide the resources for a physical home as well as a cognitive sense of home that will allow people to become ecological citizens rather than environmental injustice victims.

Michael is another East Washington resident for whom "home" also plays an important role in his vision of ecological citizenship. An African-American, middle-class man in his early thirties, Michael is an attorney and accountant in neighboring Virginia and lives in the historic district of Anacostia, where he is active in civic life. A relative newcomer to the community, he is one of a growing influx of young, professional African Americans attracted to the community's low housing costs and potential for redevelopment. Michael was drawn in particular by the affordability and aesthetic appeal of the Victorian houses in the Historic Anacostia neighborhood.

Since moving to Anacostia, Michael has helped found two community-based organizations. Influential in bringing grant funding into the community, these organizations encapsulate features of Michael's understanding of ecological citizenship: homeownership, neighborhood improvement, and being a good neighbor. Participating in and partaking of "the common wealth" for Michael hinge on being a good neighbor and working for neighborhood improvement, both of which he sees as closely tied to homeownership: "Any time a community has homeowners, it's always gonna improve. Right now I think it's like 30% homeownership, so there's definitely room for improvement. You want people to come in who are gonna care about the property, fix up their homes, and become good neighbors."[6] Increasing homeownership is clearly an important component of Michael's vision of cultivating "common wealth," and his understandings of neighborhood improvement and being a good neighbor tend to be grounded in aesthetic and economic values. An improved neighborhood would have less crime, less trash on the streets, fewer abandoned homes, and fewer kids hanging out on street corners; likewise, being a good neighbor involves working to make those changes happen. When asked whether these visions of neighborhood improvement would be shared by longer-term residents of the community, Michael is optimistic: "How we verbalize it might be different," he says, "but I think we all want the conveniences that most people are used to in other neighborhoods."

The large population of low-income residents in East Washington does not figure prominently into Michael's understanding of home and neighborliness, and he acknowledges that changes that seem like improvements to affluent residents might not be welcomed by their low-income neighbors. "If you're poor, it's like, okay, am I gonna be able to stay when all this development comes? [. . .] so it is scary for some people." In spite of his sympathy, however, he concedes that they are right to be concerned, since poorer residents are really not part of the aesthetic and economic equation of the community that he and many other newer residents are working to create:

> You don't need to tear it down to put the same people back in, it's not gonna work. [. . .] And for us to sit there and tell our poor residents that it's gonna be wonderful on replacement is a lie, and it's a injustice. So it's up to the government to help and it's up to them to take advantage of it.

Michael's vision of ecological citizenship, like Sharon's, is rooted in the idea of home, but how the two of them understand "home" is quite different. While both desire aesthetic improvement and greater amenities, Sharon is more troubled by the negative consequences of such changes for marginalized residents. Her vision of home and of "common wealth" in the East Washington community, whether ultimately realistic or not, focuses on ensuring that even the most impoverished residents can reap new developments' benefits. Michael, in spite of his acknowledgment of entrenched poverty and disinvestment, does not see the most destitute residents as redeemable neighbors or ecological citizens. Although both Sharon and Michael highlight cleanliness as important, Sharon speaks of it in terms of residents' efforts to cultivate environmental cleanliness, while Michael speaks of it in terms of their disregard for it. He says the following about residents' attitudes toward neighborhood cleanliness: "throwin' trash on the street, in your own neighborhood, I mean, that's how you feel about your community, like it's dirty, and you just make it dirtier. [. . .] Would you walk into Georgetown and throw a chicken bone on the street? No. But it's okay to do it in Anacostia?" While it's clear that Michael recognizes the despair evident in such attitudes and behaviors, his interest lies more in addressing the neighborhood's aesthetic improvement than in attacking poverty and despair's root causes.

While it would be unfair to reduce Sharon's perspective to an exclusive focus on social justice and Michael's to an exclusive focus on aesthetics, it is nonetheless clear that Sharon's vision of home and of the local common wealth is more expansive, while Michael's is more focused on his immediate Anacostia neighborhood. Both wield the conceptual tool of "home" in active and creative ways but toward differing visions of the ideal. Examining these individuals' perspectives provides ample evidence of the ideological tensions at play in the impending redevelopment of the east of the Anacostia community.

I turn now to exploring how "environment" is articulated by two Letcher County residents, particularly in terms of how it relates to recent changes in the community's landscape and surrounding environment. Keith is a middle-aged, white, working-class man who has spent most of his life in Letcher County. He is an underground coal miner and mine electrician by trade but is better known as one of the most independent-minded county judge-executives eastern Kentucky has ever known.[7] While in office, Keith, who is a social conservative and lifelong Republican, fought for such traditionally left-wing causes as a minimum wage increase and a smoking ban in restaurants. He also refused to be financially subservient to the coal industry and worked to curb the industry's negative environmental impacts on the county, particularly with regard to mountaintop removal.[8]

The notion of ecological citizenship is of profound significance for Keith, since it comprises the two concepts that best summarize his understanding of what it means to be a responsible adult. The first is the concept of active citizenship—being involved in and monitoring one's governing bodies, holding elected officials accountable, and being willing to do the work involved in exercising one's rights and responsibilities. He argues that it is not only commendable for people to participate actively in civic life but in fact necessary. He explains that he was once told by his mine supervisor to be less vocal in raising concerns at staff meetings because in speaking out he was agitating the other employees; his frank retort was that "there's too many people died for my right to free speech for me to slap them in the face by not exercisin' it!"[9] In the following excerpt, Keith reiterates active citizenship as a defining feature of ecological citizenship and touches on the other defining feature—environmentalism: "If you don't exercise your rights [. . .] where is that leadin' to? If you don't demand good government, or good environmentalism [. . .] if you're not willin' to stand up, then you're just as much at fault as the person that's doin' it [i.e. practicing incompetent governance or causing ecological damage]."

Over the years, Keith has seen his fair share of environmental degradation and neglect. Familiarity with these ills and with the pattern of causation that leads to them has convinced him that to turn a blind eye is shortsighted and selfish. Ignoring these ills violates his understanding of common sense, honesty, and fairness. In discussing the fact that Letcher County contains the headwaters of several waterways, for example, Keith argues that it is common sense that damage incurred in one place does not remain isolated in that place, though we may like to think it does:

> I think that if we had these dyes that would illustrate to people what was really happenin', and when you damage the environment over here, you drink it over here, and when this drinkin' water turned a different color, then they had to go over there and fix whatever was turnin' it green, but as long as their water's clear, then there's not a problem.

Ignoring environmental ills violates Keith's understanding of honesty and fairness because it denies what he sees as an obvious reality concerning our role in degrading the environment and because it prioritizes our own short-term needs above the long-term needs of others and of future generations.

While he reserves his harshest criticism for the coal industry and its infliction of massive environmental damage on Appalachia, he does not exempt the American public from its part in enabling that damage:

> Us as hypocrites demand cheap energy, and as a result of that we allow terrible acts against nature and against the environment and justify it to ourselves because our electric bill is cheap. [. . .] Because if we're not willing to [. . .] pay our fair share instead of passing it to our children and our grandchildren, we're hypocrites.

Citizenship and environmentalism for Keith are in many ways one and the same, as they both involve the willingness to stand up and speak the truth, to participate actively in public life with fairness and unselfishness, and to hold those in power accountable. The environment, as he sees it, is the arena in which our well-being as people and citizens is negotiated and maintained, our common wealth articulated and strengthened. It follows that "wielding" common wealth, for Keith, entails engaging in that arena as an active citizen.

Judy is a middle-aged, white, middle-class resident of Letcher County, and like Keith, she has strong opinions about the problems facing her community. As a retired teacher, community quilter, and mother and grandmother, Judy is active in the life of her family and community, and she feels that maintaining strong bonds of family and community commitment serves as the centerpiece of ecological citizenship: "I think the best part of living here is just that you know everybody and everybody knows you, and most people are very kind and helpful and caring. [. . .] We just help each other, we do for each other and for our neighbors, and that's what I like most about eastern Kentucky."[10] She agrees with Keith that the environment is the arena in which our well-being as people and citizens is negotiated.

Judy is deeply troubled by the recent proliferation of drug activity and addiction in eastern Kentucky and sees this as a component of the community's environment that is sorely in need of improvement. She also feels some sense of guilt for exposing her children to these elements:

> What I came back to [after living in a nearby metropolis] that I had not expected was the drug problem [. . .] and that is the most disturbing aspect of life here. [. . .] They both [her children] had problems because of the kind of environment that they grew up in, and I did everything I could to guide them in the right way, but still they chose some of the wrong friends.

Judy also views the depressed local economy as a negative feature of the Letcher County environment and wishes there were more job options outside the coal industry. She does not feel that the coal industry's political and environmental practices play a part in the state of the local economy, however, and in fact she views the industry as one of the few remaining sources of county vitality. "Coal mining means everything to this area, in my opinion, for the people that are here to sustain the lifestyle that they have right now."

Like Keith, Judy views the coal industry's role in the community's environment as significant, but she is hesitant to discuss this impact in negative terms, despite being aware of the ecological damage caused by mountaintop removal. She and Keith begin from shared beliefs in active participation in community life and responsibility to one's family, but those beliefs find divergent endpoints. Keith argues that active participation and responsibility entail facing head-on the so-called externalities of ecological and other kinds of damage, while Judy argues that being a responsible adult entails some measure of tolerance for these externalities if it means that one's family and community can sustain their livelihood, at least in the immediate future:

> I know when I was 25 or 30 years old I was totally against mountaintop removal, I thought it was horrible what it was doing to the area. [. . .] But now that I'm older and my family are all involved in it [. . .] as an adult, and as a mother of someone who works in a mine [. . .] and caring about my state, I think it's a necessity.

For Judy, a healthy environment for families and communities can be maintained in the face of ecological and political ills, while for Keith this goes against the very definition of the environment. Part of this divergence stems from the fact that Judy defines environmental well-being more narrowly. In her view, individuals and communities can have a healthy environment, in an immediate sense, in spite of the fact that tremendous ecological and cultural destruction may be occurring nearby. Citizenship, for her, is negotiated on individualized and immediate terms, and a flourishing community is more a collection of discrete, if connected, individuals than an organic entity of its own. For Keith, citizenship and belonging are collective goods that cannot flourish when the health and well-being of any of their constituent parts are threatened.

In wielding the conceptual tool of the environment in Letcher County, Keith and Judy construct divergent images of an ideal environment, images grounded in contrasting understandings of "common wealth." Just as with the comparison between Sharon's and Michael's views on home, examining Keith's and Judy's views on the environment offers evidence of the ideological tensions faced by residents of Letcher County as they work to protect their human and physical environment from the upheavals inflicted by extractive industry.

CONCLUSIONS

"How will this affect our common wealth?" This is the question that Berry urges all communities facing or considering major structural changes to ask of themselves. In my ethnographic analysis of residents' perspectives in Washington, DC, and eastern Kentucky, I have attempted to illuminate some of the myriad responses of local citizens to that question. "Home," "environment," and "ecological citizenship" all serve as important touchstones in these responses, and in weaving these concepts in and out of their discussions, residents inevitably compose rich, complex narratives of both their current "common wealth" and their imagined common futures. Some of those narratives, visions, and imaginings are more communally "common" than others, and some have been more fully enacted into concrete social practice than others. All hinge, however, on a commitment to exploring and nurturing the literal and metaphorical spaces that we all hold in common as ecological citizens. And in this sense, Cresswell's "conditions of possibility for creative social practice" are alive and full of promise (Cresswell 39), pointing us toward imagining and wielding into being a shared future of true "common wealth."

NOTES

1. The names traditionally favored by residents include "East Washington" and "East of the River," while a cadre of newer residents has recently argued that "rebranding" the community with the moniker "River East" could help to revitalize its local image. Unsurprisingly, debates have ignited over who in the community has the right to decide what to call it and, more fundamentally, whose claims to ownership of the community are most compelling. This issue is significant in its own right and a rich arena of discourse surrounding ideas of local citizenship.
2. For an overview of the DC government's long-range plans for the east of the Anacostia community, particularly along the banks of the river, see the District Department of Transportation's website on the Anacostia Waterfront Initiative: http://www.ddot.dc.gov/awi.

3. Pseudonyms have been used for all of the individuals featured in this chapter. For political reasons, each of my interviewees prefers to remain anonymous.
4. Name withheld. Personal interview, October 27, 2009. All subsequent quotes in this section were recorded in my interview with "Sharon."
5. Gentrification in Washington, DC, neighborhoods has been a growing area of interest in recent years, both in scholarly work and in the DC metropolitan area's local press. For a thoughtful examination of gentrification and displacement in one DC neighborhood, see Gabriella Gahlia Modan, *Turf Wars: Discourse, Diversity, and the Politics of Place.* (Malden, MA: Blackwell, 2007. Print.)
6. Name withheld. Personal interview, September 18, 2009. All subsequent quotes in this section were recorded in my interview with "Michael."
7. The county judge-executive position is the highest administrative position in the Kentucky county system and, in small, rural counties such as Letcher, functions much like the mayoral position.
8. Keith was an extremely rare, if not singular, example of a successfully elected county judge-executive in eastern Kentucky who refused all campaign contributions from the coal industry.
9. Name withheld. Personal interview, July 20, 2009. All subsequent quotes in this section were recorded in my interview with "Keith."
10. Name withheld. Personal interview, July 29, 2009. All subsequent quotes in this section were recorded in my interview with "Judy."

14 Climate Justice Now!

Imagining Grassroots Ecocosmopolitanism

Giovanna Di Chiro

At the conclusion of the 16th Conference of the Parties of the UN Framework Convention on Climate Change held at the seaside resort town of Cancún, Mexico, La Vía Campesina, one of the largest and most internationally diverse non-governmental organizations (NGOs) in attendance, declared:

> We must go beyond the anthropocentric model. We must rebuild the *cosmovision* of our peoples, based on a holistic view of the relationship between the cosmos, Mother Earth, the air, the water and all living beings. Human beings do not own nature, but rather form part of all that lives. . . . [We must] alert the social movements of the world about what is happening on the planet to defend life and Mother Earth, because we are defining the model for future generations. . . . We call on humanity to act immediately to rebuild the life of all of nature, applying the concept of "life in balance." The small farmers, peasants, and indigenous agriculturalists from the four corners of the Earth hold in their hands *thousands of solutions to climate change*. . . . [We support] the people's solutions to defend life and Mother Earth. (La Vía Campesina, italics added) (2010)

Representing millions of small- and medium-scale farmers from 150 local organizations in 70 countries, La Vía Campesina ("the peasant's/small farmer's way of life") challenged what they considered to be the conference's unacceptable agenda for mitigating global warming and instead initiated a campaign calling for "1,000 Cancún for Climate Justice." Rejecting the *mono*-vision behind the "false and dangerous global solutions" to climate change like the Clean Development Mechanism (CDM), the Reduction of Emissions for Deforestation and Forest Degradation (REDD+) initiative, and geo-engineering, the organizers called for sustainable forms of agriculture and economic development to restore a "life in balance" and to protect future generations.[1] Rather than investing in these false solutions, the members of La Vía Campesina exhorted the world's leaders attending the conference to learn from the millions of peasant and small-scale farmers and indigenous communities throughout the world whose traditional lifeways and practices of sustainability in agriculture, forestry, and energy production have for years helped to "cool down the earth" (Conant, "Peasant Farming").

The many post-mortems produced by climate justice advocates that have emerged since Cancún (or, "Can't-Cún," as some called it) have lamented the dearth of critical analyses on the relative merits of different "sustainable solutions" to curb global warming or on what would be the most effective scale on which to take action.[2] Discussions about global climate change inevitably revolve around the question of scale, and as was the case at the UN Climate Conference and in many other environmental science, economics, and policy arenas, most conventional approaches to the climate problem tend to concentrate on *global*-scale analyses, on macro-level frameworks of organized power. Drawing on the scholarship and activism of many environmental justice advocates, as well as my own experience in the movement, in this chapter, I explore the issue of scale—from "household to planet"—invoked in diverse efforts to tackle climate change and reflect on which worlds and futures are imagined, produced, and reproduced at which scales of action.[3]

BRINGING CLIMATE CHANGE HOME

Addressing the question of scale in environmental problem solving has always been at the core of analytical frameworks committed to environmental justice. For scholars and activists in the environmental justice movement, the environment is not considered "out there" as an abstracted, ideal, or intangible "elsewhere," but instead is mundane, "in your backyard," and corporeal; the environment is "where we live, work, play, and go to school" (Novotny, 2000; Di Chiro 1996). For residents of environmental justice communities around the world whose neighborhoods, villages, and tribal homelands have become sites of ecological degradation, the local, bodily effects of broad-scale environmental problems—like global warming—strike home in devastating ways.[4] Analyses of structural inequalities and the environment explain how the homes and neighborhoods of environmental justice communities are overburdened with environmental hazards that put their children and families at risk, and, at the same time, their homes and neighborhoods are underresourced with environmental amenities that wealthier and whiter communities take for granted, such as clean, green spaces; safe parks and playgrounds; and access to grocery stores that supply fresh, healthy foods. Drawing on the logic that "where we live, work, play, and go to school" brings the environment home, so to speak, environmental justice advocate Majora Carter argues for a multiscalar perspective to guide policies and actions on global climate change, what she refers to as "hometown security" (Carter, *TED Talks*).

In fact, mainstream environmental discourse urges us to think of the planet earth as our *home*—the place that nurtures us, feeds us, and provides us with all we need to survive and flourish. But, many environmentalists wonder whether humans have the conceptual capacity to think in such a multiscalar fashion. Are our environmental imaginations robust or capacious enough to grasp an understanding of the "close to home" issues affecting daily life (i.e., the "local scale" comprising our neighborhoods, families, children) while conceiving of the "global scale" concerns of the earth and its systems and processes (including big issues like global warming and climate change, problems that can seem overly abstract, distant, and perhaps too big to comprehend)? Thinking of the planet earth as our *home*, or embracing a "sense of planet" as literary scholar Ursula Heise has called it, in fact does mean thinking in different geographic and imaginary scales at one and the same time. In recent years, many environmental scholars and activists have argued that we need to develop such a scale-crossing environmental consciousness in order to reduce or prevent global catastrophes like climate change (e.g., Shiva, McKibben).

Earlier environmental theorists have made similar arguments. In 1972, at the first UN Conference on the Human Environment and in subsequent writings, René Dubos made the point that ecological consciousness should "begin at home."[5] Dubos argued that human consciousness and imaginaries must encompass the earth's ecological wholeness, yet our daily actions to protect the earth, to "save the planet" and its inhabitants, should be focused closer to home on the health and well-being of our everyday environments. To express this complex concept, Dubos coined the now legendary environmentalist's maxim: "Think Globally, Act Locally," which in the 1970s and 1980s became a favorite bumper sticker and rallying cry for the environmental movement (Seager).

Today, a new expression of this early environmental thinking is evolving, a new ecological consciousness that is occurring around the globe through the visionary and practical work undertaken by activists and communities that are part of a global environmental movement dedicated to advancing climate justice. This growth and flourishing of a new environmental imagination committed to concrete action to curb global warming is grounded in the proliferation of "people's solutions" to a planetary environmental crisis like climate change; people are organizing in their own neighborhoods, in their local environments, and on their native soil, but they are also thinking about and creating bridges with other communities, other environments, and groups of people organizing for environmental and climate justice in their own "hometowns" from many countries around the world. I think about this emergent movement for planetary interconnectedness bringing together struggles for everyday life at *home* with global ecological change on *earth* as the development of what I call "grassroots ecological cosmopolitanism."

My use of the term "grassroots ecocosmopolitanism" is somewhat of a recuperative project—that is, like many other critics who analyze global processes and systems, I aim to recuperate the more classic model of "cosmopolitanism," the ideal concept that we are all members of a human *cosmopolitan* community, fundamentally united as *world citizens* through a shared morality based on relationships of mutual respect and assumptions of goodwill despite differences of culture, ethnicity, nationality, religion, or political perspective. In response to the current era of global capitalism and the negative externalities of globalization, which many argue are accelerating the deterioration of our earth's ecological systems, increasing poverty rates around the world, and leading to the escalation of war and international conflict, I believe that a revitalization of this archetypal cosmopolitanism is urgently needed. Furthermore, the use of the term "cosmopolitanism" is recuperative because I, like others, am interested in challenging its more recent association with the globe-trotting lifestyles of the rich and powerful so blatantly on display at the Moon Palace Golf and Spa Resort, the luxurious setting of the UN Climate meetings in Cancún. In my use of the term, I am interested in joining together the world citizen and global interdependence perspectives of the old cosmopolitanism with a fresh version that envisions and connects with a commitment to the sustainability (and survivability) of local hometowns and local environments.

SCALE-CROSSING, SUSTAINABILITY, AND CLIMATE JUSTICE

I am interested in the recent popular attention to the problems of global warming and climate change in particular because I believe that these large-scale environmental problems require an environmental perspective and imagination that have the capacity to cross scales. One could presume we might see evidence of multiscalar, local/global thinking (or grassroots ecocosmopolitanism) engaging with a problem that is arguably the greatest threat to life on earth as we know it occurring at the various international conferences on climate change, such as, for example, the UN Climate Conference in Cancún. But, according to the members of La Vía Campesina and other climate justice organizations from around the world, the macroscale associated with elite UN Climate Conference attendees does not embrace a *cosmo*vision, a locally invested, grassroots ecological cosmopolitanism that imagines the creative processes of "acting globally"—not just thinking or deliberating globally at plush, international resorts—but acting globally through *en*-acting thousands of local scale "sustainable" solutions to protect the planet and *Madre Tierra*.

The recent upsurge of interest in the idea of sustainability in the U.S. and many other countries around the world was, I believe, *supposed* to connect the two scales, that is, it was supposed to illuminate the global consequences of local policies and the local impacts of global systems. "Living sustainably" meant focusing on eating locally produced foods or conserving energy at home by using energy-efficient light bulbs and driving a hybrid car. These local actions would, in theory, encourage people to *think globally*, to think about where their food comes from or how their electricity is generated, and these seemingly personal decisions would encourage greater awareness of the broader social and environmental impacts of our everyday lifestyles. But, many environmental justice and climate justice activists have raised the question about whether sustainability as we know it is genuinely concerned about protecting and sustaining the environments, bodies, and lives of people living in poor communities and poor nations.

Many environmental and climate justice activists argue that the mainstream focus on "sustainability" too easily slips into greenwashing and tends to contain a limited agenda: a consumerist, carbon footprint-reducing, green lifestyles agenda that all too often turns a blind eye to the environmental injustices and health disparities facing low-income and poor communities around the world.[6] The focus on policies to protect the climate in the name of sustainability without a critical intersectional analysis that spotlights the structural inequalities of gender, race, and class tends to create blind spots—blind spots such as, for example, the fact that most consumers don't know or think about what happens to one's neatly sorted recyclables—household products, laptops, cell phones—after they are picked up from the front yard or from the recycling center. Optimistically harboring the perception that these discarded products seamlessly become part of an efficient, closed-loop resource processing cycle, few people know about or ask what happens to the health of the workers who dismantle and process these electronics "recyclables." As environmental justice scholars have pointed out, the dismantling of recycled electronics products is potentially hazardous work that may expose workers to toxic materials, including heavy metals, adhesives, and lubricants. In many cases, recycling dismantlers are poor women and children from countries in the global South who are not protected by worker health and safety laws nor supplied with protective equipment (Pellow; Clapp). Recycling is one of the cornerstones of sustainability, yet, despite its good intentions, it relies on keeping out of sight and out of mind the harm being done to the bodies of poor women's and children's bodies and the poisoning of their local environments.

Another way the discourse of global sustainability remains oblivious to the local impacts on bodies marked by racial, gendered, and class disparities is not about the *invisibility* of the bodies of women and children in the global South but instead about their *excess*. For example, a recent revival of the perspective that "overpopulation" is the major threat to the planet and the cause of global warming has led to increasing anti-immigrant policies supported by a number of international environmental organizations, and it has created the fear that the planet will soon be inundated by an oversupply of poor, carbon-emitting people from the developing world (Hartmann and Barajas-Roman, "The Population Bomb is Back"; Fisher and

Newman, "People, Population, and Climate Change"). In response to this alarmist rhetoric, some international groups, including the UK-based organization Population Matters, have begun to promote carbon offset options that are different from the more familiar offset programs typically available to environmentally conscientious air travelers (i.e., programs that fund green energy projects or afforestation and reforestation efforts in developing nations such as Bangladesh or Colombia). Instead, Population Matters offers carbon offset options to fund "family planning" programs in countries in Africa and Asia.[7] By purchasing population offsets or "PopOffsets" to prevent poor women from overreproducing in the name of the progressive liberal notion of "family planning," the elite "ecocosmopolitan" can feel pleased about mitigating climate change and promoting global sustainability while flying off on holiday to, say, Cancún.

Focusing on population growth as the major cause of climate change places the blame on the world's poorest people, particularly women, who are the least responsible for global warming, and it conveniently shifts the blame away from the inequitable and ecologically destructive consumption and production patterns of the rich countries (Angus and Butler, "Panic Over 7 Billion"). This focus on the global threats of poor women's fertility has also justified the design and implementation of aggressive and coercive population control mechanisms and contraceptive technologies that restrict women's reproductive rights and endanger their health. For example, in the aftermath of the social and environmental devastation wreaked by Hurricane Katrina in 2005, Louisiana State Representative John LaBruzzo recommended a sterilization program for low-income African-American women on welfare since they and their children made up the majority of people who were stranded and homeless in New Orleans after the levees broke and the city was flooded.[8] As the impending problems of catastrophic climate change and economic crises are amplified in the popular media, this resurgence of sexist, racist, anti-immigrant, and eugenics explanations and solutions functions to displace the responsibility for ecological degradation and climate change onto the bodies of women of color and poor women around the world. In the name of creating global "sustainable solutions" to the climate change problem, this putative global approach represents the darker side of "planetary thinking"; it represents the danger of the flight from the local and the lure of embracing a macroscale, mono-vision focus on "the global" or "the planetary" as the definitive environmental imagination for the current era of environmental crisis.

The lack of attention to the bodily scale of experiences of environmental degradation and climate change, the *everyday* material effects of breathing toxic air, drinking polluted water, being stranded, or becoming a climate refugee as a result of social and economic disinvestments in your city's storm management systems and transportation infrastructure—this invisibility of the bodies of people from environmental justice communities in part reflects an inattention to the local-scale devastation wrought by a globally framed problem and in part reflects the structural injustices that undergird the popular notions of sustainability. Many environmental justice activists and scholars adopt a more relational and *embodied* approach to environmental politics and pay attention to the *everyday,* material experiences of global environmental problems like climate change (Harcourt and Escobar; Alaimo). A focus on the interlocking scales of the crisis of climate change creates an intersectional framework for global environmental cooperation that some have referred to as "just sustainability" (Agyeman, Bullard, and Evans; Barnett and Penn). The envisioning of a more *just* sustainability that accounts for the bodily scale of the problem of climate change can benefit from decades of feminist research and insights about bodies and reproduction. Sustainability *is* in fact about reproduction, although it is rarely framed as such. Elsewhere I have argued for a critical dialogue between the proponents of sustainability and activists who support reproductive justice. In particular, I've examined the Marxist-feminist concept of "social reproduction" in terms of imagining a more just sustainability (Di Chiro, "Living Environmentalisms").

In brief, feminist critics define social reproduction as the social and material conditions necessary for reproducing viable bodies (which includes biological reproduction) and for reproducing or *sustaining* everyday life (which includes access to healthy food, clean air, and clean water). The analysis of social reproduction enables deeper understandings of the underlying structures of power and race, gender, and class inequalities that determine what happens to different bodies: who lives and who dies, who is healthy and who is sick, whose environment is polluted and whose is clean, and who is responsible for global warming and who suffers most from its consequences (Brennan; Katz, "Bad Elements").

"LOOKING BOTH WAYS": ASIAN COMMUNITIES FOR REPRODUCTIVE JUSTICE

One example of an organization that develops such an intersectional ecopolitics by joining together issues of reproductive health and environmental justice is Asian Communities for Reproductive Justice (ACRJ), based in Oakland, California.[9] Activists in the organization argue for a critical analytical framework based on "looking both ways" through the dual lenses of environmental sustainability and reproductive justice in order to create innovative strategies and social policies that, at the same time, mitigate climate change and address the reproductive rights, environmental health, and social reproduction needs of, in their case, the predominantly low-income Asian and Pacific Island residents of the city of Oakland.

One way the organization "looks both ways," for example, is to examine the multiple risks to both women's reproductive health and the stability of the climate that are associated with mid-level industries such as microelectronics manufacturing and nail salons. These industries, which employ

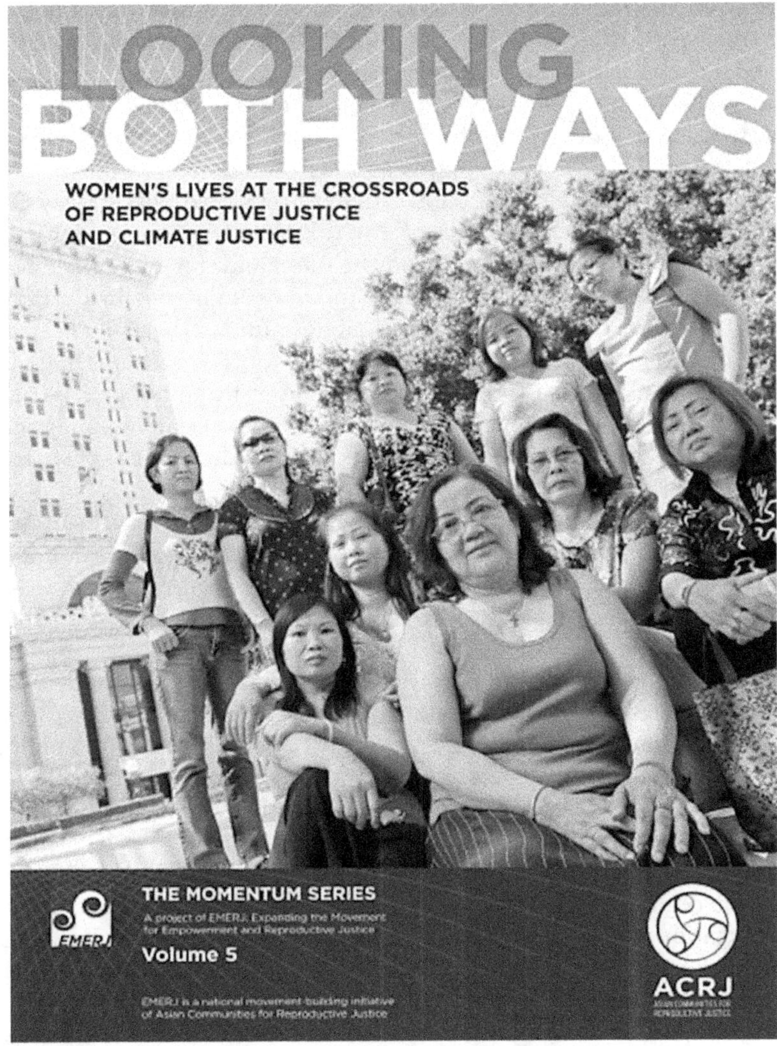

Figure 14.1 *Looking Both Ways* cover image. Credit: Forward Together.

large numbers of Asian American and Asian Immigrant women, are not widely identified as the main targets for climate change mitigation as are, for example, coal, oil and gas production, commercial and residential heating, or the transportation sector. But, in fact, they do produce significant greenhouse gas emissions in their production processes and in the chemical feedstocks used in their products.[10] At the same time, both the microelectronics industry and nail salons represent workplaces that are known to put the health of women workers at risk (Smith et al.; Ngai).

The women leaders of ACRJ have documented how women working in the microelectronics and nail salon industries are exposed regularly to industrial chemicals such as perfluorocompounds (PFCs) and the so-called "toxic trio"—dibutyl phthalates, toluene, and formaldehyde—an amalgam of hazardous compounds all of which are classified by the EPA as potent carcinogens and reproductive toxins and also recognized as potent greenhouse gases contributing to global warming.[11] By "looking both ways," the organization has built coalitions of environmental, women's rights, and labor organizations that advocate, on the one hand, for workplace health and safety in the electronics and semiconductor industries in California, and, on the other hand, for climate change solutions that advance social justice. In recent years, these "looking both ways" coalitions have succeeded in convincing the California State legislature to adopt regulations and phase out several harmful chemicals used in microchip manufacturing that contribute to global warming and pose reproductive health risks for women workers.[12]

Similarly, ACRJ has developed advocacy networks with Asian and Asian-immigrant women working in the growing and lucrative nail salon industry, 80% of which are owned and staffed by Vietnamese women (Kang 23). As documented by ACRJ activists and their scientific partners, the largely unregulated chemicals and products used in nail salons, including solvents, hardeners, fragrances, polishes, and drying agents, are associated with higher rates of multiple myeloma, stomach cancer, liver disease, and asthma in salon workers. Likewise, the array of volatile organic compounds (VOCs) and the metals processing techniques used to manufacture these products emit high levels of greenhouse gases. In 2005, the organization helped to start a nail salon worker's advocacy group known as Participatory Research, Organizing, and Leadership for Safety and Health (POLISH), which has organized throughout the city and the state to provide multilingual educational materials promoting healthier nail salons, and they have lobbied for a Safer Alternatives Bill in California to phase out and replace the chemicals and products used in nail salons that endanger workers and consumers, pollute the environment, and contribute to global warming.[13]

NUESTRAS RAÍCES: TAKING ACTION ON FOOD SOVEREIGNTY, GREEN ENERGY, AND ENVIRONMENTAL JUSTICE

A second example of an intersectional, grassroots ecocosmopolitanism producing "just sustainability" is the work of Nuestras Raíces, a community organization that focuses on urban agriculture, food justice and healthy foods policy, and environmental justice and serves the low-income Puerto Rican/Latino residents of Holyoke, Massachusetts.[14] The leaders of Nuestras Raíces (Our Roots) recognize the multiple risks to the community's capacity to sustain itself: the high rates of diabetes and obesity and the lack of access to healthy, fresh foods in the downtown neighborhoods and inner-city schools; the social and economic disinvestment in urban infrastructure resulting in limited access to safe parks and green spaces for children to play; and the legacy of environmental racism that has left a blighted urban landscape strewn with polluting factories and scores of contaminated brownfields, all of which contribute to the city's poor air quality and disproportionately high asthma rates while providing few jobs or economic security.

To address these diverse and interlocking problems, Nuestras Raíces's organizers work with local residents and partners to create a local foods infrastructure in the city through a network of community gardens and inner-city farmers' markets. This urban foods infrastructure provides the low-income Puerto Rican communities in Holyoke with access to fresh, organic produce, to Puerto Rican specialty foods, including ajices dulces chili peppers, herbs, and vegetables used in Caribbean cooking that are not available in local supermarkets, and to sustainable economic opportunities through culturally based food microenterprises and business start-ups including Mi Plaza (a Puerto Rican Café), La Lechonera (traditional Puerto Rican barbeque), and a newly forming, women's-run food cooperative that will stock locally produced foods that can be purchased with federal Women, Infant, and Children's (WIC) Supplemental Nutrition Program vouchers.

Figure 14.2 Nuestras Raices greenhouse. Credit: Giovanna Di Chiro.

Figure 14.3 Nuestras Raices main office. Credit: Giovanna Di Chiro.

Figure 14.4 Aijces dulces for sale at farmers' market. Credit: Giovanna Di Chiro.

The leaders of Nuestras Raíces have also adopted an intersectional or "looking both ways" approach to their community organizing by linking the expansion of community gardens and urban farms to an environmental justice and climate justice framework. Nuestras Raíces organizers have built coalitions with a wide range of environmental organizations promoting locally produced food because, they argue, local agriculture reduces the greenhouse gas emissions associated with large-scale industrial agriculture (it helps "cool the planet"), eliminates the use of harmful chemical pesticides and hormones used in factory farms, and improves the city's air quality and environmental health by increasing urban green space and safe places for children to get exercise and play outdoors (Gottlieb and Joshi).

Connecting the struggles for community health, sustainable economic development, and climate change mitigation, in 2010, Nuestras Raíces launched a new, locally owned energy services company called Energía. Energía provides energy efficiency upgrades and retrofits including weatherization, insulation, and solar hot water system installation for homeowners, multifamily housing projects, and commercial buildings in the city. By improving the energy efficiency of the aging nineteenth-century building stock in industrial cities such as Holyoke, Nuestras Raíces, which is the non-profit majority owner of this new for-profit, 24% worker-owned company, is creating economic opportunities and career-path green jobs for local youth *and* reducing the greenhouse gases associated with fossil fuel energy use in residential and commercial buildings.[15]

This concrete, solutions-based approach to climate change mitigation has energized local Puerto Rican youth, who have historically been unconvinced by the apocalyptic discourse on global warming favored by much of the environmental movement or the elite concept of sustainability circulated throughout the mainstream media. With the introduction of a concrete, proactive climate justice framework, many young people now say that they "see themselves in the picture."[16] In October 2010, a group of youth organizers—Los Protectores de la Tierra—led an enthusiastic, bilingual community event celebrating the "global day of action" organized by Bill McKibben's 350.org, the international web-based movement to encourage communities to make changes in their everyday lives to reduce their carbon footprint and to help lower global atmospheric CO_2 levels to below 350 ppm, widely considered by climate scientists to be the safe level of the gas in the atmosphere. The youth group's program—"350 Actions for Holyoke"—embraced a highly abstract, chemical representation of the global environmental crisis to promote their commitment to home-grown activism in support of local environmental sustainability.

Similarly, in April 2010, at the media launch of the company Energía, 19-year old Yamil Brito, one of Nuestras Raíces's green jobs trainees who had been recently hired as a junior energy technician by the company, voiced his

Figure 14.5 Energía grease-powered trucks. Credit: Giovanna Di Chiro.

particular expression of grassroots ecocosmopolitanism when he proudly announced to a TV reporter, "Energía is good for young people because we can get good jobs, support our community, and protect the earth—I'm part of the green revolution!" While Yamil was most likely unaware of the problems associated with the *first* global green revolution—a U.S.- and World Bank-invented, postwar economic modernization plan that further entrenched and expanded fossil fuel-driven industrial agriculture across the globe—he expressed his pride to be part of a new global movement supporting and celebrating the emergence of "green" communities in small hometowns like his.

These brief sketches describing the work of organizers from Nuestras Raíces and Asian Communities for Reproductive Justice (now, Forward Together) are examples, among many others, of practical, solutions-based approaches to climate change grounded in social justice that use a multiscalar analytical framework bridging the bodily/household scale with the planetary one. Such creative ecological actions and *cosmo*visions embodied in the "1,000 Cancún" emerging around the world represent just a few of the thousands of people's solutions for climate justice and just sustainability.

Figure 14.6 Mark Tajima and Yamil Brito. Credit: Giovanna Di Chiro.

NOTES

1. As defined in the Kyoto Protocol in 1997 and further elaborated in subsequent UNFCCC documents, the Clean Development Mechanism (CDM) specifies the range of "flexible" greenhouse gas mitigation approaches that should be adopted by Annex I (industrialized) countries to meet their carbon emissions reduction commitments with the least impact on their economic growth. Moreover, CDM aims to support "Non Annex I" (developing) countries to move toward cleaner development strategies and achieve sustainable development as they expand their economies. REDD (Reducing Emission from Deforestation and Forest Degradation) is a clean development mechanism whose objective is to support activities that enable reductions in CO_2 emissions that are caused by deforestation and forest degradation. REDD+ refers to programs that strengthen and expand the role of forests as carbon sinks, which are achieved by investing in forest conservation and sustainable forest management practices and expanding the use of forests as carbon stocks. Critics of the CDM and REDD+ (including La Vía Campesina and many other environmental justice groups) argue that these mechanisms designed to curb global warming are skewed in favor of Annex I nations and violate environmental justice principles since the "flexibility" of the CDM essentially allows rich countries to continue polluting as usual while expanding their operations by investing in (and sometimes imposing) cleaner development projects, land use prioritization,

and sometimes engaging in land grabbing practices in poor countries in the developing world. For more detailed analyses, see Posner and Weisbach (2010) and *Carbon Trade Watch* available at http://www.carbontradewatch.org/.

2. For example, see *Climate Connections: Global Justice Ecology Project.* "After Cancún." Accessed on 3 Mar 2011. < Available at http://climatevoices.wordpress.com/2011/02/01/after-cancun-fsm-in-dakar-g8-g20-durban-how-to-build-the-movement-for-climate-justice/>.
3. Earlier versions of sections of this article appeared in Di Chiro, "Acting Globally" (2011).
4. For substantive analyses of the disproportionate impact of climate change on poor communities of color, see Hoerner and Robinson (2008), Park (2009), and Barnett and Loh (2010).
5. For a fuller treatment of this idea, see Dubos and Ward, *Only One Earth* (1972).
6. For a critique of the discourse of sustainability, see Parr, *Hijacking Sustainability* (2009) and *The Sustainability History Project.* Available at http://sustainabilityhistory.org/.
7. *Population Matters*, Carbon Offset Programs. Available at http://populationmatters.org/action/connections/offset-carbon/
8. Women's Health & Justice Initiative and the New Orleans Women's Health Clinic, *New Orleans Indymedia.* "Reproductive Justice Feminist Response to Louisiana State Rep. Sterilization Plan." Available at http://neworleans.indymedia.org/news/2008/09/13113.php. Also see Joni Seager, "Noticing Gender (or not) in Disasters," *Geoforum* 37(1) 2006: 2–3.
9. In early 2012, ACRJ concluded a strategic planning process and decided on a name change due to the recognition of the organization's broadened mission over the years. The new name of the organization is *Forward Together* (see http://forwardtogether.org/). In this chapter, I retain the organization's former name (ACRJ) in the interest of being consistent with the historical framework of the issues I discuss.
10. See the scientific report from the International Panel on Climate Change (IPCC). Solomon et. al. *Climate Change: The Physical Science Basis* (2007).
11. See Campaign for Safe Cosmetics. Available at http://safecosmetics.org/article.php?id=224.
12. Looking Both Ways: Women's Lives at the Crossroads of Reproductive Justice and Climate Justice. Available at http://reproductivejustice.org/assets/docs/ACRJ-MS5-Looking-Both-Ways.pdf.
13. In 2011, the activists and community researchers from POLISH published an extensive guide supporting the reproductive health and environmental justice rights of nail salon workers. See *Keeping Our Families Strong: A Health and Safety Handbook for Nail Salon Workers.* Oakland, CA: ACRJ (2011). Available at http://reproductivejustice.org/assets/docs/ACRJ-Nail-Salon-Health-and-Safety-Handbook-English.pdf.
14. See the organization's website, http://www.nuestras-raices.org. For a more detailed history of the organization, see Kleindienst, "The Urban Gardens of Nuestras Raíces" and Tumber, Small, Gritty, and Green (2012).
15. See the company's website (www.energiaus.com).
16. See Diana Pei Wu, Julie Quiroz-Martinez, and Kristen Zimmerman.*ReGeneration: Youth Organizing and Leadership Development in Environmental Justice.* Oakland, CA: Movement Strategy Center, 2005. <http://www.movementstrategy.org/research.html> and Jade Sasser. "Justice for All? Youth

Environmental Activism and the New Framings of Social Justice." *Differen-Takes*. 72 (2011). <http://popdev.hampshire.edu/sites/popdev/files/uploads/u1149/DT_72_Sasser.pdf>.

15 The Los Angeles Urban Rangers, Trailblazing the Commons

Stephanie LeMenager

Imagine a campfire circle, winsome campers telling stories, and a Ranger, seated outside the circle, strumming her guitar. Then add the following elements to the scene: the pyramidal peaks of the Los Angeles Museum of Contemporary Art (MOCA), the vertical cliff of a Wells Fargo corporate tower, and stories whose ghosts still walk, like the rat that one camper recalls from her recent hike through LA's impoverished Central City East neighborhood, popularly known as Skid Row. In the midst of the camper's rat story, a second Ranger intervenes. He's an African American man, about forty years old. As a long-time resident of Skid Row, he knows how to handle *rattus rattus* (L.), the urban rat. The proximity of LA's Bunker Hill with Skid Row makes the region an urban *ecotone*, a transition area between two biomes where we find overlapping communities of fauna. Bunker Hill is home to public venues like MOCA, the Cathedral of Our Lady of Los Angeles, and the Walt Disney Concert Hall. The populations of Skid Row and Bunker Hill mingle uneasily as gentrification gobbles up Skid Row properties, converting single-room-occupancy hotels (SROs) into galleries. When our Ranger finishes interpreting the rat, another camper asks him if he doesn't get frustrated with ignorant tourists, particularly museum people. He answers confidently, "I'm an educator. I tell people what I know. That's my job." He adds that when he walks through Skid Row at night, he appreciates its quietness.

I offer this scene from a recent public art event called Critical Campout (2011) to introduce the Los Angeles Urban Rangers, an art collective founded in 2004. The LA Urban Rangers designed and performed Critical Campout as the culmination of a summer-long collaboration with MOCA that also featured a stroll into the channelized Los Angeles River and an evening of downtown hikes along freeways, up the "peaks" of the Bonaventure Hotel (via its glass elevators), and into outdoor office plazas which the Rangers poetically renamed "corporate meadows." The River Ramble, and the specter of the LA River that hangs over the Rangers' project, will figure later in this chapter. For the moment, I'll return to the Critical Campout, where visitors hiked the Skid Row/Bunker Hill ecotone, gathered in campfire circles, built a utopian street shelter, and slaked their thirst at a tap water bar that lent a gustatory dimension to environmental injustice. The tap water from wealthier west LA tasted "clean," as one camper put it, in comparison to the waters of less affluent areas. The Rangers' printed *Water Bar Menu* accentuates these differences, for instance describing East LA's water as characterized by "a big nose, a rich vein of sulfate, and exceptional turbidity" ("Water Bar Menu"). As night deepened, a group of campers returned to the tents they'd pitched in the MOCA plaza for an asphalt sleepover. This chapter's opening recollection is drawn from my own experience as a critical camper, and I think it highlights the effort of translation that is central to the LA Urban Rangers' appeal. Critical campers contemplated extreme wealth discrepancies, racialized poverty, and the potentially parasitic relationship of arts communities to the urban poor through temperate, ecological metaphors. The metaphors, and the hospitable Rangers, moderated tense conversations between the museum's public and the Skid Row activists who participated in the hike and the campfire chats.

As an art collective, the LA Urban Rangers can be understood within the traditions of community arts practice, temporary public art, the conversational practice that critic Grant Kester calls "dialogical art" (9–10, 13) and "relational aesthetics," the French curator and critic Nicolas Bourriaud's term for artworks whose goal is "to actually be ways of living and models of action" (13). California has been a hotbed for this kind of engaged art since the 1960s, and currently the LA Urban Rangers share practices and commitments with a robust community of Los Angeles-based groups such as Invisible Five, Fallen Fruit, and Finishing School. All of these collectives investigate what the artist and critic Sarah Kanouse calls "social nature." By "social nature," Kanouse means the socio-ecological relationships that make up modernity as we live and know it, with its injustice, waste, pollution, wit, and beauty ("A Post-Naturalist" 168).[1] Finishing School, for example, presented a lively project called M.O.L.D. (2009), which the group describes as "a hot zone-themed installation and workshop that investigates food in crisis." Audience members were invited to join in a variety of playful experiments, including building their own "amateur bio-indicators" (Finishing School).

The founders of the LA Urban Rangers, whom I interviewed for this chapter, recognize the extremities of Los Angeles as an impetus for the city's strong arts focus on postnatural ecologies. Ranger Sara Daleiden notes that "what LA has given us . . . is *so much room* to ask what urban nature is" (S. Daleiden, personal interview, September 1, 2011). This regional strength also reflects the influence of the Center for Land Use Interpretation (CLUI), which was founded in 1994. The CLUI became a gathering place in LA for people interested in interpreting the built environment and experimenting with presentation strategies drawn from both popular culture traditions like the bus tour and avant-garde practice like the Situationist dérive.[2] The CLUI describes itself as a politically disinterested "educational organization," and its various media—from its flagship on-line archive, *Land Use*

Database, to its guide books, interactive CD-ROMs, and tours—offer deadpan delivery of geographical information that falls out of conventional maps, from nuclear test sites to natural gas infrastructure (The Center for Land Use Interpretation).[3] In roughly the same moment when academic historians like William Cronon and Jenny Price were dismantling the mythos of "wilderness" and "nature," the CLUI's Culver City gallery space nurtured a group of academics, activists, and infrastructure geeks who remade themselves as collaborative artists.

In the case of the LA Urban Rangers, the intellectual movement toward the nature of modernity lives particularly close to home. Jenny Price, author of the paradigm-shifting environmental history *Flight Maps: Adventures with Nature in Modern America* (1999), is one of the group's founders, and another founder, Emily Scott, moved to LA with the intention of following in Price's footsteps after picking up *Flight Maps* in a bookstore in Moab, Utah, where she was working as a National Park Service Ranger. Scott reinvented herself in LA as a different kind of Ranger, inspiring the group's trademark persona. The four founders of the LA Urban Rangers are Scott, Price, Sara Daleiden, and Therese Kelly. Daleiden works primarily as an artist, Kelly is an architect and urban designer, Price a nonfiction writer and historian, and Scott now holds a doctorate in art history, describing herself as a "creative scholar" (E. Scott personal interview, September 8, 2011). When these four women "put on the Ranger hat" and became an arts collective in 2004, they recognized, in Daleiden's words, that they had found a way to "open up how things can get talked about, which can also mean *where* they get talked about" (S. Daleiden, personal interview, September 1, 2011). I'll delineate how I see the group reinventing the idea of "the commons" below. For now, suffice it to say that since 2004 two new Rangers have joined the group and several volunteers have donned the hat to test the possibilities of common ground. Our hike leader at the Critical Campout was a guest Ranger from the wryly named LAPD, or Los Angeles Poverty Department, which is an art collective based in Skid Row.[4]

The story of the LA Urban Rangers inevitably revolves around the Urban Ranger persona, which the group calls "the delivery mechanism" for its explorations of urban ecologies. As noted, Emily Scott first suggested the Ranger as a platform, although all group members have contributed to its development—from seasonal uniforms (hats, badges, and khaki pants or shorts) to an irrepressibly friendly affect. Scott spent years working as a National Park Service Ranger in Alaska and Utah, where in a sense she previewed the Urban Rangers project by pushing the limits of the Park Service program. "I was always interested in heady ideas," she reflects.

> I did a program at Arches National Park that was on Hollywood representations of canyon country and how they framed that landscape. . . . I was taking this theoretically inflected set of questions and translating it into a language and a form that would be engaging for a really broad

Figure 15.1 Los Angeles Urban Rangers, *Malibu Public Beaches* 2007–2010. Core LA Urban Rangers members, from left to right: Therese Kelly, Sara Daleiden, Emily Scott, and Jenny Price. Credit: Tom Queally.

> lay public, which also would include people from across the political spectrum. Lots of Mormons traveling down from Salt Lake, and lots of environmental activists coming to go backpacking, [and] recreationists. As a Ranger, I needed to translate what were historical-conceptual questions into very accessible terms. I did a related program in Glacier Bay National Park in Alaska that looked at a history of visual images of the park and the kinds of technologies that have been used to picture and investigate that landscape, and how they have shaped our understanding of the place: everything from early maps and engravings to contemporary cutting-edge scientific imagery. Not your typical, run-of-the-mill ranger programs. (E. Scott, personal interview, September 8, 2011)

Although the Park Service's claims to objectivity irritate Scott—"part of my larger project is to explode that notion of objectivity," she laughs—she recognizes "Ranger etiquette" as an effective communication tool. The Ranger persona invites trust because of its seemingly apolitical, open stance. "As a civil servant, your job is to speak to a diverse park-going public and let them make their own decisions" (E. Scott, personal interview, September 8, 2011). The Ranger radiates "hospitality," "making people feel at home" in a way that summons a sense of belonging, of *being in public*, for diverse crowds (E. Scott, personal interview, September 8, 2011).[5]

COMMON GROUND

> *common.* c. 1300, "belonging to all, general," from O.Fr. comun "common, general, free, open, public" (9c., Mod.Fr. commun), from L. communis "in common, public, general, not pretentious, shared by all or many," from PIE *ko-moin-i- "held in common," compound adjective formed from *ko- "together" + *moi-n-, suffixed form of base *mei- "change, exchange" (see mutable), hence lit. "shared by all." Second element of the compound also is the source of L. munia "duties, public duties, functions," those related to munia "office." ("common, n." *Online Etymology Dictionary*)[6]

Given the vexed history of "the commons" in U.S. environmental history, the concept has to be reworked to introduce the questions of environmental justice that undergird much of the LA Urban Rangers' relational practice. When the biologist Garrett Hardin published the influential article "The Tragedy of the Commons" in 1968, he aligned enduring environmental concerns (pollution, overconsumption) with a faddish horror of "personal liberty" linked to the social experimentation of the Sixties (1249).[7] With Paul Ehrlich, author of *The Population Bomb* (1968), Hardin promoted the idea that only population control could redeem depleted resource commons such as ocean fisheries and the U.S. national parks. "Injustice is preferable to total ruin," he intoned, referring to the necessity of private property and legal inheritance (Hardin 1249). While Hardin did not advocate the privatization of the national parks, he imagined "allocating" the right to enter them, perhaps through a lottery (Hardin 1245). His misinterpretation of the English commons and the U.S. parks as unregulated communal property complemented an ideological assault on public use that still undergirds the elite bias of mainstream U.S. environmentalism. The national parks were a symbolic pivot for Hardin and for more charismatic environmentalists like Ed Abbey (Abbey 423).[8] In the parks, public place in the U.S. reached an ideal form—and betrayed its impracticalities. When the Indian historian Ramachandra Guha delivered his shot across the bow of the American wilderness aesthetic in the late 1980s, he identified the U.S. national park system with an anti-local, anti-human bias: "environmentalism by the state and the conservation elite" (73). With the origins of some North American national parks tangled in the displacement of indigenous Americans, the parks suggest a complex North American response to the dream of a common place, shared by all.

The layered meanings of the national parks as an American commons inflect the LA Urban Ranger persona, which typically presides over contested ground. The Urban Rangers gravitate toward places where the idea of the public has become untenable. The Malibu beaches are a prime example of a public resource withheld from the commons by super-elites. The LA Urban Rangers' *Malibu Public Beaches* project (2007–2010) wittily reclaimed this space, leading approximately 1,200 people on "safaris" on

Malibu's beaches and equipping them with a how-to map guide of beach access points and public easements. The *Malibu Public Beaches* map guide offers instruction about fake signage ("Visit your local hardware store to make your own 'no parking' sign for as little as $25"), beach fauna ("while the residents are 89% Caucasian, day-use weekend visitors include a more diverse array"), and self-defense against irate security guards ("a copy of the CA Coastal Act is not necessary but can be useful") (*Malibu Public Beaches* guide).[9] Maps have been part of the LA Urban Rangers project since their first appearance at the artist Fritz Haeg's and architect Francois Perrin's *gardenLAb experiment* exhibition back in 2004.[10] Therese Kelly argues that "maps are an important tool for our project, especially because the project is talking about things that are invisible, all these invisible infrastructures that inform the way we behave and use the city, and maps . . . make visible these systems" (T. Kelly, personal interview, December 1, 2011). In the broadest sense, the maps facilitate what Sara Daleiden describes as the group's twin goals of "translation and distribution" (S. Daleiden, personal interview, September 1, 2011). All of the LA Urban Rangers' maps are available on the group's website. The California Coastal Commission has used the Rangers' *Malibu Public Beaches* map in their efforts to open up beach access (J. Price, personal interview, August 5, 2011).[11] Collaboration with state agencies underlines the civic purpose integral to the LA Urban Rangers' art.

Dialogue with state agencies, engineers, hydrologists, politicians, and developers has been a feature of so-called eco-art since the pioneering work of Helen Mayer Harrison and Newton Harrison, California-based artists who began staging ecological interventions in the 1970s. The site-specific, collaborative work of artists like the Harrisons spawned contemporary social service entities like New York City's Center for Urban Pedagogy, a non-profit educational organization that uses "the power of design and art to improve civic engagement" ("What We Do" 2012).[12] Conversation with government and business people, according to historian Peter Selz, is a crucial component of "social sculpture"—meaning action-oriented art that aims to restructure society (Selz 226).[13] The LA Urban Rangers fell into this larger civic effort somewhat accidently, when they were discovered by real park rangers. Jenny Price explains:

> One of the things that has been incredibly gratifying over the course of the group's life is this wonderful relationship we have with the real rangers, who are the Santa Monica Mountains Conservancy. Their operating arm, the Mountains Recreation and Conservation Authority, funded our Malibu safaris. Initially we were a little bit worried that they would think that we were making fun of them. So we didn't alert them or ask them for money before the summer, because I thought they might try to shut us down. Then they came to us and said, "We really like what you're doing on the beaches." Because they do a lot of work

> trying to open up the beaches in Malibu—and [they asked], "Do you want some funding?" So then they funded us. And then we worked with them to actually consult, taking their rangers to the beaches to show them what we were doing, because they want to start doing their own beach programs, and just passing on all that knowledge that we have. And so there's been this wonderful slippage—almost—between the actual, real rangers and the fake Rangers. (J. Price, personal interview, August 5, 2011)

The Santa Monica Conservancy also contributed funds to the Urban Rangers' Los Angeles River Ramble, part of the 2011 MOCA series. Therese Kelly notes how important these partnerships have been in creating lasting infrastructure out of time-bound performances.[14]

Although the Ranger persona is the lynchpin to the group's collaborative practice and the delivery mechanism for its many translating tools—e.g., ecological metaphors, interpretive maps, directed walks—Price acknowledges that Ranger rhetoric doesn't work for everyone: "It's really important to ask, *Who exactly participates in this rhetoric?* It's not for all Americans, necessarily. It's not an accident that the four co-founders are Midwesterners from a certain generation" (J. Price, personal interview, August 5, 2011). When the LA Urban Rangers collaborated with the Los Angeles Poverty Department at the Critical Campout, they repurposed the Urban Ranger as a guardian of precisely the sort of human life (non-white, poor) that sometimes has been disregarded for the sake of the national parks. Hiking through Skid Row also functioned as an antidote to the old-fashioned genre of the slum tour, with hikers forbidden from photography and from the unself-conscious spectatorship typical of nineteenth- and early twentieth-century forays into so-called ghettos like the Five Points area of New York City.[15] With a less edgy style than the Lesbian Rangers, a Canadian collective that points out the unnaturalness of conventional gender performance, the LA Urban Rangers dismantle "nature" to reveal occluded histories.[16] They also tactically use the "nature" idea to make urban environments more accessible and recognizably public. The group's presence in corporate plazas with restrictions on public use, for instance, makes the unlikely statement that such places should be conceived as natural. In an American context, "natural" implies belonging to everyone, even if the inclusivity of "everyone" has been undermined by the elitism of some environmentalists.

Jenny Price elaborates on how the group came to see itself as not only reclaiming public places but also reclaiming the idea of the public.

> The group in general learned the value of the Urban Ranger for emphasizing "public," and creating publics in public spaces, public activities in public spaces. The Ranger is the ultimate guardian of public spaces, because the national parks are where there still is a sense of the public,

> that this is our great national heritage, and it belongs to all of us. That rhetoric is still strong in ways that, I think, it has been weakened so much in the past thirty years in almost every kind of space or geography. So here we are, we're the great guardians of our most treasured public spaces, but we're doing it in Los Angeles. It's actually turned out to be a really powerful character for talking about a public—What's "public"? Why is it not "public"? It's a powerful tool for re-public-izing LA spaces. (J. Price, personal interview, August 5, 2011)

Price adds that part of the "re-public-izing LA" project involves simply placing people in areas deemed off-limits, abandoned, or unsafe. Speaking of the MOCA series, she notes that "both for Bunker Hill, and then particularly the LA River Ramble—these are places that clear out at night. They're desolate at night. These are great, big public spaces (though so much of Bunker Hill isn't truly public, it's supposed to be *for* the public). We populated those spaces" (J. Price, personal interview, August 5, 2011). Price recognizes the dysfunctional public space in LA's downtown as a byproduct of the Community Reinvestment Act, which encourages private development. The more than 50-mile-long Los Angeles River presents an especially dramatic appropriation of an ostensibly public resource. In the 1930s, the Army Corps of Engineers began paving the river's channel and banks, turning LA's primary water source into a glorified "storm drain," in the words of the advocacy group Friends of the Los Angeles River (FoLAR) ("About FoLAR"). Price calls the LA River "one of the greatest disappearing acts in environmental history" (J. Price, personal interview, August 5, 2011).

The Urban Rangers' LA River Ramble originated at MOCA's Geffen Contemporary, located in the Arts District that abuts the channelized river. To enter the LA River through the underpass at the 6th Street bridge, urban ramblers applied to the Rangers for an "LA River Trail Access Permit," which did double duty as a pedagogical tool. "Acceptance of Full Responsibility for Trail Usage" included our signed endorsement of the following:

- I understand that I am entering a major public space.
- I understand that the LA River is a river and not a flood control channel.
- I understand that I can ask my federal, state, county, or city representatives at any time to open this essential public space for safe and consistent public use. ("Backcountry Permit")

Getting the river permits required standing in line at a "Riverside Ranger Station" with fellow ramblers, and inevitably we broke into conversations about the river—among ourselves and with guest Rangers from FoLAR and other advocacy groups. Such spontaneous sociability typifies Urban Rangers' events. Walking into the river at the 6th Street accessway mapped for us by the Rangers created another opportunity to feel oneself becoming public in response to a potentially public place. At 6th Street the river looks like a concrete speedway. Yet when I entered it in the company of hundreds of eager pedestrians, the industrial bridge overhead assumed the emotional valence of a cathedral. The mere presence of others expecting something in the line of the sublime—the sort of thing we'd see at Yosemite—changed the look of this misspent place, or at least my reading of what is still there, its light and its scale. Price adds that the first goal of LA River activists is to get people to experience the river: "When people ask me, just me, not Ranger Jenny, 'Come talk to us about the River,' I say, 'No, come to the River' " (J. Price, personal interview, August 5, 2011). This emphasis on embodied experience harkens back to the CLUI bus tours and, deeper into art history, the psycho-geographical mapping of the Situationists.

When I spoke with Sara Daleiden about how she thinks that art acts in the world, she began by noting that "artists are good at . . . taking language as material, whether you want to use a visual language, or a verbal one, or a performative one, or some combination" (S. Daleiden, personal interview, September 1, 2011). This movement beyond text-based pedagogy also anchors Therese Kelly's sense of how the LA Urban Rangers create public affects that last longer than their discrete performances. She identifies the public as the primary medium through which the group realizes itself.

> For instance, during our Downtown project, the normally deserted streets of LA were filled with people walking at night and feeling safe. Even if they didn't understand what our overall metaphorical project was about, they just were out enjoying the night, the summer evening, with strangers in the city, in a place that's not usually inhabited by pedestrians. That is successful. I feel like that's enough—we've done something simply by enabling people to collectively experience and personally discover their own city. (T. Kelly, personal interview, December 21, 2011)

Most simply, I might argue that artists like the LA Urban Rangers "make" experience.

Jenny Price chooses the term "reimagination" to describe the fundamental action that the group performs. "Art is particularly good at going after basic assumptions," she says. "It's very good at juxtaposing what we know and what we don't know, or what we assume and what we don't tend to think about" (J. Price, personal interview, August 5, 2011). The LA Urban Rangers have been allied to the active reimagining of D.I.Y. art like Safari 7, a self-guided tour of "urban wildlife" along the 7 subway line in New York City, and PARK(ing) Day, which was originated in San Francisco by the collective Rebar. In 2005, Rebar's Matt Passmore unfurled living sod in a street parking place, put a tree and bench on it, and sat out the duration of his meter. Since then, PARK(ing) Day has gone viral, thanks to an open-source guide on how to make parks in metered spaces. A recent issue of *Public Art Review* features the LA Urban Rangers' MOCA series and PARK(ing) Day under the heading "DIY Park" and also recognizes the Occupy movement in terms of the reimagination of places and privileges withheld from the commons (A. Foster 29). While the overtly political Occupiers summon a different public than the hospitable LA Urban Rangers, both groups experiment with temporary common practice, avoiding the solidification of their gestures into systemic norms. The relationship between "being public" and time, or the problem of being public in time, has been important to artists and activists who want to encourage new spatial habits without foreclosing on possible futures.

For Therese Kelly, it's important to distinguish between activism, conventionally understood as taking action *for* others, and "activation," by which she means preparing people to act for themselves, ask questions, and develop their own commitments. "When people ask if we're activists, I say, 'No, we're not activists. We're activating a site, we're asking people to look and question, but we're asking questions, too.' We try to leave room for self-discovery and personal investigation" (T. Kelly, personal interview, December 21, 2011). Sara Daleiden's emphasis on the civic nature of the Rangers' art offers a deeper gloss on what the group intends by "activation." When I asked Daleiden what "civic" means for her, she defined civic practice as opening possibilities for who we can be in a common place. "Here's an interesting notion of the civic—keep finding temporary gestures to explore what your identity can be" (S. Daleiden, personal interview, September 1, 2011). Following Daleiden, I enjoy considering the commons as *practice* not only in the sense of acting but also in the sense of making assays, where we assume that the gesture isn't finished, that we might do it better or differently.[17] Whenever a concept has as much hope packed into it as does "the commons," it resists settling into definition.

SPECULATION GROUND

> *speculation* (n.) late 14c., "contemplation, consideration," from O.Fr. speculation, from L.L. speculationem (nom. speculatio) "contemplation, observation," from L. speculatus, pp. of speculari "observe, from specere "to look at, view" (see scope (1)). Disparaging sense of "mere conjecture" is recorded from 1570s. Meaning "buying and selling in search of profit from rise and fall of market value" is recorded from 1774; short form spec is attested from 1794. ("Speculation, n.")[18]

This second section of my chapter takes its name from a remarkable feature in the city of Almere in the Netherlands. Almere is the site of the LA Urban Rangers' most extensive international project. For the Museum de Paviljoens in Almere, the Urban Rangers collaborated to create a trail system in a vacant lot. Daleiden speaks about her experience at the site, leading hikes for the program. "It was very phenomenological, about wandering in this vacant lot," she says. "We had this beautiful phrase, 'When can a dead end wander?'" (S. Daleiden, personal interview, September 1, 2011). For the six months out of the year that Dutch weather allows, Almere's meticulous mowers create the trails, and since they were installed (2008), other artists have responded by making new gestures in the space. In a culture that is "used to being public," as Daleiden describes the Netherlands, an installation like this one met with less bureaucratic resistance than it might have in Los Angeles. Moreover, the vacant lot where the installation developed isn't exactly a vacant lot, as we might understand that term in the U.S. It's a space called a "speculation ground," set aside for thinking like an artist. Daleiden explains:

> This was extremely valuable land, it was right by the central train station and around attractive houses. A major architect/urban designer in the Netherlands had designed the city center abutting it, and so it was a space lying in wait. It was a beautiful premise; they call it a "speculatie grond," a speculation ground. They planned for what they didn't know. The Dutch are such amazing planners they even said, we'll put a city block's worth of space in the center for what we don't know about where our identity is going to go. (S. Daleiden, personal interview, September 1, 2011)

This "calculated gesture of leaving things open" appealed to Daleiden's sense of civic practice, and it invites comparison with U.S. cities where such gestures are rarely made. "We have all of these leftover spaces here, too," Daleiden says of Los Angeles, "but I don't think we decide to value them. Whereas in the Netherlands they decided they were going to leave the space open. *We're going to admit what we don't know*" (S. Daleiden, personal interview, September 1, 2011).

The slippage between thought and spatial practice here compels—a speculation ground makes literal space out of speculating, which means either contemplating things or betting on the future value of things. Daleiden assures me that "speculation" in Dutch holds a similar double valence. I turn toward both senses of speculation—contemplating and investing in the future—for the next few paragraphs. Specifically, I'll wonder alongside the LA Urban Rangers about how the translation of their site-specific work across cultures comments on the viability of a transnational notion of the commons.

The LA Urban Rangers have performed aspects of their work in the Netherlands and Sweden, and they have exhibited in the Netherlands, Mexico, and Canada. Some of their projects translate fairly smoothly. For example, the *Malibu Public Beaches* project tells a story of the predations of extreme wealth that proves resonant in other countries. Yet the Ranger persona, the master key to the group's accessibility, has few equivalents outside of the U.S. and Canada. When Sara Daleiden worked in the Netherlands, she wore the Urban Ranger uniform, she led hikes in the uniform, and she was interpreted by her local audience—as a "forester": "They really associate 'rangers' with Westerns, like cowboy and Indian movies. The closest thing that they have in their culture is a forester. So they understood having a character that could guide a hike, but the sense of wilderness is not present" (S. Daleiden, personal interview, September 1, 2011). For the Dutch, the forester suggests federal-level efforts to manage the Dutch land in a country where state design reaches as far as the sea bottom. The city of Almere sits on a polder, low-lying land that has been reclaimed from the sea and is protected by dikes and dams. "It's one of the few countries that makes more of its country without conquering others," Daleiden remarks. There's an almost poetic redundancy to the idea of land art in a country of polders. The forester role didn't take Daleiden too far away from her everyday persona as an artist. "Going on a walk as an art project was a common concept for a lot of people," she says (S. Daleiden, personal interview, September 1, 2011). The sympathy for the project already present in Dutch culture made for a different kind of pleasure than what the Urban Rangers evoke in Los Angeles, where the group assumes its art to be premised on, again, the reimagination of place and of spatial practices like walking.

When Therese Kelly and Jenny Price brought the LA Urban Rangers to Sweden, they held a workshop with students where they explicitly sought authority figures equivalent to U.S. park rangers. Kelly recalls a series of unexpected translations: "One person said Pippi Longstocking, because she's a thing-finder." The students objected to the park ranger as a person who "interferes" and "regulates." "In most of the Scandinavian countries they have this understood law that you can go anywhere in nature—including on other people's properties—to camp for a night, and pick berries and mushrooms. So, pretty much the whole land is yours to explore" (T. Kelly, personal interview, December 21, 2011). Without the wilderness concept, the ranger figure loses charisma. The idea of "the commons" also fails to excite where "commons" aren't extraordinary. Eventually the Swedish students settled on the figure of the "hut keeper," which comes from Lapland, as a translation for "ranger." Hut keepers are mythic, elderly figures who keep cabins for visitors in remote areas of the far north and who give strangers guidance. Swedish students imagined hut keepers outside of metro stations in suburban neighborhoods, guiding confused city dwellers. In short, the most privatized living areas they could conceive, suburbs, represented the greatest likeness to Lapland, the most mysterious place they could imagine. In Sweden, Urban Ranger translates to Suburban Hut Keeper. All of this tells us a good deal about the U.S.—where we read both city and wilderness as extraordinary and potentially public, while suburbia is a normative landscape.

The LA Urban Rangers offer distinct opinions about whether their work should be conceived as not only site-specific but also explicit to the U.S. For Daleiden, "the gestalt is rarely applicable" in other countries, but some elements of the project can be exported. Emily Scott, who now lives and works in Switzerland, argues that "local knowledge, site-specific knowledge, takes a long time to accrue and accumulate." She doesn't imagine donning her Ranger hat as an artist-theorist abroad. "I'm really an Americanist, which I wasn't fully aware of until I left the States. It's a specific kind of expertise—at least my interests in the history of the National Parks Service and of notions of landscape in the US—that does not easily translate" (E. Scott, personal interview, September 8, 2011). Yet when Scott speaks of her current project, *Supply Lines*, she loops back to her work with the LA Urban Rangers. *Supply Lines* is a visual-research collaboration among a core group of artists and theorists (including the video essayist Ursula Biemann) spread across the globe and devoted to exploring human interactions with natural resources and the socio-spatial relations ensuing from them.[19] The *Supply Lines* platform eventually will be a web archive, which can be accessed by anyone—from students to government policymakers to the artists themselves, who might use the research others produce to deepen their own contributions. The global scale of this project differentiates it sharply from the local, low-tech, street-level performances of the LA Urban Rangers. Yet Scott finds the scalar extremes of "local" and "global" less interesting than what the projects have in common, which is—as I would phrase it—how they act in the world. She describes both as "intervening into top-down flows of information" and raising questions that "have no real end, or that become a jumping-off point for other people to continue their own investigations" (E. Scott, personal interview, September 8, 2011).

I think it would be a mistake to assume that the public anticipated by *Supply Lines* is necessarily larger than the public created by the LA Urban Rangers, whose delivery mechanism (the Ranger persona) enters into the channels of popular culture in a way that a more theoretically nuanced platform cannot. Scott acknowledges that some kinds of projects demand a level of discourse more readily associated with academia: "In order to write about certain kinds of practices, which are theoretically complex, the only way to do it is to write at the level of the work." I make note of this scalar difference in implied publics not to critique either project, but to point out the tendency that I've seen in my own academic circles to judge the scale of a critical work in terms of what or whom it attempts to represent rather than who will be likely to receive it, read it, or be prompted by its concerns. Scott makes a similar call for "attentiveness to *where* geographical work happens" in an article touching on the *Malibu Public Beaches* project: "This project compels us to consider the destination of our labors, by asking: 'Where will my work most effectively operate, especially in terms of the communities/publics I intend to engage?'" ("Undisciplined Geography" 56). For me, the questions "How does it act?" and "Whom does it activate?", to use the LA Urban Rangers' language, are questions of method and media—and really first questions in the effort to conceive the scale of our work and thought.

CONCLUSION

Given how hard it is to find common ground in the U.S. these days, an art collective that generates temporary "commons" offers a rich model for both academic and political practice. I interviewed the four founders of the LA Urban Rangers because I felt they had something to teach me, as a North American academic and an environmental critic who sees scholarly work as sustainable insofar as it builds things, where "things" might mean intangibles such as social relationships or expressive styles. The LA Urban Rangers have been described as a project of "applied American Studies," meaning, I suppose, that they are a critical and historical project that lives in performance, through specific sites and actors.[20] To an extent, American Studies is always applied, whether performed by artists or environmental critics. But accessibility haunts my own academic practice—for instance, how to write as a scholar for a larger public and to teach my graduate students to do the same. While I won't insult art collectives or academics by suggesting that academics can or should be artists, I admire the ways in which the LA collectives that I've experienced collaborate, translate, and distribute their often acute reimaginings of the world.

My thinking between "academic" and "arts" practice makes up the primary transcultural dimension of this interview/chapter, and I thank the

Figure 15.2 Los Angeles Urban Rangers, Critical Campout 2011, tent view, dawn. Credit: Stephanie LeMenager.

founders of the LA Urban Rangers for their generous participation. I conclude with a few of their ideas about academic-arts collaboration. "Our group wouldn't be what it is without our academic backgrounds," Jenny Price says flatly. "We bring a depth of experience with critical thinking in particular fields that you could not get without going to graduate school" (J. Price, personal interview, August 5, 2011). Sara Daleiden encourages "thoughtful experiments in merging language, exploring language. Activists, artists, and academics tend to have radically different language sets. Actually, the merging of those is potentially where power comes." Price adds, "We [the LA Urban Rangers] are all about communication. And that's ultimately what academia is supposed to be about, even though I think that often gets lost. It's supposed to be about communication" (J. Price, personal interview, August 5, 2011). Of course, "communication" shares an etymological root with "commons" in the Latin *communis*, meaning "in common, public, general, not pretentious, shared by all or many." When the pursuit of the deep contexts of social nature assumes a common tongue, there's no telling what the scale of reimagination will be, or when it tips toward remaking.

NOTES

1. I thank Emily Scott for directing me to the work of Sarah Kanouse.
2. Of the situationist practice of the derive ("drift"), Guy Debord writes, "In a dérive one or more persons during a certain period drop their relations, their work and leisure activities, and all their other usual motives for movement and action, and let themselves be drawn by the attractions of the terrain and the encounters they find there. Chance is a less important factor in this activity than one might think: from a dérive point of view cities have psychogeographical contours, with constant currents, fixed points and vortexes that strongly discourage entry into or exit from certain zones."
3. I owe some of my broader insights about the CLUI to Sarah Kanouse's "Touring the Archive, Archiving the Tour: Image, Text, and Experience with the Center for Land Use Interpretation."
4. For more information, visit "About LAPD" at the LAPD website: http://www.lapovertydept.org/about-lapd/index.php
5. In a discussion of the Urban Ranger persona, Emily Scott described a lecture that she gave at the University of Wisconsin–Madison, where an audience member pointed to "hospitality" as a primary quality of the park ranger. Scott feels that "hospitality" best conveys the feeling that the LA Urban Rangers attempt to offer to their audiences.
6. Because of its efficient and even lyrical treatment of the multiple trajectories of the usage of "common" in a single concise entry, the *Online Etymology Dictionary* is cited here (Harper). For scholarly purposes, I suggest that the reader cross-reference this etymology with that of the *Oxford English Dictionary,* which notes the disparate dates of usage of "common" as in "the common body of the people of any place" (c. 1300) and "common" as in "common land or estate" (c.1479), meaning "the undivided land belonging to the members of a local community as a whole. Hence, often, the patch of

unenclosed or 'waste' land which remains to represent that." See "common, n." in *Oxford English Dictionary*.

7. For a discussion of the historical inaccuracies of Hardin's influential article, see Susan Jane Buck Cox's "No Tragedy on the Commons."
8. See Edward Abbey's "Industrial Tourism and the National Parks" in *American Earth: Environmental Writing since Thoreau.*
9. LA Urban Ranger maps can be accessed at www.laurbanrangers.org.
10. For a record of this and other gardenLAb installations and events, see Fritz Haeg's website: http://www.fritzhaeg.com/garden_main.html.
11. Jenny Price described both the California Coastal Commission and the Coastal Conservancy "using our maps when they're having meetings and [having] people look" at the beach access points.
12. See the Center for Urban Pedagogy's mission statement, "What We Do": http://welcometocup.org/.
13. The term "social sculpture" was coined by the artist and politician Joseph Beuys, who uses it with a more explicit ideological valence than I convey here.
14. Kelly described the Ranger figure as complementary to the consensus building that she does in her professional life as an architect, saying "the Ranger persona itself plays really well with that, [as a] very democratic, accessible figure that's asking everyone what they think and inviting all kinds of viewpoints" (T. Kelly, personal interview, December 21, 2011).
15. For a classic example of the literary equivalent of the "slum tour," the "mysteries of the city" exposé, see George G. Foster's *New York by Gas-Light, and Other Urban Sketches.*
16. Jenny Price offered the Lesbian Rangers and the New York City Park Rangers—a methodologically "straight" group that leads hikes and campouts in urban parks—as examples of other collectives that utilize the Ranger persona ("The Los Angeles Urban Rangers Enact the Megalopolis!").
17. I want to note some suggestive points of congruence between Daleiden's notion of the commons in arts practice and certain movements within an elegant conference paper I had the pleasure to hear Professor Lauren Berlant offer in October 2011. See Lauren Berlant, "Sensing the Commons: This Connection of Everyone with Lungs."
18. Again, this online source offered the most compressed and therefore poetic rendering, although for scholarly purposes I would suggest cross-referencing it with the *Oxford English Dictionary*, which breaks down the varied meanings of the term with more precise attention to usage dates, variants, and so on.
19. For more on *Supply Lines,* check out the "curatorial" link at http://www.geobodies.org/.
20. Jenny Price mentioned the "Applied American Studies" descriptor during her lecture at UC-Santa Barbara. See note 16.

References

"25 Stories from the Central Valley." 2012. Web. 6 June 2012.

Abbey, Edward. "Immigration and Liberal Taboos." *One Life at a Time, Please.* New York: Holt Paperbacks. 1988. Print.

———. "Industrial Tourism and the National Parks." *American Earth: Environmental Writing since Thoreau.* Ed. Bill McKibben. 1968. New York: Literary Classics of the United States, 2008. Print.

"About FoLAR." *The Friends of the Los Angeles River.* The Friends of the Los Angeles River. 2012. Web. 25 Jan. 2012.

Abraham, Chad. "For Sale: Nation's Most Expensive Home." *The Aspen Times.* 12 July 2006. Print.

Adams, Rachel. *Continental Divides: The Remapping of North America.* Chicago: University of Chicago Press, 2009. Print.

Adamson, Joni. *American Indian Literature, Environmental Justice, and Ecocriticism: The Middle Place.* Tucson: University of Arizona Press, 2001. Print.

———. "Encounter with a Mexican Jaguar: Nature, NAFTA, Militarization, and Ranching in the U.S.-Mexico Borderlands." *Globalization on the Line: Culture, Capital, and Citizenship at U.S. Borders.* Ed. Claudia Sadowski-Smith. New York: Palgrave, 2002. Print.

———. "Literature-and-Environment Studies and the Influence of the Environmental Justice Movement." *A Companion to American Literature and Culture.* Ed. Paul Lauter. Oxford, UK: Wiley-Blackwell Publishing, 2010. 593–607. Print.

———. "'*¡Todos Somos Indios!*': Revolutionary Imagination, Alternative Modernity, and Transnational Organizing in the Work of Silko, Tamez and Anzaldúa." *The Journal of Transnational American Studies* 4.1 (2012): 1–28. Web. 25 June 2012.

———, Mei Mei Evans, and Rachel Stein, eds. *The Environmental Justice Reader: Politics, Poetics Pedagogy.* Tucson: University of Arizona Press, 2002. Print.

Agyeman, Julian, Robert Bullard, and Bob Evans. *Just Sustainabilities: Development in an Unequal World.* Cambridge, MA: MIT Press, 2003. Print.

Aki, Rimuy. *Saninghua de guxiang (The Homeland of Mountain Sakura).* Taipei: Rye Field, 2010. Print.

Alaimo, Stacy. *Bodily Natures: Science, Environment, and the Material Self.* Bloomington, IN:

Indiana University Press, 2010. Print.

"Aliens Play Havoc With Song-Birds." *New York Times.* 22 Oct. 1922. n. pag. Print.

Allen, Chadwick. *Blood Narrative: Indigenous Identity in American Indian and Maori Literary and Activist Texts.* Durham: Duke University Press, 2002. Print.

"The Anchorage Declaration." *Indigenous Peoples' Global Summit on Climate Change*. Alaska, Anchorage. 24 April 2009. Web. 1 Feb. 2012.
Anderson, Benedict. *Imagined Communities: Reflection on the Origin and Spread of Nationalism*. Revised Edition. London: Verso, 2006. Print.
Andreas, Peter. "The Mexicanization of the U.S.-Canada Border: Asymmetric Interdependence in a Changing Security Context." *International Journal*. Spring (2005):450–462. Print.
Angus, Ian, and Simon Butler. "Panic Over 7 Billion: Letting the 1% Off the Hook." *DifferenTakes*. Fall (2011). Web. 07 June 2012.
Anholt, Simon. "Branding Places and Nations." *Brands and Branding*. New York: Bloomberg Press, 2004. 213–226. Print.
———. "Editorial." *Place Branding and Public Diplomacy* 1.1 (2004): 4–11. Print.
Anzaldúa, Gloria. *Borderlands/La Frontera: The New Mestiza*. San Francisco: Aunt Lute Books,1999. Print.
Axelrod, Jeremiah B. C. *Inventing Autopia: Dreams and Visions of the Modern Metropolis in Jazz Age Los Angeles*. Berkeley: University of California Press, 2009. Print.
Azuma, Eiichiro. *Between Two Empires: Race, History, and Transnationalism in Japanese America*. Oxford: Oxford University Press, 2005. Print.
"Backcountry Permit." Los Angeles Urban Rangers. *Public Access 101: Downtown L.A.* in collaboration with The Museum of Contemporary Art. Los Angeles' *Engagement Party*. 2011. Pamphlet.
"Background on Disturbances." *NASA-CASA Project*. NASA. n.d. Web. 21 June 2012.
Baker, Houston A., Jr. *Modernism and the Harlem Renaissance*. Chicago: University of Chicago Press, 1987. 79–93. Print.
Balazs, Carolina, Rachel Morello-Frosch, Alan Hubbard, and Isha Ray. "Social Disparities in Nitrate-Contaminated Drinking Water in California's San Joaquin Valley." *Environmental Health Perspectives* 119.9 (2011): 1272–1278. Print.
Barber, Alan. Letter to the editor. *Aspen Times*. 7 Jan. 2000. Print.
Barnett, Kalila, and Penn Loh, eds. "Environmental Justice and the Green Economy." Roxbury, MA: Alternatives for Community and Environment, 2010.
Bath, Richard C. "Resolving Water Disputes."*Proceedings of the Academy of Political Science* 34.1 (1981): 181–188. Print.
Baumli, Mildred. Letter to the editor. "Bleeding hearts." *Valley Journal*. 3 Feb. 2000. Print.
Bean, Michael J. *The Evolution of National Wildlife Law*. New York: Praeger/Environmental Defense Fund, 1982. Print.
Beck, John. *Dirty Wars: Landscape, Power, and Waste in Western American Literature*. Lincoln, NE: University of Nebraska Press, 2009. Print.
Becker, Marc. "Third Continental Summit of Indigenous Peoples and Nationalities of AbyaYala: From Resistance to Power." *Latin American and Caribbean Ethnic Studies* 3.1 (March 2008): 85–107. Print.
Benítez-Rojo, Antonio. *The Repeating Island: The Caribbean and the Postmodern Perspective*. Trans. James Maraniss. Durham: Duke University Press, 1996. Print.
Bennett, Michael. "From Wide Open Spaces to Metropolitan Places: The Urban Challenge to Ecocriticism." *ISLE: Interdisciplinary Studies in Literature and Environment* 8.1 (2001): 31–52. Print.
———. "Manufacturing the Ghetto: Anti-urbanism and the Spacialization of Race." *The Nature of Cities: Ecocriticism and Urban Environments*. Eds. Michael Bennett and David W. Teague. Tucson: University of Arizona Press, 1999. 169–188. Print.

Berger, Judson. "Border Patrol Charged Millions for Habitat Damage, Republicans Say Enough 'Extortion'." *Fox News.com.*21 June 2010. Web. 12 Dec. 2011.

Berlant, Lauren. "Citizenship." *Keywords for American Cultural Studies.* Eds. Bruce Burgettand and Glenn Hendler. New York: New York University Press, 2007. 37–42. Print.

———. "Sensing the Commons: This Connection of Everyone with Lungs." *Professor Lawrence Buell: A Symposium,* Harvard University. 14 Oct. 2011. Lecture.

Berry, Wendell. "Conserving Communities." *Another Turn of the Crank: Essays by Wendell Berry.* Washington, DC: Counterpoint, 1995. Print.

———. "Simple Solutions, Package Deals, and a 50-Year Farm Bill." *What Matters? Economics for a Renewed Commonwealth.* Washington, DC: Counterpoint, 2010. Print.

Billig, Michael. *Banal Nationalism.* London: Sage, 1995. Print.

Boas, Franz. "The Methods of Ethnology." *American Anthropologist* 22.4 (Oct.–Dec. 1920): 311–322.

———. *Race Language and Culture.* Chicago: University of Chicago Press, 1940. Print.

Boelhower, William. "Side-by-Side with You: The Common as Foundational Figure." *Redefinitions of Citizenship and Revisions of Cosmopolitanism.* Special issue of *Journal of Transnational American Studies* 3.1 (2011): 47–53. Print.

Botkin, Benjamin A., ed. *Lay My Burden Down: A Folk History of Slavery.* Chicago: University of Chicago Press, 1945. Print.

Bourriaud, Nicolas. *Relational Aesthetics.* Trans. Simon Pleasance and Fronza Woods. n.p.: Les presses du réel, 2002. Print.

Boyle, A. E., and M. R. Anderson. *Human Rights Approaches to Environmental Protection.* Oxford: Oxford University Press, 1998. Print.

Brady, Lois Smith. "A Birthday Party in a Trailer Park Is Completely Different in Aspen." *New York Times.* 26 May 2002. Print.

Braz, Albert. "Reconstructing the Border: Jim Lynch and the Return of the Canada-US Boundary." *Comparative American Studies* 9.3 (2011): 191–203. Print.

Brennan, Teresa. *Globalization and Its Terrors: Daily Life in the West.* New York: Routledge, 2003. Print.

Brickhouse, Anna. *Transamerican Literary Relations and the Nineteenth-Century Public Sphere.* Cambridge: Cambridge University Press, 2004. Print.

Briggs, Laura. *Reproducing Empire: Race, Sex, Science, and US Imperialism in Puerto Rico.* Berkeley: University of California Press, 2002. Print.

Brown, Lester. *Reinventing Malthus for the 21st Century Conference.* Sponsored by Negative Population Growth and the Federation for American Immigration Reform. National Press Club, Washington, DC. 14 July 1997. Speech.

Brown, Russell. "The Written Line." *Borderlands: Essays in Canadian-American Relations.* Ed. Robert Lecker. Toronto: ECW Press, 1991. 1–27. Print.

Buell, Lawrence. "Ecoglobalist Affects: The Emergence of U.S. Environmental Imagination on a Planetary Scale." *Shades of the Planet: American Literature as World Literature.* Eds. Wai Chee Dimock and Lawrence Buell. Princeton: Princeton University Press, 2007. 227–248. Print.

———.*The Environmental Imagination: Thoreau, Nature Writing, and the Formation of American Culture.* Cambridge, MA: Belknap of Harvard University Press, 1995. Print.

———. *The Future of Environmental Criticism: Environmental Crisis and Literary Imagination.* Oxford: Blackwell, 2005. Print.

———. "Introduction: In Pursuit of Ethics." *PMLA* 114 (1999): 7–19. Print.

———. "Ecocriticism: Some Emerging Trends." *Qui Parle: Critical Humanities and Social Sciences* 19.2 (2011a): 87–115. Print.

———. "Some Emerging Thoughts on Ecocriticism." *Qui Parle* 19.2 (Spring/Summer 2011b): 87–115. Print.

———. "What We Talk About When We Talk About Ethics." *The Turn to Ethics.* Eds. Marjorie Garber, Beatrice Hanssen, and Rebecca L. Walkowitz. New York and London: Routledge, 2000. 1–15. Print.

Bullard, Robert. D. *The Quest for Environmental Justice: Human Rights and the Politics of Pollution.* San Francisco: Sierra Club Books, 2005. Print.

Bullock, Heather, Karen Fraser Wyche, and Wendy R Williams. 2001. "Media Images of the Poor." *Journal of Social Issues* 57.2 (2001): 229–246. Print.

Burns, Shirley Stewart. *Bringing Down the Mountains: The Impact of Mountaintop Removal on Southern West Virginia Communities, 1970–2004.* Morgantown: West Virginia University Press, 2007. Print.

Burrows, Edwing G., and Mike Wallace. *Gotham: A History of New York to 1898.* New York: Oxford University Press, 1999. Print.

Burtynsky, Edward. *Burtynsky: Oil.* Göttingen: SteidlVerlag, 2009. Print.

———. *Edward Burtynsky: Photographic Works.* Web. 30 May 2012.

Bustamante, Jorge A. "Demystifying the US-Mexico Border." *The Journal of American History* 79.2 (1992): 485–490. Print.

CAIRCO.org. Colorado Alliance for Immigration Reform. n.d. Web. July 2004.

Caldwell, Alicia A. "Border Fence Could Cut through Backyards." *USA today.com.* Associated Press. 8 Nov. 2007. Web. 8 Nov. 2011.

Carroll. Rick. "Strange Bedfellows Made in Quest for Immigration Reform." *Aspen Daily News.* 19 Aug. 2002. Print.

Carter, Majora. "Hometown Security." *Ted Talks.* 10 Jan. 2011. Web. 22 Mar. 2011.

Cartwright, Keith. "'To Walk with the Storm': Oya as the Transformative 'I' of Zora Neale Hurston's Afro-Atlantic Callings." *American Literature* 78.4 (2006): 741–767. Print.

Cassidy, Thomas. "Janie's Rage: The Dog and the Storm in *Their Eyes Were Watching God.*" *CLA Journal* 36.3 (March 1993): 260–269. Print.

"CBS Seeks Public Input on Northern Border Environmental Impacts." *CBP.gov news.* 12 July 2010. Web. 13 July. 2010.

Ceasar, Stephen. "Along the Border Fence, and Environment Fractured." *The New York Times.* 10 Sept. 2009. Web. 8 Nov. 2011.

"CEC Home Page." *Commission for Environmental Cooperation (CEC).* 2007. Web. 12 June 2007.

The Center for Land Use Interpretation. The Center for Land Use Interpretation. n.d. Web. 21 Jan. 2012.

Chang, Kornel. "Enforcing Transnational White Solidarity: Asian Migration and the Formation of the U.S.-Canadian Boundary." *American Quarterly* 60.3 (2008): 671–696. Print.

Charles, Ron. "An Agent of Understanding." *Washington Post.* 17 June 2009. Web. 17 June 2009.

Cherokee v. Georgia. 30 U.S 1. Supreme Courth of the United States. 1831. *Lexis-Nexis Academic.* Web. 30 Sep. 2012.

Chiang, Connie Y. "Imprisoned Nature: Towards an Environmental History of World War II Japanese American Incarceration." *Environmental History* 15 (2010): 236–267. Print.

"Cholera." *Partners in Health.* 2009–2012. Web. 3 Mar. 2012.

Chopin, Kate. "Development of the Literary West." *St. Louis Republic.* 9 December 1900. Sunday magazine section, 1. Print.

Christian, Jonette. "Population, Immigration and Global Ethics." The Myth of Sustainable Growth Conference. Aspen Institute, Aspen, Colorado. 9 Oct. 1999. Presentation.

Cihung, Kaji. "Truku People about Asia Cement Event." *Dictionary of Taiwanese Aboriginal People's History, Language, and Culture.* Web. 1 Feb. 2012.

Clapp, Jennifer. *Toxic Exports: The Transfer of Hazardous Wastes from Rich to Poor Countries.* Ithaca, NY: Cornell University Press, 2010. Print.

Clifford, Hal. "Aspen's Extremes." *Ski Magazine* (January 1999): 33–37. Print.

CNN Live. Turner Broadcasting System, Inc. 28 May 2009. Television.

CNN Wire Staff. "Gulf Oil Spill Is Worst Accidental Spill Ever" *CNN U.S.* 3 August 2010. Web. 4 August 2010.

Collier, John. *From Every Zenith: A Memoir; and Some Essays on Life and Thought.* Denver: Sage, 1963. Print.

Comer, Krista. *Landscapes of the New West: Gender and Geography in Contemporary Women's Writing.* Chapel Hill: University of North Carolina Press, 1999. Print.

Conant, Jeff. "'Peasant Farming Can Cool Down the Earth': An Interview with Chavannes Jean-Baptiste, Executive Director of Mouvement Paysan de Papaye, Durban South Africa." *Climate Connections: Global Justice Ecology Project.* 9 Jan. 2012. Web. 28 Jan. 2012.

Conniff, Michael. "Natural High." Advertisement. Mountain Marketplace. *Aspen Daily News.* 21 July–Aug. 3 2004. Print.

Connor, Walker. *Ethnonationalism: The Quest for Understanding.* Princeton, NJ: Princeton University Press, 1994. Print.

Conover, Ted. *Whiteout: Lost in Aspen.* New York: Random House, 1991. Print.

Constitution of Ecuador. *Asamblea Nacional Constituyente.* 2008. Web. April 20, 2011.

Correspondence Relative to the Emigration to Hayti, of the Free People of Colour, in the United States, Together with the Instructions to the Agent Sent Out by President Boyer. New York: Mahlon Day, 1824. Print.

Cosco, Joseph J. *Imagining Italians: The Clash of Romance and Race in American Perceptions, 1880–1910.* Albany, NY: SUNY, 2003. Print.

"Court Tosses Conviction of Arizona Man Who Left Water for Migrants." *Arizona Republic.* 2 Sept. 2010. Web. 8 Nov. 2011.

Cox, Susan Jane Buck. "No Tragedy on the Commons." *Environmental Ethics* (Spring 1985): 49–62. Print.

Creef, Elena Tajima. *Imagining Japanese America. The Visual Construction of Citizenship, Nation and the Body.* New York: New York University Press, 2004. Print.

Cresswell, Tim. *Place: A Short Introduction.* Malden, MA: Blackwell Publishing, 2004. Print.

Cronon, William. "The Trouble with Wilderness." *Uncommon Ground: Rethinking the Human Place in Nature.* Ed. William Cronon. New York: W. W. Norton, 1996. 69–90. Print.

———. "The Trouble with Wilderness: Or, Getting Back to the Wrong Nature." *Environmental History* 1.1 (January 1996): 7–28. Print.

———. "Revisiting the Vanishing Frontier: The Legacy of Frederick Jackson Turner." *Western Historical Quarterly* 18.2 (1987): 157–176. Print.

Crutzen, Paul J., and Eugene F. Stoermer. "The Anthropocene." *Global Change Newsletter.* 41 (2000): 17–18.

Daleiden, Sara. Personal interview by Stephanie LeMenager. 1 Sept. 2011.

Daniels, Rogers. *America's Concentration Camps.* New York: Garland, 1989. Print.

Darwin, Charles. *On the Origin of Species by Means of Natural Selection: Or, the Preservation of Favoured Races in the Struggle for Life.* London: Humphrey Milford Oxford University Press, 1914. Print.

Da Silva, Denise Ferreira. *Toward a Global Idea of Race.* Minneapolis: University of Minnesota Press, 1998. Print.

Davis, Allen. "The Politics of American Studies." *American Quarterly* 42.3 (1990): 353–374. Print.

Dayan, Joan. "A Few Stories About Haiti, or, Stigma Revisited." *Research in African Literatures* 35.2 (Summer 2004): 157–172. Print.

Debord, Guy. "Theory of the Dérive."*Internationale Situationniste* 2 (1958): n. pag.

———. *Situationist International Anthology*. Ed and Trans. Ken Knabb. *Bureau of Public Secrets*. Web. 13 Jan. 2012.

De la Cadena, Marisol. "Indigenous Cosmopolitics in the Andes: Conceptual Reflections beyond Politics.'" *Cultural Anthropology* 25.2 (2010): 334–370. Print.

del Moral, Roger, and Lawrence R. Walker. *Environmental Disasters, Natural Recovery and Human Responses*. Cambridge, UK: Cambridge University Press, 2007. Print.

Deleuze, Gilles, and Felix Guattari. *A Thousand Plateaus: Capitalism and Schizophrenia*. Trans. Brian Massumi. London: The Athlone Press, 1992.

Deloria, Philip. "Presidental Address the American Studies Association: Broadway and Main: Crossroads, Ghost Roads, and Path to an American Studies Future." *American Quarterly* 6.1 (2009): 1–25. Print.

———. *Playing Indian*. New Haven, CT: Yale University Press, 1998. Print.

Deloria, Vine, Jr. *The Nations Within: The Past and Future of American Indian Sovereignty*. New York: Pantheon, 1984. Print.

DeLoughrey, Elizabeth, and George Handley. *Postcolonial Ecologies: Literature of the Environment*. Oxford and New York: Oxford University Press, 2011. Print.

DeLuca, Kevin, and Anne Demo. "Imagining Nature and Erasing Class and Place: Carleton

Watkins, John Muir, and the Construction of Wilderness." *Environmental History* 4.6 (2001): 541–560. Print.

Denetdale, Jennifer. *Reclaiming Diné History: The Legacies of Navajo Chief Manuelito and Juanita*. Tucson: University of Arizona Press, 2007. Print.

Denis, Claude. *We Are Not You: First Nations and Canadian Modernity*. Toronto: University of Toronto Press, 1997.

"Destroying the Borderlands to Secure the Border." 5 Aug. 2010. Web. 10 Nov. 2011.

Dewahare, Anthony. *Nationalism, Marxism, and African American Literature Between the Wars: A New Pandora's Box*. Oxford, MS: University Press of Mississippi, 2003. Print.

Dewey, John. *Experience and Nature*. Chicago: Open Court, 1925. Print.

Di Chiro, Giovanna. "Acting Globally: Cultivating a Thousand Community Solutions for Climate Justice." *Development* 54.2 (2011): 232–236. Print.

———. "Nature as Community: The Convergence of Social Justice and the Environment." *Uncommon Ground: Rethinking the Human Place in Nature*. Ed. William Cronon. New York: W. W. Norton, 1996. Print.

———. "Living Environmentalisms: Coalition Politics, Social Reproduction, and Environmental Justice." *Environmental Politics* 17.1 (2008): 276–298. Print.

———. "Defining Environmental Justice: Women's Voices and Grassroots Politics." *Socialist Review* 22.4 (1992): 93–130. Print.

Dimock, Wai Chee, and Lawrence Buell. *Shades of the Planet: American Literature as World Literature*. Princeton, NJ: Princeton Paperbacks, 2007. 1–16. Print.

Dinan, Stephen. "Environmental Laws Put Gaps in Mexico Border Security." *Washington Times*. 16 Nov. 2009. Web. 8 Nov. 2011.

Diner, Hasia R. *Hungering For America: Italian, Irish, and Jewish Foodways in the Age of Migration*. Cambridge: Harvard University Press, 2001. Print.

Dinnerstein, Leonard, and David M. Reimers. *Ethnic Americans: A History of Immigration*. 5th ed. New York: Columbia University Press, 2009. Print.

Dixon, Chris. *African America and Haiti: Emigration and Black Nationalism in the Nineteenth Century*. Westport, CT: Greenwood Press, 2000. Print.
Doane, Rebecca. Personal interview with Lisa Sun-Hee Park and David Naguib Pellow. Spring 2004.
Donato, Katharine M., and Evelyn Patterson. "Women and Men on the Move: Undocumented Border Crossings." Eds. Jorge Durrand and Douglas S. Massey. *Crossing the Border: Research from the Mexican Migration Project*. New York: Russell Sage Foundation, 2004. 111–130. Print.
Dorsey, Kurkpatrick. *The Dawn of Conservation Diplomacy: U.S.-Canadian Wildlife Protection Treaties in the Progressive Era*. Seattle: University of Washington Press, 1998. Print.
Douglas, Marjorie Stoneman. *Everglades: River of Grass*. Sarasota, FL: Pineapple Press, 1997. Print.
Duany, Andres, Elizabeth Plater-Zyberk, and Jeff Speck. *Suburban Nation: The Rise of Sprawl and the Decline of the American Dream*. 2000. New York: North Point Press, 2010. Print.
Dubos, Rene, and Barbara Ward. *Only One Earth: The Care and Maintenance of a Small Planet*. New York: W. W. Norton, 1972. Print.
Dunn, Timothy J. *The Militarization of the U.S.-Mexico Border, 1978–1992: Low-Intensity Conflict Doctrine Comes Home*. Austin: CMAS Books, 1996. Print.
Eagle Woman, Angelique. "Fencing Off the Eagle and the Condor, Border Politics, and Indigenous Peoples." *Natural Resources & Environment* 23.2 (2008): 33–35. Print.
Eller, Ronald D. *Uneven Ground: Appalachia Since 1945*. Lexington: The University Press of Kentucky, 2008. Print.
Eschbach, Karl, Jacqueline M. Hagan, and Néstor Rodriguez. *Causes and Trends in Migrant Deaths along the US-Mexico Border, 1985–1998*. Houston: University of Houston, Center for Immigration Research, 2001. Print.
———. "Deaths during Undocumented Migration: Trends and Policy Implications in the New Era of Homeland Security." *Defense of the Alien* 26 (2003): 37–52. Web.
Evans, Mei Mei. "'Nature' and Environmental Justice." *The Environmental Justice Reader*. Eds. Joni Adamson, Mei Mei Evans, and Rachel Stein. Tucson: University of Arizona Press, 2002. 181–193. Print.
Feagin, Joe. "Old Poison in New Bottles: The Deep Roots of Modern Nativism." *Immigrants Out!: The New Nativism and the Anti-Immigrant Impulse in the United States*. Ed. Juan F. Perea. New York: New York University Press, 1997. 13–40. Print.
"Fellows: The Petra Foundation." 2012. Web. 6 June 2012.
Fenton, Steve, and Stephen May, eds. *Ethnonational Identities*. New York: Palgrave, 2002. Print.
Ferber, Edna. *Giant*. New York: Doubleday, 1952. Print.
Fiege, Mark. *Irrigated Eden: The Making of an Agricultural Landscape in the American West*. Seattle: University of Washington Press, 1999. Print.
Finishing School. Finishing School. 2009. Web. 25 Jan. 2012.
Fischlin, Daniel, and Martha Nandorfy. *The Community of Rights: The Rights of Community*. New Delhi, India: Oxford University Press, 2012. Print.
———. *The Concise Guide to Global Human Rights*. New Delhi, India: Oxford University Press, 2007. Print.
Fisher, Sarah, and Karen Newman. "People, Population, and Climate Change: Opportunities for Advancing Climate Resilience and Reproductive Right." *RH Reality Check*. Population and Sustainability Network. 27 Oct. 2011. Web. 07 June 2012.
Fishkin, Shelley F. "Crossroads of Cultures: The Transnational Turn in American Studies—Presidential Address to the American Studies Association." *American Quarterly* 57.1 (2005): 17–57. Print.

Flesch, Aaron D., Clinton W. Epps, James W. Cain III, Matt Clark, Paul R. Krausman, and John R. Morgart. "Potential Effects of the United States-Mexico Border Fence on Wildlife." *Conservation Biology* 24.1 (2010): 171–181. Print.

"F. O. Mattheissen Distinguished Visiting Professorship of Gender and Sexuality Fact Sheet." Web. 19 May 2012.

Ford, Sarah. "Hurston's *Their Eyes Were Watching God*." *CLA Journal* 43.4 (June 2000): 400–419. Print.

Foster, Amelia. "DIY Parks: Two Ongoing Public Art Projects Expand the Definitions of Parkland in the City." *Public Art Review* 45 (Fall/Winter 2011): 29. Print.

Foster, George G. *New York by Gas-Light, and Other Urban Sketches*. Ed. Stuart M. Blumin. 1850. Berkeley: University of California Press, 1990. Print.

Frank, Thomas. "More Cameras for Canada Border." *USA Today*. 1 April 2009. Web 8 November 2011.

Friedman, Ellen. Personal interview with Lisa Sun-Hee Park and David Naguib Pellow. Spring 2002.

Gamber, John. "Native American Studies." *Concise Companion to American Studies*. Ed. John Carlos Rowe. New York: Blackwell, 2010. 172–189. Print.

Garrard, Greg. *Ecocriticism*. London: Routledge, 2004. Print.

Gilmore, Ruth Wilson. *Golden Gulag: Prisons, Surplus, Crisis, and Opposition in Globalizing California*. Berkeley: University of California Press, 2007. Print.

Glasby, Geoffrey P. "Abiogenic Origin of Hydrocarbons: An Historical Overview." *Resource Geology* 56.1 (2006): 83–96. Print.

Glissant, Edouard. *Caribbean Discourse: Selected Essays*. Trans. J. Michael Dash. Charlottesville: University Press of Virginia, 1989. Print.

"Globalization at the Crossroads: Ten Years of NAFTA in the San Diego/Tijuana Border Region." *Environmental Health Coalition: Globalization Cover*. 2004. Web. 12 June 2007.

Glotfelty, Cheryll, and Harold Fromm, eds. *The Ecocriticism Reader: Landmarks in Literary Ecology*. Athens: University of Georgia, 1996. Print.

Gordon, Avery. *Ghostly Matters: Haunting and the Sociological Imagination*. Minneapolis: University of Minnesota, 1997. Print.

Gottlieb, Robert. *Forcing the Spring: The Transformation of the American Environmental Movement*. Washington, DC: Island Press, 1993. Print.

———, and Peter Dreier. "Sierra Club Wrestles with the Nativism in Environmentalism." *The Los Angeles Times*. 1 March 1998. Print.

———, and Anupama Joshi. *Food Justice*. Cambridge, MA: MIT Press, 2010. Print.

Grant, Madison. *The Passing of the Great Race, or, the Racial Basis of European History*. New York: Charles Scribner's Sons, 1916. Print.

Green, Janet. "The Federal Government and Migratory Birds: The Beginning of a Protective Policy." *Historical Papers* 11.1 (1976): 207–227. Print.

Gruez, Kirsten Silva. *Ambassadors of Culture: The Transamerican Origins of Latino Writing*. Princeton, NJ: Princeton University Press, 2002. Print.

Guha, Ramachandra. "Radical American Environmentalism and Wilderness Preservation: A Third World Critique." *Environmental Ethics* 11 (Spring 1989): 71–83. Print.

———, and Juan Martinez-Alier. *Varieties of Environmentalism: Essays from North and South*. London: Earthscan Publications, 1997. Print.

Gussow, Adam. *Seems Like Murder Here: Southern Violence and the Blues Tradition*. Chicago: University Chicago Press, 2002. Print.

Hackett, Steven C. *Environmental and Natural Resources Economics: Theory, Policy, and the Sustainable Society*. 2nd ed. Armonk, NY: M. E. Sharpe, 2001. Print.

Hagen, Joel Bartholemew. *An Entangled Bank: The Origins of Ecosystem Ecology*. New Brunswick, NJ: Rutgers University Press, 1992. Print.
Hall, Stuart, Charles Critcher, Tony Jefferson, John Clarke, and Brian Robert. *Policing the Crisis*. London, UK: Palgrave Macmillan, 1978. Print.
Harcourt, Wendy, and Arturo Escobar, eds. *Women and the Politics of Place*. Sterling, VA: Kumarian Press, 2005. Print.
Hardin, Garrett. "The Case Against Helping the Poor." *Psychology Today* (September 1974): n. pag. Web. 30 May 2012.
———. "Lifeboat Ethics: The Case Against Helping the Poor." *Psychology Today*. (September 1974): Web. 5 March 2012.
———. "The Tragedy of the Commons." *Science* 162.3859 (1968): 1243–1248. Print.
Harrell, Eben. "The Changing Face of the Valley." *Aspen Times Weekly*. 12–13 June 2004. Print.
Harrison, Jill Lindsey. *Pesticide Drift and the Pursuit of Environmental Justice*. Cambridge, MA: MIT, 2011. Print.
Hartmann, Betsy. "Conserving Racism: The Greening of Hate at Home and Abroad." *Z Magazine Online*. 10 Dec. 2003. Web. Aug. 2004. Print.
———. *Reproductive Rights and Wrongs*. Cambridge: South End Press, 1995. Print.
———, and Elizabeth Barajas-Roman. "The Population Bomb Is Back—With a Global Warming Twist." *Women in Action* 2 (2009).
Harvey, Allyn. "Issue of Racism Sparks a Fierce City Council Debate." *The Aspen Times*. 12 April 2001a. Print.
———."Lamm Speaks on Foreign Labor 'Addiction.'" *Aspen Times*. 24 Sept. 2001b. Print.
———. "New Watchdog Group Puts Eye on Immigration." *Aspen Times*. 24 June 1999. Print.
Hayashi, Robert T. "Beyond Walden Pond: Asian American Literature and the Limits of Ecocriticism." *Coming into Contact: Explorations in Ecocritical Theory and Practice*. Eds. Annie Merrill Ingram, Ian Marshall, Daniel J. Philippon, and Adam W. Sweeting. Atlanta: University of Georgia Press, 2007: 58–75. Print.
"Heightened Security at the U.S.-Canada Border Catching Few Terror Suspects." *Seattle PI*. 20 April 2009. Web. 10 Nov. 2011.
Heiman, Jeremy. "City Council Passes Resolution Requesting Immigration Limits." *Aspen Times*. 20 Dec. 1999. Print.
Heise, Ursula. *Sense of Place and Sense of Planet: The Environmental Imagination of the Global*. New York: Oxford University Press, 2008. Print.
Heredia, Juanita. *Transnational Latina Narratives in the Twenty-First Century: The Politics of Gender, Race, and Migration*. New York: Palgrave Macmillan, 2009. Print.
Herrick, Francis H. "Italian Bird Life as It Impresses an American Today." *Bird-Lore* 8 (November–Dec 1906): 196–201. Print.
Hershey, Tony. Personal interview with Lisa Sun-Hee Park and David Naguib Pellow. Spring 2004.
Herzog, Lawrence A. *Where North Meets South: Cities, Space, and Politics on the U.S.-Mexico Border*. Austin: University of Texas Press, 1990. Print.
Hewitt, C. Gordon. *Conservation of the Wild Life of Canada*. New York: Charles Scribner's Sons, 1921. Print.
Higham, John. *Strangers in the Land*. 2nd ed. New Brunswick, NJ: Rutgers University Press, 1988. Print.
Hoerner, Andrew J., and Nia Robinson. *A Climate of Change: African Americans, Global Warming, and a Just Climate Policy for the U.S.* Oakland, CA: Environmental Justice and Climate Change Initiative, 2008. Web. 7 June 2012.

Hogan, Linda. *Solar Storms: A Novel.* New York: Simon and Schuster, 1995. Print.

Hooper, Troy. "EPA Lauds Aspen for Getting Around." *Aspen Daily News.* 27 April 2004. Print.

———. "Illegal Immigration Critic Jumps into Council Race." *Aspen Daily News.* 6 April 2001. Print.

Horkheimer, Max, and Theodor W. Adorno. *Dialectic of Enlightenment.* Trans. John Cumming. New York: Seabury Press, 1972. Print.

Hornaday, William T. *Campfires in the Canadian Rockies.* New York: Charles Scribner's Sons, 1906. Print.

———. *Our Vanishing Wild-Life: Its Extermination and Preservation.* New York: Charles Scribner's Sons, 1913. Print.

———. *Thirty Years War for Wild Life: Gains and Losses in the Thankless Task.* Stamford, CT: Permanent Wild Life Protection Fund, 1931. Print.

Hornig, James F., ed. *Social and Environmental Impacts of the James Bay Hydro-electric Project.* Montréal: McGill-Queen's University Press, 1999. Print.

Hornung, Alfred. "Planetary Citizenship." *Journal of Transnational American Studies* 3.1 (2011): 37–46. eScholarship University of California. Web. 20 June 2011.

Houston, Jeanne Wakatsuki. "Crossing Boundaries." *The Colors of Nature: Culture, Identity and the Natural World.* Eds. Alison Hawthorne Deming and Lauret E. Savoy. Minneapolis: Milkweed Press: 2002: 171–180. Print.

———. *Farewell to Manzanar: A True Story of Japanese American Experience during & after World War II* . New York: Doubleday, 1974. Print.

———. *The Legend of Fire Horse Woman.* New York: Kensington Books, 2003. Print.

Huhndorf, Shari M. *Going Native: Indians in the American Cultural Imagination.* Ithaca: Cornell University Press, 2001. Print.

———. *Mapping the Americas: The Transnational Politics of Contemporary Native Culture.* Ithaca: Cornell University Press, 2009. Print.

"Hurricane Dolly—Human Rights and U.S. Fraud, Waste and Abuse—FEMA and DHS Cause Further Harm Against Indigenous People." *Lipan Apache Women Defense.* 30 July 2008. Web. 1 Feb. 2012.

Hurston, Zora Neale. *Dust Tracks on a Road.* 1941. New York: Harper Perennial, 1991. Print.

———. *Every Tongue Got to Confess: Negro Folk-tales from the Gulf States.* New York: Harper Collins, 2001. Print.

———. *Go Gator and Muddy the Water: Writings.* Ed. Pamela Bordelon. New York: Norton, 1999. Print.

———. Letter to William Stanley Hoole. 7 March 1936.

———. *Zora Neale Hurston: A Life in Letters.* Collected and ed. Carla Kaplan. New York: Doubleday, 2002. Print.

———. *Mules and Men.* 1935. New York: Perennial, 1990. Print.

———. "Spunk." 1925. *The New Negro.* Ed. Alain Locke. New York: Simon and Schuster, 1997. Print.

———. *Their Eyes Were Watching God.* 1937. New York: Harper Perennial, 1998. Print.

———, and Dorothy Waring. *Polk County: A Comedy of Negro Life on a Sawmill Camp with Authentic Negro Music in Three Acts.* Registered 1944. Library of Congress, Rare Book and Special Collections Division. Web.

Hutchinson, Louise Daniel. *The Anacostia Story: 1608–1930.* Washington, DC: Smithsonian Institution Press, 1977. Print.

Information for the Free People of Colour, Who Are Inclined to Emigrate to Hayti. New York: Samuel Wood & Sons, 1824. Print.

International Forum on Globalization factsheet, Making Room for Alternatives. Web. 1 February 2012.

"Introduction to the New Enclosures." *Midnight Notes 10*. Web. 04 May 2012.

Iverson, Peter. *The Navajo Nation*. Westport, CT: Greenwood, 1981. Print.

Iverson, Peter, and Monty Roessel. *Diné: A History of the Navajos*. Albuquerque: University of New Mexico, 2002. Print.

Jay, Paul. *Global Matters: The Transnational Turn in Literary Studies*. Ithaca NY: Cornell University Press, 2010. Print.

———. "The Myth of 'America' and the Politics of Location: Modernity, Border Studies, and the Literature of the Americas." *Arizona Quarterly* 54.2 (1998): 165–192. Print.

Jefferson, Thomas. *Notes on the State of Virginia*. Ed. William Peden. Chapel Hill: University of North Carolina Press, 1982. Print.

Johnson, Kirk. "A $135 million home, but if you have to ask. . . ." *New York Times*. 2 July 2007. Print.

Johnson v. McIntosh. 21 U.S. 543. Supreme Court of the United States. 1823. *LexisNexis Academic*. Web. 30 Sep. 2012.

Jones, Thomas Jesse, et al. *The Navajo Indian Problem*. New York: Phelps-Stokes Fund, 1939. Print.

Kada, Naoko, and Richard Kiy, eds. "Blurred Borders: Trans-Boundary Impacts & Solutions in the San Diego-Tijuana Border Region." *International Community Foundation Report*. 2004. Web. 12 June 2007.

Kang, Miliann. *The Managed Hand: Race, Gender, and the Body in Beauty Service Work*. Berkeley: University of California Press, 2010. Print.

Kanouse, Sarah. "A Post-Naturalist Field Kit: Tools for the Embodied Exploration of Social Ecologies." *Mapping Environmental Issues in the City: Arts and Cartography Cross Perspectives*. Eds. Sébastien Caquard, Laurene Vaughan, and William Cartwright. Berlin/Heidelberg: Springer-Verlag, 2011. Print.

———. "Touring the Archive, Archiving the Tour: Image, Text, and Experience with the Center for Land Use Interpretation." *art journal* (Summer 2005): 79–87. Print.

Kaplan, Amy. "Manifest Domesticity." *American Literature* 70.3 (1998): 581–606. Print.

———, and Donald Pease, eds. *Cultures of United States Imperialism*. Durham, NC: Duke University Press, 1993.

Katz, Cindi. "Bad Elements: Katrina and the Scoured Landscape of Social Reproduction." *Gender, Place, and Culture* 15.1 (2008): 15–29. Print.

Kearney, Michael. "Transnationalism in California and Mexico at the End of Empire." Ed. Hastings Donnan. *Border Identities: Nation and State at International Frontiers*. Ed. Thomas M. Wilson. Cambridge: Cambridge University Press, 1998. 117–141. Print.

Kelly, Erin. "Napolitano Halts Funding for 'Virtual Fence.'" *Arizona Republic*. 16 March 2010. Web. 8 Nov. 2011.

Kelly, Therese. Personal interview by Stephanie LeMenager. 21 Dec. 2011.

Kester, Grant H. *Conversation Pieces: Community + Communication in Modern Art*. Berkeley: University of California Press, 2004. 9–10, 13. Print.

Kimes, Beverly. *Pioneers, Engineers, and Scoundrels: The Dawn of the Automotive Industry in America*. Warrendale, PA: Society of Automotive Engineers, 2005. Print.

Kleinberg, Eliot. *Black Cloud: The Deadly Hurricane of 1928*. New York: Carroll and Graf, 2003. Print.

Kleindienst, Patricia. *The Earth Knows My Name: Food, Culture, and Sustainability in the Gardens of Ethnic America*. Boston: Beacon Press, 2007. Print.

Kluckhohn, Clyde, and Dorothea Leighton. *The Navaho*. Garden City, NY: Anchor Books, 1962. Print.

Knighton, Jose. "Ecoporn and the Manipulation of Desire." *Wild Earth: Wild Ideas for a World Out of Balance*. Ed. Tom Butler. Minneapolis: Milkweed, 2002. 165–171. Print.

Kolodny, Annette. *The Lay of the Land: Metaphor as Experience and History in American Life and Letters*. Chapel Hill: University of North Carolina, 1975. Print.

———. "Rethinking the 'Ecological Indian': A Penobscot Precursor." *ISLE: Interdisciplinary Studies in Literature and Environment* 14.1 (2010): 1–23. Print.

Konrad, Victor, and Heather N. Nicol. *Beyond Walls: Re-inventing the Canada-United States Borderlands*. Aldershot: Ashgate, 2008. Print.

Kosek, Jake. *Understories: The Political Life of Forests in Northern New Mexico*. Durham, NC: Duke University Press, 2006. Print.

Kovarik, William. "Niles' Weekly Register." *Encyclopedia of American Journalism*. Ed. Stephen L. Vaughn. New York: Routledge, 2008. 366. Print.

Krech, Shepard, III. *The Ecological Indian: Myth and History*. New York: Norton, 2000. Print.

Kristeva, Julia. "Women's Time." Trans. Alice Jardine and Harry Blake. *Signs: Journal of Women in Culture and Society* 7.1 (1981): 13–35. Print.

Kroeber, Karl. *Ecological Literary Criticism: Romantic Imagining and the Biology of Mind*. New York: Columbia University Press, 1994. Print.

Krupat, Arnold. *Red Matters: Native American Studies*. Philadelphia: University of Pennsylvania Press, 2002. Print.

LaDuke, Winona. *All Our Relations: Native Struggles for Land and Life*. Cambridge, MA: South End Press, 1999. Print.

"La Via Campesina Declaration in Cancún: The People Hold Thousands of Solutions in their Hands." 2010. Web. January 15, 2011.

Lamm, Richard. "The Agonizing Dilemma of Immigration." Presentation at the *Myth of Sustainable Growth Conference*. Aspen Institute, Aspen, Colorado. 9 Oct. 1999. Presentation.

Lamm, Richard. *Myth of Sustainable Growth Conference*. Aspen Institute, Aspen, Colorado. 9 Oct. 1999. Presentation.

Lamothe, Dorothy. "Vodou Imagery, African American Tradition, and Cultural Transformation." *Zora Neale Hurston's Their Eyes Were Watching God: A Casebook*. Ed. Cheryl A. Wall. Oxford, UK: Oxford University Press, 2000. Print.

Lauter, Paul. *From Walden Pond to Jurassic Park: Activism, Culture, and American Studies*. Durham and London: Duke University Press, 2001. Print.

Lawrence, Jane. The Indian Health Service and the Sterilization of Native American Women. *American Indian Quarterly* 24:3 (Summer 2000): 400–419. Print.

Lektionen in Finsternis. Dir. Werner Herzog. Canal+ and Premièr, 1992. Film.

Lengell, Sean. "Border Patrol Has Bear of Time Stopping Terrorists from North." *Washington Times*. 6 June 2010. Web. 8 Nov. 2011.

Lenz, Günter H. "Redefinitions of Citizenship and Revisions of Cosmopolitanism—Challenges of Transnational Perspectives." *Journal of Transnational American Studies* 3.1 (2011): 4–17. Print.

Leopold, Aldo. *A Sand County Almanac and Sketches Here and There*. Oxford, UK: Oxford University Press, 1968. Print.

"Letter." Jean-Pierre Boyer, President of Hayti, to Mr. Dodge, at North Salem, Massachusetts. *Niles' Weekly Register* (1814–1837) 22.571 (August 17, 1822): 391. American Periodical Series Online.

Lewis, David, and David Mosse, eds. *Development Brokers and Translators: The Ethnography of Aid and Agencies*. Bloomfield, CT: Kumarian Press, Inc., 2006. Print.

Liglav, Awu. *Hong zuiba de vuvu* (*Vuvu with a Red Mouth*). Taichung: Morning Star, 1997. Print.

———. *Mulidan buluo shouzha* (*Mulidan: Tribal Notebook*). Taipei: Fembooks, 1998. Print.

Lillios, Anna. "'The Monstropolous Beast': The Hurricane in Zora Neale Hurston's *Their Eyes Were Watching God.*" *The Southern Quarterly* 36.3 (Spring 1998): 89–93. Print.

Limerick, Patricia. *The Legacy of Conquest: The Unbroken Past of the American West.* New York: Norton, 1987. Print.

LipanApacheCommunityDefense.blogspot. Lipan Apache Women Defense. Web. 1 February 2012.

Lipsitz, George. *The Possessive Investment in Whiteness: How White People Profit from Identity Politics.* Philadelphia: Temple University Press, 1998. Print.

Locke, Alain, ed. *The New Negro.* New York: Touchstone, 1925. Print.

Lofgren, Charles A. "Missouri v. Holland in Historical Perspective." *The Supreme Court Review* (1975): 77–122. Print.

Logan, Rayford W. *The Diplomatic Relations of the United States with Haiti, 1776–1891.* Chapel Hill: The University of North Carolina Press, 1941. Print.

Loh, Penn, and Kalila Barnett. "'Towards 'Justainability': A Colored Perspective on the Green Economy." *Ohio State University Kirwan Institute for the Study of Race and Ethnicity.* 22 Apr. 2010. Web. 7 June 2012.

Loo, Tina. *States of Nature: Conserving Canada's Wildlife in the Twentieth Century.* Vancouver: University of British Columbia Press, 2006. Print.

Los Angeles Poverty Department. Los Angeles Poverty Department. n.d. Web. 21 Dec. 2011.

Loustaunau, Martha Oehmke, and Mary Sanchez-Bane, eds. *Life, Death, and In-between on the US-Mexico Border: AsiEs La Vida.* Westport, CT: Bergin and Garvey, 1999. Print.

Lovecraft, Amy Lauren. "Transnational Environmental Management: U.S.-Canadian Institutions at the Interlocal Scale." *American Review of Canadian Studies* 37.2 (2007): 218–245. Print.

Lye, Collen. *America's Asia: Racial Formation and American Literature, 1893–1945.* Princeton: Princeton University Press, 2004. Print.

Lynch, Jim. *Border Songs.* New York: Alfred A. Knopf, 2009. Print.

Magocsi, Paul R., ed. *Encyclopedia of Canada's Peoples.* Toronto: University of Toronto Press, 1999. Print.

Malibu Public Beaches Guide, Public Access 101, Malibu, California 2007–2008. Los Angeles Urban Rangers. PDF file.

Mann, Charles C. *1491: New Revelations of the Americas before Columbus.* New York: Knopf, 2005. Print.

"Mannahatta Project." Wildlife Conservation Society. n.d. Web.21 September 2009.

Manson, Bill. "Danger at Quick Death Canyon." *San Diego Reader.* 2 Mar. 2000. Web. 12 June 2007.

Maquilapolis: City of Factories. Dir. Vicky Funari, Sergio De La Torre, and Group Factor X. 2006. Web. 12 June 2007.

"Marijuana and Methamphetamine Trafficking on Federal Lands Threat Assessment." *National Drug Intelligence Center.* Feb. 2005. Web. 8 Nov. 2011.

Marx, Leo. *The Machine in the Garden: Technology and the Pastoral Ideal in America.* London and New York: Oxford University Press, 1964. Print.

Masumoto, David Mas. *Harvest Son.* New York: Norton, 1999. Print.

Matthiessen, F. O. *American Renaissance: Art and Expression in the Age of Emerson and Whitman.* London: Oxford University Press, 1941. Print.

McDonald, Hugh P. *John Dewey and Environmental Philosophy*. Albany: SUNY Press, 2004. Print.

McGarry, Mike. Letter to the editor. "Ingrates Don't Deserve Citizenship." *Aspen Daily News*. 22 October 2002. Print.

McKibben, Bill. *Eaarth: Making a Life on Tough New Planet*. New York: Times Books, 2010. Print.

McLaurin, John J. *Sketches in Crude-Oil*. Franklin, PA: Self-published. Web. 1902.

Meyer, Eugene L. "A Comeback Story Decades in the Making." *New York Times*.30 Jan. 2008. Web. 31 Aug. 2010.

Meyer, Phillip. "Outlaws' Paradise." *New York Times*. 30 Aug. 2009. Web. 8 Nov. 2011.

Miller, Bill. "Plugging a Very Porous Northern Border." *Washington Post*. A03. 8 Apr. 2002. Web.

Miller, Peter. "Before New York." *National Geographic* (September 2009): 122–137. Print.

Miller, G. Tyler, Jr. *Environmental Science: Working With the Earth*. 9th ed. Pacific Grove, California: Brooks/Cole, 2003. Print.

Millet, Lydia. "Die, Baby Harp Seal!" *Naked: Writers Uncover the Way We Live on Earth*. Ed. Susan Zakin. New York: Four Walls, 2004. 146–150. Print.

"Minorities Will Soon Be the Majority." *La Plaza*. Latinovations. 11 March 2010. Web. 12 March 2010.

Modan, Gabriella Gahlia. *Turf Wars: Discourse, Diversity, and the Politics of Place*. Malden, MA: Wiley-Blackwell, 2007. Print.

Monroe, James. *The Writings of James Monroe*. Ed. Murray Hamilton. Vol. VI. 1817–1823. New York: AMS Press, 1902, 1960. Print.

Moral, Roger del, and Lawrence R. Walker. *Environmental Disasters, Natural Recovery and Human Responses*. Cambridge, UK: Cambridge University Press, 2007. Print.

Murray, Alice Yang. *Historical Memories of the Japanese American Internment and the Struggle for Redress*. Stanford: Stanford University Press, 2008. Print.

Mykle, Robert. *Killer 'Cane: The Deadly Hurricane of 1928*. New York: Cooper Square Press, 2002. Print.

Nash, Roderick. *Wilderness and the American Mind*. New Haven, CT: Yale University Press, 1967. Print.

"Nation, n." *OED Online*. Oxford University Press. Mar. 2012. Web. 12 May 2012.

Nevins, Joseph, and Timothy Dunn. "Barricading the Border." *Counterpunch* 41.6 (Nov./Dec. 2008): 21–25. Web. 8 Nov. 2011.

Ngai, Mae M. *Impossible Subjects: Illegal Aliens and the Making of Modern America*. Princeton, NJ: Princeton University Press, 2004. Print.

Ngai, Pun. *Made in China: Women Factory Workers in a Global Workplace*. Durham, NC: Duke University Press, 2005. Print.

Nicholls, David. *From Dessalines to Duvalier: Race, Colour and National Independence in Haiti*. Cambridge, UK: Cambridge University Press, 1979. Print.

Niezen, Robert. *The Origins of Indigenism: Human Rights and the Politics of Identity*. Berkeley: University of California Press, 2003. Print.

Nixon, Rob. *Slow Violence and the Environmentalism of the Poor*. Boston: Harvard University Press, 2011. Print.

Nordhoff, Charles. *California for Health, Pleasure, and Residence*. New York: Harper & Brothers, 1872. Print.

Norton, Dee. "Bomb Suspect Arrested Jan. 14 in Bellingham." *Seattle Times*. 2 Aug. 1997. Web. 8 Nov. 2011.

Novotny, Patrick. *Where We Live, Work and Play: The Environmental Justice Movement and the Struggle for a New Environmentalism.* Westport, CT: Praeger, 2000. Print.

Nunn, Kem. *Tijuana Straits.* New York: Scribner, 2004. Print.

Okada, John. *No-No Boy.* Seattle: University of Washington Press, 1978. Print.

Olins, Wally. "Making a Nation Brand." *The New Public Diplomacy: Soft Power in International Relations.* Ed. Jan Melissen. Hampshire: Palgrave Macmillan, 2005. 169–179. Print.

"One Texas Oil Fortune." *New York Times.* 26 May 1901. A1. Print.

Panagioti. "Down with Borders, Up with Spring!" *Earth First!* July–August 2006. Print.

Park, Angela. *Everybody's Movement: Environmental Justice and Climate Change.* Washington, DC: The Environmental Support Center, 2009. Web. 7 June 2012.

Park, Lisa Sun-Hee, and David Naguib Pellow. *The Slums of Aspen: Immigrants vs. the Environment in America's Eden.* New York: New York University Press, 2011. Print.

Parman, Donald. *The Navajos and the New Deal.* New Haven, CT: Yale University Press, 1976. Print.

Parr, Adrian. *Hijacking Sustainability.* Cambridge, MA: MIT Press, 2009. Print.

Paulson, Terry, and Mike McGarry. Personal interview with Lisa Sun-Hee Park and David Naguib Pellow. Spring 2002.

Pearce, Fred. "On World Population Day, Take Note: Population Isn't the Problem." *Grist.* 10 July 2010. Web. 10 July 2010.

Pellow, David N. *Resisting Global Toxics: Transnational Movements for Environmental Justice.* Cambridge, MA: MIT Press, 2007. Print.

———, and Robert J. Brulle. "Power, Justice, and the Environment: Toward Critical Environmental Justice Studies." *Power, Justice, and the Environment: A Critical Appraisal of the Environmental Justice Movement.* Eds. David Naguib Pellow and Robert J. Brulle. Cambridge: MIT Press, 2005. 1–21. Print.

———, and Lisa Park. *The Silicon Valley of Dreams: Environmental Injustice, Immigrant Workers, and the High-Tech Global Economy.* New York: New York University Press, 2003. Print.

Perea, Juan F., ed. *Immigrants Out! The New Nativism and the Anti-Immigrant Impulse in the United States.* New York: New York University Press, 1997. Print.

Perkins, Tracy E. "Women's Pathways in Activism: Rethinking the Women's Environmental Justice Narrative in California's San Joaquin Valley." *Organization and Environment* 25.1 (2012): 76–94. Print.

Phillips, Dana. *The Truth of Ecology: Nature, Culture, and Literature in America.* New York: Oxford University Press, 2003. Print.

Phillips, John C. *Migratory Bird Protection in North America: The History of Control by the United States Federal Government and a Sketch of the Treaty with Great Britain.* Special Publication of the American Committee for International Wild Life Protection 1.4 (1934). Print.

Pohl, Walter L. *Economic Geology: Principles and Practice.* New Malden: John Wiley and Sons, 2011. Print.

Pollock, Floyd. *A Navajo Confrontation and Crisis.* Tsaile, AZ: Navajo Community College Press, 1984. Print.

Porter, Carolyn. "'What We Know That We Don't Know: Remapping American Literary Studies." *American Literary History* 6.3 (1994): 467–526. Print.

Porteus, Liza. "Border Fence Plan to Get Critical Look in Next Congress." *Fox News.* 15 Dec. 2006. Web. 12 June 2007.

Posner, Eric A., and David Weisbach. *Climate Change Justice*. Princeton, NJ: Princeton University Press, 2010. Print.

Powell, John Wesley. *Report on the Lands of the Arid Region of the United States*. Washington, DC: Government Printing Office, 1878. Print.

Preston, Julia. "Homeland Security Cancels 'Virtual Fence' After $1 Billion Is Spent." *New York Times*. 14 Jan. 2011. Web. 8 Nov. 2011.

Price, Jenny. *Flight Maps: Adventures with Nature in Modern America*. New York: Basic Books, 1999.

———. "The Los Angeles Urban Rangers Enact the Megalopolis!" Interdisciplinary Humanities Center Lecture Series. UC-Santa Barbara, California. 28 April 2011. Lecture.

———. Personal interview by Stephanie LeMenager. 5 August 2011.

Ramirez, Bruno. *Crossing the 49th Parallel: Migration from Canada to the United States, 1900–1930*. Ithaca, NY: Cornell University Press, 2001. Print.

Ramirez, Charles E., and Gregg Krupa. "Officials Offer First Look at Border Cameras." *Detroit News*. 28 April 2009. Web. 12 Dec. 2011.

Ransom, John Crowe. "Reconstructed but Unregenerate." *I'll Take My Stand: The South and the Agrarian Tradition by Twelve Southerners*. New York: Harper, 1930. Print.

Ray, Sarah Jacquette. "Endangering the Desert: Immigration, the Environment, and Security in the Arizona-Mexico Borderland." *Interdisciplinary Studies in Literature and the Environment* (2010): 709–734. Print.

Rebuilding a Community Through Healthy Green Innovation. The Green Housing Series. National Center for Healthy Housing, n.d. Web. 31 Aug. 2010.

Reese, April. "Border Fence: Smuggler's Gulch Project Is 'Disaster' for Estuary, Critics Say." *Greenwire*. 15 Jan. 2009. Web. 12 Dec. 2011.

Reiger, John F. *American Sportsmen and the Origins of Conservation*. 3rd ed. Corvallis: Oregon State University Press, 2001. Print.

"Review: *Correspondence Relative to the Emigration to Hayti, of the Free People of Colour, in the United States, Together with the Instructions to the Agent Sent Out by President Boyer*." *The North American Review* 20.1 (1825): 191–210. Print.

Review of *The Ford*, by Mary Austin. *The North American Review* 206.740 (July 1917): 132–135. Print.

Reyes, Belinda I., Hans P. Johnson, and Richard Van Swearingen. *Holding the Line: The Effect of the Recent Border Build-Up on Unauthorized Immigration*. Public Policy Institute of California, 2002. Print.

Rizzuto, Rahna R. *Why She Left Us: A Novel*. New York: Harper Collins, 2000. Print.

Robbins, William G. *Colony and Empire: The Capitalist Transformation of the American West*. Lawrence: University of Kansas Press, 1994. Print.

Roediger, David. *Working Toward Whiteness: How American's Immigrants Became White*. New York: Basic Books, 2005. Print.

Roessel, Ruth. *Navajo Livestock Reduction: A National Disgrace*. Chinle: Navajo Community College Press, 1974. Print.

Ross, Andrew. *Bird on Fire: Lessons from the World's Least Sustainable City*. New York: Oxford University Press, 2011. Print.

Rowe, John Carlos, ed. *Post-Nationalist American Studies*. Berkeley: University of California Press, 2000. Print.

———, ed. *Concise Companion to American Studies*. New York: Blackwell, 2010.

Ruffin, Kimberly. *Black on Earth: African American Ecoliterary Traditions*. Athens and London: University of Georgia Press, 2010. Print.

Sadowski-Smith, Claudia. "Unskilled Labor Migration and the Illegality Spiral: Chinese, European, and Mexican Indocumentados in the United States, 1882–2007." *American Quarterly* 60.3 (2008): 779–804. Print.

———, and Claire F. Fox. "Theorizing the Hemisphere: Inter-Americas Work at the Intersection of American, Canadian, and Latin American Studies." *Comparative American Studies* 2.1 (2004): 41–74. Print.

Saldívar, José David. *Border Matters: Remapping American Cultural Studies.* Berkeley: University of California Press, 1997.

———. *The Dialectics of Our America: Genealogy, Cultural Critique, and Literary History.* Durham: Duke University Press, 1991.

Sanderson, Eric W. *Mannahatta: A Natural History of New York City.* Illus. Markley Boyer. New York: Abrams, 2009. Print.

Sasser, Jade. "Justice for All? Youth Environmental Activism and the New Framings of Social Justice." *DifferenTakes* 72 (2011).

Schlosberg, David. *Defining Environmental Justice: Theories, Movements, and Nature.* Oxford: Oxford University Press, 2007.

Schmitt, Eric. "Whites in Minority in Largest Cities, the Census Shows." *New York Times.* 30 April 2001. Print.

Schrag, Peter. *Not Fit for Our Society: Nativism and Immigration.* Berkeley: University of California Press, 2010. Print.

Scott, Emily Eliza. Personal interview by Stephanie LeMenager. 8 Sept. 2011.

———. "Undisciplined Geography." *Geohumanities: Art, History, Text at the Edge of Place.* Eds. Michael Dear, Jim Ketchum, Sarah Luria, and Douglas Richardson. New York: Routledge, 2011. Print.

Scott, James. *Seeing Like a State: How Certain Schemes to Improve the Human Condition Have Failed.* New Haven, CT: Yale University Press, 1998. Print.

Seager, Joni. *Earth Follies: Coming to Feminist Terms with Global Environmental Crisis.* New York: Routledge, 1993. Print.

———. "Noticing Gender (or Not) in Disasters." *Geoforum* 37.1 (2006): 2–3.

Selz, Peter. *Art of Engagement: Visual Politics in California and Beyond.* Berkeley: University of California Press and San Jose Museum of Art, 2006. Print.

Shaw, Kari Thorene. "Border Cameras too Close for Some." *Bellingham Herald.* 29 May 2002. Web. 8 Nov. 2011.

Sheller, Mimi. "Arboreal Landscapes of Power and Resistance." *Caribbean Land and Development Revisited.* Eds. Jean Besson and Janet Momsen. Gordonsville, VA: Palgrave Macmillan, 2007. 207–218. Print.

———. "Virtual Islands: Mobilities, Connectivity, and the New Caribbean Spatialities." *Small Axe* 24 (October 2007): 16–33. Print.

Shepardson, Mary. "The Gender Status of Navajo Women." *Women and Power in Native North America.* Eds. Laura F. Klein and Lillian A. Ackerman. Norman: University of Oklahoma Press, 1995. Print.

Shiva, Vandana. *Earth Democracy: Justice, Sustainability, and Peace.* Cambridge, MA: South End Press, 2005. Print.

Simpson, Mark. "Powers of Liveness: Reading Hornaday's *Camp-Fires.*" *The Culture of Hunting in Canada.* Eds. Jean L. Manore and Dale G. Miner. Vancouver: University of British Columbia Press, 2007. 56–85. Print.

Singh, Nikhil Pal. "Disciplining American Studies?: A Response to the Presidential Address." *American Quarterly* 61. 1 (March 2009): 27–32. Print.

A Sketch of the Origin and Progress of the American Colonization Society, with Some Notice of the Slave Trade, and of the Interior Condition of Africa, by a Friend of the Cause. Hartford: P. Canfield, 1833. Print.

Smith, Andrea. *Conquest: Sexual Violence and American Indian Genocide.* Cambridge, MA: South End Press, 2005. Print.

Smith, Henry Nash. *Virgin Land: The American West as Symbol and Myth.* Cambridge, MA: Harvard University Press, 1950. Print.

Smith, Lindsey Claire. *Indians, Environment, and Identity on the Borders of American Literature: From Faulkner and Morrison to Walker and Silko*. New York: Palgrave, 2008. Print.

Smith, Marian L. "The Immigration and Naturalization Service (INS) at the U.S.-Canadian Border, 1893–1993: An Overview of Issues and Topics." *Michigan Historical Review* 26.2 (2000): 127–147. Print.

Smith, Ted, David A. Sonnenfeld, and David N. Pellow. *Challenging the Chip: Labor Rights and Environmental Justice in the Global Electronics Industry*. Philadelphia: Temple University Press, 2006. Print.

Smith, Paul Chaat. *Everything You Know about Indians Is Wrong*. Minneapolis: University of Minnesota Press, 2009. Print.

Smythe, William Ellsworth. *The Conquest of Arid America*. New York: Harper & Brothers, 1900. Print.

Solnit, Rebecca. *Savage Dreams: A Journey into the Landscape Wars of the American West*. New York: Vintage, 1995. Print.

Solomon, S. D. et al., eds. *Climate Change: The Physical Science Basis*. Contribution of Working Group I to the Fourth Assessment Report of the Intergovernmental Panel on Climate Change. Cambridge, England, and New York: Cambridge University Press, 2007. Print.

Sone, Monica. *Nisei Daughter*. Seattle: University of Washington Press, 1979. Print.

Sorensen, Leif. "Modernity on a Global Stage: Hurston's Alternative Modernism." *MELUS* 30.4 (Winter 2005): 3–24. Print.

"Speculation, n." *Online Etymology Dictionary*. Douglas Harper. n.d. Web. 21 Dec. 2011.

Spence, Mark David. *Dispossessing the Wilderness: Indian Removal and the Making of the National Parks*. New York: Oxford University Press, 1999. Print.

Spiro, Jonathan. *Defending the Master Race: Conservation, Eugenics, and the Legacy of Madison Grant*. Burlington, VT: University Press of New England, 2009. Print.

———. "Patrician Racist: The Evolution of Madison Grant." Diss. University of California, Berkeley, 2000. Print.

Spivak, Gayatri Chakravorty. *Death of a Discipline*. New York: Columbia University Press, 2003. Print.

Staudenraus, P. J. *The African Colonization Society 1816–1865*. New York: Columbia University Press, 1961. Print.

Stegner, Wallace. *Discovery! The Search for Arabian Oil*. Vista, CA: Selwa Press, 2007. Print.

Stein, Rachel. *Shifting the Ground: American Women Writers' Revisions of Nature, Gender, and Race*. Charlottesville, VA: University Press of Virginia, 1997. Print.

Steingraber, Sandra. *Having Faith: An Ecologist's Journey to Motherhood*. Cambridge: Perseus, 2001. Print.

Stiny, Andrew. "Former Governor Lamm Heads Growth Conference." *Aspen Daily News*. 7 Oct. 1999: A1. Print.

Sullivan, Robert. "Island in the Stream." *New York Times*. 24 May 2009. BR 13. Print.

Suzack, Cheryl, Shari M. Huhndorf, Jeannne Perreault, and Jean Barman. *Indigenous Women and Feminism: Politics, Activism, Culture*. Vancouver: University of British Columbia Press, 2010. Print.

Sweeting, Adam W. "Writers and Dilettantes: Central Park and the Literary Origins of Antebellum Urban Nature." *The Nature of Cities: Ecocriticism and Urban Environments*. Eds. Michael Bennett and David W. Teague. Tucson: University of Arizona Press, 1999. 93–110. Print.

Sze, Julie. *Noxious New York: The Racial Politics of Urban Health and Environmental Justice*. Cambridge: The MIT Press, 2007. Print.

———. "From Environmental Justice Literature to the Literature of Environmental Justice." *The Environmental Justice Reader: Politics, Poetics Pedagogy*. Tucson: University of Arizona Press, 2002. 163–180. Print.

Szeman, Imre, and Maria Whiteman. "The Big Picture: On the Politics of Contemporary Photography." *Third Text* 23.5 (2009): 551–556. Print.

Tamez, Margo. *The Daughter of Lightning*. Unpublished manuscript. Cited with permission.

———. *Raven Eye*. Arizona: University of Arizona Press, 2007.

———. *Naked Wanting*. Tucson: University of Arizona Press, 2003.

———. "Restoring Lipan Apache Women's Laws, Lands, and Strength in El Calaboz Ranchería at the Texas-Mexico Border." *Signs: Journal of Women in Culture and Society* 35.3 (2010): 558–570. Print.

"Tancredo: If They Nuke Us, Bomb Mecca." Associated Press. 18 July 2005. Print.

Taylor, Alf. Letter to the editor. "You Stopped the INS, Now Stop the Cocaine." *The Aspen Times*. 31 Jan. 2000. Print.

Tedlock, Dennis, trans. *Finding the Center: Narrative Poetry of the Zuni Indians*. Lincoln: U of Nebraska P, 1972. Print.

Than, Ker. "Manhattan 1609 vs. 2009: Natural Wonder to Urban Jungle." *National Geographic*. n.d. Web. 23 September 2009.

"The Free Blacks—Hayti and Africa." *Niles' Weekly Register* (1814–1837). 22.669 3rd ser. 2.18 (July 3, 1824): 283. Print.

Thirsty for Justice: A People's Blueprint for California Water. 2012. Web. 6 June 2012.

Thompson, Edward Palmer. *Customs in Common: Studies in Traditional Popular Culture*. New York: New, 1991. Print.

———.*The Making of the English Working Class*. New York: Vintage, 1966. Print.

———. *Whigs and Hunters: The Origin of the Black Act*. London: Allen Lane, 1975.

Tober, James A. *Who Owns the Wildlife? The Political Economy of Conservation in Nineteenth-Century America*. Westport, CT: Greenwood Press, 1981. Print.

Treuer, David. *Native American Fiction: A User's Manual*. Saint Paul, MN: Graywolf Press, 2006. Print.

Trouillot, Michel-Rolph. *Silencing the Past: Power and the Production of History*. Boston: Beacon Press, 1995. Print.

Tumber, Catherine. *Small, Gritty, and Green: The Promise of America's Smaller Industrial Cities in a Low-Carbon World*. Cambridge, MA: MIT Press, 2012. Print.

"Tunnel Discovered Between Canada and U.S." U.S. Immigration and Customs Enforcement news release. 21 July 2005. Web. 8 Nov. 2011.

Turner, Frederick Jackson. *The Frontier in American History*. New York: Henry Holt, 1920. Print.

"US Border Patrol Home Page." 2012. Web. 6 June 2012.

Universal Declaration on the Rights of Mother Earth and Climate Change. World People's Conference on Climate Change and the Rights of Mother Earth. 22 April 2010. Web. September 17, 2010.

University of South Carolina. "New Evidence Puts Man in North America 50,000 Years Ago." *Science Daily*. 18 Nov. 2004. Web. 25 July 2010.

Urry, John. *Sociology beyond Societies: Mobilities for the Twenty-First Century*. London: Routledge, 2000. Print.

Varner, Gary R. *The Owens Valley Paiute: A Cultural History.* Morrisville, NC: Lulu Press, 2009. Kindle.

"Via Campesina Declaration in Cancún: The People Hold Thousands of Solutions in Their Hands." *La Vía Campesina International Peasant Movement.* 10 Dec. 2010. Web. 15 Jan. 2011.

Vidal, John. "Bolivia Enshrines Natural Worlds' Rights with Equal Status for Mother Earth." *guardian.co.uk.* Gaurdian News and Media Ltd. 10 April 2011. Web. 15 April 2011.

Vitalis, Robert. "Wallace Stegner's Arabian Discovery: Imperial Blindspots in a Continental Vision." *Pacific Historical Review* 76.3 (2007): 405–437. Print.

Wagman, Paul. "U.S. Goal: Sterilizations of Millions of World's Women." *St. Louis Post-Dispatch.* 22 April 1977. Print.

Wald, Priscilla. "American Studies and the Politics of Life." 2011 Presidential Address to the American Studies Association. *American Quarterly* 64.2 (June 2012): 185–204. Print.

———. "Minefields and Meeting Grounds: Transnational Analyses and American Studies." *American Literary History* 10.1 (Spring 1998): 199–218. Print.

Waldie, Angela. "Challenging the Confines: Haiju from the Prison Camps." *Coming into Contact: Explorations in Ecocritical Theory and Practice.* Eds. Annie Merrill Ingram, Ian Marshall, Daniel J. Philippon, and Adam W. Sweeting. Atlanta: University of Georgia Press, 2007. 39–57. Print.

Walker, William. "Canada, U.S. Eye Scrapping Border." *The Star.* 28 July 2001: A1 and A25. Print.

Walz, Eric. "From Kumamoto to Idaho: The Influence of Japanese Immigrants on the Agricultural Development of the Interior West." *Agricultural History* 74.3 (2000): 404–418. *JSTOR.* Web. 17 Dec. 2008.

Warren, Louis. *American Environmental History.* Oxford: Blackwell Publishing, 2003. Print.

———. *The Hunter's Game: Poachers and Conservationists in Twentieth-Century America.* New Haven, CT: Yale University Press, 1997. Print.

Warrior, Robert. 2010 Native American and Indigenous Studies Association (NAISA), Presidential Address. Speech.

Washington, Booker T. *Up from Slavery: An Autobiography.* NuVision Publications. 2007. Web. 21 June 2012.

Washington, Mary Helen. "Disturbing the Peace: What Happens to American Studies If You Put African American Studies at the Center?" *American Quarterly* 50.1 (1998): 1–23. Print.

"Water Bar Menu." Los Angeles Urban Rangers. *Public Access 101: Downtown L.A.* in collaboration with the Museum of Contemporary Art. Los Angeles' *Engagement Party.* 2011. Pamphlet.

Weaver, Jace, ed. *Defending Mother Earth: Native American Perspectives on Environmental Justice.* Maryknoll, NY: Orbis, 1996. Print.

———, Craig S. Womack, and Robert Warrior. *American Indian Literary Nationalism.* Albuquerque: University of New Mexico Press, 2005. Print.

Webester, Paul. "Quebec Inc. Unplugged." *The Nation.* 27 Apr. 1992. Print.

Weisiger, Marsha. "Gendered Injustice: Navajo Livestock Reduction in the New Deal Era." *Western Historical Quarterly* 38 (Winter 2007): 437–455. Print.

———. *Dreaming of Sheep in Navajo Country.* Seattle, WA: University of Washington Press, 2011. Print.

Westling, Louise H. *The Green Breast of the New World: Landscape, Gender, and American Fiction.* Athens: University of Georgia Press, 1996.

"What We Do." *The Center for Urban Pedagogy.* The Center for Urban Pedagogy. 2012. Web. 23 December 2011.

White, Richard. "Are You an Environmentalist or Do You Work for a Living?" *Uncommon Ground: Rethinking the Human Place in Nature*. Ed. William Cronon. New York: Norton, 1995. 171–185. Print.

———. *The Roots of Dependency: Subsistence, Environment, and Social Change Among the Choctaws, Pawnees, and Navajos*. Lincoln: University of Nebraska Press, 1983. Print.

Williams, John Alexander. *Appalachia: A History*. Chapel Hill: University of North Carolina Press, 2002. Print.

Williams, Michael. *Americans and Their Forests: A Historical Geography*. Cambridge, UK: Cambridge University Press, 1989. Print.

Winch, Julie. *A Gentleman of Color: The Life of James Forten*. Oxford: Oxford University Press, 2002. Print.

Wise, Gene. "'Paradigm Dramas' in American Studies: A Cultural and Institutional History of the Movement." *American Quarterly* 31.3 (1979): 293–337. Print.

Wister, Owen. *The Virginian*. New York: Macmillan, 1902. Print.

Witschi, Nicolas. *Traces of Gold: California's Natural Resources and the Claim to Realism in Western American Literature*. Tuscaloosa: University of Alabama Press, 2002. Print.

Wolfe, Patrick. "Settler Colonialism and the Elimination of the Native." *Journal of Genocide Research* 8.4 (2006): 387–409. Print.

Womack, Craig. *Red on Red: Native American Literary Separatism*. Minneapolis: University of Minnesota Press, 1999. Print.

Woodard, Colin. "Far from Border, U.S. Detains Foreign Students." *The Chronicle of Higher Education*. 9 Jan. 2011. Web. 8 Nov. 2011.

Wu, Diana Pei, Julie Quiroz-Martinez, and Kristen Zimmerman. *ReGeneration: Youth Organizing and Leadership Development in Environmental Justice*. Oakland, CA: Movement Strategy Center, 2005. Yellow Robe, and William S., Jr. *The Council. Where the Pavement Ends: Five Native American Plays*. Norman: University of Oklahoma Press, 2000. 71–126. Print.

Zarsky, L., ed. *Human Rights and the Environment: Conflicts and Norms in a Globalizing World*. London: Earthscan, 2002. Print.

Zhang, Patrick. "Mining and Benefication." *Florida Industrial and Phosphate Research Institute*. Florida Industrial and Phosphate Research Institute. 2010. Web. 21 June 2012.

Ziser, Michael, and Julie Sze. "Climate Change, Environmental Aesthetics, and Global Environmental Justice Cultural Studies." *Discourse* 29.2 (2007): 384–410. Print.

Contributors

Joni Adamson is Associate Professor of English and Environmental Humanities in the School of Letters and Sciences, Senior Sustainability Scholar at the Global Institute of Sustainability, and Program Faculty in Human and Social Dimensions of Science and Technology at Arizona State University. She is serving as 2012 President of ASLE and worked for more than ten years as the Liaison between the American Studies Association and the Environment and Culture Caucus.

Kirsten Crase is a Ph.D. candidate in American Studies at the University of Maryland. Her dissertation uses ethnography and cultural landscape studies analysis to explore local responses to environmental changes within marginalized communities.

Philip J. Deloria is Professor of History in the Program in American Culture and Native American Studies and Associate Dean of Undergraduate Studies at the University of Michigan. Deloria was the President of the American Studies Association (May 2008–May 2009) and winner of the John C. Ewers Prize in Ethnohistory, Western History Association, 2006 (for *Indians in Unexpected Places*) and a Gustavus Myers Outstanding Book Award in 1999 (for *Playing Indian*).

Giovanna Di Chiro is Environmental Justice Policy Advisor at Nuestras Raíces, Inc. and the Lang Professor for Issues of Social Change at Swarthmore College. She is completing a book titled *Embodied Ecologies: Science, Politics, and Environmental Justice*. Di Chiro collaborates with environmental justice organizations to conduct community-based research on environmental health concerns and developing culturally relevant sustainability initiatives.

John Gamber is Assistant Professor in the Department of English and Comparative Literature and the Center for the Study of Ethnicity and Race at Columbia University. He is the author of *Positive Pollutions and*

Cultural Toxins: Waste and Contamination in Contemporary U.S. Ethnic Literatures (University of Nebraska Press, 2012).

Ivan Grabovac is Assistant Professor of English at Mount Royal University in Calgary, Alberta. His chapter in this collection is part of a book project on "ecological modernism," which situates early efforts to preserve wildlife and wilderness in the context of modernism in the arts.

Hsinya Huang is Professor of American and Comparative Literature and Vice President for Student Affairs at National Sun Yat-Sen University, Taiwan. In addition to numerous articles, her book publications include *Huikan beimei yuanzhumin wenxue: duoyuan wenhua de shengsi (Native North American Literatures: Reflections on Multiculturalism*, 2009), the first Chinese essay collection on Native North American literatures.

Stephanie LeMenager is Associate Professor of English at UC-Santa Barbara, where she holds affiliate appointments in Environmental Studies and Comparative Literature. She is lead editor of *Environmental Criticism for the Twenty-First Century* (Routledge, 2011). She is currently at work on a book arguing the importance of the Humanities in the era of Tough Oil.

Jeffrey Myers is Associate Professor of English at Manhattan College, where he teaches nineteenth-century and multiethnic American literature along with environmental literature. He is the author of *Converging Stories: Race, Ecology, and Environmental Justice in American Literature* (University of Georgia, 2005).

Susan Scott Parrish is Associate Professor in the English Department at the University of Michigan. Her current book-length project, titled *Noah's Kin: Southern Floods and Forms of Modern Experience*, is an environmental and cultural history of two major southern floods (1927–1928).

David Naguib Pellow is Professor and Don A. Martindale Endowed Chair of Sociology at the University of Minnesota. Among his publications are *The Treadmill of Production: Injustice and Unsustainability in the Global Economy* (with Kenneth Gould and Allan Schnaiberg, Paradigm Press, 2008); *Resisting Global Toxics: Transnational Movements for Environmental Justice* (MIT Press, 2007); and *The Silicon Valley of Dreams: Environmental Injustice, Immigrant Workers, and the High-Tech Global Economy* (with Lisa Sun-Hee Park; New York University Press, 2002).

Kimberly N. Ruffin is Associate Professor of English and Associate Provost of Graduate Studies at Roosevelt University. Awarded an American Association of University Women Postdoctoral Research Leave Fellowship for her research in ecoliterature, she authored *Black on Earth: African-American Ecoliterary Traditions* (University of Georgia Press, 2010).

Claudia Sadowski-Smith is Associate Professor of English at Arizona State University. She is the author of *Border Fictions: Globalization, Empire, and Writing at the Boundaries of the United States* (University of Virginia Press, 2008) and the editor of a special issue of *Comparative American Studies* on "Comparative Border Studies" as well as of *Globalization on the Line: Culture, Capital, and Citizenship at U.S. Borders* (Palgrave, 2002).

Karen Salt is a Lecturer in the School of Divinity, History, and Philosophy at the University of Aberdeen, Aberdeen, Scotland, specializing in nineteenth-century African Diaspora Studies. She is also an Associate for the Centre for Sustainable International Development. She has presented at several international conferences devoted to early and transnational American Studies.

Lisa Sun-Hee Park is Professor of Sociology and Asian American Studies at the University of Minnesota. She is the author of several works, including *The Slums of Aspen: Immigrants vs. the Environment in America's Eden* (with David N. Pellow; New York University Press, 2011). In 2006, she was awarded the "Outstanding Book Award" from the American Sociological Association's Asia and Asian America Section for *Consuming Citizenship: Children of Asian Immigrant Entrepreneurs* (Stanford University Press, 2005).

Julie Sze is Associate Professor of American Studies at UC-Davis as well as the founding director of the Environmental Justice Project for UC-Davis's John Muir Institute for the Environment. Sze's book, *Noxious New York: The Racial Politics of Urban Health and Environmental Justice*, won the 2008 John Hope Franklin Publication Prize.

Traci Brynne Voyles is Assistant Professor of Women's Studies at Loyola Marymount University, where she teaches courses on gender, race, environmental justice, and environmental history. Her current book manuscript explores the history of the uranium industry on Navajo land.

Sarah D. Wald is Assistant Professor of English and Environmental Studies and Sustainability at Drew University. She is currently completing *The Nature of Citizenship: Race, Nature, and Citizenship in Representations of Californian Agricultural Labor.*

Michael Ziser is Associate Professor of English at UC-Davis, where he codirects the Environments and Societies Research Initiative.

Index

O

P

Q

R

Y